Bach: The Mass in B Minor

BACH

The Mass in B Minor

(The Great Catholic Mass)

George B. Stauffer

Hunter College and the Graduate Center
City University of New York

Monuments of Western Music

George B. Stauffer, Series Editor

SCHIRMER BOOKS
An Imprint of Simon & Schuster Macmillan
NEW YORK

Prentice Hall International
LONDON   MEXICO CITY   NEW DELHI   SINGAPORE   SYDNEY   TORONTO

Schirmer Books
An Imprint of Simon & Schuster Macmillan
1633 Broadway
New York, NY 10019

Library of Congress Catalog Number: 96–27495

Printed in the United States of America

Printing number

1 2 3 4 5 6 7 8 9 10

Library of Congress Cataloging-in-Publication Data

Stauffer, George B., 1947–
    Bach, the Mass in B minor: the great Catholic Mass / George B. Stauffer.
        p. cm. — (Monuments of western music)
    Includes index.
    ISBN 0–02–872475–5 (alk. paper)
    1. Bach, Johann Sebastian, 1685–1750. Masses, BWV 232, B minor.
I. Title.   II. Series.
ML410.B1S77 1996
782.32'32—dc20   96–27495
                                                              CIP
                                                              MN

This paper meets the requirements of ANSI/NISO Z39.48–1992 (Permanence of Paper).

For Marie and Matthew

Contents

Foreword

✂

$\mathscr{I}$t was the Swiss publisher Hans Georg Nägeli who first declared the
B-Minor Mass a masterpiece, hailing it in 1818 as "the greatest musical art-
work of all times and all people." To a certain extent Nägeli was speaking
out of self-interest: he had purchased the original manuscript of the work
from C. P. E. Bach's heirs some years earlier, and he now wished to realize
his investment by bringing out the first edition. Still, his statement was an
audacious claim, coming at a point when the B-Minor Mass had never been
performed in public and was scarcely known. Bach's vocal works still lay in
obscurity, and audiences were no longer looking to Mass settings for musical inspiration.

Yet time has proven Nägeli close to the mark. Although another twenty-
seven years were to pass before his edition was completed, and another
forty-one before the B-Minor Mass received a full performance, the work
gradually made its way into the standard repertory and has remained there
ever since. It is not difficult to understand why. No other work displays
Bach's powers of compositional refinement and stylistic synthesis so clearly and on such a grand scale. The B-Minor Mass is a church work that tran-
scends the church. Its text is Catholic, but its music, catholic—as Nägeli
rightly perceived. Beethoven, Mahler, Stravinsky, Bernstein, and other
nineteenth- and twentieth-century composers have turned to the Latin texts
and music of the ancient church in search of transcendence. But it was
Bach, in the B-Minor Mass, who most successfully joined ecclesiastical
past with worldly present to create a work of enduring universality.

At the same time, the B-Minor Mass has emerged as an enigmatic piece.
When was it composed? What was its purpose? How is it to be performed?
How much of its music is original? Historians have wrestled with these
questions for over one hundred years, and to date they have reached gener-
al agreement only on the first (thanks to the "new" Bach chronology).
Recent research has raised further issues. Wolfgang Horn's study of
Dresden Mass practices, completed in 1987, suggests that Bach may have

paid homage to contemporary Catholic models to a greater degree than pre-
viously thought. Joshua Rifkin's controversial "one on a part" theory of
Bach's choir has brought into question the appropriateness of traditional
large-scale performances. And Peter Wollny's discovery just four years ago
of an early version of the "Credo in unum Deum" movement opens anew the
question of compositional process.

These developments, plus the approach of the 250th anniversary of
Bach's death, lead one to believe that this is a good time to take stock of the
B-Minor Mass, to reevaluate its complex history and remarkable music.
That is the goal of the present volume. Chapter 1 surveys the roots of the
Mass Ordinary text and its treatment in late-Baroque musical settings that
were known to Bach. Chapter 2 examines the composer's activities in
Leipzig and traces the events that led to the writing of the B-Minor Mass.
Chapters 3 through 5 are devoted to a detailed inspection of the music
itself, taking into account the new knowledge of Bach's late compositional
habits and Mass conventions in Dresden. Chapter 6 follows the resurrection
of the B-Minor Mass after Bach's death and looks at the changing approaches to performance. Chapter 7 weighs specific issues of performance practice, and Chapter 8 attempts to pinpoint those qualities that give the
B-Minor Mass its universal appeal, that render it an "art-work of all times
and all people" indeed.

When one writes about the B-Minor Mass, one does not take the road
less traveled. Most Bach specialists eventually make their way to the work,
attracted by its central position in Bach's oeuvre and the riddles it poses.
The extensive literature on the B-Minor Mass has been greatly enhanced by
the writings of Carl Hermann Bitter and Philipp Spitta in the nineteenth
century and Albert Schweitzer, Arnold Schering, Friedrich Smend, Georg
von Dadelsen, Christoph Wolff, Robert L. Marshall, and Joshua Rifkin, in
particular, in the twentieth. Charles Sanford Terry, Walter Blankenburg,
Helmut Rilling, and John Butt have penned B-Minor Mass monographs,
and in very recent times Yoshitake Kobayashi has performed an inestimable
service by clarifying the chronology of Bach's late performances and compositions. One is indebted to these historians, and the present study stands
upon the foundation they labored so diligently to build.

For assistance with the present volume I would like to thank the Music
Divisions of the Austrian National Library in Vienna, the Berlin State
Library in Berlin, the New York Public Library in New York City, and the
Saxon State Library in Dresden for allowing me to examine manuscripts and
prints in their collections and providing microfilms of relevant items. I am

equally grateful to the Research Foundation of the City University of New York (CUNY) for financial support and to Hunter College for a fellowship leave that facilitated a year of uninterrupted research and writing.

I would also like to extend thanks to Alexander Blachly, Ruth DeFord, Alfred Dürr, Robin A. Leaver, Hans-Joachim Schulze, Christoph Wolff, and Peter Wollny for their thoughts on a variety of issues; to the students in my masters seminar on Dresden Mass practices given at Hunter College— Frank McGarry, Marilyn Niebuhr, Patricia Ruffin, Brad Stoller, and Pamela Vera—whose transcriptions proved most helpful in sorting out the court repertory; and to the students in my Ph.D. seminar on the B-Minor Mass given at the CUNY Graduate Center—Carlos Coelho, Risa Freeman, Lauren Longo, Karen Mandelbaum, Anthony Netz, Rebecca Pechefsky, and the late Milton Setzer—for preparing a performance edition of C. P. E. Bach's arrangement of the *Symbolum Nicenum* that allowed theory to be tested in practice. Robert L. Marshall gave the entire manuscript a close reading and offered sage counsel on many points (in addition to catching a number of errors), George Ritchie looked over the chapter on performance issues and made many useful suggestions, and Lynn Hall stepped in with practical advice on computers when I was in deepest need. I owe a special debt to Joshua Rifkin, whose personal letters and public reproach (in *Journal of Musicological Research* 14 [1995], 223–234) prompted me to rethink several ideas in a fruitful way. I am grateful, too, to Maribeth Payne, formerly of Schirmer Books and now of Oxford University Press, and Jonathan Wiener of Schirmer Books for backing this volume and the *Monuments* series in general, and to Laurie H. Ongley for copyediting the final manuscript and James Hatch for guiding it through production.

My greatest debt, however, is to my wife Marie and my son Matthew, who have shown remarkable patience with my musicological undertakings over the years. Without their continual support and encouragement I would not have been able to bring the present project to completion.

Abbreviations

---------------------------- ✂ ----------------------------

Am.B.   Amalien-Bibliothek. Abbreviation for "Library of Prin-
                    cess Anna Amalia" used by the Berlin State Library.

Bach Compendium   *Bach Compendium: Analytisch-bibliographisches Reper-*
                    torium der Werke Johann Sebastian Bachs, ed. Hans-
                    Joachim Schulze and Christoph Wolff (Frankfurt: C. F.
                    Peters; Leipzig: Edition Peters, 1985-present).

Bach-Dokumente   *Bach-Dokumente,* issued under the auspices of the
                    Neue Bach-Gesellschaft, ed. Werner Neumann and
                    Hans-Joachim Schulze (Kassel: Bärenreiter Verlag;
                    Leipzig: VEB Deutscher Verlag für Musik, 1963–
                    1979).

The Bach Reader   *The Bach Reader,* ed. Hans T. David and Arthur
                    Mendel (rev. ed. New York: W. W. Norton, 1966).

BG   *Johann Sebastian Bach's Werke (Bach-Gesamtausgabe),*
                    issued under the auspices of the Bach-Gesellschaft
                    (Leipzig, 1851–1899).

BWV   *Thematisch-systematisches Verzeichnis der musik-*
                    alischen Werke von Johann Sebastian Bach (Bach-
                    Werke-Verzeichnis), ed. Wolfgang Schmieder (rev. ed.,
                    Wiesbaden: Breitkopf & Härtel, 1990).

H.   *Thematic Catalogue of the Works of Carl Philipp*
                    Emanuel Bach, ed. E. Eugene Helm (New Haven,
                    Conn.: Yale University Press, 1989).

KB   *Kritischer Bericht.* Critical report of the *Neue Bach-*
                    Ausgabe.

NBA   *Johann Sebastian Bach: Neue Ausgabe sämtlicher*
                    Werke (Neue Bach-Ausgabe), issued under the aus-
                    pices of the Neue Bach-Gesellschaft (Kassel:
                    Bärenreiter Verlag; Leipzig: VEB Deutscher Verlag
                    für Musik, 1954–present).

P   Partitur. Abbreviation for "musical score," used by
                  the Berlin State Library. In Bach studies, "P" is com-
                  monly employed as an abridgment for the full library
                  siglum, *Mus.ms.Bach P.*

St   Stimmen. Abbreviation for "performance parts," used
                  by the Berlin State Library. In Bach studies, "St" is
                  commonly employed as an abridgment for the full
                  library siglum, *Mus.ms.Bach St.*

Z.   *Jan Dismas Zelenka. Thematisch-systematisches
                  Verzeichnis der musikalischen Werke,* ed. Wolfgang
                  Reich (Dresden: Sächsische Landesbibliothek, 1985).

All music examples have been edited from the original manuscripts. All
translations are by the author unless otherwise marked.

In the text, musical pitch is indicated by the standard system of c-based
octaves: c' = middle c; c = the c one octave below middle c; C = the c two
octaves below middle c; c'' = the c one octave above middle c; c''' = the c
two octaves above middle c.

Libraries have been translated as follows:

Austrian National Library = Österreichische Nationalbibliothek (Vienna)

Berlin State Library = Staatsbibliothek zu Berlin—Preussischer
   Kulturbesitz (Berlin)

Saxon State Library = Sächsische Landesbibliothek (Dresden)

Bach: The Mass in B Minor

Chapter 1

THE LATE BAROQUE CHURCH MASS: CATHOLIC AND LUTHERAN

THE CATHOLIC MASS ORDINARY

The Roman Catholic *Ordinarium Missae,* or Ordinary of the Mass, which Bach set to music in his late masterpiece, consists of the liturgical items of the Mass whose texts remain the same throughout the church year. The Proper of the Mass, by contrast, consists of the items whose texts vary from day to day according to the occasion. In the earliest centuries of the Christian church the Ordinary and Proper were set to chant with equal fervor, and from the tenth century onward we find extensive notated repertories for both.

The advent of polyphony in the twelfth century brought multivoice settings of Ordinary and Proper texts. Two of the earliest known writers of church polyphony, Léonin (c. 1135–1201) and Pérotin (c. 1160–1225) of the Cathedral of Notre Dame in Paris, composed elaborate contrapuntal music for the Gradual, Alleluia, and other Proper chants, to embellish Mass and Office services on special feast days of the Christmas season. As the art of polyphony blossomed in the centuries that followed, however, composers turned increasingly to the Ordinary, undoubtedly because they wished to focus their creative efforts on texts that could be used for more than one day of the church year.

Polyphonic music from the thirteenth century shows the emergence of the Ordinary, and by the fourteenth century, collected cycles begin to appear that include Kyrie, Gloria, Credo, Sanctus, and Agnus Dei. (The sixth item of the Ordinary, Ite, missa est, was often included in early cycles but was generally omitted by the time of the Renaissance.) The initial polyphonic cycles—the Mass of Tournai, the Mass of Toulouse, and the Mass of Barcelona—are transmitted without attributions and probably represent compilations. Guillaume de Machaut's *Messe de Nostre Dame* of c. 1350, the first Mass cycle known to be written by one person, set the stage, figuratively speaking, for the great Ordinary settings of the Renaissance and subsequent eras.

Although the five portions of the Ordinary (we are going to omit the Ite missa est, since it was not set by Bach and most other Baroque composers) follow one another without a break in polyphonic settings, they occur at different times within the Roman Catholic Mass. The Kyrie is sung immediately after the Introit, which opens the service. The Gloria follows the Kyrie without pause (it is not performed, however, during Advent and Lent—the penitential periods leading up to Christmas and Easter, respectively—and a few other occasions). The Credo is sung toward the middle of the service, after the Gospel and Homily; it is the last, and climactic, item of the Synaxis, or preparation portion, of the Mass. The Sanctus and Agnus Dei are sung during the Eucharist, or Communion portion, of the Mass. The Sanctus emerges from the Preface, after the opening Offertory, and the Agnus Dei is sung during the elevation of the Host, just before Communion is administered. The position of the Ordinary elements within the Mass service can be summarized as follows:

	PROPER	ORDINARY
Synaxis	Introit	
		Kyrie
		Gloria (except during Advent and Lent)
	Collects	
	Epistle	
	Gradual	
	Alleluia/Tract	
	Gospel	
	[Sermon]	
		Credo

	PROPER	ORDINARY
Eucharist	Offertory	
	Preface	
		Sanctus
		Agnus Dei
	Communion	
	Post-Communion	
		Ite, missa est

The parts of the Ordinary have different liturgical roots. The Kyrie, a solemn supplication in Greek, is not, as one might think, a vestige of the first few centuries of the Roman church, when the liturgy was celebrated in Greek. According to Joseph A. Jungmann, it can be traced instead to the Eastern church—to Jerusalem, Antioch, and other religious centers, where it was used as a response to various petitions.[1] It may have been introduced into the Roman rite by Gelasius I (pope from 492 to 496), who ordered a long litany with "Kyrie eleison" attached as a repeated response. By the time of Gregory the Great (590–604), both "Kyrie eleison" and a second phrase, "Christe eleison," were sung without petitions on normal feast days. By the eighth century, the phrases were grouped into units of threefold "Kyrie," threefold "Christe," and threefold "Kyrie." In early liturgies all phrases referred to Christ, not God. Trinitarian symbolism emerged only in the late Middle Ages and early Renaissance, as witnessed in contemporary tropes (liturgical glosses, which were eliminated by the Council of Trent in the sixteenth century).

The Gloria, an exuberant prose hymn of praise written in imitation of the Psalms, consists of several distinct elements. It opens with an angelic hymn from the New Testament (Luke 2:14), continues with acclamations and petitions, and concludes with a short doxology, or expression of adoration to God. Like the Kyrie, the Gloria has origins in the Eastern church. It appears in Greek in the Apostolic Constitutions of c. 380 and the *Codex Alexandrinus* of the fifth century. The earliest Latin version can be found in the Antiphonal of Bangor, from the late seventh century. By the sixth century, the Gloria had entered into the Mass, but initially it remained the exclusive property of bishops and could be used by common priests on Easter only.[2] It became a fixed part of the Ordinary by the eleventh century, to be sung at all Masses of a festive character.

The Credo, or Nicene Creed, dates from the fourth century, when Constantine summoned a council of bishops to Nicaea[3] to counter the rise of the heretical sect of Arianism. The text was formulated by the bishops as a statement of faith; it was revised by the First Council of Constantinople (381) and incorporated into Eastern liturgies by the fifth century. Its use in the Carolingian Mass was mandated by Charlemagne in 798, but it did not enter the Roman rite until the eleventh century, when Henry II requested its performance at his imperial coronation in Rome in 1014. Jungmann explains that in the early church, it was used as a profession of faith by the individual Christian about to undergo baptism, hence the use of the singular, "*I believe in one God. . . .*" The tradition of genuflecting at the phrase "Et incarnatus" ("And he was incarnate by the Holy Ghost . . .") emerged in the eleventh century. As we shall see in Chapter 4, Baroque composers normally highlighted the "Et incarnatus" with unusually expressive music—a convention to which Bach adhered after rethinking his initial plans.

The Sanctus joins an Old Testament vision of God (Isaiah 6:30) with a New Testament acclamation of Christ's sovereignty (Matthew 21:9, for the "Osanna" and "Benedictus") to form what the French theologian François Amiot has termed "a heartfelt exclamation proclaiming the greatness of God and Christ and an Act of Faith in the mysteries about to be accomplished."[4] It is one of the oldest elements in the Roman Mass. The *Liber Pontificalis* of 530 attributes its use in Rome to Sixtus II (119–128), who proclaimed that it be sung by the people as a communal prayer. This seems to have become universal practice by the fourth century, though it is clear that the "Osanna" and "Benedictus" were added at a later point. According to Jungmann, the Sanctus remained a congregational chant until the twelfth century, when it was transferred to the choir in conjunction with the composition of newly elaborate melodies and, within a century or two, of polyphonic settings.[5]

The Agnus Dei, a succinct supplication that accompanies the breaking of the bread during the Eucharist, seems to have entered the Roman Mass in the late seventh century. Scholars generally credit its introduction to Sergius I (685–701), who decreed that it should be sung "by the clergy and the people . . . during the Fraction of the Body of the Lord."[6] Sergius, a Syrian, probably appropriated it from Eastern practice. The text is derived from John 1:29: "Behold the Lamb of God. Behold the Lamb who taketh away the sins of the world." Initially, the phrase "Lamb of God, who taketh away the sins of the world, have mercy upon us" was repeated any number of times until all the bread was divided. By the twelfth century, the petitions were pruned to three, and "grant us peace" substituted for the third "have mercy upon us."

The Roman Catholic Ordinary, then, is an eclectic collection of texts which made their way into the Mass over a period of ten centuries. Its parts have different origins and display different characters. The Kyrie, Gloria, Sanctus, and Agnus are communal acclamations; the Credo is an individual affirmation. It was only with the polyphonic cycles of the late Middle Ages and to an even greater extent the monumental settings of the Renaissance that the five parts of the Ordinary were firmly united.

MUSICAL DEVELOPMENTS IN THE BAROQUE

By the beginning of the Baroque Era (which we will take here to mean the years from approximately 1600 to 1750), the polyphonic Mass Ordinary had passed its zenith as the preeminent musical art form. After 1600, the opera, the concerto, the sonata, and other secular genres began to supplant the Ordinary as the supreme test of a composer's skills. The Baroque nevertheless offered an unusual array of creative choices for the writers of Mass settings, for it was an age that fostered not one but two distinct styles of church composition: a progressive, expressive style that reflected the aesthetics of the time, and a conservative, more objective style that paid tribute to the great sacred works of the Renaissance. This dichotomy was first described by Claudio Monteverdi, who in 1607 termed the Renaissance-oriented approach (in which "music rules the words") the "First Practice," and the Baroque method (in which "words rule the music") the "Second Practice."[7] The two practices enjoyed a dynamic coexistence throughout the Baroque, as the contemporary classifications of Marco Scacchi, Johann Joseph Fux, and others demonstrate. Bach's contemporary Johann Mattheson, writing about church music in 1739—almost a century and a half after Monteverdi—still emphasized the fundamental difference between "Moteten-Styl" and "Madrigal-Styl," as he termed the retrospective and modern styles.[8] Other phrases used to express the contrast between the old and the new include *stylus gravis* vs. *stylus luxurians, stile antico* vs. *stile moderno,* and most commonly, *stile da cappella* vs. *stile concertato* (the word *allabreve,* too, was often connected with Renaissance-style pieces). The creative tension between the two approaches—and the advocates of each—lent Baroque Ordinary settings much of their vitality. There can be no question that Bach, looking for new compositional worlds to conquer late in life, found the diverse stylistic possibilities of the Ordinary highly attractive.

As Mattheson pointed out in his description, the modern style was closely associated with instrumental writing, and in church music the most striking product of the Second Practice was the *Missa concertata,* the concerted Mass or Mass with instruments. Historians generally view the concerted Mass as an outgrowth of Venetian polychoral style. The use of vocal *cori spezzati* (split choruses) at San Marco in Venice during the late Renaissance led to the employment of choruses of voices and instruments in the Baroque. The text of the Ordinary was treated sectionally, and the sections were differentiated by timbre, forces, figurations, and meter, according to the *Affekt,* or emotional nature, of the words. In Monteverdi's 1640 setting of the Gloria,[9] for instance, the florid, animated sixteenth-note figures presented by the chorus, soloists, and violins for the opening words "Glory be to God on high" suddenly give way to slower, restful quarter-note chords on the phrase "And on earth peace, good will toward men," sung by the full chorus. The musical contrast vividly underlines the word "peace," and it is not surprising that many composers after Monteverdi, including Bach, employed a similar effect at the same point in the Gloria text.

The success of the early-Baroque Mass settings led, by the beginning of the eighteenth century, to a style dominated by instrumental figurations and sectional contrasts. In such pieces, produced by the hundreds in Catholic centers such as Rome, Venice, Bologna, Vienna, and Dresden, the chorus writing commonly consists of stylized declamations that reflect the rhythm of the words. The "Gratias agimus tibi" from Jan Dismas Zelenka's *Missa votiva,*[10] Z. 18, written in Dresden in 1739, is representative of this approach: the chorus, accompanied by pulsating eighth notes in the strings, sounds forth with black-note, instrumental figurations whose rhythms mirror the speech pattern of the Latin text (Example 1–1). Solo passages generally show greater flexibility and nuance. Historians have often termed this type of concerted setting, which tended to be short, sectional (rather than multimovement), and eminently pragmatic, the "Venetian Mass" or "Viennese Mass." Although it certainly thrived in Venice and Vienna, and we will use the term Venetian/Viennese for want of a better label, by 1700 it could be found throughout Italy and Austria and in Southern and Middle Germany as well (as Zelenka's Mass, written in Dresden, demonstrates).

The most common setting for the turn-of-the-century Venetian/Viennese Mass was four-part strings (violin 1, violin 2, viola, basso with continuo) and four-part chorus, often with a quartet of soloists for solo passages and

Example 1–1. Zelenka: "Gratias agimus tibi" from *Missa votiva.*

textural contrasts within choral sections. In Austria and Germany two oboes were often added to the ensemble, mostly as doubling reinforcement for the violin parts. The "Gloria in excelsis Deo" from Antonio Caldara's *Missa dicta reformata*,[11] a Mass imported from Vienna to Dresden by Zelenka (who seems to have added the oboes), is a typical example of this vocal and instrumental scoring (Example 1–2). Larger instrumental forces were frequently used on special festival days. In Germany composers favored more colorful ensembles, with batteries of brass and wind instruments and less orthodox string and chorus combinations. As we shall see in Chapter 3, Bach united the Venetian/Viennese and German scoring traditions in the B-Minor Mass.

With regard to terminology, manuscript scores of the time reveal that the word *Missa* was applied not just to full Ordinaries but also to Kyrie and Gloria pairs and other partial settings. *Missa tota* was sometimes used for a complete Ordinary, to distinguish it from an incomplete arrangement, and *Missa brevis* was commonly linked with a markedly succinct setting.

The most critical development in the evolution of the late-Baroque concerted Mass was the growing influence of the so-called Neapolitan style. As much an attitude as a specific school, the Neapolitan approach called for setting the Ordinary text as a series of large, more-or-less independent movements rather than as a chain of connected sections—the route normally taken in the more modest Venetian/Viennese Mass. The new style reflected the strong influence of late-Baroque opera and resulted in a "numbers" Mass of choruses and arias, often utilizing ritornello and da capo techniques (recitative was viewed as too overtly operatic for use in the Mass; da capo procedure may have been frowned upon for the same reason but managed to find its way, despite its general inappropriateness for the text of the Ordinary, into many works, including the B-Minor Mass). In the Neapolitan Mass—and we will use this term, too, for want of a better one—individual movements fulfilled affective, operatic roles: the "Christe" appears as an amorous love duet, the "Et incarnatus" and "Crucifixus" as baleful laments, the "Cum Sancto Spiritu" and "Et vitam venturi" (which conclude the Gloria and Credo, respectively) as act finales. As Walther Müller nicely explained it in his classic study of Hasse's church music, while the old contrapuntal style moved the soul to thoughtful listening, the new Neapolitan style spoke directly to the emotions.[12] It brought the opera into the church, and therein lay its great appeal.

In such settings the emphasis shifted from instrumental-derived motives to more expressive vocal writing, in choruses as well as arias, with instru-

Example 1–2. Caldara: "Gloria in excelsis Deo" from *Missa dicta reformata*.

ments playing a distinctly supporting role. To create a simpler, more appealing melodic style, composers writing in the Neapolitan vein increasingly utilized homophonic textures, straightforward harmonies, symmetrical phrases, and memorable melodies. The *style galant*, as the new, lighter idiom was termed, was refreshingly direct and tuneful. As in the Neapolitan opera, instrumental forces usually consisted of no more than a four-part string body, with or without oboes, and continuo. The sprightly, balanced phrases (4 + 4 + 2 bars), tonic-dominant harmonies, and string accompaniment of the alto aria "Domine Fili Unigenite" from Francesco Durante's *Missa concertata* in C Major[13]—another Italian work performed in Dresden—are typical (Example 1–3).

In Naples, Durante, Alessandro Scarlatti, Francesco Mancini, Domenico Sarri (or Sarro), and others writing concerted Masses in the new style concentrated on settings of the Kyrie and Gloria alone, perhaps because there was little call for polyphonic Credo, Sanctus, and Agnus Dei settings in the local rite or because with the use of full-length movements, the Kyrie and Gloria grew to such great size that it was no longer possible to accommodate the Credo, Sanctus, and Agnus Dei as well. The Kyrie and Gloria had been singled out for independent concerted settings since the days of Monteverdi; now they came into still greater prominence. With the arrival of Neapolitan style and the introduction of discrete movements, the Ordinary was commonly divided into separate portions that were set to music independently and then compiled to form "pasticcio" Masses. For the abovementioned *Missa votiva*, Zelenka imported a Credo from another work, his *Missa Eucharistica*, Z. 15. Bach wrote the "Christe eleison," BWV 242, for insertion into a *Missa* in C Minor by Durante,[14] and it is possible that the "Credo in unum Deum" of the B-Minor Mass, too, originated as an interpolation (see Chapter 4). Such inserts were, in a way, the liturgical equivalent of an operatic *aria di baule*, a trunk aria that could be transported from one work to another. The Neapolitan approach greatly facilitated the compilation practice that produced the B-Minor Mass. During the Late Baroque the Neapolitan Mass flourished with many regional variations. In Venice and Vienna composers incorporated choruses with solo interludes. In Germany, composers wrote works with more variegated instrumental bands.

But even as the concerted Mass prospered, the Renaissance *a cappella* style—Monteverdi's First Practice—remained in use. Palestrina's works, in particular, were preserved and elevated as models of classical vocal counterpoint. They were accorded canonic status and performed on a regular basis not only in Rome, but in Catholic centers elsewhere, including

Example 1–3. Durante: "Domine Fili Unigenite" from *Missa Concertata* in C Major.

Vienna and Dresden. Even in progressive Naples, composers studied
Renaissance vocal style and employed it as a matter of course in church
music: Alessandro Scarlatti wrote Palestrina-style Masses (the two *Missa
clementina* settings for Pope Clement XI, for instance) while simultaneously helping to forge the progressive Neapolitan opera. Fux's famous treatise
Gradus ad Parnassum, in which Palestrina's idiom is codified as species
counterpoint, summarized a practice of long standing. First issued in
Vienna in 1725, *Gradus* enjoyed a wide circulation despite the fact that its
text was—appropriately—in Latin. Bach owned a copy and may have
helped to spur the German translation issued in Leipzig in 1742 by his
friend and admirer Christoph Lorenz Mizler.[15] As Christoph Wolff has
shown in his important work on the *stile antico,*[16] Bach not only studied
Renaissance vocal style with great intensity in the 1730s and 1740s (we
will return to this in Chapter 2) but also performed the Kyrie and Gloria
from Palestrina's *Missa sine nomine* in the Leipzig worship service around
1742—that is, close to the time that Mizler published his translation.

Writing in 1700, the influential French music lexicographer Sébastien
de Brossard defined the Renaissance-style Mass, or *Messa da Capella,* as a
Mass which is "sung entirely by the full choir and usually filled with
fugues, double counterpoint, and other artful devices."[17] Although Baroque
composers emulated the writing of their Renaissance predecessors by using
allabreve time signatures, white-note notation, and the contrapuntal devices
mentioned by Brossard, they did not hesitate to dress the early idiom in
more modern garb. The counterpoint in Baroque *a cappella* pieces is normally more chord-oriented and tonal than that of Renaissance works. In
addition, in Dresden and other northern centers Renaissance-style works
were performed with instrumental doubling as a matter of course. As
Wolfgang Horn has shown, the vocal parts of Palestrina's compositions were
reinforced with strings, oboes, bassoons, and continuo in Dresden performances[18]—an approach to Renaissance scoring that Bach followed in
Leipzig (see Chapter 7).

Equally important was the expansion of the "Palestrina" style into two
schools. Some composers, including Fux and Alessandro Scarlatti, maintained the austere approach of the Renaissance. Others, including Durante
and Antonio Lotti, spiced the vocal counterpoint with more expressive chromatic writing at appropriate spots—that is, they updated the *a cappella*
idiom with Baroque affectation. In *Gradus ad Parnassum* Fux noted the difference between the two approaches, relating the first to works devoid of
intense chromaticism (such as Palestrina's Masses) and the second to works

showing greater freedom in melody and modulation.[19] Bach wrote comfortably in both idioms: the Kyrie "Christe, du Lamm Gottes," BWV 233, illustrates the former, and the opening chorus of Cantata 38, *Aus tiefer Not schrei ich zu dir*, with its pungent chromaticism reflecting the text "Out of the depths have I cried unto thee" (Psalm 130), illustrates the latter. As we shall see, Bach achieves a balance between the two approaches in the B-Minor Mass.

The most remarkable feature of the late-Baroque Catholic Mass was its happy accommodation of concerted and *a cappella* writing in the same work. In the Masses of the Venetian/Viennese School, especially, we find sections in retrospective Renaissance style standing next to sections in Baroque concerted style, producing what some scholars have called *stile misto*, or mixed style. This, too, was turned to expressive advantage, for it provided composers with additional means of presenting musical contrasts. Even a musician as steeped in *galant* style as Hasse turned to Renaissance writing in his church works, as attested by the "Kyrie eleison" II of his Mass in D Minor, composed in Dresden for the dedication of the new Hofkirche in 1751 (Example 1–4). The retrospective movement, a vocal fugue with doubling instruments, comes after an opening "Kyrie eleison" in *galant* concerted style and a "Christe eleison" written in the fashion of a love duet. This pattern—"Kyrie" I in concerted style, "Christe" as fashionable duet, and "Kyrie" II in *a cappella* style—was almost a Kyrie cliché in Dresden Masses. We find it often in the works of Heinichen, Zelenka, and Hasse, and in many of the Masses they imported from Vienna and Italy. And we find it, of course, in Bach's B-Minor Mass.

LUTHERAN PRACTICES IN LEIPZIG

The Reformation was—as the name implies—a movement to rectify Roman Catholicism rather than to reject it outright, and when Luther initially formulated a liturgy for the new Protestant *Hauptgottesdienst*, or the Principal Sunday Service, he retained the basic outline of the Latin Mass. In the *Formula missae et communionis* of 1523 he proposed an evangelical service that was essentially a "purified" Catholic Mass, in Latin except for the sermon and several hymns. The *Formula* included the traditional Kyrie, Gloria, Credo, Sanctus, and Agnus Dei, which were to be chanted in Latin by the choir. In 1526, in response to the publication of German Masses by

Example 1–4. Hasse: "Kyrie eleison" II from Mass in D Minor.

Kaspar Kantz and Thomas Münzer, Luther issued the *Deutsche Messe,* a vernacular service for "unlearned lay folk." Here he dropped the Gloria and presented alternatives for the remaining four portions of the Ordinary: for the Kyrie he proposed a new, simplified melody, with the text in Greek but without the threefold repetition of each supplication; for the Credo, now repositioned between the Gospel and the Sermon (rather than after both), he proposed his own 1524 paraphrase of the Creed, the German hymn "Wir glauben all' an einen Gott"; for the Sanctus he presented a new German hymn, "Jesaja dem Propheten das geschah"; and for the Agnus Dei he suggested singing "the German Agnus Dei" (probably the hymn "Christe, du Lamm Gottes"). In time, the hymn "Kyrie, Gott Vater in Ewigkeit" (a German paraphrase, first published in Naumburg in 1537, of the troped Kyrie *Kyrie fons bonitatis*) took the place of Luther's abridged Kyrie, and the hymn "Allein Gott in der Höh sei Ehr" (Nicolaus Decius, 1522) was adopted for the Gloria.

Luther voiced caution about celebrating the Mass solely in German, however. In the preface to the *Deutsche Messe* he warned:

> For in no wise would I want to discontinue the service in the Latin language, because the young are my chief concern. And if I could bring it to pass, and Greek and Hebrew were as familiar to us as the Latin and had as many fine melodies and songs, we would hold Mass, sing, and read on successive Sundays in all four languages, German, Latin, Greek, and Hebrew. I do not at all agree with those who cling to one language and despise all others. . . . It is also reasonable that the young should be trained in many languages; for who knows how God may use them in times to come?[20]

Despite this admonition, rural congregations, especially, fully embraced the vernacular service. But in Leipzig, Luther's vision of a polyglot liturgy remained strong, and at St. Thomas and St. Nikolai, the town's two main churches, *Hauptgottesdienst* continued to be a rich blend of Latin, German, and Greek elements far into the eighteenth century. The principal accounts of the Leipzig liturgy in Bach's day—Vopelius's New Leipzig Hymnal of 1682, various printed church and town almanacs, and the manuscript notes of St. Thomas Sexton Johann Rost[21]—show that the Ordinary was set to music in the form of Latin chants, German hymns, and Latin polyphonic settings of the Kyrie, Gloria, and Sanctus, depending on the occasion.[22]

The Kyrie was chanted in Greek or, on special festivals, performed polyphonically, in the church in which the "First Choir" was present.[23] In the other church on such occasions the congregation sang the German hymn "Kyrie, Gott Vater in Ewigkeit." The Gloria was chanted in Latin or performed polyphonically on festival Sundays; otherwise the congregation sang "Allein Gott in der Höh sei Ehr." The Creed was normally performed in its "Wir glauben" form. Yet according to Rost, during the last three Sundays of Advent and the four Sundays of Lent—the two periods when cantatas were not performed—the congregational singing of "Wir glauben" was preceded by the chanting of the Latin Credo by the choir.[24] Although the Sanctus seems to have been omitted on normal Sundays, on special feast days it was sung in polyphony (without the "Benedictus" and "Osanna") by the choir as the climax of the Preface (which was chanted in Latin by the officiant and choir). Finally, on special festivals when there were many communicants, the Latin Agnus Dei was sometimes chanted by the choir during the Eucharist, or the German "Christe, du Lamm Gottes" was sung, together with other hymns, by the congregation.

In short, the Latin Ordinary continued to play a substantial role in the Leipzig worship service in Bach's day, even though it had long since been replaced by German equivalents in most other Lutheran congregations. In Leipzig—a conservative bastion—all five portions were chanted in Latin at one time or another during the church year,[25] and on high feasts the Kyrie, Gloria, and Sanctus (without the "Osanna" and "Benedictus") were performed in polyphonic arrangements, which Bach, like his immediate predecessors and successors, presented as part of his Kantor duties.[26] Polyphonic settings of the Credo, Sanctus (in its full form), and Agnus Dei lay outside Lutheran practice, however.[27] For these, one had to look to the Catholic tradition, and for Bach, that undoubtedly meant the Dresden Court.

MASS WRITING IN DRESDEN

Dresden, the seat of the Saxon Elector, was both a Lutheran and a Catholic center in Bach's time. Its citizenry was staunchly Lutheran, having embraced the Protestant cause during the Reformation, when Elector Frederick the Wise offered Luther asylum in Wartburg Castle near Eisenach following the Diet of Worms. The Court, by contrast, was Catholic, in accordance with the decree of Elector Friedrich August I ("August the Strong," ruled 1694–1733), who converted to Catholicism in 1697 in order to extend his domain to Poland (where he reigned as August II). August's proclamation ushered in a period of awkward transition: his wife, the Electress Christiane Eberhardine, refused to become Catholic and remained steadfastly Lutheran until her death in 1727 (when a large memorial service, featuring Bach's "Trauer-Ode," BWV 198, was held in Protestant Leipzig), and the conversion of Crown Prince Friedrich August II in 1712 went unannounced for five years, for fear of unrest.[28] The religious situation at the Court stabilized only in 1719 with the Prince's marriage to a Catholic, Maria Josepha, the daughter of Emperor Joseph I of Austria. The nuptial agreement stipulated that the couple's children and grandchildren would be raised in the Roman Catholic religion.[29] The union greatly strengthened the Court's ties with Vienna and Rome, and this in turn led to the importation of large quantities of Latin-texted church music from those cities. By the time Friedrich August II ascended to the throne in 1733, Dresden had become, as Wolff has nicely phrased it, a Catholic Diaspora in the middle of the Lutheran heartland.[30]

Together, Friedrich August I and Friedrich August II built Dresden into the music capital of Germany. Friedrich August I, a Francophile, appointed the French-trained Jean Baptiste Volumier to serve as concertmaster of the Royal "Capell- und Cammer-Musique." Under Volumier's direction, the instrumental band became one of the most celebrated ensembles in Europe, boasting a host of renowned players, including violinist Johann Georg Pisendel, cellist A. A. de Rossi, flautists Pierre-Gabriel Buffardin and Johann Joachim Quantz, and lutanist Silvius Leopold Weiss. In 1708 August converted the court opera house into a Catholic chapel in order to demonstrate to Rome his firm commitment to Catholicism. The "Hofkirche im Theater" (Plate 1–1), as the reconstructed space was termed, served for Catholic worship until a new Hofkirche was built in 1751 (see Chapter 8). Weekly service music was entrusted to Kapellmeister Johann David Heinichen and, following his death in 1729, Zelenka, who gained the title of Church Composer in 1735. Protestant services continued at the Court, first under the musical direction of Kapellmeister Johann Christoph Schmidt (until 1728) and then under Vice-Kapellmeister Pantaleon Hebenstreit, who was, however, in fragile health. But Friedrich August I assigned the Court Capella to the Hofkirche, and hence it was the music for the Catholic service that attained unprecedented magnificence.

The opening of a new opera house in 1719, a majestic and sumptuously equipped theater built in the Zwinger complex by the famous architect Matthäus Daniel Pöppelmann, led to an era of operatic opulence and the further augmentation of the Court Capella with virtuoso singers, who not only appeared on stage but also took part in services at the Hofkirche. By 1730 young female singers and male castratos, specially trained for six years in Italy, were in place,[31] and within three years the immensely successful composer of Neapolitan operas Johann Adolf Hasse was working in residence as Kapellmeister. Friedrich August II (ruled as Elector 1733–1763, and in Poland, as August III, from 1735 to 1763), who as Crown Prince had traveled extensively in Italy, vigorously promoted Italian opera and church music and filled the Capella with Italian-trained musicians and composers. Pisendel, who succeeded Volumier as concertmaster

Plate 1-1. The "Hofkirche im Theater," Dresden (drawing by Raymond Le Plat, 1719; Dresden, Kupferstich-Kabinett, Staatliche Kunstsammlungen, *C 6691*).

in 1728, had studied with Vivaldi in Venice; Hasse had worked with Alessandro Scarlatti in Naples; Zelenka had studied with Lotti in Venice (as well as with Fux in Vienna). The Court's Italian vocalists, which by the mid-1730s included sopranos Faustina Bordoni (Hasse's wife) and Anna and Maria Negri, alto Margheritta Ermini, bass Cosimo Ermini, and castrato Giovanni Bindi, brought fame and glamor to opera productions and lent an air of the spectacular to Catholic service music in the Hofkirche.

Bach enjoyed close ties with music circles in Dresden. It was there that he challenged and vanquished (by default) the French organist Louis Marchand in 1717 and presented publicly acclaimed organ recitals in 1725, 1731, and 1736. During the 1731 visit he also performed at the Court and in all likelihood attended the premiere of Hasse's *Cleofide*. Bach was personally acquainted with many of the Capella's leading musicians, including Volumier, Heinichen, Zelenka, Hasse, Pisendel, and Weiss, and he counted among his patrons Count Hermann Carl von Keyserlingk, the Russian Ambassador to Dresden and alleged dedicatee of the "Goldberg" Variations. During his heated dispute with the Leipzig Town Council in 1730 over performance conditions, Bach pointed to the Dresden ensemble as an exemplary model ("One need only go to Dresden and see how the musicians there are paid by His Royal Majesty . . . [and consequently] relieved of all concern for their living, free from chagrin, and obligated each to master but a single instrument. It must be something choice and excellent to hear"[32]). After his son Wilhelm Friedemann's appointment as organist of the Sophienkirche in 1733, Bach's visits to Dresden became more frequent and prolonged, and in 1736, three years after submitting the Kyrie and Gloria that were later incorporated into the B-Minor Mass, he obtained the title of Court Composer.

Bach's increasingly close association with the Dresden Court in the 1730s and 1740s undoubtedly contributed to his late interest in Latin-texted church music, for as Horn has shown in his excellent survey, the Hofkirche repertory included not only works by Heinichen, Zelenka, and occasionally Hasse, but an attractively rich assortment of Italian and Viennese pieces as well.[33] The *a cappella* Masses of Palestrina held a prominent position and were performed on a regular basis.[34] Equally important were Baroque settings from the seventeenth and eighteenth centuries. Venetian practice was represented by music of Caldara, Lotti (who had served as Court Composer in Dresden from 1717 to 1719), and Antonio Vivaldi; Viennese practice by music of Fux, Caldara (again), Georg von Reutter Sr., and Francesco Conti; and Neapolitan practice by music of Alessandro Scarlatti, Mancini, Durante, Sarri, and Nicolò Jommelli. In addition, there was music from Bologna (Giuseppe Aldrovandini), Rome (Orazio Benevoli and Giuseppe Pitoni), and other Catholic music centers. The Hofkirche's inventory of Latin-texted church music was unsurpassed in Germany, and its contents could not have escaped Bach's attention. That he explored its resources is verified by Carl Philipp Emanuel Bach's well-known comment that his father "esteemed highly" in his final years "Fux, Caldara, Händel, Kayser, Hasse, both Grauns, Telemann, Zelenka, Benda, and in general everything that was worthy in Berlin and Dresden."[35] The inclusion of Fux, Caldara, and Zelenka points directly to the Hofkirche, for in Dresden it was their sacred works that held special prominence.

Viewed as a whole, the Dresden Mass settings display a number of general features that are highly pertinent to the B-Minor Mass (we will look at more specific details in Chapters 3 through 5):[36]

First, the range of Renaissance vocal style is remarkably impressive. Palestrina's Masses—Horn counts over twenty-five settings in Zelenka's possession[37]—include such learned pieces as the *Missa ad fugam*, the *Missa L'homme armé*, and the *Missa Ut re mi fa sol la*. One also finds Fux's

Missa canonica, a complete eighteenth-century setting of the Ordinary in Palestrina style, as well as a host of *a cappella* movements within concerted works. The movements within "mixed-style" Masses extend from the *galant* idiom of Hasse (illustrated by the "Kyrie eleison" II from his Mass in D Minor, cited above) to the more austere writing of Caldara. Wolff has shown that Bach was particularly attracted to Caldara's *stile antico* music, adding newly composed violin lines to the vocal parts of the Renaissance-style "Suscepit Israel" of his Magnificat in C Major.[38] The Hofkirche inventory, which includes almost a dozen Masses by Caldara, shows that Caldara himself liked to blend *a cappella* and *concertato* elements, as the obbligato violin parts that accompany the Renaissance-style vocal lines in the "Kyrie eleison" II from his *Missa Providentiae*[39] demonstrate (Example 1–5). As the "Credo" of the B-Minor Mass attests, this type of stylistic synthesis was not lost on Bach.

Second, the Dresden concerted settings display many recurring features—features that obviously reflect long-standing traditions of Catholic Mass writing. Gestures such as prefacing the "Kyrie eleison" with a slow introduction, setting the "Christe eleison" as a soprano-alto duet, ending the "Crucifixus" with a pianissimo passage to set the stage for a forte "Et resurrexit," and scoring the "Dona nobis pacem" as a Renaissance-style chorus fugue appear time and time again in the Dresden works, and one sees them carried to a new level of sophistication in the B-Minor Mass (we will look at specific examples in Chapters 3–5). The Hofkirche music served as a reliable guide for Bach as he studied the polyphonic Catholic Ordinary to familiarize himself with its conventions.

Third, the concerted Masses, both the sectional works of the Venetian/Viennese type and the multimovement works of the Neapolitan school, show a strong emphasis on chorus writing, a characteristic that most probably stems from the Renaissance roots of the genre. Of the thirty-one distinct sections in Caldara's *Missa Providentiae,* for instance, all but six are scored for chorus. When composing concerted church works Bach normally called for a preponderance of solo writing—that is, aria and recitative. The new weight given to chorus movements in the late portions of the B-Minor Mass, a tendency that we will examine in Chapters 4 and 5, may well reflect his growing familiarity with the scoring of the Dresden Ordinaries.

Fourth, Zelenka in particular took a very pragmatic approach toward Mass composition and performance. Vast quantities of music were needed to fulfill weekly Hofkirche requirements, and Zelenka commonly rounded

Example 1–5. Caldara: "Kyrie eleison" II from *Missa Providentiae*.

out incomplete settings of his own or of other composers by retexting music from existing portions, by composing new music, or by appropriating required segments from another Mass. For Durante's *Missa Modestiae*,[40] a large Neapolitan Kyrie-Gloria setting, for example, he fashioned a Sanctus and Agnus Dei by retexting selected passages drawn from the Kyrie and Gloria.[41] Many Dresden Masses display this type of patchwork. The "pastiche" nature of the Ordinary—the excerpt and insertability of its parts—is mirrored in the local custom of storing various portions of a given setting in separate folders. Zelenka's *Missa votiva*, for instance, is handed down in four folders: one for the Kyrie, one for the Gloria, one for the Credo (which, as we have noted, stems from Zelenka's *Missa Eucharistica*), and one for the Sanctus and Agnus Dei. The fact that the individual portions of an Ordinary setting could be treated as separate entities fit in well with Bach's inclination toward compilation in his late years. It allowed him to assemble a full Ordinary by using preexistent music for some portions and new (or newly arranged) music for others, much in the way that he had compiled the second volume of the Well-Tempered Clavier some ten years earlier. Moreover, the multifunctional nature of the Ordinary—one could perform an entire setting or extract just one or two portions (which were conveniently stored in separate folders)—paralleled Bach's desire, late in life, to create multifunctional collections: *Clavierübung* III, with its extractable duets and prelude and fugue, or the Musical Offering, with its extractable trio sonata,[42] for instance.

Finally, one is astonished at the scale of the largest Dresden Masses. A number of Neapolitan or Neapolitan-oriented Kyrie-Gloria settings, most written for five-part, SSATB chorus, approach or exceed forty-five minutes in duration. Sarri's *Missa Adjutorium*,[43] a Kyrie and Gloria for five-part chorus, strings, oboes, trumpet, and continuo, is representative. It consists of the following sections and dimensions:

Kyrie
    "Kyrie eleison"—D major
        [Andante?]; 74 mm. in $\frac{4}{4}$; chorus with solos; ritornello movement
    "Christe eleison"—B minor
        [Allegro?]; 71 mm. in $\frac{3}{4}$; chorus with solos; concerted movement
    "Kyrie eleison"—D major
        Largo; 11 mm. in $\frac{4}{4}$; chorus with solos; concerted movement

Gloria
    "Gloria in excelsis"—D major
        Vivace; 135 mm. in $\frac{2}{4}$; chorus with solos; ritornello movement

"Et in terra pax"—B minor
  Larghetto; 120 mm. in $\frac{3}{8}$; chorus with solos; concerted movement
"Domine Deus"—D major
  Andante; 70 mm. in $\frac{4}{4}$; tenor and soprano solos with chorus;
  ritornello movement
"Qui tollis"—G minor
  Andante ma non troppo; 71 mm. in $\frac{4}{4}$; soprano solo with oboe
  obbligato; ritornello movement.
"Qui sedes"—B minor
  Largo; 51 mm. in $\frac{4}{4}$; solos with chorus; ritornello movement
"Quoniam tu solus sanctus"—D major
  Vivace; 72 mm. in $\frac{4}{4}$; bass solo with trumpet, oboes, and strings;
  ritornello movement
"Cum Sancto Spiritu"—D major
  Largo/allegro; 4 mm. in $\frac{4}{4}$; 91 mm. in $\frac{3}{8}$; chorus with solos;
  ritornello movement

Mancini's *Missa* in E Minor and *Missa* in G Major are equally large, and Sarri's *Missa Divi Nepomuceni* is larger still.[44] All are Kyrie-Gloria settings, performed by Zelenka in the Hofkirche. The dimensions of such pieces must have impressed Bach. Here, obviously, was not only the prototype for his own Kyrie and Gloria but also the challenge for composing a *Missa tota* with music of similarly grand proportions.

Chapter 2

THE COMPOSITION OF THE B-MINOR MASS

— ∞ —

BACH IN LEIPZIG (1723–1750)

*W*hen Bach arrived in Leipzig in the spring of 1723 to take up his duties as Kantor of St. Thomas and Town Music Director, he stepped into one of the oldest and most prestigious music positions in Germany. Although he later claimed, in a moment of disenchantment, that he had been blissfully happy in Cöthen and had planned to spend the rest of his days there, the move to Leipzig was a step up the professional ladder, and not just in terms of salary. In Leipzig Bach was answerable to a stable, self-perpetuating Town Council rather than to an autocratic prince; he could compose both sacred and secular music; he had at his disposal a small but able band of professional musicians; and his sons could attend the university—an educational opportunity he himself had not been able to enjoy. In addition, Leipzig was an international trade city. With its three annual fairs and prosperous citizenry, it bustled with commercial and cultural activity.

Bach had not been the first choice for the job. The Town Council initially approached Telemann, whose musical accomplishments as a university student in Leipzig were well remembered (he had composed operas, established a collegium musicum, and lured singers and instrumentalists into the New Church). By the fall of 1722, when the Thomaskantor search was launched, Telemann was Kantor and Music Director in Hamburg and had written over 400 church cantatas—far more than the four dozen or so Bach had composed in Mühlhausen and Weimar. When Telemann declined, the

Leipzig Council approached Darmstadt Kapellmeister Christoph Graupner, who by that time had produced over 600 cantatas. It was only after Graupner declined, too, that the town overseers turned to Bach. Councilman Abraham Platz complained: "Since the best men can't be obtained, mediocre ones will have to be accepted." Platz may have overstated the case, but there can be little doubt that the Council offered Bach the job with a certain air of resignation. He was a famous keyboard player and concertmaster, to be sure, but his skills as a Kantor were untested. Moreover, he was uninterested in teaching Latin and less than enthusiastic about giving private singing and instrumental lessons to the boys of the school. Nevertheless, an agreement was reached, and on Sunday, May 30, 1723, Bach began his weekly duties with Cantata 75, *Die Elenden sollen essen.*

As if to put the Council's misgivings to rest, Bach initially approached his new responsibilities as Kantor with remarkable industry. The Obituary of 1754, compiled by his son Carl Philipp Emanuel and his student Johann Friedrich Agricola, states that he compiled five annual cycles of church cantatas,[1] and scholarship since World War II has shown that he seems to have assembled all five during the first six years in Leipzig.[2] From 1723 to 1724 he drew heavily on preexistent pieces from Weimar and Cöthen, refashioning texts and music wherever necessary. During the second year, 1724–1725, he compiled a cycle of new works, chorale cantatas written on hymn melodies and texts. From 1725 to 1727 he assembled a third annual cycle, often relying, once again, on earlier music. And from 1728 to 1729 he seems to have composed a fourth cycle, to texts by the local poet Christian Friedrich Henrici, called Picander. Little is known about the now-lost fifth cycle, yet most of it, too, appears to have been in place by 1729.[3] Bach wrote the vast majority of his church cantatas, then—up to 300 works—during the first six years of his Leipzig tenure. To this extraordinary period of vocal composition we can also add the St. John and St. Matthew Passions, the Magnificat (in its Eb form, BWV 243a), the Sanctus in D Major, BWV 232[III], the "Trauer-Ode," BWV 198, and most of the motets.

Bach's steady production of church works appears to have come to an abrupt halt in 1729, never to resume again. His decision to step back from cantata writing was surely influenced by increasing differences with the Town Council over the prerogatives of the Thomaskantor. From 1723 to 1726 Bach argued for the traditional right of the Kantor to direct the old and new services in the University Church. When the Council rejected his claim, he took the matter to Saxon Elector Friedrich August I, who awarded him jurisdiction over the old services only. In 1728 Bach protested that

the subdeacon was being allowed to choose hymns for the Vespers service—a privilege that usually fell to the Kantor. Here, too, he was unable to
win support. The poor performance conditions at the St. Thomas School
added to his disgruntlement. Bach claimed that the school was accepting
boys who were unusable for singing and that the Council was no longer
awarding honoraria to student instrumentalists. The issue reached a climax
in 1730, when Bach sent the authorities a stinging letter, the famous "Short
but Most Necessary Draft for a Well-Regulated Church Music,"[4] complain-
ing about the lack of capable choirboys and instrumentalists at his disposal. By August 1730 Bach found himself out of favor with the Council, which
voted to restrict his incidental income because of his "incorrigible" indifference toward his job.

    It could also be that Bach turned away from cantata writing in response
to an inner artistic need. Having written or revised some 300 works, he may
have yearned for a new compositional challenge. In March 1729 he took a
decisive step in that direction by becoming the director of the Collegium
Musicum founded by Telemann twenty-seven years earlier. The ensemble of
university students had been led since its inception by the organist of the
New Church. Now, as New Church organist Georg Schott left to become
Town Kantor in Gotha, Bach broke past tradition and stepped into the lead-
ership position himself. The Collegium presented public readings weekly,
indoors in Zimmermann's Coffee House in the winter months and outdoors
in Zimmermann's Coffee Garden in the summer. During the trade fairs, the
performances increased to twice per week. Bach may well have continued
to compose at the same demanding pace as earlier, but he now produced
secular cantatas, instrumental works, and keyboard pieces instead of sacred
cantatas, passions, and motets. He appears to have provided enormous
quantities of music for the Collegium, rearranging Cöthen pieces for different forces (violin concertos resurfaced as harpsichord concertos, for
instance) and writing new works altogether (the gamba sonatas, for example). Most striking is his flirtation with opera composition: Cantata 201,
Geschwinde, ihr wirbelnden Winde ("The Contest between Phoebus and
Pan," possibly written for the St. Michael's Fair, 1729), Cantata 213, *Laßt
uns sorgen, laßt uns wachen* ("Hercules at the Crossroads"), and other
Collegium vocal works border on chamber opera; Cantata 211, *Schweigt
stille, plaudert nicht* ("Coffee Cantata") displays the conventions of *opera
buffa*. Bach's involvement with progressive instrumental and vocal idioms
in the 1730s had a decisive effect on the works of his final decade, including the B-Minor Mass.

Bach directed the Collegium until 1737, and then again from 1739 to 1741 or so. From that time until his death in 1750 he increasingly withdrew from both church and collegium and devoted his attention to private projects: the publication of selected keyboard works, the study of Latin church music, the sorting of earlier compositions, and the compilation of encyclopedic compendia. He traveled more frequently to Berlin and Dresden, lingering even when duty and family required a timely return to Leipzig.[5] During the very last years of his life, Bach appears as an almost Beethoven-like figure, working independently on projects destined—it would seem—only for himself or posterity. The most ambitious of these projects was the B-Minor Mass.

NEW DIRECTIONS: BACH'S LATE COMPOSITIONAL PRACTICES

The years after 1729 were also critical for Bach with regard to his compositional practices. A number of new developments bear directly on the composition of the B-Minor Mass.

The first is his growing reliance on parody technique to produce vocal works. By the late Baroque, parody procedure—the art of underlaying a new text to old music—had become part and parcel of a composer's trade. In Germany, the increased use of "madrigal" poetry (that is, specially written verse) in concerted vocal works allowed composers to interchange texts in the same poetic meter, as long as the new text fit the character of the old music.[6] The steady demand for new pieces made recycling preexistent material an attractive and even necessary compositional option. As we noted in Chapter 1, Jan Dismas Zelenka used parody technique extensively in Dresden to expand short Masses into *Missa tota* settings. Parody also drew on the German penchant for *Verbesserung*, or improvement. In architecture, for instance, new buildings were commonly constructed by expanding old ones, rather than razing the original and starting from the ground up. The "new" St. Thomas School of 1732 (Plate 4–2 in Chapter 4) resulted from Georg Werner's upward extension (by one story) and remodeling of the older edifice. Werner retained the positioning of the windows and doors but fully recast the facade and roof. Bach's refashioned home was, in a sense, a parody of the earlier structure.

In music, parody technique was by no means frowned upon. When carried out with finesse, it was greatly admired. We find Bach's Weimar colleague Johann Gottfried Walther praising Braunschweig Kapellmeister Georg Caspar Schürmann for also being a skilled poet, who knew, among other things, "how to lay a well-made text to another's composition."[7] Some, such as Johann Adolph Scheibe, voiced uneasiness about deriving church music from salacious secular scores:

> He [Pater Präses] had a sheaf of Italian opera arias stocked up, so whenever he needed a sacred aria for a *Gloria,* he made a parody out of a lovesick and voluptuous opera aria, and performed it with all devotion, just as if opera and church music were all one and the same, and as if one could sigh just as voluptuously, tenderly, and basely over the highest being as to an insensible beauty.[8]

Such borrowings were nevertheless tolerated—indeed, they carried the imprimatur of Luther himself, who, as it is well known, remarked that the Devil should not have all the good tunes. As we shall observe, Bach did not hesitate to draw on the techniques—and in the "Et in unum Dominum" seemingly the notes, too (see Chapter 4)—of the Neapolitan love duet when he wished to portray the intimate relationship between Christ and humankind.

Bach first used parody procedure extensively during the initial Leipzig years, when under the pressure of weekly deadlines he turned to Weimar and Cöthen works for material that could be converted quickly to sacred cantatas. For instance, Cantata 208, *Was mir behagt, ist nur die muntre Jagd,* most probably composed for the birthday of Prince Christian of Weissenfels in 1713, provided music for Cantata 68 of 1725 and Cantata 149 of c. 1729. Some of the most inventive sacred parodies appear in the third cantata cycle, in which Bach returned to copious borrowing after a year of new composition in the chorale-cantata cycle. According to recent calculations, at least twenty percent of the music in the extant cantata cycles stems from earlier material,[9] and since much of the Cöthen repertory is lost, which prevents comparison, the actual figure is surely higher.

Bach's reliance on parody continued when he took over the Collegium Musicum in 1729. In need of new music on a weekly basis once again, he drew heavily from the Cöthen instrumental pieces, revising the scores to fit the resources of his student ensemble.

What had been a necessity for church and collegium became, during the 1730s, a standard approach for Bach. The St. Mark Passion, the Christmas Oratorio, the four short Masses, and most other vocal pieces written after

1730 appear to stem largely from parody procedure. As Hans-Joachim Schulze has shown, the direction of the parodying was invariably secular to sacred,[10] suggesting that Bach was also motivated by the desire to preserve ephemeral, occasional works in a more enduring form—namely, as liturgical pieces that could be performed repeatedly. The conversion was not unlike turning a Proper into an Ordinary.

The ease with which Bach transformed Cantatas 213, 214, and 215 into the Christmas Oratorio and the close chronological proximity of the models and product (the cantatas were composed in 1733–1734, the oratorio in 1734–1735) have led scholars to suspect that Bach wrote certain secular works with the sacred parodies already in mind. Such parodying may have been a labor-saving device. But elsewhere his transformation of the chorus "Jauchzet, ihr erfreuten Stimmen" of Cantata 120 into the "Et expecto" of the B-Minor Mass, or Pergolesi's *Stabat mater* into *Tilge, Höchster, meine Sünden,* BWV 1083, involved so much revision that one wonders whether it would not have been easier to start from scratch. These pieces suggest that Bach began to view parodying as an end in itself, as a creative art that he pursued with increasing vigor in the later Leipzig years.

It is possible, of course, that as Bach reached his forty-fifth birthday in 1730 he experienced what we would term today a mid-life crisis and began to suffer from *horror vacui*—from fear of the blank page (as Hans-Joachim Schulze has put it).[11] A significant number of newly composed masterpieces—the organ works of *Clavierübung* III, the "Goldberg" Variations, the Art of Fugue, and others—put that explanation to rest, however. It is more likely that Bach's strong desire for perfection, witnessed in the ongoing refinement of details in the Well-Tempered Clavier or the Great Eighteen Chorales, may have led naturally to parody technique, which offered extensive opportunity for reworking earlier scores. Bach viewed his vocal parodies as "new" creations, commonly imploring Christ's help at the top of the scores with the invocation "J.J." ("Jesu Juva"—"With Jesus's help"). For Telemann and others, parody appears to have been more burdensome than writing new music. For the aging Bach, parody became a central part of the creative process, enabling him to be increasingly self-critical. The supreme refinement of the B-Minor Mass is due in large part to the parody process.

The second shift after 1730 is Bach's expanded interest in Latin church music. As we noted in Chapter 1, Latin-texted music remained a part of the Lutheran worship service in Leipzig: Renaissance *a cappella* motets were performed weekly, and concerted settings of the *Missa* (Kyrie and Gloria), the Sanctus (minus "Osanna" and "Benedictus"), and the Magnificat were offered on high feasts, especially those of Christmas and Easter. In Weimar, Bach seems to have had limited need for Latin pieces, apparently composing only one Kyrie (the Kyrie "Christe, du Lamm Gottes," BWV 233a) and depending mostly on *Missae* or single Kyries by Johann Ludwig Bach, Christoph Pez, Marco Giuseppe Peranda, and others. He also copied out the score of Francesco Bartolomeo Conti's concerted motet *Languet anima mea.* Presumably, he assembled these works after his promotion to concertmaster in 1714, when he first gained the opportunity to write church music for the court chapel.

It was in Leipzig that Bach began in earnest to assemble a collection of Latin pieces. He composed the E♭ version of the Magnificat, BWV 243a, for Christmas 1723, inserting among the verses of Mary's Canticle to Elizabeth four German-texted interpolations for the holiday season. The next year he wrote the six-voice Sanctus in D Major, BWV 232^{III}, which he later appropriated for the B-Minor Mass. During the first Leipzig years he also arranged two smaller Sanctus settings, BWV 237 and 238, and reused a number of the Latin pieces assembled in Weimar.

After the yearly flow of church cantatas had ceased in 1729, Bach started to focus on Latin-texted church music in a more concentrated way. Between 1730 and 1740 we find him gathering additional Sanctus settings (BWV 239 and BWV Anh. 28), *Missae* by Johann Hugo von Wilderer, Francesco Durante, Antonio Lotti, and an unidentified composer (possibly Johann Ludwig Bach or Lotti, again), and six more encompassing Masses (Kyrie through Sanctus) from Giovanni Battista Bassani's *Acroama missale.* Among the Mass composers, Wilderer was a Mannheim Kapellmeister. But Durante was stationed in Naples, Lotti in Venice, and Bassani in Bergamo; through studying the works of these composers Bach kept abreast of Catholic church music in Italy.

Bach's heightened interest in Latin-texted church music in the 1730s reflects his preoccupation with the Catholic Court in Dresden, to which he submitted the five-voice *Missa* of 1733, BWV 232^{I}, and probably the revised, D-major version of the Magnificat, BWV 243, as well,[12] in the hope of receiving an appointment as Court Composer. The *Missa* was followed by a flurry of congratulatory compositions for the royal family (Cantatas 205a, 213, 214, 215, and two lost works), suggesting that Bach was intent on winning favor with Friedrich August II in every possible way. After he attained the title of *Hofcompositeur* in 1736, his study of the Latin repertory intensified, presumably because he was now fulfilling his promise to provide the Elector with music "for the church as well as the orchestra"—a point to which we will return shortly.

In the 1740s Bach presented additional *Missa* and Magnificat settings in Leipzig, including Palestrina's *Missa sine nomine* (Bach had the entire Mass copied out, but he performed only the usable Kyrie and Gloria). More importantly, he fashioned arrangements of Antonio Caldara's Magnificat in C Major, Bassani's *Acroama missale* Masses (which had been copied earlier), Johann Kaspar Kerll's eight-voice Sanctus from the *Missa superba,* and Pergolesi's *Stabat mater.* As the sources show, the Kerll and Pergolesi arrangements, at least, were performed. But the revisional work in general, which sometimes involved adding obbligato instrumental parts or writing new music altogether,[13] undoubtedly served as private study for Bach as well, much as his keyboard transcriptions of instrumental music by Vivaldi, Torelli, and Corelli had done in earlier years. The vocal arrangements provided firsthand experience in the Renaissance *a cappella* style (the Palestrina Mass, especially), the Baroque concerted style (the Bassani, Caldara, and Kerll pieces), and the most progressive *galant* church style (the Pergolesi *Stabat mater*). Like the keyboard transcriptions, the Latin arrangements paved the way for a shift in Bach's personal idiom.

The third late change is Bach's increased enthusiasm for encompassing, "encyclopedic" compendia. By 1729 Bach was no stranger to systematic collections. The *Orgelbüchlein,* with chorales arranged by liturgical function, dates from the Weimar years, and the first volume of the Well-Tempered Clavier, with preludes and fugues ordered by ascending keys, dates from 1722. But beginning with *Clavierübung* I (the Six Partitas) of 1726–1731, Bach focused not just on logical organizational plans but on assembling pieces that methodically—in some cases, exhaustively—illustrated the diverse stylistic possibilities of a specific genre. In *Clavierübung* I, for instance, he commenced each of the Partitas with a different type of prelude (Praeludium, Sinfonia, Fantasia, Ouvertüre, Praeambulum, and Toccata) and used a different meter in each of the five gigues ($\mathbf{C}$, $\frac{12}{8}$, $\frac{3}{4}$, $\frac{6}{8}$, and $\pmb{\phi}$). Four years later, in *Clavierübung* II, Bach juxtaposed a French Overture with an Italian Concerto to demonstrate the difference between the two leading national styles of the day (to emphasize the point, he set the Overture in B minor and the Concerto in F major, keys a tritone apart).

In *Clavierübung* III (1739) Bach illustrated the various ways of writing an organ chorale, from the *stile antico* of *Aus tiefer Not, schrei ich zur dir,* BWV 686, to the *galant* idiom of the *Fughetta super Dies sind die heil'gen Zehn Gebot,* BWV 679. The second volume of the Well-Tempered Clavier, assembled around the same time, shows an equally wide stylistic range. The extraordinary diversity of prelude and fugue types and the abundance of dance music distinguish volume two from volume one, written twenty years before. In the Art of Fugue (c. 1740–50), *Clavierübung* IV (the "Goldberg" Variations; 1741), the Musical Offering (1747), and the Canonic Variations on "Vom Himmel hoch" (c. 1747) Bach explored increasingly sophisticated organizational plans.[14] In the Canonic Variations and the Art of Fugue his self-criticism became so great that he produced two equally valid versions of each work—seemingly because he could not settle on a single, definitive scheme.

During the Weimar years, Bach created an innovative, cosmopolitan idiom by amalgamating the chief national styles of the time: Italian, French, German, English, and Polish. As Robert L. Marshall has recently proposed,[15] in the projects of the 1730s and 1740s Bach achieved yet another major synthesis by bringing together the principal historical styles of the day—Renaissance, Baroque, and Preclassical—and displaying them in compilations arranged with brilliantly calculated logic. It is the B-Minor Mass that displays this new transcendence and order on the grandest possible scale.

PREPARATORY STEPS: THE SANCTUS OF 1724, THE *Missa* OF 1733, CREDO STUDIES

The oldest music in the B-Minor Mass is found in the "Crucifixus," which is derived from the chorus "Weinen, Klagen, Sorgen, Zagen" of Cantata 12 of 1714. If one takes 1714 as the starting point for the B-Minor Mass, it follows that Bach evolved the work over a period of thirty-five years, a gestation longer than that of Beethoven's Ninth Symphony (thirty-two years)[16] or that of Wagner's Ring (twenty-six years). But to make such a claim would be stretching a point, for when Bach wrote Cantata 12 in Weimar he surely had no inkling that he would one day appropriate the music for a monumental *Missa tota*. One is on safer ground to begin with the Sanctus in D Major, BWV 232[III], not only because the piece was later incorporated into the B-Minor Mass with very little change, but also because it is the first work in which Bach's great ambitions for the Mass Ordinary come to the fore.

The Sanctus was composed for Christmas Day 1724. For Bach, it was a time of remarkable productivity: he was in the midst of compiling the chorale-cantata cycle, and for the fourteen-day stretch from Christmas to the First Sunday after Epiphany (January 7) he wrote, prepared, and performed not only the Sanctus but seven other new works—Cantatas 91 (first version), 121, 133, 122, 41, 123, and 124. Presumably, he was able to carry out much of the composing during the *tempus clausum*, the period between the Second Sunday in Advent and Christmas, when concerted music was not performed in church. Still, it must have been a daunting task to produce so many new pieces in so short a time. In the case of the Sanctus, three small sketches in the margins of the relatively neat original score (*P 13* in the Berlin State Library) suggest that Bach wrote the seventeen-part work quickly and without the aid of a preliminary draft.[17]

The Sanctus calls for six voices (three sopranos, alto, tenor, and bass), three trumpets and timpani, three oboes, strings, and continuo. It was Bach's most ambitiously scored vocal work before the St. Matthew Passion, and he seems to have been justly proud of his handiwork, for sometime after Christmas 1724 he lent the original performance parts (or at least most of them) to Count Franz Anton Sporck, a Bohemian nobleman and music enthusiast based in Prague. Sporck apparently failed to return the parts, and when Bach performed the Sanctus again, most probably on Easter Day 1727, he had to have his St. Thomas School scribes write out a new set.[18] Bach performed the Sanctus at least once more in Leipzig, sometime between the years 1743 and 1748—that is, during the time he began to contemplate the composition of the B-Minor Mass.

Nine years after penning the six-voice Sanctus, Bach composed the most important segment of music that ended up in the B-Minor Mass, the five-voice *Missa* that he presented, together with a letter requesting a court title, to Saxon Elector Friedrich August II in Dresden in the summer of 1733. Friedrich August I had died on February 1, and Bach must have felt that the new ruler, who as Elector Prince had helped to build the Court Capella into one of the finest ensembles in Europe, would be especially receptive to his request. Bach's petition to Friedrich August II reads as follows:

Most Gracious Lord, Most Serene Elector, Most Gracious Lord!

To Your Royal Highness I submit in deepest devotion the present slight labor of that knowledge which I have achieved in *musique*, with the most wholly submissive prayer that Your Highness will look upon it with Most Gracious Eyes, according to Your Highness's World-Famous Clemency and not according to the poor *composition*; and thus deign to take me under Your Most Mighty Protection. For some years and up to the present moment I have held the *Directorium* of the Music in the two principal churches in Leipzig, but have innocently had to suffer one injury or another, and on occasion also a diminution of the fees accruing to me in this office; but these injuries would disappear altogether if Your Royal Highness would grant me the favor of conferring upon me a title of Your Highness's Court Capella, and would let Your High Command for the issuing of such a document go forth to the proper place. Such a most gracious fulfillment of my most humble prayer will bind me to unending devotion, and I offer myself in most indebted obedience to show at all times, upon Your Royal Highness's Most Gracious Desire, my untiring zeal in the composition of music for the church as well as for the orchestra, and to devote my entire forces to the service of Your Highness, remaining in unceasing fidelity,

    Your Royal Highness's most humble and most obedient slave,

Johann Sebastian Bach
Dresden, July 27, 1733[19]

Precisely when the *Missa* was written and where it was performed—if indeed it was performed at all—have been the subjects of considerable scholarly debate. Arnold Schering proposed that Bach wrote the work soon after Friedrich August I's death and performed it before Friedrich August II on April 21 in St. Nikolai in Leipzig, where the new Elector was honored with a special fealty celebration.[20] More recently, scholars have ruled out such a performance on several grounds. First, an April performance would have fallen in the middle of the five-month mourning period for Friedrich August I, a time when concerted music was forbidden in Saxon churches. Second, the materials submitted to Friedrich August II (*Mus. 2405-D-21* in the Saxon State Library) point more clearly to a performance in Dresden: the parts are written on a type of paper found only in Dresden documents; the figured continuo part (Plate 2–1), presumably for organ, is untransposed, reflecting Dresden practice rather than Leipzig (where the organ was normally notated down a step);[21] the oboe d'amore parts are notated in French violin clef rather than treble clef (as was customary in Leipzig); and both the title on the wrapper of the parts and the petition to Friedrich August II are in the hand of Dresden amanuensis Gottfried Rausch, who copied documents for Zelenka and others at the court.[22] In addition, when producing the performance parts Bach turned for assistance principally, if not wholly, to family members—Anna Magdalena, Wilhelm Friedemann, and Carl Philipp Emanuel[23]—rather than to St. Thomas School students, whose services he normally employed in Leipzig for church works. The absence of St. Thomas copyists hints at a special, out-of-town event.

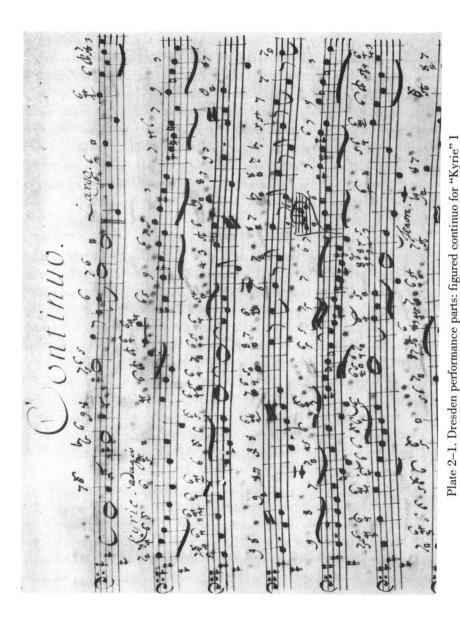

Plate 2–1. Dresden performance parts: figured continuo for "Kyrie" I (Dresden, Saxon State Library, *Mus. 2405-D-21*).

The appearance of the *Missa* parts suggests an imminent performance. Bach carried out the bulk of the copying himself, interceding several times in parts started by others.[24] Articulation marks and tempo indications are plentiful but inconsistent (see Chapter 7), and the vocal cues in the continuo part are incomplete. The first page of oboe 1 shows a change of notation: the copyist first drew treble clefs, which Bach scratched out and replaced with French violin clefs for d'amore instruments. These factors point to haste, to copying carried out in Dresden on short notice. One cannot prove that the Kyrie and Gloria sounded, for there are no contemporary reports of a performance (though such reports were rare for music events at the time). However, it makes little sense for Bach to have produced a set of performance parts—parts which contain a wealth of details that are meaningful only within the context of playing the piece—unless a performance was at hand.

Shifting the performance of the *Missa* from April in Leipzig to July in Dresden affects not only the date but also the circumstances of composition. Since Bach normally wrote vocal works just before they were needed,[25] it is likely that he did not begin to compose the Kyrie and Gloria until shortly before the July 27 visit, and then only when the prospect of a trip to Dresden became evident.[26] That first occurred toward the end of May, when the death of Sophienkirche organist Christian Petzold opened a position for which Wilhelm Friedemann was eminently qualified. Bach wasted no time aggressively seeking the post for his oldest son, writing letters in Friedemann's name on June 7 to the Dresden Town Council and to Council Advisor Paul Christian Schröter. In addition, Bach probably wrote out the final version of the Prelude and Fugue in G Major, BWV 541, for Friedemann to use during his audition, as Schulze has recently argued.[27] The audition took place on June 22, and the Church Council awarded Friedemann the Sophienkirche post the next day. It would have been at that point that Bach could predict a family trip to Dresden to help Friedemann settle in.

One can theorize, then, that Bach wrote the *Missa* between June 23 and July 27—a span of only four and a half weeks. It is also possible that although he planned to present the work to Friedrich August II during the July visit, he did not anticipate a performance of the music (since he seems to have left for Dresden without performance parts or paper on which to copy them). The performance may have materialized only after Bach reached the Saxon center.

Assuming that a performance occurred, where did it take place? The petition of July 27 points, of course, to the Catholic Hofkirche (see Plate

1–1 in Chapter 1), and a number of recent writers have linked the virtuosic style of the *Missa*'s arias with soprano Faustina Bordoni, castrato Giovanni Bindi, and other illustrious members of the Court Capella.[28] The use of two obbligato bassoons in the "Quoniam tu solus sanctus," too, points to the Hofkirche ensemble, which included five specialists on the instrument (see Chapter 7). Bach had good connections with the Capella—as we have noted, composers Jan Dismas Zelenka and Johann Adolf Hasse, concert-master Johann Georg Pisendel, lutenist Silvius Weiss, and others were per-sonal friends—and the group may in fact have performed the *Missa* in the Hofkirche.

It is also possible, however, that the work was performed in the Sophien-kirche, where Wilhelm Friedemann was now ensconced. The untransposed continuo part of the Dresden materials would have worked equally well in the Sophienkirche, since its Silbermann organ, like the instrument in the Hofkirche im Theater (and later those in the Frauenkirche and the new Hofkirche), was tuned in chamber pitch.[29] If the *Missa* was given in the Sophienkirche, however, one must ask what group performed it. The church had no resident ensemble, since concerted music was presented there only on the feasts of Christmas, Easter, and Pentecost. Members of the Court Capella played in the Sophienkirche on occasion, at least,[30] and may have done so for the *Missa* during the Bachs' July visit, to honor the recent appointment of Friedemann as Organist. Containing the Kyrie and Gloria only, the *Missa* would have been suitable in the Lutheran Sophienkirche as well as in the Catholic Hofkirche.

Two aspects of the performance parts further becloud the issue. First, the principal violin 1, which contains the violin solo of the "Laudamus te," shows no indication of having been earmarked for Court Concertmaster Pisendel. It was customary in Hofkirche performance materials to inscribe the principal violin 1 "Monsieur Pisendel" or "Signor Pisendel."[31] If Pisendel played in the *Missa* performance, why didn't he or Bach, a friend from Weimar days, mark the violin 1 part in the usual way? Second, as we have noted, the *Missa* continuo part (Plate 2–1, above) contains vocal cues. This suggests not only that Bach did not participate in the performance (since he would not have required such cues), but that the ensemble was led by the keyboard continuo player. That would point to Friedemann rather than Pisendel. In sum, the location and ensemble of the Dresden perfor-mance—if there truly was one—are issues that must remain open.

The use of a *Missa* for the Dresden submission was a fine stroke of diplomacy on Bach's part, for the Kyrie and Gloria paid homage to both the

Catholic and the Lutheran traditions in the Saxon capital. The five-part vocal texture, which Bach had used for the E♭ Magnificat of 1723, shows that he was aiming not at German models but rather at the large Neapolitan-style Mass settings that crowned the Dresden Court Mass repertory. The "Gratias agimus tibi" and the "Qui tollis" are demonstrably parodies, and it is quite likely that many—if not all—of the other movements stem from earlier material as well. The high degree of borrowing would accord with Bach's work patterns in the 1730s and with the idea that the piece was composed in a relatively short period of time.

Despite the extraordinary nature of the 1733 *Missa*, Bach's request for a court appointment was tabled until 1736, when a second letter of application, combined with the intercession of Count Hermann von Keyserlingk, persuaded the Elector to grant the desired Hofcompositeur title. On December 1, 1736, Bach celebrated his new appointment with a recital on the Silbermann organ in the recently completed Frauenkirche.

Bach returned to Mass composition around 1738, penning the short *Missa* settings in A major, BWV 234, and G major, BWV 236, and probably those in F major, BWV 233, and G minor, BWV 235, as well.[32] These works, which each contain a Kyrie and Gloria, are entitled "Lutheran Masses" in the *Neue Bach-Ausgabe*, and the A-major setting, at least, seems to have been performed in Leipzig.[33] There is a good possibility, however, that the short Masses were composed for Dresden as part of Bach's promise to provide Friedrich August II with works "for the church as well as for the orchestra"—as Philipp Spitta already proposed in the nineteenth century.[34] The works have been the target of much criticism because of their high degree of parody,[35] yet as we observed in Chapter 1, many of the Masses performed at the Dresden Court by Zelenka have a patchwork origin, with movements fashioned hastily out of preexistent music and a certain insouciance toward text underlay. Bach's short Masses have a similar background, and it is easier to see them fitting positively into the Dresden Mass tradition than negatively into Bach's oeuvre. But no matter what their purpose, they demonstrate Bach's continued interest in the Latin Mass.

A half-decade or so after composing the short Masses, most probably in December 1745, Bach returned to the *Missa* of 1733 to borrow three movements for the Latin-texted work *Gloria in excelsis Deo*, BWV 191.[36] The new piece consists of the chorus "Gloria in excelsis Deo" (transferred with little change from the *Missa*) followed, after a pause for an oration, by the small doxology in the form of the duet "Gloria Patri" (derived from the A section of the "Domine Deus") and the chorus "Sicut erat in principio" (taken from the "Cum Sancto Spiritu," with six measures and fully independent flute and oboe parts added).[37] The relationship of the two scores is as follows:

1733 *missa*		*gloria in excelsis deo*
Chorus: "Gloria in excelsis" (176 mm.)	→	Chorus: "Gloria in excelsis" (176 mm.)
Duet: "Domine Deus" (95 mm.)	→	Duet: "Gloria Patri" (74 mm.)
Chorus: "Cum Sancto Spiritu" (128 mm.)	→	Chorus: "Sicut erat in principio" (134 mm.)

Fashioning the *Gloria in excelsis Deo* gave Bach the opportunity to review the 1733 *Missa* and may well have spurred him to consider using the score in still other ways. Indeed, it could have been at this moment, midwinter 1745, that he first envisioned setting the entire Mass Ordinary, for soon afterward we see the first concrete signs that he was moving beyond Kyrie and Gloria movements to the music of the Credo. Around 1747–1748 he returned to the manuscript copy (*Mus.ms. 1160* in the Berlin State Library) of Bassani's *Acroama missale* that a St. Thomas School scribe had written out a dozen years earlier. Issued in Augsburg in 1709, the *Acroama* collection ("Acroama" means "that which is heard with pleasure") consisted of six small concerted Mass settings of the Venetian/Viennese type, each composed of Kyrie, Gloria, Credo, and Sanctus (through the "Osanna" I). Bach now focused on a specific compositional issue in the Credo movements. Although the Credo music of Mass 3 began with the words "Credo in unum Deum," that of the other Masses commenced with the second phrase of the Latin text, "Patrem omnipotentem," leaving the "Credo in unum Deum" to be provided in chant by a precentor. It was to the "Patrem" Credos that Bach turned, in order to experiment with ways of inserting the "Credo in unum Deum" phrase into the polyphony.

In Masses 1, 2, 4, and 6 he was able to squeeze the words into the existing "Patrem omnipotentem" music by altering the text underlay. Such a procedure was not possible in Mass 5, however, and for this piece Bach composed a short, polyphonic "Credo in unum Deum" insert, BWV 1081. The interpolation, which we will discuss further in Chapter 4, displays the same amalgamative style as the "Credo in unum Deum" of the B-Minor Mass: Renaissance *a cappella* vocal parts supported by a Baroque walking-bass ostinato. In addition, the music leads directly into Bassani's concerted "Patrem omnipotentem," forming a pair of contrasting movements much like the *stile antico* "Credo" and *stile moderno* "Patrem" of the B-Minor

Mass. The new "Credo" setting is only sixteen measures long; nevertheless, it has all the earmarks of a miniature "dry run" for the "Credo in unum Deum"/"Patrem omnipotentem" section of the Credo of the B-Minor Mass.

It is reasonable to assume that the early version of the "Credo in unum Deum" movement of the B-Minor Mass, discovered only in 1992 by Peter Wollny, dates from the same period as the *Acroama missale* revisions.[38] Written a whole step lower than the final version, the movement appears to have been conceived for a purpose outside the B-Minor Mass. Was it a polyphonic preface to another composer's five-voice Credo, one beginning with "Patrem omnipotentem" in the fashion of the five Bassani Masses? The fact that the score contains continuo figures (Plate 2–2) hints at a performance of some sort, perhaps one outside Bach's immediate circle. Or was it an isolated study, the expansion of an idea first tested in the Bassani interpolation? The stylistic similarity to the Bassani insert and the larger, more complex setting points to such a connection. What seems certain is that the Credo studies of 1747–1748 were soon followed by the B-Minor Mass itself.

Plate 2–2. Early version of the "Credo in unum Deum" (Gotha, Landes- und Forschungsbibliothek, *Mus 2° 54c/3*).

Missa tota: THE COMPOSITION
OF THE B-MINOR MASS

There is general agreement among specialists today that Bach assembled the B-Minor Mass during the last two years of his life. In the most recent scholarly assessment of his late activities, the Mass is assigned to the specific period August 1748-October 1749.[39] It has taken historians almost a century to arrive at this conclusion, for reasons that become clear when one considers the difficulties surrounding the dating of the piece.

Neither Bach's letters nor contemporary documents contain any mention of the B-Minor Mass—a circumstance not at all unusual in an age when composers were largely considered craftsmen rather than artists. The sole source of information about the Mass's origin is its autograph, *P 180* in the Berlin State Library, a complex manuscript that has been slow to yield its secrets.

P 180 is a 188-page compilation consisting of four parts, each with a title page. There is no title page or title for the complete work; the individual title pages read as follows:

"No. 1. Missa" [Kyrie and Gloria]

"No. 2. Symbolum Nicenum" [Credo]

"No. 3. Sanctus" [Sanctus, without "Osanna" and "Benedictus"]

"No. 4. Osanna/Benedictus/Agnus Dei et Dona nobis pacem" ["Osanna" and "Benedictus" of the Sanctus, and Agnus Dei]

The earliest editions of the B-Minor Mass, the Nägeli-Simrock print of 1833–1845 and the highly influential *Bach-Gesamtausgabe* of 1856–1857, glossed over the unusual division of the *P 180* manuscript and presented Bach's masterpiece as a Catholic Mass Ordinary with the traditional five parts: Kyrie, Gloria, Credo, Sanctus, and Agnus Dei.

It was Spitta who first recognized the heterogeneous nature of *P 180* as the key to unlocking the compositional history of the B-Minor Mass. Writing in 1880, he noted that the manuscript contained two different types of paper, one in the *Missa* section and one in the remaining portions. Using watermarks as a guide, Spitta linked the first paper with the mid-1730s and the second with the early 1730s, and proposed that Bach commenced by writing the Credo (No. 2) around 1732, continued by composing the

"Sanctus" and "Osanna" to "Dona nobis pacem" (Nos. 3 and 4) around 1735, and finished by writing out a new copy of the Dresden *Missa* (No. 1) around 1736.[40] In Spitta's account, the B-Minor Mass emerged as a product of Bach's middle Leipzig years, with the Art of Fugue taking the place of honor as the composer's final project. This view held sway for seventy-five years.

In the early 1950s, Friedrich Smend fully reevaluated *P 180* in conjunction with editing the *Neue Bach-Ausgabe*. Smend concluded that the Credo was written in 1732, as Spitta had proposed, but suggested slightly different dates for the other parts. In his opinion, Bach composed the "Sanctus" in 1736 and the "Osanna" to "Dona nobis pacem" portions in 1738–1739 before using the original 1733 score of the Dresden *Missa* to complete the Mass.[41] More controversial was Smend's proposal that Bach never viewed the work as a united whole. Pointing time and time again to the variegated nature of the autograph manuscript and the absence of an encompassing title, Smend argued that there was no such thing as a unified B-Minor Mass. As a consequence, he printed the piece in four parts in the *Neue Bach-Ausgabe*, with the title "Missa/Symbolum/Nicenum/Sanctus/Osanna, Benedictus, Agnus Dei et Dona nobis pacem (later called 'Mass in B Minor')." Smend's "so-called B-Minor Mass" theory sent shock waves through the music world.[42]

The shock waves were short-lived, however, for within two years another German scholar, Georg von Dadelsen, refuted Smend's theory.[43] Armed with new, encompassing studies of the watermarks, handwriting, and scribes of Bach's manuscripts,[44] Dadelsen demonstrated that the B-Minor Mass was conceived as a unified whole (the numbered title pages are indeed in Bach's hand) and that the contents of the *P 180* autograph date from two distinct periods (reflecting the two watermarks discerned by Spitta).[45] In Dadelsen's dating, the *Missa* was composed in 1733, as Smend observed. But the remaining portions—Nos. 2, 3, and 4—and the title pages were written not in the 1730s, as Spitta and Smend had believed, but in the 1740s, and probably in the very last years of Bach's life.

Dadelsen's dating of the late portions was initially challenged by Wolff, who proposed on stylistic grounds that Bach may have composed the *Symbolum Nicenum* around 1742–1745, in conjunction with several *stile antico* projects.[46] More recently, however, Dadelsen's chronology has been upheld by Yoshitake Kobayashi, who was able to link the labored handwriting that appears in parts of the Credo, Sanctus, and Agnus Dei portions of *P 180* with that found in other Bach manuscripts and documents dating from August 1748 to October 1749.[47] As Kobayashi convincingly shows, this fourteen-month span seems to have been Bach's last active period. During this time, the aging Kantor of St. Thomas appears to have had difficulty manipulating a pen (his script is uncharacteristically stiff and stilted), and by the summer of 1749 his eyesight was failing seriously (to judge from the fact that on June 8 the Town Council auditioned a potential replacement, Johann Gottlob Harrer). By the end of October, Bach seems to have lost the use of his eyes altogether, since from that time onward there are no written documents in his hand. At the Bursar's Office his son Johann Christian signed pay receipts on his behalf. In the spring of 1750 Bach submitted to two eye operations by the English oculist John Taylor, and on July 28 he died of complications from the surgery. In the "new" chronology of the final decade, the Art of Fugue is moved back to the early 1740s.[48] The B-Minor Mass, by contrast, emerges as one of Bach's final projects. It may have been his very last.

When Bach settled on the idea of assembling a complete setting of the Mass Ordinary, the decision to use the five-voice *Missa* of 1733 as the cornerstone of the new work was unquestionably his most critical compositional choice, for it determined both the scoring and the scale of the music that would follow. Since Bach normally wrote vocal works from start to finish,[49] it is logical to assume that he began with the Kyrie and Gloria and then moved to the Credo and other portions. Although he no longer owned the Dresden performance materials of the *Missa* in which he had refined many details (see Chapter 7), he still possessed the manuscript score, which, as we have seen, probably stems from the early summer of 1733 and displays the elegant, flowing handwriting of his middle years (Plate 2–3). He appropriated the manuscript for the first part of his new *Missa tota* score. Although Bach made no substantive alterations in the Kyrie and Gloria, he appears to have reviewed the music and changed a few details here and there. Refinements in the vocal line of the "Qui sedes" are not reflected in the Dresden parts, for instance, and the dotted rhythm of the "Et in terra pax" fugue theme postdates both the Dresden parts and the *Gloria in excelsis*, BWV 191, of c. 1745.

It is most likely that Bach turned to the Credo next. Using the same ambitious setting as the *Missa*—five voices, three trumpets and timpani, two oboes, two flutes, strings, and continuo—he composed a companion piece of equal weight, deriving most—possibly all—of the music from earlier pieces. After completing the music, Bach reviewed the score and made a number of crucial structural alterations: he added a four-bar instrumental

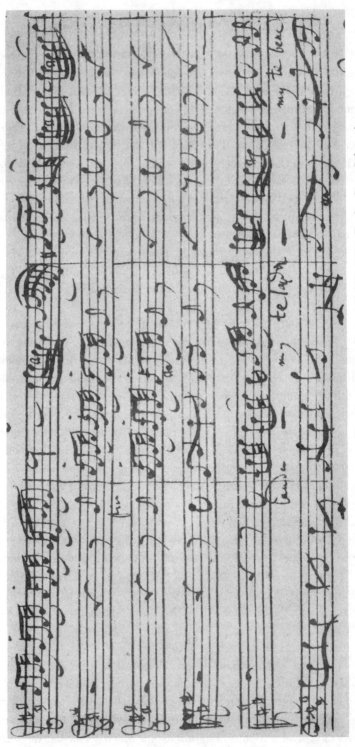

Plate 2–3. "Laudamus te": excerpt from the *Missa* portion of *P 180*, 1733 (Berlin State Library).

introduction to the "Crucifixus," and at a still later point, it seems, he added a separate "Et incarnatus" movement and retexted the "Et in unum Dominum." He accomplished these modifications by inserting a new page for the "Et incarnatus" and by writing out new vocal parts for the "Et in unum Dominum" on empty pages that followed the "Et expecto." The large-scale changes reflect Bach's working habits in the 1740s, when he altered the design of a number of seemingly completed scores in order to investigate additional organizational possibilities. The Credo forms a parallel to the Canonic Variations on "Vom Himmel hoch" and the Art of Fugue, which are also passed down in first and second versions.

When Bach reached the Sanctus, he appears to have encountered a dilemma. He had neither a preexistent five-voice Sanctus setting, as far as one can tell, nor any other five-voice music that could be readily parodied. To form a piece with the same setting as the Kyrie, Gloria, and Credo, he faced the prospect of revising a four-voice work or writing new music altogether. Instead, he appropriated the Sanctus from 1724 even though it called for different vocal and instrumental forces from those of the preceding portions—six voices instead of five, three oboes instead of two, and no flutes. He had never before changed vocal or instrumental forces during the course of a work (the Christmas Oratorio calls for a switch in instrumentation, it is true, but each of its six parts was performed on a different day of the holiday season). The break from five-part vocal writing, especially, is striking. Bach may have wished to explore other choral textures in the final sections of the Mass—a possibility we will consider in Chapter 5. But it may also be that impending blindness, or growing motor difficulties caused by diabetes, as has recently been proposed,[50] compelled him to take an expedient route and adopt the existing Sanctus even though it was not an exact fit. He may have felt that he was running out of time.[51]

Whatever the case, Bach revised the Sanctus music, altering the voice parts from three sopranos, alto, tenor, and bass to two sopranos, two altos, tenor, and bass. The new vocal setting reflected more closely that of the Kyrie, Gloria, and Credo, and nicely foreshadowed that of the "Osanna," in which the forces are expanded still further, to two sopranos, two altos, two tenors, and two basses. The changes in the Sanctus prevented Bach from appropriating the 1724 manuscript and forced him to write out a new score for insertion into his growing *Missa tota* compilation. The labored handwriting of the revised Sanctus in *P 180* suggests that this was not an easy task.

For the remaining parts of the Sanctus and for the Agnus Dei, Bach turned mostly—if not exclusively, once again—to earlier music. Some stretches of writing show a more graceful hand than others. Kobayashi, one of the few scholars to examine the fragile *P 180* score in recent times, claims to see light ink lines under the notes of the "Benedictus," suggesting that Bach sketched parts of the music first and thus was still capable of finely controlled handwriting.[52] But the text of the "Dona nobis pacem" seems especially coarse and stiff (Plate 2–4) when compared with Bach's earlier script (Plate 2–3, above) and stands as a stirring testament to his physical struggle. Bach concluded the score of the "Dona nobis pacem" with "Fine" and the colophon "DSGl"—Deo Soli Gloria, "To God Alone the Honor." The handwriting matches that of his last signed receipts from the second half of 1749.

As assembled by Bach, the *P 180* manuscript was not an "integral" score in the modern sense, for it appears to have been neither continuous nor bound. Rather, it seems to have been a collection of loose leaves, divided into four parts by the numbered title pages. The title pages, single sheets today, are probably the remnants of folders whose back pages were removed and discarded in the nineteenth century, when the autograph was bound. Bach normally stored the scores of his music as loose leaves within folders: the unbound format facilitated the copying of performance parts, and the folders allowed the parts to be stored conveniently with the score. Bach customarily wrote a work's forces on the folder cover so that one could see at a glance the voices and instruments required for performance. When C. P. E. Bach produced performance parts for the Credo of the B-Minor Mass in 1786, he seems to have followed his father's practice and stored them in the folder marked No. 2, to judge from the 1790 description of the manuscript in his estate catalogue.[53]

In this same catalogue we find the B-Minor Mass called "Die große catholische Messe"—the "Great Catholic Mass." This is the earliest title for the work, and it is the only title to come directly from the Bach family (the appellation "B-Minor Mass" first appears in the late 1820s, when it emerged in reviews and letters, and was consequently cast in stone in the *Bach-Gesamtausgabe* edition of 1856). There is no reason to doubt that J. S. Bach viewed the music as a five-part Mass Ordinary. Indeed, the earliest copies of *P 180—Am.B. 3* and the manuscript complex *P 572/P23/P 14*, both made under C. P. E. Bach's supervision—preserve the work in its entirety. We shall treat it as a full five-part Ordinary in the chapters to come.

Still, why did Bach divide the B-Minor Mass into four sections in *P 180*? The most plausible answer is that since the piece was of impractical length, Bach wished to preserve the option of performing—or possibly even renting

Plate 2–4. "Dona nobis pacem": excerpt from the final page of *P 180*, c. 1748–1749 (Berlin State Library).

out—individual portions of it. Within *P 180*, Nos. 1 and 3, the *Missa* and Sanctus, could be used in a Lutheran or Catholic service, and Nos. 2 and 4, the *Symbolum Nicenum* and the "Osanna" to "Dona nobis pacem," in a Catholic service. The one-time presence of individual folders suggests that Bach weighed the possibility of making performance parts for all four portions at a future point. As we noted in Chapter 1, Dresden Ordinary settings were commonly stored in several folders—one for the Kyrie, one for the

Gloria, etc. Bach may have been adhering to a pragmatic practice of long standing with Mass Ordinaries.

Bach's use of the term "Symbolum Nicenum" may be significant in this regard. In Mass Ordinary settings of the time, "Credo" was normally used for the Creed portion. "Symbolum Nicenum," by contrast, appears more commonly in independent Credo settings, perhaps to identify the text definitively as the Nicene rather than the Apostles' Creed. Zelenka's independent Credo in D Major, Z. 201, mentioned in Chapter 4, is entitled "Credo sive Symbolum Nicaenum" in its Vienna manuscript, for instance. Such verification was unnecessary within a *Missa tota* setting, since it was the Nicene Creed that was used in the Ordinary. The word "Credo" sufficed. The use of "Symbolum Nicenum" in the *P 180* autograph reinforces the idea proposed in Chapter 1, that Bach wished to create a multifunctional work—a work that could be contemplated in its entirety as a "Great Catholic Mass" or, on a more pragmatic level, divided up and performed part by part in whichever service was appropriate, Lutheran or Catholic. By emphasizing the parts at the expense of the whole—the *Missa* to the detriment of the *Missa tota*—Smend failed to give proper recognition to Bach's grand plan for the B-Minor Mass, just as one would do by looking at the prelude and fugue, the chorale preludes, and the duets of *Clavierübung* III as separate pieces without considering their subtle roles and relationships within the full collection.[54] We will examine the subtle roles and relationships of the five portions of the B-Minor Mass in Chapter 8.

How much of the B-Minor Mass is derived from earlier music? Specific models or fragments can be pinpointed for eleven of the work's twenty-seven movements:

MOVEMENT	MODEL
"Gratias agimus tibi	"Chorus "Wir danken dir, Gott," BWV 29/2 (1731), or an earlier common source
"Qui tollis"	"A" section of chorus "Schauet doch, und sehet," BWV 46/1 (1723)
"Credo in unum Deum"	Chorus "Credo in unum Deum" in G (c. 1747–1748?)
"Patrem Omnipotentem"	Chorus "Gott, wie dein Name," BWV 171/1 (c. 1729), or an earlier common source
"Et in unum Dominum"	Lost duet, considered for "Ich bin deine," BWV 213/11 (1733)
"Crucifixus"	"A" section of chorus "Weinen, Klagen, Sorgen, Zagen," BWV 12/2 (1714)

"Et expecto"	Chorus "Jauchzet, ihr erfreuten Stimmen," BWV 120/2 (c. 1728)
"Sanctus"	"Sanctus," BWV 232III (1724)
"Osanna"	"A" section of chorus "Es lebe der König," BWV Anh. 11/1 (1732), or "Preise dein Glücke," BWV 215/1 (1734)
"Agnus Dei"	Aria "Entfernet euch, ihr kalten Herzen," BWV Anh. 196/3 (1725) or "Ach, bleibe doch," BWV 11/4 (1735?)
"Dona nobis pacem"	Chorus "Gratias agimus tibi," BWV 232/7 (1733), "Wir danken dir, Gott," BWV 29/2 (1731), or an earlier common source

To this we can add two other movements that are most probably derived from specific, now-lost sources:[55]

"Domine Deus"	Duet "Ich will (du sollt) rühmen," BWV 193a (1727)
"Et resurrexit"	"A" section of chorus "Entfernet euch, ihr heitern Sterne," BWV Ahn. 9/1 (1727)

This brings the total number of parody movements to thirteen—approximately half the work. But there is undoubtedly much more borrowing than even this. The four-part vocal writing of "Kyrie" II, for instance, points to a model conceived outside the context of a five-voice Mass. In addition, the regular gatherings of the *P 180* manuscript—bunches of four pages in the *Missa* and four, six, or eight pages in the remaining sections[56]—and the carefully planned layout of the pages (which aside from the "Dona nobis pacem" contain the precise number of staves)[57] point to very little fully "ad hoc" composition on Bach's part. He seems to have had a good idea how he was going to proceed before he set pen to paper. As we shall see when we examine the music itself, strong cases can be made in favor of parody for most of the remaining movements. Klaus Häfner has speculated that two-thirds of the B-Minor Mass is drawn from earlier music; Joshua Rifkin envisions earlier models for the entire score except the Introduction to "Kyrie" I and the "Confiteor."[58] The present writer suspects that only the introduction to "Kyrie" I and the "Et expecto" bridge are completely new, in the sense of being composed on the page without a preexistent model or draft. Indeed, in recent times Bach scholars seem to agree that the B-Minor Mass contains very little, if any, fully original music.

Such a possibility was not considered by early writers, who were unaware of Bach's fondness for parody in his later years. Instead, Spitta,

Carl Hermann Bitter, and most other commentators before Dadelsen preferred to cast the St. Thomas Kantor in the Beethovenian mold, as a genius
creating new music rather than reworking old. However, viewing the B-
Minor Mass as the product of parody brings the work into line both with the
four short Mass settings and with the common practice of Mass production
in Dresden. Moreover, as we shall see in the coming chapters, Bach's transformation of earlier scores was a stunningly ingenious process. That he
could take music of such high quality and lift it to further heights is a
supreme testament to his creative powers.

Chapter 3

THE KYRIE AND GLORIA

GENERAL CONSIDERATIONS

*I*t is not surprising that Bach turned to the Dresden *Missa* of 1733 for the Kyrie and Gloria of the B-Minor Mass. By using a completed score he was able to procure ready-made music for two-fifths of his ambitious Mass Ordinary project. At the same time, he gained the opportunity to revive a magnificent work that in all likelihood had not been performed in its entirety since the year he wrote it.

In the four short Masses, BWV 233–236, Bach paid homage to the modest week-to-week settings of his Lutheran and Catholic contemporaries. In the 1733 *Missa* he aimed at something quite different: the monumental celebratory settings that were performed on special occasions in the Dresden Hofkirche. There can be little doubt about this, for the extraordinary scale of the *Missa*—it contains twelve fully developed movements and lasts approximately three-quarters of an hour in performance—points in that direction. While Kyrie-Gloria settings of such dimensions were rare in Protestant Germany, the Catholic repertory of the Dresden Hofkirche, as we noted in Chapter 1, contained over half a dozen, including Antonio Lotti's *Missa Vide Domine*, Francesco Mancini's *Missa* in G Major and *Missa* in E Minor, Domenico Sarri's *Missa Adjutorium nostrum* and *Missa Divi Nepomuceni*, and Jan Dismas Zelenka's *Missa Judica me* and *Missa Dei Filii*.[1] Without question it was these or similar works, imported from Naples or written elsewhere along Neapolitan lines, that inspired Bach's ambitious plan. Strengthening this notion is the fact that the *Missa* contains many gestures that reflect Dresden Mass conventions (as we shall see shortly, when we look at the music in detail).

The five-part vocal scoring of the *Missa*—soprano 1, soprano 2, alto, tenor, and bass (SSATB)—also points to Dresden models. Bach used the combination in only five sacred works: Cantata 31, *Der Himmel lacht! die Erde jubilieret;* the Magnificat (in its E♭- and D-major forms); the *Missa;* the *Gloria in excelsis Deo,* BWV 191; and the B-Minor Mass. It was an impractical chorus texture, for in Leipzig, at least, two soprano parts sorely taxed the vocal resources of the St. Thomas School choirs (see Chapter 7). In Cantata 31, a work written in 1715, the use of five voices probably represents a Weimar experiment in colorful scoring, a carryover from the heterogeneous North German settings of the Mühlhausen years. In the Latin-texted works, however, it is more likely that Bach adopted SSATB texture in imitation of the Dresden Catholic repertory, in which it appears frequently as a more ambitious alternative to SATB settings. Among the works Zelenka performed in the Hofkirche we find a good number of SSATB pieces, most cast in the style of the Neapolitan "numbers"-Mass: Lotti's *Missa Vide Domine* and Sarri's *Missa Adjutorium nostrum* and *Missa Divi Nepomuceni,* mentioned above, and Alessandro Scarlatti's *Missa Magnanimitatis,* Baliani's *Missa* in A Major, Durante's *Missa Modestiae,* and other works.[2] Bach may have associated the richer vocal texture with large Latin-texted compositions in the Neapolitan vein and perhaps for that reason chose it for the Magnificat of 1723 and the *Missa* of 1733.

In contrast to the vocal scoring, the instrumental scoring of the *Missa* has a distinctly German stamp. Bach goes beyond Italian works, which normally call for a four-part string ensemble, two oboes, and sometimes one or two trumpets or horns, to include both a larger wind group—two flutes, two oboes (or oboes d'amore in some movements), and two bassoons—and a larger brass group—three trumpets and timpani. The presence of these instruments reflects the German tradition of woodwind and brass writing, a penchant that surfaces in the heterogeneous ensembles of seventeenth-century North German church works (which, as we mentioned earlier, were strongly influenced by Gabrieli's Venetian polychoral scoring). Nevertheless, the instrumental ensemble of the *Missa* has a distinctly modern hue. Aside from the oboe d'amore, the alto oboe greatly loved in Thuringia (but not used in more cosmopolitan Saxony), Bach avoids the specialized instruments that produce unusual colors in his cantatas, such as the violino piccolo, viola d'amore, or viola pomposa.[3] By excluding these instruments from the *Missa* ensemble and pairing the woodwind instruments, he produced a scoring that is markedly in step with progressive trends of the time. Although he employed this combination in the Magnificat of 1723, he used it most frequently in the 1730s and 1740s, in the Ascension Oratorio, Cantatas 30a, 34, 214, 215, and other pieces. It seems to have been his personal response to the growing movement toward homogeneous ensembles that marked the advent of the Preclassical era. That he later called for the same instrumental band in the *Gloria in excelsis Deo* and all the remaining portions of the B-Minor Mass except the Sanctus (which dated from 1724) suggests that he may have viewed it as especially appropriate for celebratory Latin-texted works.

Bach's personal mark is also seen in the distinct separation of chorus and aria (in Dresden Masses, composers liked to exploit the effect of solo singers within chorus movements, as we noted in Chapter 1) and the virtuosic writing for obbligato instruments in the arias (the instrumental parts in Dresden arias are seldom taxing, from a technical standpoint).[4] Whether by dint of habit, design, or parody, the music of the *Missa* strongly reflects Bach's Leipzig cantata style.

THE MUSIC OF THE KYRIE

The Kyrie impresses us not just with its monumental scale but also with its deeply serious nature. Arnold Schering's idea that the music was originally intended as a "Trauer-Ode" for Friedrich August I would explain the unusual gravity of the score,[5] but as we observed in Chapter 2, it is unlikely that the work served that function. Luther's writings, so often a source of clarification, here fail to explain Bach's approach: in the German Mass of 1526 Luther advocated the use of the Latin Kyrie in the worship service, but he (uncharacteristically) did not elaborate on the meaning of its text. A clue to Bach's thinking is provided by his Weimar colleague Johann Gottfried Walther, who described writing a solemn Kyrie on the chorale "Aus tiefer Not schrei ich zu dir" ("Out of the depths have I cried unto thee, O Lord"), Luther's paraphrase of Psalm 130.[6] It seems to have been in the same spirit of imploring God's compassion *de profundis* that Bach composed the Kyrie of the B-Minor Mass, with its somber shades of B minor and F♯ minor (the key of "Aus tiefer Not, schrei ich zu dir," BWV 687, in *Clavierübung* III).

"Kyrie eleison" I

Kyrie eleison, Kyrie eleison, Kyrie eleison. (Lord have mercy upon us, Lord
   have mercy upon us, Lord have mercy upon us.)

Chorus: five-part choir (SSATB), 2 flutes, 2 oboes d'amore, strings,
   bassoon, continuo.

"Kyrie" I begins with a short *adagio* introduction that serves as an invoca-
tion for both the movement and the entire Kyrie-Christe-Kyrie complex.
Christoph Wolff has proposed a specific model for the opening: Johann
Hugo von Wilderer's Mass in G Minor, a work Bach copied out and performed in Leipzig around 1730, just a few years before composing the
Missa.[7] The Wilderer Mass commences with a concise *adagio* which, like
Bach's introduction, displays tutti scoring, declamatory chords in dactylic
rhythm, three melodic phrases, and a phrygian cadence leading to the Kyrie
proper. Alfred Dürr has pointed to another possible prototype: an anonymous movement in E minor—most probably a Kyrie performed by Bach in
Weimar—that starts in much the same way.[8] Either piece may well have
influenced the composer. At the same time, it is clear that the Mass settings
performed in Dresden in Bach's day commonly began with some sort of succinct introduction. This gesture was so firmly established that it appears
even in works that begin in a purely instrumental fashion. For instance, the
six-measure *adagio* that opens the sinfonia to Antonio Caldara's *Missa
Providentiae*[9] (Example 3–1), a work presented by Zelenka in the late
1720s, exhibits the three phrases and dactylic rhythm of the Kyrie text
while dispensing with the words themselves.

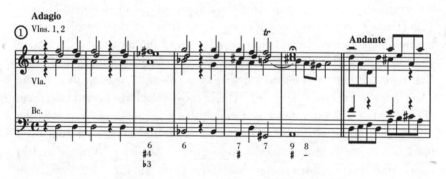

Example 3–1. Caldara: *Missa Providentiae,* Sinfonia to "Kyrie" I.

The *adagio* of "Kyrie" I from the B-Minor Mass reflects this tradition. Bach imbues the music with much greater drama than is present in Caldara's work, however. The first phrase moves to a jolting seventh chord, whose pungent arrival is enriched by an appoggiatura in soprano 2, flute 2, and oboe 2. The second phrase is marked by syncopation in soprano 2 and additional rhythmic activity in the alto and tenor. The third phrase, extended over two measures, contains still more syncopation and sixteenth-note motion that includes the slurred second (in violin 1) that plays such an important role in the fugue proper. During the course of the passage the two sopranos emerge with free, cadenza-like lines that link the three chordal sequences. In Baroque church music, the soprano voice traditionally represented the Christian soul. In the opening measures of "Kyrie" I it is thus the soul that cries out in anguish over the other voices.

The result is an astonishing "contrapuntalization" of the traditional Kyrie introduction. The steady increase in polyphonic complexity gives growing urgency to the plea for mercy—it is as if the vocal and instrumental voices, united in the initial measure, set out on different paths, to meet again only at the conclusion of the fugue. It is not surprising that the *adagio* was the first passage of the B-Minor Mass to be praised in print after Bach's death (see Chapter 6) or that it fired the imagination of Romantic writers. "The heart opens," the early Bach biographer Carl Hermann Bitter wrote rhapsodically, "and it leads us to the passion hill of the crucified one. We see the Savior and how he died, amidst a thousand pains, to fulfill the offering of redemption."[10]

The *largo* that follows the *adagio* is an immense *fuga gravis*—a slow, solemn fugue with extended chromatic development. We find a similar *largo* fugue in the same key in Well-Tempered Clavier I, and it may be that Bach viewed B minor, the tonality described as "morose" and "lonely and melancholy" by Baroque theorists,[11] as ideal for grave fugal writing.[12] The theme of the "Kyrie" I fugue displays a number of traditional figures. It begins with a *repercussio,* or repeated-note motive, with a dactyl rhythm (Example 3–2, "x"). The advantages of this motive are clear: it reinforces the natural declamation of the word "Kyrie," it creates an almost hypnotic, chant-like sound (especially in a slow tempo), and it firmly establishes the tonic. The *repercussio* is followed by a gradually widening wedge ("y"),   which expands upward, step-by-step, toward the dominant note, f♯". The wedge twice incorporates an expressive "sigh," the slurred, falling second, g→f♯. Instead of reaching the dominant, the common goal of wedge figures (compare the subject of the famous "Wedge" Fugue in E Minor, BWV

Example 3–2. "Kyrie" I, fugue theme.

548/2), the Kyrie theme suddenly digresses, first falling chromatically downward and then jumping upward, with two poignant leaps, before concluding on the dominant ("z"). The leaps represent yet another figure, the *exclamatio,* or exclamatory cry, which adds further intensity to the line. Bach, then, combines five figures in one theme: the *repercussio,* the wedge, the sigh, the chromatic digression, and the *exclamatio.* And by concluding the theme on the dominant, he leaves the music open-ended, like the introduction. The passion unleashed by this complex, emotionally charged subject will be resolved only in the fugue's final measure, with its picardy-third (major-mode) cadence.

We can outline the structure of the "Kyrie" fugue as follows:

Orchestral exposition 1: 25 measures
    Exposition (mm. 5–15), with final cadence on v
    Episodic material, "a" (mm.15–18) and "b" (mm. 19–21)
    Exposition (mm. 22–30), with final cadence on i

Vocal exposition 1: 42½ measures
    Exposition (mm. 30–57), with final cadence on v/v
    Episodic material, "a" (mm. 58–61) and "b" (mm. 62–64)
    Exposition (mm. 65–72½), with final cadence on v

Orchestral exposition 2: 8½ measures
    Exposition (mm. 72½–74)
    Episodic material, "b" (mm. 75–76½)
    Exposition (mm. 76½–79)
    Episodic material, "b" (mm. 79–80)

Vocal exposition 2 (mm. 81–126): 46 measures
    Exposition (mm. 81–102), with final cadence on i
    Exposition (mm. 102–111), with final cadence on v
    Episodic material, "a" (mm. 112–115) and "b" (mm. 116–118)
    Exposition (mm. 119–126), with final cadence on i

This plan contains an element of symmetry as well as an element of development. The symmetrical element is the reappearance, at m. 102, of the opening orchestral exposition, now with chorus and instruments sharing the parts (Bach camouflages the arrival of this climactic moment by delaying the cadence to the tonic until m. 103). The developmental element is the growing crescendo that results from doubling the vocal lines with instruments after m. 45. If we view the "Kyrie" as a plea for mercy from the depths, it is a plea that proceeds with rising strength and momentum.

Joshua Rifkin has suggested that "Kyrie" I is a parody movement.[13] He points out that the text is cleanly written in the *P 180* autograph, with little evidence of compositional activity except for the introduction, which contains several compositional corrections and may have been penned on the spot.[14] Numerous transposition mistakes of an upper second hint that Bach may have been copying from a model in C minor, which Rifkin believes to be a lost cantata movement from around 1726, the time when Bach wrote a number of large, concerted chorus fugues.[15] Bach's standard for cantatas was four voices, however, and it is difficult to believe that the vocal texture of "Kyrie" I was not five-part from the start. If the "Kyrie" stems from pre-existent music, its prototype may have been an unusually ambitious piece, possibly a lost Kyrie written for a special occasion.[16] Until further evidence surfaces, the prehistory of "Kyrie" I remains unclear.

"Christe eleison"

Christe eleison, Christe eleison, Christe eleison. (Christ have mercy upon us, Christ have mercy upon us, Christ have mercy upon us.)

Duet: soprano 1 and soprano 2, violins 1 and 2 in unison, continuo.

In the "Christe eleison" Bach moves from the elevated world of the chorus fugue to the intimate realm of the love duet. There can be no question about the nature of the "Christe," for its music displays, as Robert L. Marshall has shown, the "gentle" affections—the *affetti amorosi*—that appear in love duets of the Neapolitan opera: dulcet parallel thirds and sixths (emphasized here through sustained notes), diatonic melodic lines, a *galant* mixture of duple and triple figures, straightforward harmonies, expressive appoggiaturas, and weak-beat phrase endings that resolve downward as "sighs" (Example 3–3).[17] The unison violin line reinforces the sense of happy concord.

Bach used such duets in sacred and secular works. Wolff has pointed to the similarities between the "Christe" and the duet "Ich bin deine/Du bist meine" from the Hercules Cantata, *Laßt uns sorgen, laßt uns wachen,* BWV

Example 3–3. "Christe eleison," principal vocal theme.

213, of September 1733.[18] In "Ich bin deine," Hercules and Virtue sing
rhapsodically of their affection for one another: "I am yours" (Hercules),
"You are mine" (Virtue), "Kiss me, I shall kiss you" (both), etc. The ease
with which such pieces could be transferred from coffee garden to church is
demonstrated by this movement, which Bach soon recycled in Part 3 of the
Christmas Oratorio with the text "Herr, dein Mitleid, dein Erbarmen"
("Lord, thy compassion and mercy console and free us").

In casting the "Christe" as a love duet for high voices, Bach was following a well-established tradition. The Wilderer Mass in G Minor that he
copied around 1730 contains a "Christe" alto-tenor duet in a similar style.[19]
More tellingly, in Dresden, "Christe" duets for two sopranos or soprano and
alto were standard fare. The "Christe" from Caldara's *Missa Providentiae* is
typical. A duet for soprano and alto accompanied by strings and continuo,
it features sweet parallel thirds and sixths, weak-beat phrase endings,
transparent textures, and a chamber meter ("3") that conspire to create a

score of pleasing lightness and charm (Example 3–4).[20] The music sounds like an amorous opera excerpt, and that is typical of Dresden "Christe" movements.

Walter Blankenburg and other commentators have suggested that the duet setting of Bach's "Christe" portrays the unity of God and Christ: the two voices in the same range, as well as unison violins, serve to highlight the idea of "two in one."[21] It is also possible that Bach wished to portray the intimate relationship of Christ and humankind. In Lutheran theology, Christ is the compassionate, approachable emissary of God; he assumes the role of confidant for humankind, a loving friend addressed in the familiar form of the second-person pronoun, "du." In Bach's cantata texts, Christ is often represented allegorically as a lover who courts a beleaguered soul and shepherds it into the protective realm of his chambers—that is, into heaven. Hence the bride-bridegroom imagery of the soprano-bass duet "Mein

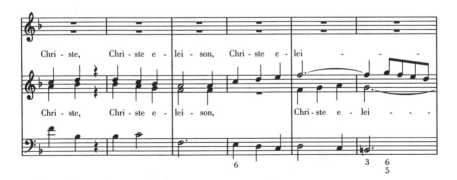

Example 3–4. Caldara: "Christe eleison" from *Missa Providentiae.*

Freund ist mein" from Cantata 140. In the "Christe," Bach may have settled specifically on two sopranos (it is the only such aria in his oeuvre) in
order to extend the symbolism of the introductory *adagio* of "Kyrie" I, in
which sopranos 1 and 2, as icons for the soul, seem to lead the cry for God's
mercy (see discussion, above). If we extend that idea, the same souls now
seek Christ's mercy in the highly personal language of the duet.

Structurally, the "Christe" is a ritornello form, a convenient alternative
to the da capo design that was skirted in Mass settings. In the classic
Vivaldian concerto, harmonically stable ritornello sections alternate with
modulatory episodes. Bach's aria follows this pattern, with ritornello sections, played by the instruments alone, marking the tonic, dominant, submediant, and tonic. The vocal sections, featuring the soprano soloists, serve
as modulatory "interludes." The straightforward design (the most straightforward of any ritornello aria in the B-Minor Mass) parallels the direct
nature of the music:

	MEASURES	HARMONY
Ritornello	1–10	I — I
Vocal section	10–33	I → V
Ritornello	33–42	V — V
Vocal section	42–53	V → vi
Ritornello (abbreviated)	53–58	vi — vi
Vocal section	58–76	vi → I
Ritornello	76–85	I — I

Bach's treatment of the vocal sections is especially remarkable. In love
duets, the two voices often enter separately, with individual comments,
before joining together with a shared phrase—a sequence that creates the
pleasing effect of growing accord. Indeed, such convergence appears in the
Hercules Cantata duet and "Mein Freund ist mein" ("My friend is mine") of
Cantata 140. In Mozart's famous dialogue on the power of love, "Bei
Männern, welche Liebe" from the Magic Flute, Pamina opens the discussion, Papageno politely adds his view, and the two then voice their agreement together, singing mainly in parallel thirds and sixths. In the "Christe,"
by contrast, the voices enter together with concordant material (mm. 10–13;
Example 3–3, above), separate in imitation (mm. 14–17½), and then join
for the cadence (mm. 17½–18½). This nicely balanced sequence, which
creates a sensation of accord → discussion → accord, is repeated several

times in the movement (mm. 18½–26, 42–53). The final vocal section (from m. 58) begins in B minor with imitative material that evolves, little by little, into consonant homophony as the harmony moves toward the bright D major of the tonic. Hovering over the voices throughout, in magnificent counterpoint, is the unison violin line, with fragments or direct quotations from the ritornello.

Does the music of the "Christe" stem from a lost aria? The clean appearance of the autograph manuscript and the abundance of performance indications point in that direction. John Butt, citing the alto clefs that appear several times by mistake in the soprano 2 part, has proposed that the "Christe" was derived from a soprano-alto duet of some sort.[22] Alfred Dürr has pointed to corrections in the violin part (which, like the unison violin line of the Agnus Dei, is written in soprano clef) that hint at transposition from a model in more conventional treble clef.[23] And Klaus Häfner has suggested as a model the duet "Seid zu tausend mahl willkommen" from *Entfernet euch, ihr heitern Sterne,* BWV Anh. 9, for which only the printed libretto has survived.[24] While "Seid zu tausend mahl willkommen" is certainly of the love-duet type ("Let the glorious hours of August be kissed," say Apollo and Philuris), the text begins as a dialogue, with the voices entering separately, and the overall form is that of a da capo aria. Both aspects would have required considerable reworking to produce the "Christe." Parody seems likely for the "Christe," but the model remains obscure.

"Kyrie eleison" II

Kyrie eleison, Kyrie eleison, Kyrie eleison. (Lord have mercy upon us, Lord have mercy upon us, Lord have mercy upon us.)

Chorus: four-part choir (S1 and S2 combined, ATB), continuo; other instruments (2 flutes, 2 oboes d'amore, strings, and bassoon) *colla parte.*

After the "Christe" Bach turned to the genre commonly used by Dresden composers for the second "Kyrie eleison"—the Palestrina-style chorus fugue. The music of "Kyrie" II displays the distinguishing characteristics of Renaissance *a cappella* writing: a "white-note," conjunct theme; a ₵ time signature and *allabreve* designation (which in Bach's German circles meant Renaissance style as much as it indicated tempo; see Chapter 7); a thick web of vocal imitation; dissonances carefully prepared through suspensions and anticipations; a steady, almost accentless pulse; and, toward the end, the use of stretto for contrapuntal intensification.

"Kyrie" II is thus patterned after the sixteenth-century motet and serves as a perfect foil for "Kyrie" I, with its concerted idiom and obbligato instrumental parts. In the *P 180* manuscript, "Kyrie" II resembles Palestrina: the score contains nothing more than the four vocal parts and the continuo line (Bach's addition to the otherwise Renaissance-style setting). The other instruments, which double the vocal lines in *colla parte* fashion (that is, they play with the appropriate vocal part), are indicated solely through the designation "Stromenti in unisono"—"instruments at the unison" (see Plate 7–2 in Chapter 7). Unfortunately, the vocal nature of Bach's scoring is obscured in modern editions, which notate the instruments on separate staves, giving them an unwarranted look of independence.

As we noted in Chapter 1, Renaissance vocal style remained a viable option for Baroque composers and was especially popular in Mass settings. In choosing the Palestrina idiom, Bach not only paid respect to the church writing of his forebears but also followed the contemporary fashion of combining old and new in sacred works. Of the two approaches to Palestrina style discerned by Christoph Wolff, the freer *allabreve* style and the more severe *stile antico*, it is the latter that obtains in "Kyrie" II: the music is dominated by sixteenth-century linear principles.[25] That did not stop Bach from animating the score with elements of Baroque emotionalism, however. If "Kyrie" II is Palestrina, it is highly personalized Palestrina.

Bach's choice of key and his shaping of the fugue subject make his individuality clear from the outset. For Baroque composers, F♯ minor was a highly expressive tonality. Bach's contemporary Johann Mattheson described it as "leading to great distress . . . it has something abandoned, singular, and misanthropic about it."[26] Bach used F♯ minor selectively in his church works, reserving it for moments of passionate intensity, such as the "Deposuit potentes" from the Magnificat ("He hath put down the mighty from their seats . . .") or the aria "Ach Herr, was ist ein Menschenkind" from Cantata 110 ("O Lord, what is a child of man that Thou wouldst redeem him through such pain?"). In setting the "Kyrie" II in F♯ minor Bach chose an emotionally charged Baroque key rather than a more neutral Renaissance-oriented tonality such as D minor, which Hasse used for the Palestrina-style "Kyrie" II fugue in his Mass for the 1751 inauguration of the new Hofkirche in Dresden.

The fugue theme of "Kyrie" II forms a classic Palestrina arch, rising gently from the note f♯ to the note b and then descending, step-by-step, back to f♯ (Example 3–5). The subject of the "Gratias agimus tibi" (Example 3–10, below) has the same vaulted shape; but in the "Kyrie" II

Example 3–5. "Kyrie" II: principal theme.

subject, the g♮ on the second note, harmonized with a Neapolitan sixth
chord, produces a purely Baroque "jolt" that energizes the line and propels
it forward. The g♮, emphasized by a syncopated bass, is followed by the
leading tone, e♯, which is prolonged through a dot and not fully resolved
until the final note of the theme, two measures later. These elements,
together with a second bass syncopation at the beginning of the third measure, color the line with a sense of anxious urgency. As in "Kyrie" I, the
plea to God is a fervent one, shaded with dissonant reminders of humankind's sinful state.

Bach's treatment of the continuo line is also calculatedly dramatic. At
the beginning of the movement, the continuo moves independently of the
vocal bass most of the time. But as the fugue unfolds, the continuo doubles
the vocal bass more and more, especially in thematic and cadential passages. Twice the continuo climbs upward by chromatic half steps in a star-
tlingly tense Baroque sequence (mm. 16–18 and 27–29). The entries of the
fugue subject reflect the conservative harmonic scheme of a sixteenth-century church work: aside from a single entry in the subdominant (m. 40), all
are in the tonic or dominant. But Bach's chromaticism—in the subject, in
the bass, and in the accompanying voices—exceeds anything known to
Palestrina. Within the generally straightforward harmonic plan, it augments
the drama of the linear counterpoint.

Although the "Kyrie" II fugue is through-composed, unfolding in a continuous, developmental way, it nevertheless falls into two roughly equal
parts in terms of procedure. Bach devotes the first half of the movement to
normal entries of the theme, first in tonic-dominant pairs (bass and tenor,
mm. 1–5; alto and sopranos, mm. 9–14), then individually (alto, m. 18; bass
with continuo, m. 25; tenor, m. 29). In the second half, Bach intensifies the
counterpoint, beginning in m. 31 with a circle-of-fifths sequence based on
a motive derived from the rising fourth and falling third of the fugue theme.
The motive appears in stretto—that is, narrowly spaced, overlapping

entries—beginning with the bass and moving upward to the sopranos. This sets the stage for stretto entries of the theme itself (alto and tenor, mm. 35–38; sopranos and bass, mm. 40–43; bass and sopranos, mm. 54–57). The sequential motive reappears, too, first in the bass alone (mm. 37–40), then in two stretto passages (mm. 43–46 and 51–54). The last stretto passage forms a mirror image of the initial stretto passage of sequential material: the entries now descend in order, from the sopranos to bass, rather than ascend. The two passages thus act as a framing element for the second half of the fugue. The introduction of stretto toward the end of an imitative work is a hallmark of Renaissance *a cappella* style. Bach's use of it to highlight a sequential episode as well as the principal subject adds a Baroque twist to the Renaissance technique.

Is "Kyrie" II a parody? Rifkin and Häfner, pointing to the relatively clean appearance of the autograph manuscript, the inconsistent declamation of "eleison" ("e-le-i-son" at some spots, "e-lei-son" at others), and the four-part vocal texture, have proposed that "Kyrie" II is derived from a lost cantata movement.[27] The inconsistent declamation cannot be taken as a clear sign of parody, however, since one commonly finds mixed declamation in Kyrie settings of the time.[28] Wolff has discussed the difficulty of parodying Palestrina-style pieces, since the shape of the thematic material is so intimately related to the text. This might lead one to conclude that if "Kyrie" II was based on earlier music, which it seems to be, its model was a now-lost, four-voice Kyrie setting or possibly a well-worked-out compositional draft. Still, Bach parodied a Renaissance *a cappella* movement with a German text for the "Gratias" and "Dona nobis pacem," so it is possible that he did so here as well.

THE MUSIC OF THE GLORIA

With the Gloria, we encounter an abrupt and shocking change of mood. Bright D major, the Baroque key of trumpets and drums, sweeps away the brooding B minor and F♯ minor of the Kyrie; extroverted concerto writing replaces introverted fugal development; and springy, dance-like rhythms, notated in the chamber meter of $\frac{3}{8}$, supplant the *allabreve* gravity of Renaissance vocal style.

Schering, in proposing a fealty-service origin for the *Missa*, attributed the remarkable shift in *Affekt* from the Kyrie to the Gloria to political considerations: the Kyrie paid homage to the deceased Friedrich August I, while the Gloria celebrated the forthcoming reign of Friedrich August II.[29] As attractive as Schering's explanation may be, it is much more likely that Bach was guided by liturgical concerns, wishing to highlight the theological contrast between the beseeching, Greek-texted Kyrie, perhaps the oldest part of the Mass, and the joyful, Latin-texted Gloria, a later entry into the Ordinary. That Bach viewed the Kyrie and Gloria as dichotomous—"ancient and somber" on the one hand and "modern and joyful" on the other—is suggested by the pedal settings of *Clavierübung* III: the Kyrie is represented by three restrained, thick-textured *stile antico* movements (BWV 669–671), while the Gloria (in its German form, *Allein Gott in der Höh sei Ehr'*) is set as a bright, airy Italian trio (BWV 676). The calculated contrast between Kyrie and Gloria is similar here.

"Gloria in excelsis"

Gloria in excelsis Deo. (Glory be to God on high.)

Chorus: five-part choir (SSATB), 3 trumpets & timpani, 2 flutes, 2 oboes, strings, bassoon, continuo.

As we observed in Chapter 1, the Gloria text opens with the *Hymnus angelicus* from Luke 2:10–14, the "Angelic Hymn" sung by the angel of the Lord and the heavenly host as they proclaim the birth of Christ to the shepherds. The proclamation had been a favorite Christmas setting since Medieval times, one depicted with great enthusiasm in paintings, frescoes, and miniatures. Bach seems to draw on this iconographical tradition in the "Gloria" (and his later assignment of the music in its Cantata 191 form to "The Feast of Christ's Birth" leaves no doubt that he associated the score with the Nativity), painting the scene with rich musical imagery. The rapid shift in mode and idiom parallels the "sudden" appearance of the heavenly host of angels, whose energetic acclamations are mirrored in the performance designation *vivace* ("lively"). The sumptuous texture, with a total of sixteen independent instrumental and vocal parts, reflects the "multitude" that joins the announcing angel. Contemporary composers sometimes began the "Gloria" with a vocal solo or duet. Bach, by contrast, seems to have felt that tutti chorus was the most appropriate scoring. He used it in three of his four short Mass settings, and when he revised the Gloria of his cousin Johann Ludwig Bach's *Missa* in E Minor on *Allein Gott in der Höh sei Ehr'*, BWV Anh. 166, he went so far as to cross out the original solo opening and substitute a newly composed chorus passage in its place.

Other aspects of the "Gloria" relate to the Biblical scene as well. The trumpets, musical representatives of heavenly and earthly rulers in the Baroque, appear for the first time in the Mass and herald Christ's arrival. The fanfare shape of the opening motive strengthens the trumpet imagery. In the vocal parts the recurring sequence of imitation → declamatory chords suggests the exuberance and growing unanimity of the angelic praise (Handel employed the same textural progression in "For unto us a child is born" from *Messiah*). The Italian giga-like dance idiom, similar to that of the $\frac{3}{8}$-meter gigues of English Suite No. 5 in E Minor, BWV 810, Cello Suite No. 3 in C Major, BWV 1009, and the Pastorella in F Major, BWV 590, expresses the earthly pleasure and joy to be experienced by humankind.[30] And in contrast to the more neutral vocal writing of "Kyrie" II, Bach employs pictorial figures: twisty, sixteenth-note melismas of a purely instrumental nature to represent angelic bliss and upward melodic leaps on the phrase "in excelsis" (mm. 49–56 and 85–91) to paint "in the highest."

Structurally, the "Gloria" is a ritornello form. It is a somewhat unusual ritornello form, however, since it is composed almost entirely of ritornello segments, with very little episodic material. The ritornello itself, presented initially by the instruments alone, displays the classic tripartite design cultivated so successfully by Vivaldi: an opening segment (mm. 1–8) establishes the tonic and concludes, in open-ended fashion, with a half cadence; a middle segment (mm. 9–16) carries the music through a series of sequences; and a final segment (mm. 17–24) moves to a closing cadence.[31] The balance and symmetry of the three ritornello segments—each contains eight measures that subdivide naturally into units of 4 + 4 bars—reflects the strong influence of dance music. After the opening, Bach repeats the ritornello three times in the orchestra while "layering in" the voices over the instrumental parts in constantly varying ways.

The only episodic passage in the "Gloria" occurs in mm. 65–77, a modulatory passage with intensified vocal imitation. Bach dovetails the last entry of the episode (soprano 2, in m. 77) with the beginning of the final ritornello segment, thus making the return of the latter and the final assertion of the tonic a surprising—and delightful—event.

The instrumental nature of the "Gloria" led Smend to propose that the music was derived from a lost concerto movement, perhaps a piece from Bach's Cöthen years.[32] None of Bach's extant concerto movements has such a striking lack of episodic material, however. Certainly the clean appearance of the "Gloria" in the original score points to the possibility of parody, and Rifkin has suggested that the music represents the A section of a four-voice da capo movement from a now-lost Leipzig cantata.[33] Butt has pointed more specifically to the da capo opening movements from a series of secular, trumpet-and-drums vocal works that Bach wrote in the late 1730s and early 1730s: Cantatas 201, 206, 207, 214, and 215.[34] Of these movements, the chorus "Schleicht, spielende Wellen" of Cantata 206, composed in 1734, hints most clearly at the possible cantata roots of the "Gloria." Like the "Gloria," "Schleicht, spielende Wellen" is a $\frac{3}{8}$-meter giga-like piece built on symmetrical, eight-bar units. The A section is composed almost entirely of ritornello, and the final return of the ritornello is disguised by imitation. The "Gloria" could well stem from a similar celebratory work. Smend first noted that most of the corrections in the *P 180* score occur in the vocal parts. The emendations may reflect the revision of existing vocal parts (and the addition of a fifth voice), however, rather than the composition of new vocal material altogether.

"Et in terra pax"

Et in terra pax hominibus. (And on earth peace, good will toward men.)

Chorus: five-part choir (SSATB), 3 trumpets & timpani, 2 flutes, 2 oboes,
  strings, bassoon, continuo.

In many Dresden Masses we find the second phrase of the *Hymnus angelicus* set off from the first by a change in music. In Sarri's five-voice *Missa Divi Nepomuceni,*[35] one of the immense Neapolitan settings performed by Zelenka, a festive, concerted "Gloria" (marked *allegro*) is suddenly interrupted by an expressive, chorale-like "Et in terra pax" (marked *adagio*). Bach takes a similar approach, ushering in the "Et in terra pax" with an abrupt shift: the upper instruments drop out, leaving the chorus to sing alone with the continuo; the meter switches from dance-related $\frac{3}{8}$ time to neutral $\frac{4}{4}$; the rhythmic pulse decelerates from sixteenth- to eighth-note motion; and animated arpeggiated lines are supplanted by more subdued conjunct motives. There is also a distinct "flattening" of D major towards the subdominant, G major, a harmonic turn that seems to bring one—as Wilfrid Mellers has aptly put it—"down to earth."[36]

The sensation of earthly peace is created by the pastoral-like qualities of the music as well. The pastoral stood as a Christmas genre throughout the Baroque, a tender dance specifically linked with the Nativity. Composers writing pastorals commonly used slurred, conjunct note pairs to simulate the rocking motion of the cradle, consonant thirds and sixths to depict sweet, soothing "lullaby" music, and pedal tones to mimic the drones of the bagpipes associated with the shepherds. These gestures can be seen in the "Pifa" of Handel's *Messiah* or the Sinfonia to Part 2 of Bach's Christmas Oratorio, two instrumental pastorals preceding shepherd scenes. In "Schlafe, mein Liebster, genieße der Ruh" from Part 2 of the Christmas Oratorio (Example 3–6), an aria with thematic material much like that of the "Et in terra," words are put to the image: "Sleep my dear one, enjoy the rest." In the "Et in terra," the sudden disappearance of the instruments at the beginning of the movement strengthens the pastoral mode, creating an appropriately "hushed" effect.

Example 3–6. "Schlafe mein Liebster" from the Christmas Oratorio, Part 2.

In terms of overall design, the "Et in terra pax" is a chorus fugue with three expositions:

mm. 1–20 (101–120)	Introduction
mm. 21–37 (121–137)	Exposition 1
mm. 37–42 (137–142)	Episode
mm. 43–60 (143–160)	Exposition 2
mm. 60–70 (160–170)	Episode
mm. 70–78 (170–178)	Exposition 3

The introduction, with the phrase "Et in terra" treated in gentle imitation and the word "pax" ("peace") emphasized through sustained notes, wanders harmonically, with pedal points on G, B, and E. Harmonic "peace," though sought, is not fulfilled until the initial fugal exposition, in which D major is reestablished for the first time since the end of the "Gloria." The subject of the fugue is derived from the opening motive of the introduction and displays the same flirtation with the subdominant: the C♮ in the first measure hints at G major, but the C♯ in the second measure confirms D major (Example 3–7). Its almost fully conjunct, expressive note-pairs make it an ideal vocal motive. The dotted figure for the word "hominibus" appears to have been a late refinement on Bach's part. It is not found in the Dresden parts of 1733 or the Cantata 191 music of c. 1745, and Bach seems to have added it to the score only in the late 1740s, probably in conjunction with expanding the 1733 *Missa* into a *Missa tota*. Unfortunately, it is not reproduced in the *Bach-Gesamtausgabe* and editions derived from it.

et   in   ter   -   ra   pax   ho - mi - ni - bus   bo - nae   vo - lun - ta   -   tis

Example 3–7. "Et in terra pax": final version of fugue theme.

Against the fugue theme soon appears a memorable, contrasting counter-subject on the words "bonae voluntatis." This idea, with arpeggiated leaps and running sixteenth notes (and, for the singers, little place to breathe), harks back to the instrumental motives of the "Gloria." It enlivens the counterpoint of the fugue and paradoxically links the "peace" of the "Et in terra pax" with the "joy" of the "Gloria." The voices of the fugue enter one by one, each with a string of countersubjects (or pseudo-countersubjects). This methodical procedure, dubbed "permutation technique" by Werner Neumann in his classic study of Bach's chorus fugues, results in a canon-like scheme:[37]

soprano 1	a	b	c	d	e
soprano 2					a
alto		a	b	c	d'
tenor			a	b	c'
bass				a	b
harmony	I	V	I	V	ii

   The second exposition is structured similarly. It does not seem the same, however, since the first thematic entry, of soprano 1 at m. 43 (or 143), coincides with the last block of homophonic material in the episode and is thus disguised. The same overlap occurs in exposition 3, rendering the permutation process less mechanical. Bach also dresses up the repetitive plan through additive instrumentation, replacing the detached accompanimental chords of exposition 1 with weightier instrumental doubling in expositions 2 and 3. And in expositions 2 and 3 he adds trumpet 1 to the final vocal entry, creating a brilliant dynamic climax.

   In the *P 180* autograph manuscript, the "Et in terra pax" has the appearance of a revision copy—to use the term coined by Marshall.[38] The musical text is confidently written on the whole—that is, there are no large-scale cross-outs. However, patches of stiff, untidy handwriting, not just in the vocal parts but also in the instruments (the oboe and flute in the second episode, or the trumpet and timpani throughout), suggest that Bach was reworking a sketch or an earlier piece. Rifkin, pointing to the revisions in the vocal parts, has proposed that Bach derived the music from a cantata movement for four-voice chorus.[39] Neumann has likened the permutation procedure of the "Et in terra pax" to that of the chorus "Lob, und Ehre, und Preise, und Gewalt" of Cantata 21, written in Weimar around 1713.[40] In the *P 180* score, the "disguised" beginnings of expositions 2 and 3 show considerable revision. Perhaps this reflects Bach's desire to spruce up an otherwise straightforward model from the Weimar years, the period of his greatest infatuation with permutation technique.

   When Bach borrowed the music of the "Et in terra pax" for *Gloria in excelsis Deo*, BWV 191, around 1745, he made only minor changes. Two are of special interest from the standpoint of performance practice, however. First, he consistently filled in the initial third of the "bonae voluntatis" countersubject, producing livelier note motion (Example 3–8a). Second, when the countersubject appears in doubling instruments, he used two-note slurs for the sixteenth notes, echoing, in diminution, the paired groupings of the fugue theme (Example 3–8b). Both refinements merit consideration in modern performances of the B-Minor Mass.

"Laudamus te"

Laudamus te. Benedicimus te. Adoramus te. Glorificamus te. (We praise
Thee. We bless Thee. We adore Thee. We glorify Thee.)

Aria: soprano 2, solo violin, strings, continuo.

In the "Laudamus te" Bach continues the festive instrumental style of the "Gloria," writing an elaborate, virtuosic aria for soprano 2 and obbligato violin (termed "Violino concertato" in the *P 180* manuscript). The fourfold praise of the "Laudamus te" text is expressed through exuberant *Spielfiguren,* or instrumental figurations, notated with meticulous care in the score. This is the only movement of the B-Minor Mass to feature solo violin (the obbligato instrument of the "Benedictus" is most probably flute, as we shall see in Chapter 5), and Bach's finely detailed part, with its precisely placed slurs and dots and wealth of ornaments and dynamic marks, is reminiscent of the unac-

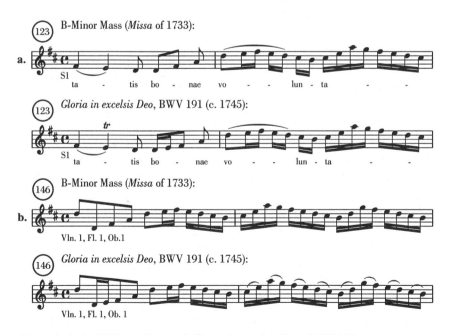

Example 3–8. B-Minor Mass and *Gloria in excelsis Deo,* BWV 191: motives compared.

companied violin sonatas and partitas. Similar writing also appears in the solo violin parts of a number of cantata arias, where, in major mode, it is commonly linked with joyous praise. In "Lobe den Herren, der alles so herrlich regieret" ("Praise to the Lord, who rules over all so gloriously") from Cantata 137, an alto aria that Bach later transferred to the organ as the sixth Schübler Chorale, BWV 650, the solo violin sets forth an equally lively, well-articulated line. The voice then enters with a contrastingly simple, unadorned chorale melody. In the "Laudamus te," the voice picks up the ornate line of the solo violin and embellishes it further, producing an aria of unbridled mirth.

The mirth stems from careful calculation on Bach's part. Indeed, the "Laudamus te" is a study in the Baroque art of diminution, of making "small notes" or, as Walther colorfully expressed it, *fioretti* ("little flowers").[41] If we examine the opening two measures of the violin line, for instance, we find that the underlying melody is a simple, almost folk-like tune (Example 3–9a and b), one that nicely complements the relaxed pastoral idiom of the "Et in terra pax." Bach decorates the principal notes of the melody with sixteenth- and thirty-second-note figuration: auxiliary tones, turns, passing tones, and appoggiaturas. The opening vocal line is based on the same melody; Bach now extends the phrase to more than twice its original length in order to accommodate increasingly extravagant figures (Example 3–9c). The autograph manuscript shows that he reworked this passage on the page. Initially, the soprano 2 line was simpler, with a sustained half note on g' (an unexpected flattening of g♯', reflecting, perhaps, the flattening found in the "Christe eleison" and the "Et in terra") and an eighth-note upbeat e" for the cadence (Example 3–9d).[42] This he revised, ornamenting the g' through neighbor notes and the e" through an arpeggiated figure. Although Bach was criticized during his lifetime for writing out diminutions of this type, thereby usurping the prerogatives of the performer, it is hard to imagine that spontaneous embellishment would yield such extraordinarily well-crafted results.

Marshall, pointing to the soprano line's trill-studded nature and low tessitura (c♯'–e"), has suggested that the part seems to have been intended specifically for Faustina Bordoni, whom Bach undoubtedly heard in the first performance of *Cleofide* in Dresden in 1731.[43] Bordoni is known to have had a mezzo-soprano range, and her specialty was coloratura singing. Her technique, as described by Quantz, does seem to match perfectly the demands of the "Laudamus te":

> Her execution was articulate and brilliant. She had a fluent tongue for pronouncing words rapidly and distinctly, and a flexible throat for divisions, with so beautiful and quick a shake, that she could put it in

motion upon short notice, just when she would. The passages might be smooth, or by leaps, or consist of iterations of the same tone—their execution was equally easy to her.[44]

Underscoring the music's connection with Dresden, if not with Bordoni in particular, is the predominance of short-long lombardic rhythmic figures, which were highly fashionable in Dresden circles. The operatic character of the vocal part, too, points in a general way to Dresden, where, as we have seen in Chapter 1, soloists from the court opera were enlisted to sing Mass arias in the Hofkirche. The virtuosic solo violin, by contrast, is more characteristic of Bach's style alone. As we noted earlier, Dresden composers tended to avoid exceedingly difficult solo instrumental lines in their Mass arias.

If the vocal writing of the "Laudamus te" is operatic, so is the form. Bach casts the music in the mold of a modified da capo aria: A (mm. 1–30), B (mm. 31–46), A' (mm. 47–62). The opening A is framed by the instru-

Example 3–9. "Laudamus te": aspects of the principal theme.

mental ritornello, which appears first in the tonic and then, in an abridged
form that overlaps with the end of the soprano material, in the dominant.
The B section, with thinner texture, touches on the dark hues of the submediant, F♯ minor, and mediant, C♯ minor. All that is conventional enough. It
is in the A' section that Bach reinterprets da capo tradition. Here he dis-
penses with the introductory ritornello—the soprano, rather than the violin,
initiates the return to A major and the opening material (m. 47)—and trans-
poses the stepwise-rising violin line (mm. 56–58) into the tonic in such a
way that it now climbs to the highest note in the movement, a'''. This not
only creates the climax of the "Laudamus te" as a whole but enhances the
e" of the soprano 2—the highest note of its mezzo range—and makes it
seem more magnificent than it actually is. In the A' section, Bach com-
presses the material of the original A to half its original length, intensifying
the music and at the same time disguising the formal outlines of the da capo
structure that was generally avoided in Mass settings.

Bach's treatment of the accompanimental strings is no less ingenious.
Much of the time the strings provide chordal harmonic support, their
expected role in the context of an aria with a solo instrument. But sometimes they take on a thematic function, echoing the motivic material of the
solo violin (mm. 4, 18, 38, etc.) or developing, in imitation, the slurred note-
pair motive of m. 2 (mm. 13–14 or 19–20). Occasionally the first violin of
the accompanimental group doubles the solo violin, adding emphasis to
critical cadential figures (mm. 2, 16, and 50). The shifting roles of the
strings add still another layer of intricacy to the finely detailed score.

Both Marshall and Rifkin see the "Laudamus te" as a parody of an existing aria, perhaps a piece selected because of its specific appropriateness for
Bordoni.[45] Dürr feels that the music is adopted from *something*—the generally neat nature of the autograph manuscript points in that direction—but
does not rule out the use of sketches.[46] While the instrumental parts of the
"Laudamus te" are elegantly and immaculately written in the *P 180* score,
the soprano 2 line displays numerous reworkings and stretches of a stiff
compositional hand—a strong indication of parody. It is likely that Bach was
either adapting an existing cantata aria or working from drafts in which the
soprano 2 part was insufficiently realized (since many of the erasures in the
soprano 2 involve the spontaneous embellishment of the vocal line). Gerhard
Herz has shown that Bach was strongly infatuated with lombardic figures in
the 1730s, between 1732 and 1735 in particular (see Chapter 7). Thus if the
"Laudamus te" is the parody of a now-lost cantata movement, the model may
have been written only a short time before the Mass segment.

"Gratias agimus tibi"

Gratias agimus tibi propter magnam gloriam tuam. (We give thanks to
   Thee for Thy great glory.)

Chorus: four-part choir (S1 and S2 combined, ATB), 3 trumpets and
   timpani, continuo; other instruments (2 flutes, 2 oboes, strings, and
   bassoon) *colla parte.*

In the "Gratias agimus tibi" Bach turns for a second time to Renaissance *a
cappella* vocal style, the retrospective idiom encountered in "Kyrie" II. The
music stems from the chorus "Wir danken dir, Gott, wir danken dir" of
Cantata 29, a work written to celebrate the change of Town Council in
Leipzig on August 27, 1731. The ceremony was an annual event, held each
August in St. Nikolai, and Bach used Cantata 29 at least two more times, in
1739 and 1749. "Wir danken dir, Gott" is the second movement of Cantata
29, coming directly after the well-known sinfonia for organ solo based on
the prelude of the Partita in E Major, BWV 1006, for unaccompanied violin. The sinfonia is derived from an intermediary arrangement (lacking
brass) from Cantata 120a, and the clean appearance of the "Wir danken dir,
Gott" chorus in the autograph score hints that it, too, may be a parody.[47]

It is not difficult to see why Bach was attracted to "Wir danken dir" for
the "Gratias." The music is appropriately dignified and majestic. The text,
taken from verse 1 of Psalm 75, is similar in meaning to that of the
"Gratias," so much so that the German and Latin could almost be translations of one another. In addition, the German text, like the Latin, falls naturally into two phrases, which are set to complementary themes in the music:

Cantata 29:
    Wir danken dir, Gott, wir danken dir   und verkündigen deine Wunder.
    (We give thanks unto Thee, O God   and proclaim Thy wonders.)

"Gratias":
    Gratias agimus tibi   propter magnam gloriam tuam.
    (We give thanks to Thee   for Thy great glory.)

In forming the "Gratias" Bach retained the four-voice setting of "Wir
danken dir" and the movement's overall structure. At the same time he
altered the meter from 𝄵 with whole-note measures to 𝄵 with breve measures and reshaped the thematic material to accommodate the new text.

The revisions are revealing. The first theme, in both its original and
revised forms, is a classic Palestrinian arch, rising step-by-step from D to G

(in its initial appearance) and then falling back, stepwise again, to D
(Example 3–10). The conjunct note motion and harmonic emphasis on the
subdominant rather than the dominant give the theme a chant-like, modal
quality. It is possible, in fact, that Bach based the idea on the concluding
phrase, "Deo dicamus gratias" ("Let us give thanks to God"), of the
Benedicamus dominicale chant that was sung at the end of the worship service each Sunday in Leipzig—a point to which we will return when we discuss the "Dona nobis pacem" in Chapter 5. As Wolff has demonstrated, in
the "Wir danken dir" chorus the 𝄵 meter provides a steady flow of half-
note accents, endowing the theme with a clear upbeat-downbeat pattern
that is ideal for the declamation of the German text: "Wir dán-ken dir."[48] In
the "Gratias" the initial upbeat of the cantata music would have been inappropriate, since it would have worked against the dactylic declamation of
the Latin text, "Grá-ti-as." The larger, less pronounced beats of the breve
measures of 𝄵 time better suit the softer accentuation of the Latin. Bach
more commonly emphasizes strong syllables through duration ("Grá-tias,"
"ág-imus," "tí-bi") rather than metric accent, in imitation of spoken Latin.

The second theme of the fugue displays qualities that hint at Baroque
instrumental style: repeated notes, decorative eighth-note flourishes, and a
clear tonal shape (Example 3–11). Bach altered the figuration of the "und
verkündigen deine Wunder" theme for the "Gratias," replacing the two small
melismas on the words "verkündigen" ("proclaim") and "Wunder" ("wonder") with a single, larger melisma for the word "gloriam" ("glory"). The
changes strengthen the melody's tonal qualities: the leading tone G♯ is
stressed more starkly through unembellished quarter notes, and the cadential progression ii$^6_5$→V^7→I (in A major) seems stronger because the note D
is given downbeat emphasis. The shift of eighth-note motion to the second
half of the theme imbues the line with an accelerando quality that is found
in many of Bach's purely instrumental ideas, such as the theme from the

Cantata 29:

Wir   dan -   - ken dir   Gott, Wir dan -   -   -   ken dir

"Gratias":

Gra   -   -   ti - as   a   -   -   gi - mus ti   -   bi

Example 3–10. "Gratias agimus tibi": derivation of the first theme.

Cantata 29:

"Gratias":

Example 3–11. "Gratias agimus tibi": derivation of the second theme.

well-known Fugue in G Minor ("Little") for organ, BWV 578. The instrumental qualities of the "Gratias" led Wolff to classify it as a Renaissance-
type piece in the freer *allabreve* manner rather than in vocally purer *stile
antico* style of "Kyrie" II.[49] Numerous corrections in the *P 180* manuscript of
the B-Minor Mass show that Bach made the changes in the "Wir danken dir"
music as he wrote out the "Gratias." There was no intermediary source.

Like the thematic material, the scoring of the "Gratias" reflects
Renaissance practice with Baroque updating. The movement is fundamentally a four-part vocal motet, with the strings, flutes, oboes, and bassoon
doubling the voices *colla parte*. The continuo is not an independent line, as
it is in "Kyrie" II, but rather a Renaissance *basso seguente*, following the
lowest vocal part from measure to measure. The brass and timpani play a
dual role: sometimes trumpets 1 and 2 alone double thematic entries, in
Renaissance *colla parte* fashion; other times, the three trumpets and timpani together present independent material in a Baroque manner, expanding the texture to as many as nine real parts.

The "Gratias" unfolds in a dense web of Renaissance vocal polyphony.
Bach begins the movement with three short overlapping points of imitation,
devoted respectively to the first theme, the second theme, and then the first
theme once again. In each case, the voices enter with thematic material in
ascending order, from bass to soprano. At m. 13, Bach combines the two
ideas in double counterpoint for the first time. This sequence of events is
capped in m. 15 by the entrance of trumpet, which doubles theme 1 as it
appears in the soprano. From here Bach intensifies the imitation even further. A rush of entries of both themes produces a climax in m. 31, when
trumpets 1 and 2 present theme 1 in stretto. The full trumpet and timpani
battery enters for the first time four measures later. In m. 41 the trumpets
and timpani appear again, doubling the thematic entries of theme 1 in the
alto and tenor and bringing the movement to a brilliant close.

No verbal description can depict the concentration of Bach's counter-point. In the course of forty-six measures, theme 1 appears twenty-nine times, theme 2, seventeen times. There is no episodic material whatsoever. The trumpets and timpani add Baroque coloration to the idiom of the Renaissance motet, highlighting and expanding the imitative fabric at climactic moments. This is Renaissance *a cappella* writing at its Bachian best.

"Domine Deus"

Domine Deus, Rex coelestis, Deus Pater omnipotens. Domine Fili unigenite Jesu Christe altissime. Domine Deus, Agnus Dei, Filius Patris. (O Lord God, heavenly King, God the Father almighty. O Lord God, the only-begotten Son, Jesus Christ, the most high. O Lord God, Lamb of God, Son of the Father.)

Duet: soprano 1 and tenor, solo flute, strings, continuo.

In the "Domine Deus," Bach returns to the intimate realm of the "Christe eleison" and the "Laudamus te." The choice of transverse flute as solo instrument sets the tone: as a pastoral instrument, the flute commonly represented Christ, the "Lamb of God." By the late Baroque it was also associated with the delicate trio and quartet settings of the emerging *galant* style.

The scoring and style of the "Domine Deus" are delicate indeed. The violins and viola, playing *con sordino* ("with the mute"), are sometimes legato, sometimes detached. The cello and violone (which one assumes is present)[50] perform pizzicato, and the flute sounds in lightly nuanced arpeggios and slurred note pairs, which in Dresden, at least, were performed with fashionable lombardic rhythms (see Chapter 7). In the *P 180* manuscript, Bach assigned the obbligato line to flutes 1 and 2 in unison; in the Dresden parts, he gave it to flute 1 alone. The subtle articulations of the instrumental ensemble act as a foil for the solo voices, which present longer, more sustained lines. The vocal writing, like that of the "Christe eleison," shows many characteristics of the Neapolitan love duet: "sweet" parallel thirds and sixths; gentle, weak-beat phrase endings; long, expressive appoggiaturas; and a catchy downbeat figure ♬ ♩　♪ that has lombardic overtones.

The "Domine Deus" illustrates once again Bach's skill in avoiding overt da capo form. The outlines of da capo design are clear: a lengthy, fully rounded A section (mm. 1–74), beginning and ending with ritornello segments, leads to a B section (mm. 75–95) that touches on the submediant, E minor, and mediant, B minor. The B section is followed not by a return of the A material, however, but by the "Qui tollis" chorus, and it is this truncation that effectively removes the "Domine Deus" from the realm of the da capo aria. But Bach obviously had textual considerations in mind as well. The major mode of the A section was fully appropriate for the first two lines of text, which speak of God the almighty and Christ the most high. The darker hues of the B section were apt for the third phrase, with its reference to Christ, the sacrificial lamb. But a return of the cheerful A section would have clashed with the next line, "Qui tollis peccata mundi," with its allusion to "the sins of the world." Introducing new music instead of returning to A solved the structural and textual dilemmas.

In the A section, Bach presents the "Domine Deus, Rex coelestis" and "Domine Fili unigenite" lines simultaneously, rather than one after the other. Polytextuality was common in love duets, and in the second half of the eighteenth century it was used in Mass settings as a means of covering the lengthy texts of the Gloria and Credo quickly. Succinctness does not seem to have been the concern in the rather expansive "Domine Deus," however. As Spitta first suggested, Bach probably juxtaposed the two lines to portray the "mysterious Unity of the Father and Son, on which the possibility of atonement depends."[51] Musically, Bach presents the lines of text in imitative counterpoint, with the tenor sometimes leading the soprano and the soprano sometimes leading the tenor. But the first voice always carries the "Domine Deus" line and the second the "Domine Fili," thus preserving the theological image of the Father preceding the Son. The autograph manuscript shows that for a moment, at least, Bach toyed with the idea of setting the Latin text more conventionally.[52] At the initial entry of the voices in mm. 17–18, he used the "Domine Deus, Rex coelestis" phrase in both the tenor and soprano, employing an underlay that soon united the two voices on the "-us" of "Deus"—a marvelously concordant love-duet effect (Example 3–12a). This he scratched out and replaced with the dual-text reading (Example 3–12b), which prevails for the rest of the A section.

Much has been made of the fact that the word "altissime" in the "Laudamus" text does not appear in the Roman Catholic Ordinary. Spitta located the accretion in Vopelius's hymnbook of 1682 and suggested that it was a Leipzig variant.[53] More recent research has shown that "altissime" is probably the remnant of a medieval trope from the Leipzig area, since it appears in Glorias found in the famous St. Thomas Gradual of the late thirteenth century.[54] Bach later omitted the word in the Glorias of his four short Masses, BWV 233–236, presumably because he had become more famil-

Example 3–12. "Domine Deus": original (a) and revised (b) text underlay of opening vocal theme.

iar with the Roman rite in the intervening years (or because he intended to use the pieces outside Leipzig). It is also possible, however, that Bach deliberately used "altissime" in the "Domine Deus" of the 1733 *Missa* because it facilitated the polytextuality of the A section: "altissime" extended the length of the "Domine Fili" phrase, bringing it closer in length to the "Domine Deus" phrase and making it easier to join the two lines in parallel counterpoint. "Altissime" also formed a four-syllable equivalent to "omnipotens," a happy circumstance that Bach exploited in striking fashion in m. 48. This parallel, too, bolsters the image of unanimity between the Father and Son (even without the editorial exclamation marks that are found in all modern editions, including the *Neue Bach-Ausgabe*).

In the B section, the soprano and tenor share the "Agnus Dei" line of the "Domine" text, and Bach drops the imitative entries suggestive of the Father and Son. The accompanimental strings are silent for the first six measures, thrusting the flute into the foreground to sharpen the image of Christ as paschal lamb. The music here is firmly in E minor, the key Bach often employed in vocal works to portray the Passion.[55] The approach of B minor (the key of the "Qui tollis"), the sustained dominant-pedal F♯ in the flute, the ensuing silence of all the upper instruments, and the appearance of the "Qui tollis" motive itself (F♯-D-B) in the last soprano-tenor entry (m. 93) make a compelling transition to the new movement.

Several factors strongly suggest that the "Domine Deus" is a parody. The music is neatly written in the *P 180* manuscript, hinting that Bach was copying rather than composing. The straightforward da capo structure, minus the return of A, points to a lost A-B-A da capo aria. That Bach would not hesitate to abridge a preexistent piece is clear from the "Qui tollis," the "Crucifixus," and the "Osanna," which are demonstrably segments of larger movements. In fact when Bach later drew from the "Domine Deus" for the Latin-texted work *Gloria in excelsis Deo,* BWV 191, he took only the A section. The B section, with its dark minor mode, was no longer useful for the cheerful setting of the doxology. Häfner has proposed a specific model for the "Domine Deus": the polytextual da capo duet "Ich will/Du sollt rühmen" ("I will boast/You should boast") from the lost *dramma per musica Ihr Häuser des Himmels, ihr scheinenden Lichter,* BWV 193a.[56] While only the text of the work survives, the words of the duet match both the structure and character of the "Domine Deus" very closely.

"Qui tollis"

*Qui tollis peccata mundi, miserere nobis. Qui tollis peccata mundi, suscipe
deprecationem nostram.* (Thou who takest away the sins of the world,
have mercy upon us. Thou who takest away the sins of the world,
receive our prayer.)

Chorus: four-part choir (S2,ATB), 2 flutes, strings, continuo.

While the "Domine Deus" *appears* to be the torso of a lost aria, the "Qui tollis" is verifiably borrowed music: it is derived from the opening chorus, "Schauet doch, und sehet ob irgendein Schmerz sei," of Cantata 46, a work Bach composed in Leipzig for the Tenth Sunday after Trinity, 1723.

The Gospel reading for that day, Luke 19:41-48, speaks of both weeping and vengeance: Christ laments over the sins of Jerusalem ("And when he was come near, he beheld the city, and wept over it . . .") and then predicts the city's future demise ("Thine enemies shall cast a trench about thee . . . and shall lay thee even with the ground, and thy children with thee . . ."). The text of the "Schauet doch" chorus is drawn from a parallel passage in the Old Testament, Lamentations of Jeremiah 1:12: "Behold and see if there be any sorrow like unto my sorrow, which is done unto me, wherewith the Lord hath afflicted me in the day of his fierce anger." The reinterpretation of Old Testament proclamations in terms of New Testament events was a favorite exegetical activity of Baroque librettists (one thinks of Jennens's blending of Isaiah and Luke for Handel's Messiah), and in Cantata 46, Christ's words are linked with Jeremiah's in the recitative that follows the opening chorus: "Though thou wouldst not heed Jesus's tears, thou wilt now heed a tidal wave of passion."

In the "Schauet doch" chorus, Bach cast Jeremiah's lamentation in the form of a large prelude and fugue.[57] The mournful opening phrase, "Schauet doch und sehet, ob irgendein Schmerz sei . . ." ("Behold and see if there be any sorrow . . .") is represented in the prelude; the wrathful second phrase, "Den der Herr hat mich voll Jammers gemacht . . ." ("Wherewith the Lord hath afflicted me . . .") is represented in the fugue. It is the prelude, an expressive, imitative lament, that Bach appropriated for the "Qui tollis." The weeping *Affekt* of the music made it extremely appropriate for the Mass text. No less significant, however, was the theological context of Cantata 46: although the words of "Schauet doch" are drawn from the Old Testament, they are linked with the object of the "Qui tollis": Christ's compassion.

A comparison of the "Schauet doch" and "Qui tollis" scores shows that Bach made numerous revisions in the music. He transposed the chorus from D minor to B minor, a key more appropriate for the Gloria, and dropped the prefatory instrumental sinfonia. He retained the four-part vocal texture but specifically assigned the soprano part to soprano 2, creating a dark scoring foreshadowing that used later in the "Crucifixus." He modernized the instrumentation, substituting transverse flutes for recorders and deleting the horn and oboes that doubled the upper vocal parts in the cantata.

Bach's changes in the vocal material are more extensive. The main theme of the "Schauet doch" lament consists of three parts: a descending minor triad; a longer middle phrase, beginning with a plaintive, minor-sixth leap (the emotionally charged rhetorical figure termed *exclamatio* in Bach's day) and ending with a highly dissonant, falling diminished fourth, b♭' to f♯'; and a final phrase consisting of another descending diminished fourth, f' to c♯' (Example 3–13a). Bach used the diminished interval to underscore the

Cantata 46:

Example 3–13. "Qui tollis": derivation of vocal theme.

anguish of the word "Schmerz"—"sorrow," or more literally, "pain"—which
is emphasized in each case by a sustained half note. The "Schauet doch"
theme has a symmetrical balance, since the outer phrases are the same
length and share the same ♩ ♩ ♩ rhythm.

For the "Qui tollis," Bach retained the melodic contour of the "Schauet
doch" line but adjusted the rhythmic values. In the first phrase, the upbeat
is shortened and quickened, and the downbeat is subdivided into two quarter notes, to produce an appropriate declamation for "Qui tól-lis"; in the
second phrase, the passionate leap of the minor sixth receives greater
stress, since the upper note is sustained for four beats. This properly
accents the "-ca-" of "peccata"—"sin"—and serves to highlight this critical word; in the final phrase, the falling diminished fourth is subdivided
into eighth and quarter notes, not only accommodating the six syllables of
"miserere nobis" but also creating new chromatic seconds (Example
3–13b). As Marshall has pointed out, Bach's subtle alterations transform
the nature of the theme.[58] The original "Schauet doch" idea is serene, even-
moving, balanced. The "Qui tollis" is, as Marshall expresses it, more
"organic." It begins with a quick upbeat, slows down, and ends with a rush
of small notes—notes that impart a sense of urgency to "miserere nobis,"
the plea for mercy. This pliancy makes the theme less Baroque and more
Romantic—almost Beethovenesque, if you will.

The autograph score of the B-Minor Mass shows that Bach made these
and other refinements as he wrote out the "Qui tollis." The manuscript
looks almost like a composition draft. While the flute parts, which remained
essentially the same, are neatly penned, the string and vocal parts show
extensive cross-outs and erasures. The compelling "Qui tollis" theme was
reworked on the page: Bach's first thought called for a descending semitone
on "mundi" (which would have usurped the surprise of the D♮ of "miserere") and the use of the final phrase for the word "miserere" alone (Bach,

less familiar with the text of the Mass than his Dresden contemporaries, seems to have forgotten the word "nobis" for a moment; Example 3–14).

Qui tol - lis pec - ca - ta mun - di, mi - se - re - re

Example 3–14. "Qui tollis": original version of vocal theme.

Another *ad hoc* change was the institution of a differentiated bass line. The continuo stresses the downbeat with the ♩ ♪ ♪ figure found in the "Schauet doch" score, while the cello plays a new, more animated line ♩ ♩ ♩ (see Example 7–1 in Chapter 7). Like the revisions in the vocal theme, this alteration increases the urgency of the music. In addition, it introduces a new hierarchy of note values in the instrumental parts:[59]

in the flutes
in the upper strings
in the cello
in the continuo

The regular pulsations of the instruments provide a plush, murmuring background for the highly expressive vocal material.

Finally, there is the matter of form. The prelude of the "Schauet doch" chorus can be divided into three sections:

mm. 1–17	orchestral sinfonia	i —— i
mm. 17–45	"Schauet doch" vocal material (first imitative, then more homophonic, with the first half of the sinfonia superimposed)	i —— i
mm. 45–67	"Schauet doch" vocal material (first imitative, then more homophonic, with the entire sinfonia superimposed)	v —— v

This is a developmental form, becoming more complex as it unfolds. By dropping the opening sinfonia, Bach produced a more evenly balanced two-part form that was fully appropriate for the two-line "Qui tollis" text. The F♯-major chord that closes the second segment forms a harmonic spring-board to the B minor of the "Qui sedes."

In short, the music of "Schauet doch" is framed by new elements in the "Qui tollis." It is preceded by the "Domine Deus" instead of the sinfonia and followed by the "Qui sedes" instead of the fugue. It is compellingly joined with both. As Smend rightly pointed out, the "Qui tollis" is far from a "torso" of the "Schauet doch" score. The cantata music emerges greatly enhanced, as part of a greater whole.[60]

"Qui sedes"

Qui sedes ad dextram Patris, miserere nobis. (Thou who sittest at the right hand of the Father, have mercy on us.)

Aria: alto, solo oboe d'amore, strings, continuo.

The "Qui sedes" completes the supplication portion of the Gloria that began with the "Domine Deus." In Dresden Mass settings, the "Qui sedes" often appears as part of the "Qui tollis," and that is how Bach treated it in his four short Masses, BWV 233–236. Here he arrived at a different solution, casting the two text passages as contrasting movements—the first a chorus, the second an aria for alto and obbligato oboe d'amore—but linking the music tonally (both segments are in B minor). Spitta felt that the juxtaposition of chorus and aria resulted from Bach's desire to distinguish atonement from mediation.[61] In his view, the "Qui tollis" represents humankind's massed plea for propitiation, and the "Qui sedes" represents Christ's role in winning the propitiation through personal intervention with God.

There may be something to this. The text of the "Qui sedes" has both Old and New Testament roots. In the Old Testament, David declared: "The Lord said unto my Lord, 'Sit thou at my right hand, until I make thine enemies thy footstool'" (Psalm 110:1). In the New Testament, Mark described Christ ascending to heaven and assuming a similar position: "So then after the Lord had spoken unto them, he was received up into heaven, and sat on the right hand of God" (Mark 16:19). The "Qui sedes" phrase of the Ordinary seems to combine Mark's words with those of Peter and the Apostles: "Him hath God exalted with his right hand to be a Prince and a Saviour, for to give repentance to Israel, and the forgiveness of sins" (Acts 5:31). Christ is thus portrayed as mediator, sitting at the right hand of God and offering forgiveness. There is also a vengeful aspect to this role, however. The Old Testament words of David continue: "The Lord at thy right hand shall strike through the kings in the day of his wrath. He shall judge among the heathen, he shall fill the places with dead bodies; he shall wound the heads over many countries" (Psalm 110:5–6).

Bach's music for the "Qui sedes" has a touch of vengeance to it. The idiom is that of a gigue, the dance Mattheson characterized as showing "a heated and volatile passion, a wrath, that passes quickly."[62] In Cantata 40 Bach used a gigue to portray a wrathful *Affekt* in the aria "Höllische Schlange, wird dir nicht bange?" ("Hellish Snake, aren't you afraid?"), which describes Christ crushing the head of the snake of sin for the redemption of humankind. In the "Qui sedes," the $\frac{6}{8}$ meter, the leaping motives and twisty figures, the strong rhythmic accents, and the periodic cadences all point to the same sort of passionate, minor-mode gigue.

Bach modified gigue conventions considerably, however. Gigues normally have symmetrical phrases, and the ritornello of the "Qui sedes" begins that way, with a four-measure phrase ending on a half cadence in the mediant. But then follow phrases of 6 bars, 2½ bars, and 5½ bars—highly irregular units for a gigue. The melodic contour, too, bypasses one's expectations. The theme begins with gigue-like leaps that serve to accent the downbeat (mm. 1–2; Example 3–15a). But the tie in m. 3, which later offsets the word "ad" when the theme is picked up by the alto, produces a jarring hemiola, a device indeed common in gigues, but at cadences, not mid-phrase points. The theme of the Fugue in F Major from Well-Tempered Clavier II shows the more usual approach in gigues: uninterrupted strong-beat accents (Example 3–15b). The asymmetrical phrases and the hemiolas of the "Qui sedes" ritornello offset the impetuous, "wrathful" qualities of the gigue. It may be that these irregularities are no more than Bach's playing with dance traditions, something one can observe in the gigues of the *Clavierübung* collection of 1726–1731 or the famous gigue of the B-Minor Flute Sonata, BWV 1030, of the mid-1730s. But it may also be that he wished to symbolize the ameliorating effect of Christ's "mediation" (as Spitta put it) on behalf of humankind while sitting in judgment at the right hand of God.

More difficult to interpret are the instrumental echoes (mm. 4, 16, etc.), which Bach notated with unusual care. Detached notes are answered by slurred notes (because an echo, sounding in the distance, would be

Example 3–15.   a. "Qui sedes."   b. Fugue in F Major, BWV 880/2, from Well-Tempered Clavier II.

blurred?), and two levels of dynamics come into play: *forte* and *piano* when the instruments sound alone, and *piano* and *più piano* when the alto is present (the markings are especially consistent in the violin 2 and viola parts of the Dresden materials). Always appearing after the word "Patris," the echoes could mean that Christ is a reflection of God, his father. Or they could represent the self-doubt of humankind's supplication—mercy is sought, but will it be granted?—as in the famous echo aria "Flößt, mein Heiland, flößt dein Namen" from Part 4 of the Christmas Oratorio. "Flößt, mein Heiland" is a parody, and that may be the case with the "Qui tollis" as well. But even if the "Qui tollis" is borrowed music, Bach must have viewed the echoes as somehow appropriate for the Latin text.

Like the "Christe eleison," the "Qui sedes" is a ritornello form of considerable sophistication. As we have already mentioned, the opening ritornello can be divided into four irregular segments, the last two of which cadence in the tonic. The alto enters in m. 18 with the theme from the first segment and then begins the second segment before veering off into free material. The instrumental ritornello returns three times in the movement, in the dominant, the mediant, and the tonic. With each appearance it becomes more concise, creating the sensation of growing intensity. At the same time, at m. 69, during the final "episode," the alto recapitulates the principal theme in the tonic, marking the beginning of a concluding section that balances the opening ritornello (both are eighteen measures in length). This return invests the ritornello form with a da capo quality (A = mm. 1–43; B = mm. 43–68; and A' = mm. 69–87), as does the *adagio* on the word "miserere nobis" in m. 74, which emphasizes the final return to the tonic. A number of Dresden Masses display a similar slowing of tempo on the words "miserere nobis," and it is possible that Bach was following a long-standing tradition. In the *Missa Divi Nepomuceni,* Sarri used a series of fermatas at the end of the "Qui sedes" (which in this huge *Missa* is set as an aria for soprano and oboe solo) to create a dramatic, halting effect (Example 3–16).

The almost flawless appearance of the "Qui sedes" in the *P 180* manuscript and the abundance of articulation and dynamic indications suggest that Bach was working either from sketches or from a now-lost parody model. The few corrections in the "Qui sedes" score appear mainly in the inner string parts and the vocal line. Häfner has proposed that the music was derived from the aria "Soll des Landes Segen wachsen" of the secular cantata *Entfernet euch, ihr heitern Sterne,* BWV Anh. 9, for which a printed libretto alone survives.[63] The text of "Soll des Landes," with its allusions to "our ardent supplication," does conjure up the same sort of mood as the

Example 3–16. Sarri: conclusion of "Qui sedes" from *Missa Divi Nepomuceni.*

"Qui sedes." But the cantata poetry does not line up with the "Qui sedes" music as well as it might,[64] and it offers no reason for echo effects. Thus the model for "Qui sedes"—if there was one—remains elusive.

"Quoniam tu solus sanctus"

Quoniam tu solus sanctus. Tu solus dominus. Tu solus altissimus, Jesu Christe. (For Thou only art holy. Thou only art the Lord. Thou only, Jesus Christ, art most high.)

Aria: bass, corno da caccia, bassoons 1 and 2, continuo.

With the "Quoniam tu solus sanctus" the Gloria text turns from supplication to praise, and Bach's music correspondingly moves from somber B minor to bright D major, where it remains for the rest of the *Missa*.

The "Quoniam" is one of Bach's most extraordinary arias. The setting— bass voice, horn, two bassoons, and continuo—is unique in his oeuvre. Indeed, one is hard pressed to find the combination elsewhere in the Baroque repertory. Bach seems to have gathered such improbable forces to create an elaborate iconographical conceit. The horn, a brass instrument associated with kings and conquerors (both earthly and heavenly), symbolizes Christ. Sounding in the tenor-alto range, d–d" (though notated an octave higher, and in C),[65] it has the highest tessitura in the "Quoniam" and appropriately portrays the "most high" nature of Christ's sovereignty. Bach underscores the uniqueness of Christ's "highness" by placing the four other parts in the bass range.

The imagery does not stop there. The octave leap in the horn's theme was also associated with Christ: Andreas Werckmeister (1645–1706), a Thuringian whose progressive ideas on tuning and other matters seem to have had a considerable influence on Bach, stated that since the unison symbolized God, the octave, with its perfect proportional relationship of 1:2 with the unison, represented the figure of Christ.[66] In modern times, Helmut Rilling has suggested that the palindrome formed by the first five notes of the "Quoniam" octave motive (Example 3–17) may represent Christ's absolute perfection[67]—an arresting notion even if it lacks foundation in eighteenth-century theory. The word "altissimus"—"most high"—appears for the first time in the middle section of the "Quoniam" (mm. 53–89). Up to that point, the bass voice (also a representative of Christ in Baroque music) had risen no higher than the note b. In the middle section, however, it ascends to c', c#', d', and then twice, on the word "altissimus," to its high-

Example 3–17. "Quoniam tu solus sanctus": horn theme.

est note, e'. In addition, the key words "Dominus" ("Lord") and "solus"
("[Thou] only") are highlighted with exuberant flourishes. One can theorize
about Bach's imagery in the "Laudamus te" or "Domine Deus"; in the
"Quoniam," by contrast, his instrumental and rhetorical symbols seem
unequivocally clear.

The virtuosic writing for two bassoons also distinguishes the movement.
A glance at Bach's other church works reveals just four arias with obbligato bassoon, and in each case the scoring calls for a single instrument only.
The paucity of written-out bassoon parts for the Leipzig cantatas in general
points to limited expectations: normally the bassoon seems to have doubled
the continuo, at best.[68] And when outlining the requirements for church performance in the "Short but Most Necessary Draft for a Well-Regulated
Church Music" of 1730, Bach mentioned the need for "1, or even 2" players for the bassoon, a comment that seems to imply that one player was the
standard.

Matters were far different in Dresden, where the Court Capella boasted
as many as five bassoonists in Bach's time, including virtuosos Johann
Gottfried Böhme, Jean Cadet, and Caspar Ernst Quantz.[69] On an average
Sunday, two or three players took part in church performances,[70] and
Heinichen and Zelenka did not hesitate to use them in a solo capacity. The
"Quoniam tu solus sanctus" from Heinichen's *Missa Fidei* of 1723,[71] for
instance, is scored for bass, obbligato bassoons and violins, and continuo
(Example 3–18). Surely Bach knew of the special resources in Dresden,
and the sudden appearance of two demanding obbligato bassoon parts in
the "Quoniam" seems too great a departure from his usual Leipzig practice
to be purely coincidental.

The use of the corno da caccia also points to Dresden. The hunting horn,
or *Waldhorn* as Walther termed it, was a Dresden specialty, appearing ubiquitously in opera, chamber pieces, and church works. The Mass settings of
Heinichen and Zelenka represent one of the largest bodies of music with
"clarino" horn parts that include florid writing in the high register.[72] Bach
must have been impressed, too, by such colorful scorings as corno da caccia and theorbo in Alessandro's aria from Hasse's *Cleofide* (Act III, Scene
6), which he most certainly attended in Dresden in 1731.[73] In the early

Example 3–18. Heinichen: "Quoniam tu solus sanctus" from *Missa Fidei*.

1730s the Dresden Court ensemble included two famous horn virtuosos, first-chair player Johann Adam Schindler and his brother Andreas. We find the corno da caccia in Bach's Weimar and Leipzig cantatas, but it is always scored in pairs. The single horn of the "Quoniam" is unique in his music. In the Dresden performance materials the horn part is written on a separate sheet of paper, which leads one to believe that Bach intended it for a specialist rather than an unoccupied trumpet player. The specialist may have been one of the Schindlers.

The "Quoniam" displays a modified da capo design: A (mm. 1–53), B (mm. 53–89), A' (mm. 90–128). Bach might have used this tripartite structure to emphasize the tripartite nature of the text, allotting "Quoniam tu solus sanctus" to the A, "Tu solus dominus" to the B, and "Tu solus altissimus, Jesu Christe" to the A'. He chose instead to place the first two phrases in the A section, the "Tu solus altissimus" in the B section, and all three phrases in the A' section. This moderates somewhat the symmetrical effect of the da capo scheme. He also omits the instrumental ritornello at the opening of the A' section (as he did in the "Laudamus te") and begins directly with an embellished version of the vocal material (Example 3–19). Normally the diminutions that appear in m. 94 would have been improvised by the singer. Here Bach notates the variation, leaving little to chance. During the course of the movement the voice twice assumes the horn's ritornello theme (mm.

Example 3–19. "Quoniam tu solus sanctus": vocal theme at m. 12 (a) and m. 90 (b).

33–45 and 98–106), a procedure that tightens the bond between the bass and the horn, the two iconographical representatives of Christ.

A number of writers have viewed the clean appearance of the "Quoniam" and the finely detailed performance instructions in the autograph score as signs that this movement is also a parody. Rifkin has suggested that Bach appropriated the music from an aria whose text inspired the extraordinary setting of solo horn and two bassoons.[74] Häfner has proposed that the "Quoniam" is derived from an aria for bass, trumpet, two oboes, and continuo, and that the bassoon and horn lines were originally an octave higher. This proposal is seconded by Butt, who points to two spots where Bach initially notated one of the bassoons in treble clef.[75] One cannot demonstrate that Bach ever wrote an aria for bass, trumpet, two oboes, and continuo, however, or that he had two virtuoso bassoon players at his disposal in Weimar, Cöthen, or Leipzig. It may be that the "Quoniam" is new music, written with the help of a draft or sketches.

"Cum Sancto Spiritu"

Cum Sancto Spiritu, in gloria Dei Patris. Amen. (With the Holy Ghost in the glory of God the Father. Amen.)

Chorus: five-part choir (SSATB), 3 trumpets & timpani, 2 flutes, 2 oboes, strings, bassoon, continuo.

The "Quoniam" cadences directly into the "Cum Sancto Spiritu," a "triumphant hymn to Christ, who, having finished His earthly course, sits on the right hand of the Father," as Spitta expressed it.[76] Like the "Gloria in excelsis" that opened the Gloria portion, this brilliant trumpets-and-drums chorus is marked *vivace*—Bach's way of indicating that the concerted, instrumental figuration should be performed in a lively, highly articulated manner. The word "gloria" is set with exuberant melismatic flourishes (Example 3–20a). By contrast, the word "Patris"—"Father"—is stressed through serene sustained notes (Example 3–20b), much in the way the key word "pax" was highlighted with long notes in the music of the "Et in terra pax."

The "Cum Sancto Spiritu" exhibits a highly symmetrical five-part design:

A (mm. 1–37)	I → V		Free declamatory material
B (mm. 37–64)	V → vi		Vocal fugue
A (mm. 64–81)	vi → iii		Free declamatory material
B (mm. 80–111)	iii → I		Vocal fugue
A (mm. 111–128)	I — I		Free declamatory material

The declamatory material of the A sections falls into proportional units of four, six, or eight measures, which, together with the instrumental figuration and spirited *vivace* articulation, gives the music a dance-like character. The two B-section fugues are based on a single theme (Example 3–21a), an idea loosely derived from the opening vocal motive of the first A section. Against this theme Bach presents an animated countersubject, a weaving, conjunct idea on the word "Amen" (Example 3–21b), which acts as a per-

Example 3–20. "Cum Sancto Spiritu": "Gloria" and "Patris" motives.

Example 3–21. "Cum Sancto Spiritu": fugue, subject (a) and countersubject (b).

fect foil for the leap-filled main subject. As in the "Pleni sunt coeli" of the
Sanctus, Bach here sets up a dynamic climax in the fugues by scoring the
first for the voices and continuo alone and the second for voices, doubling
instruments, and continuo. In the second fugue he also surrounds the real
entries of the fugue subject with false entries in stretto. This produces
almost feverish contrapuntal activity—activity that suggests the ecstatic joy
over Christ's ascension to the glory of God. The two fugues of the "Cum
Sancto Spiritu" are not built on permutation technique, like those of the "Et
in terra pax." The writing is much less rigid. It is as if Bach wished to picture the liberation that comes from faith in the seated Trinity. The trumpets
and timpani appear in the A sections only, which as a consequence form
tutti framing elements for the more developmental fugues.

Many writers have speculated that the "Cum Sancto Spiritu" is a parody—the torso of a now-lost chorus from which Bach removed the opening instrumental ritornello in order to create an organic, uninterrupted
vocal link with the "Quoniam." Tovey was so certain of the abridgment ("I
am as sure as I can be of anything," he said emphatically) that he
attempted to show how the missing ritornello could be reconstructed by
joining together instrumental material from the opening and closing bars
of the initial A section (mm. 1–4, and mm. 25–37 transposed to the
tonic).[77] By contrast, Smend has argued in favor of the originality of the

"Cum Sancto," and Häfner, who projects a parody source for almost every movement of the B-Minor Mass, suggests in this case that the music may be new.[78]

In the *P 180* manuscript, the musical text of the "Cum Sancto" is generally tidy, with changes and corrections appearing mainly in the vocal parts. Rifkin has taken this to be a sign of parody. In his view, the twin-fugue structure of the music points to a lost cantata movement from the middle or late 1720s, the period when Bach showed great interest in choruses of this nature.[79] Rifkin reasons that the pseudo-entry of the soprano 2 in the first fugue and the reworking of the alto and tenor voices in the manuscript at that point (mm. 54–55) suggest that Bach added the soprano 2 to what was originally a four-voice composition. In the second fugue, however, the soprano 2 plays a fully equal role with the other voices. Whether the "Cum Sancto" is borrowed music or a new composition, Bach seems to have spent considerable time refining the vocal parts on the page.

When Bach revised the music of the "Cum Sancto Spiritu" for the chorus "Sicut erat in principio" of Cantata 191 a dozen years or so after completing the *Missa,* he significantly reworked a number of aspects of the score. As might be expected, he altered the vocal parts to accommodate the new Latin text (the conclusion of the Small Doxology, "As it was in the beginning, is now, and ever shall be. Amen"). In the process, he expanded each A section by two measures and changed elements of the instrumentation. The flutes, which in the "Cum Sancto" double the oboes until the final A section (mm. 111–128), are now given fully independent parts throughout the movement. In addition, in the first fugue Bach provides the voices with an instrumental accompaniment of detached, eighth-note chords, much in the fashion of the first fugue of the "Et in terra pax." Both the flute lines and the detached chords greatly enrich the score and, as original "second thoughts" on the composer's part, deserve consideration in modern performances of the B-Minor Mass. The "Sicut erat" arrangement also clarifies certain matters of slurring.[80]

SUMMARY

If we survey the entire Kyrie and Gloria portion—Bach's 1733 *Missa*—we find that it displays a structure containing elements of symmetry as well as asymmetry:

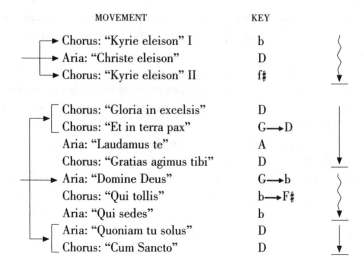

MOVEMENT	KEY	
Chorus: "Kyrie eleison" I	b	
Aria: "Christe eleison"	D	
Chorus: "Kyrie eleison" II	f♯	
Chorus: "Gloria in excelsis"	D	
Chorus: "Et in terra pax"	G→D	
Aria: "Laudamus te"	A	
Chorus: "Gratias agimus tibi"	D	
Aria: "Domine Deus"	G→b	
Chorus: "Qui tollis"	b→F♯	
Aria: "Qui sedes"	b	
Aria: "Quoniam tu solus"	D	
Chorus: "Cum Sancto"	D	

The Kyrie forms a balanced unit, with two tutti "Kyrie" choruses framing a "Christe" duet. This plan mirrors the design found in many Dresden
Mass settings of the time, as we have noted, and may represent a nod to
convention on Bach's part. The Kyrie's harmonic scheme, however, is open-
ended—that is, the music begins in B minor and ends in F♯ minor. The
resulting tonal instability offsets the symmetry of the structure and forcefully weds the Kyrie to the Gloria.

The Gloria also forms a balanced unit, if one accepts the "Domine
Deus" as the portion's center, framed on either side by four movements.
Within each group of four movements, the outer two are connected by an
elided cadence ("Gloria"→"Et in terra," "Quoniam"→"Cum Sancto")
and the inner two by a dominant cadence ("Laudamus te"→"Gratias,"
"Qui tollis"→"Qui sedes"). As in the Kyrie, the overall harmonic scheme
counteracts such elements of symmetry, however. The first four movements
of the Gloria form a closed group, in D major; the next three form a modulatory group, moving from G major to B minor; and the last two form a final
group, again in D major. This tripartite scheme may reflect Bach's desire to
distinguish praise (the D-major segments) from supplication (the middle
segment), as we noted when examining the individual movements.

In the Kyrie and Gloria, architectural and harmonic elements do not
reinforce one another in as consistent a way as they do in the Credo (in its
final form). The organizational plan of the Kyrie and Gloria, in fact, is closer to that of the Six Partitas of *Clavierübung* I (1726–1731) than to that of
the "Goldberg" Variations of *Clavierübung* IV (1741): it is logical and aes-

thetically pleasing, but it lacks the multileveled integration that is characteristic of Bach's late designs. As is true of the Six Partitas, the music of the
Missa is strongly eclectic, and it is clear that Bach wished to create an
encyclopedic work. Here, too, however, the movements in different styles
("Kyrie" II and "Gratias" in Renaissance vocal style, "Gloria" and "Cum
Sancto Spiritu" in Baroque concerted style, etc.) lack the type of organic
links that appear in the Credo.

If there is a more striking characteristic of the Kyrie and Gloria it is the
way in which Bach methodically displays the solo talents of the singers and
instrumentalists. Within the five arias of the *Missa*, he features each voice
at least once: soprano 1 in the "Christe" and "Domine Deus," soprano 2 in
the "Christe" and "Laudamus te," alto in the "Qui sedes," tenor in the
"Domine Deus," and bass in the "Quoniam tu solus." At the same time, he
highlights solo players from the string, woodwind, and brass choirs of the
instrumental band, allocating obbligato parts to the violin ("Laudamus te"),
transverse flute ("Domine Deus"), oboe d'amore ("Qui sedes"), bassoon
("Quoniam"), and horn ("Quoniam"). As many recent commentators have
noted, the "showcasing" of individual performers points to Dresden and the
exquisitely talented personnel of the Court Capella. But it also reflects the
repertory from which much of the music was derived: Bach's sacred and
secular cantatas of the 1720s and early 1730s, works that show a strong
emphasis on solo virtuosity and vocal and instrumental color. Bravura writing—for vocal soloist, instrumental player, and chorus singer—predominates over architectonic considerations. The Kyrie and Gloria represent the
apotheosis of Bach's Leipzig cantata style. In the Credo, written fifteen
years later, the composer pursued quite different principles.

Chapter 4

THE CREDO

GENERAL CONSIDERATIONS

*A*s we noted in Chapter 2, when Bach began to work on the remaining portions of the B-Minor Mass in the late 1740s, he most probably started with the Credo, or *Symbolum Nicenum,* as he labeled it. Fifteen years had passed since he had completed the Kyrie and Gloria, and the music of the Credo strongly reflects his interests of the intervening period: the intense study of the Renaissance *stile antico,* the composition of progressive vocal works for the Collegium Musicum, and the publication of large-scale, encyclopedic keyboard collections. Compared to the Kyrie and Gloria, the Credo shows a still greater stylistic synthesis and new organizational principles.

Bach had little to go on by way of models. The works that fired his imagination for the *Missa*—the immense "numbers" Masses of Durante, Mancini, Sarri, Conti, and other Neapolitan or Neapolitan-oriented composers—were of no help here, since they normally included the Kyrie and Gloria only. Concerted Credos were common in Dresden Masses and imported works of the Venetian/Viennese type, but such settings were of modest size, with segments of the text set as short sections rather than fully rounded movements. The independent Credo in D Major by Zelenka, Z. 201, preserved in the Austrian National Library in Vienna,[1] is typical:

Chorus: "Credo in unum Deum"—26 mm., ¢ meter, D major (ending on V)
Chorus: "Qui propter"—21 mm., $\frac{3}{8}$ meter, D major
Chorus: "Et incarnatus est"—27 mm., ₵ meter, G minor (ending on V)
Chorus with solos: "Et resurrexit"—48 mm., ¢ meter, D major
Chorus: "Et vitam venturi"—41 mm., ¢ meter, D major

Such pieces lasted no more than eight or ten minutes in performance—
for Bach, too small a scale, obviously, to balance the music of the 1733
Missa. The same is true of the Bassani Credos that Bach arranged during
the years 1747–1748. As we observed earlier, they surely served as
preparatory studies rather than direct models.

For the Baroque composer striving to enliven the Mass Ordinary by the
use of musical *Affekt*, the Nicene Creed was unquestionably the least grati-
fying portion of the Latin text. An objective statement of faith, it is more
doctrinal than dramatic. As Albert Schweitzer aptly observed:

> The *Symbolum Nicaenum* is a hard nut for a composer to crack. If ever
> there was a text put together without any idea of its being set to music
> it is this, in which the Greek theologians have laid down their correct
> and dry formulas for the conception of the godhead of Christ.[2]

By the late Baroque, the Nicene Creed was coming under increasing
attack by Enlightenment thinkers, who felt that it was too formal and too
emotionless to allow personal interpretation. Johann Conrad Dippel, a
Pietist writing under the pen name Christianus Democritus, asserted in his
tract *Anfang, Mittel und Ende der Ortho- und Heterodoxie* ("Beginning,
Middle, and End of Orthodox and Unorthodox Doctrine") of 1699 that the
Council of Nicea had produced nothing but "great confusion among the
orthodox" by promulgating such an arid profession of faith.[3] Ironically, it
was Bach's use, in the "Crucifixus," of music originally associated with an
emotionally charged Pietistic text that helped to infuse the Credo of the B-
Minor Mass with its high drama.

It is most probable that Bach approached the Credo text from a
Lutheran standpoint. In the Small Catechism, Luther interpreted the
Nicene Creed as a Trinitarian document, dividing it into three sections or
articles: "Of Creation," dealing with God's creation of the world ("Credo in
unum Deum" to "Patrem omnipotentem"); "Of Redemption," dealing with
the coming of Christ, his nature, and his crucifixion and resurrection ("Et
in unum Dominum" to "Et resurrexit"); and "Of Sanctification," dealing
with the nature of the Holy Spirit and the resurrection of the dead ("Et in
Spiritum Sanctum" to "Et expecto"). When Bach composed the Credo, he
seems to have drawn images from Luther's gloss, as we shall see when we
look at the music in detail. In addition, he may have based the overall
design on Luther's interpretation—a topic to which we shall return in the
summary.

THE MUSIC OF THE CREDO

"Credo in unum Deum"

Credo in unum Deum. (I believe in one God.)

Chorus: five-part choir (SSATB), violin 1 & 2, continuo; *colla parte*
instrumental doubling? (see Chapter 7).

In the "Credo in unum Deum" movement Bach achieved one of his most
remarkable feats of stylistic synthesis. The seven upper parts—the five
voices of the chorus and violins 1 and 2—represent a Renaissance *a cappella* motet. The *allabreve* meter, the abundance of white notes, the chant-
like melodic lines, the mixolydian harmony (signified by a key signature
one sharp "short"), the dense web of vocal counterpoint, and the absence of
affective figures point to the classic church style of Palestrina. The motet is
supported, however, by a quasi-ostinato, walking-bass continuo line that is
purely Baroque. The continuo provides a tonal framework, yet at the same
time preserves the modal character of the upper material by avoiding clear
cadences. By joining motet and ostinato, Bach merged the vocal tradition of
the sixteenth century with the instrumental tradition of the eighteenth.

The motet's points of imitation are based on a rhythmicized form of Credo
plainchant. The chant Bach employed is a Saxon variant of the Gregorian
"authentic tone" of the Roman rite (the Saxon chant comes closest to Credo II
in the *Liber usualis*, itself an alternate version of the authentic tone, Credo I;
Example 4–1). The variant appears in the St. Thomas Gradual from the late
thirteenth century, and Peter Wagner once raised the intriguing possibility
that Bach may have borrowed the chant directly from the medieval manuscript, which was housed in the St. Thomas School library.[4] But Bach did not
have to turn to the ancient source, for the melody was also printed in the
Vopelius Hymnbook of 1682, which he undoubtedly had on his bookshelf.

Roman rite (*Liber Usualis*, Credo II):

Cre - do   in   u - num   De - um.

Saxon rite (Vopelius, 1682):

Cre - do   in   u - num   De - um.

Example 4–1. Credo plainchant.

Quoting chant in polyphonic Credo settings seems to have been an established custom in Dresden, even in Masses written in Baroque concerted style. In the Mass in D Minor Hasse used the incipit of the authentic tone Credo chant (in the Saxon variant, once again) as a *cantus firmus* over an active, eighth-note walking bass. While this seems like the same procedure used by Bach, Hasse's music is markedly *galant* and shows no signs of the *stile antico*. In the Credo of the *Missa votiva*, Zelenka presented a chant-like melody in long held notes amidst homophonic pseudo-counterpoint. The chant appears first as a *cantus firmus,* then in stretto pairs (Example 4–2). The vocal counterpoint is accompanied by obbligato instruments, and the passage is framed by a fashionable instrumental ritornello. Like Berlioz and Liszt a century later, Hasse, Zelenka, and other Dresden composers made no more than a passing nod to ancient church ritual on the way to writing a piece in the most up-to-date style.

Bach used plainchant in a more retrospective way. The imitative entries of the "Credo" can be divided into three expositions. In the first, Bach introduces the chant theme in each voice, one by one, beginning with the tenor in m. 1 and ending with the violin 2 in m. 17. In the second exposition, which begins in m. 18 (and overlaps with the end of exposition 1), he again commences the entries in the tenor and ends in violin 2. But now the theme appears more systematically, rising in order from the lowest to the highest voice. The third exposition begins in m. 33, where the chant sounds in augmentation in the bass. Over the elongated entry the soprano 2 and alto present the chant theme simultaneously, in parallel sixths, followed a half-beat later by an entry in soprano 1 (Example 4–3). The soprano 2–alto entry represents, in Baroque nomenclature, a *canon sine pausa* ("canon without pause") and the soprano 1 entry, a stretto. Four measures later, while the bass continues to sound the theme, the violins enter with yet another stretto entry.

The contrapuntal density of the "Credo" exceeds that of "Kyrie" II and the "Gratias." Aside from the five-bar close, the theme appears in every measure, and there is no episodic material whatsoever. Although Bach ostensibly wrote the "Credo" in a neutral, objective style devoid of expressive devices, in truth he created a very intense, dramatic piece. As Christoph Wolff has pointed out, the elaborate contrapuntal manipulations of the third exposition are the *raison d'être* of the movement, and they give the music a climactic dimension normally associated with the *stile moderno*.[5]

Bach commonly used contrapuntal procedures such as canon, ostinato, and fugue as musical metaphors for the steadfastness of Christian belief: for instance, the opening chorus of Cantata 80, *Ein feste Burg ist unser Gott,*

Example 4–2. Zelenka: "Credo" from *Missa votiva*.

Example 4–2 *(continued)*.

features a canon on Luther's chorale, and the chorale prelude *Wir glauben all' an einen Gott,* BWV 680, features ostinato and fugal imitation on the German Creed hymn. The imitative writing and quasi-ostinato of the "Credo" serve a similar, symbolic purpose. In turning to a chant-derived theme and the sixteenth-century idiom of Palestrina, Bach acknowledged the roots of the Nicene Creed in the ancient church. The contrapuntal solidity of the music portrays "the eternal validity and irrevocable nature of the Creed and at the same time the recognizable firmness of confidence of faith," as Wolff has phrased it.[6]

Philipp Spitta believed that Bach's music has a distinctly Lutheran slant, one that stresses the origins of the Lutheran Church in Catholic rites: "There was yet no question of severance, but only of a reconstruction of the whole."[7] Whether or not Bach calculatedly employed the Saxon version of the Credo chant that was known to Lutherans through Vopelius's hymnbook, the fact remains that the melody would have been recognized by Lutherans and Catholics alike. This imbues the music with a certain "Evangelical Catholicity," as Jaroslav Pelikan has put it.[8]

Example 4–3. "Credo in unum Deum," mm. 33–37.

The "Credo in unum Deum" music marks the culmination of a long series of studies on Bach's part. The studies began with his growing interest in Renaissance vocal style in the late 1730s and early 1740s, and more particularly with his composition of the *stile antico* pedal settings of *Clavier-übung* III (the Kyrie-Christe-Kyrie complex and the six-part *Aus tiefer Not schrei ich zu dir*). They continued with his arrangement, around 1740, of Caldara's Magnificat in C Major, in which he augmented the four-part chorus of the "Suscepit Israel" with two obbligato instrumental voices, much in the manner of the violin lines in the "Credo" (the instrumental lines are unlabeled in the "Suscepit" score, but they seem to be for violins).[9] Around 1742, Bach studied Palestrina's *Missa sine nomine,* which includes an imitative Credo in Renaissance style. About five years later he composed the polyphonic "Credo in unum Deum," BWV 1081, for Mass 5 of Bassani's *Acroama missale.* Though only sixteen measures long, the F-major movement displays the same type of writing as the "Credo" of the B-Minor Mass: Renaissance vocal counterpoint over a quarter-note continuo ostinato (Example 4–4).[10] The setting leads without pause to Bassani's "Patrem omnipotentem," which, like the "Patrem" of the B-Minor Mass, is in Baroque concerted style. Finally, seemingly at a later point, Bach wrote the G-mixolydian version of the "Credo" that we discussed briefly in Chapter 2. Whether he intended this music, entitled "Credo in unum Deum. Fuga a 8 Voci obligate" in the only surviving manuscript (which is in the hand of his student Johann Friedrich Agricola), to serve as a preface for another composer's "Patrem," in the manner of BWV 1081, or whether he conceived it as a dry run for his own *Symbolum* (which he may have envisioned in another key at first) is an intriguing question that cannot yet be answered. The G-mixolydian version resembles the A-mixolydian version in all but a few details.[11]

"Patrem omnipotentem"

Patrem omnipotentem, factorem coeli et terrae, visibilium et invisibilium.
(The Father Almighty, Maker of heaven and earth, and of all things visible and invisible.)

Chorus: four-part choir (S1 and S2 combined, ATB), 3 trumpets & timpani, 2 oboes, strings, continuo.

The "Patrem omnipotentem," which follows the "Credo" without pause, is derived from the music of the chorus "Gott, wie dein Name, so ist auch dein Ruhm" that opens Cantata 171, a work composed for New Year's Day and

Example 4–4. Bach, "Credo in unum Deum," BWV 1081, for Mass 5 of Bassani's *Acroama missale.*

probably first performed on January 1, 1729. The cantata movement is a jubilant, D-major, four-voice vocal fugue with two main expositions. The strings and oboes mostly double the vocal parts, in the manner of a seventeenth-century motet. The trumpets, on the other hand, are fully independent and appear toward the end of the fugal expositions, bringing each to a dynamic climax. Since the chorus is a fair copy in the original manuscript of Cantata 171, it may also be a parody, derived from a still earlier, now-lost work (in which the music was perhaps preceded by an instrumental sinfonia).[12]

The text of the "Gott, wie dein Name" chorus is taken from Psalm 48, verse 10 (verse 11 in Luther's German Bible): "According to thy name, O

God, so is thy praise unto the ends of the earth." Later in the Psalm, the theme of praise is extended to allegiance: "For this God is our God for ever and ever." It is easy to see how the two ideas, adoration and fealty, nicely parallel the thoughts expressed in the "Patrem" ("Maker of heaven and earth, and of all things visible and invisible") and its "Credo" refrain ("I believe in one God").

Bach's transformation of the "Gott, wie dein Name" music into the "Patrem" is a remarkable testimony to his parody skills. First, he reshaped the fugue subject to accommodate the Latin text (Example 4–5). In the second measure, he replaced the repeated C♯s with a more interesting leap of a third, C♯ to E; in the third measure, he added a downbeat G for the "-tem" of "omnipotentem" and created a new melodic climax with an upward octave leap. Without changing any notes, Bach was able to paint "coeli" ("heaven") with appropriate upward movement (a leap from A to D) and "terra" ("earth") with a descent to the lowest note of the theme.

Second, Bach forged a strong harmonic bond with the preceding "Credo" movement by making an unusual structural change in the "Gott, wie dein Name" music (unusual because he rarely tampered with the overall design of fugues): to the beginning of the first exposition he added a new thematic entry, in the bass voice (mm. 1–6 of the "Patrem"). The entry is not in the tonic, as it ought to be at the commencement of a fugue, but rather in the dominant, A major. As a result, the "Patrem" begins in the "wrong" key. It is the "right" key, however, in terms of the "Credo in unum Deum," which concludes on an A-major chord. In addition, Bach prolonged the "bridge" effect of the new measures by rewriting the continuo line of the first tonic entry, using a B-minor chord at the beginning (m. 7 of the "Patrem") rather than a root-position tonic triad (as in the cantata) to delay the full arrival of D major until the end of the theme (m. 12 of the "Patrem").

Example 4–5. "Patrem omnipotentem": derivation of fugue theme.

Third, over the new entry of the fugue theme Bach added, in the oboes
and upper strings, off-beat quarter-note chords which continue to sound
until m. 21, where the instruments revert to the doubling role that they
played in the cantata. (After m. 8 the chords become overlapping arpeggios,
and one cannot help but notice the textural similarity to the flute and string
chords that Bach added to the "Crucifixus" when reworking the music from
the cantata chorus "Weinen, Klagen, Sorgen, Zagen.") The new instrumental parts are matched by new declamatory chords in the chorus: the soprano, alto, and tenor sound the refrain "Credo in unum Deum" with each
entry of the fugue subject until one by one each part picks up the subject
itself. A schematic comparison of the initial measures of "Gott, wie dein
Name" and "Patrem omnipotentem" shows how thoroughly, and brilliantly,
Bach reshaped and fleshed out the opening exposition, which now has five
thematic entries and consequently sounds like a five-voice fugue even
though the vocal texture remains four-part:

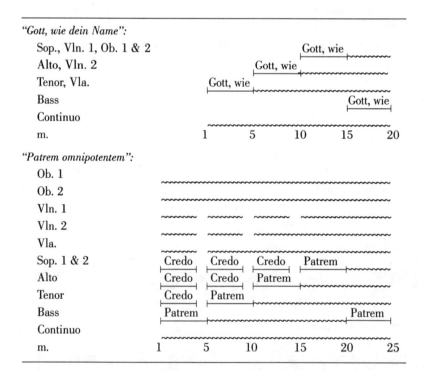

As the diagram shows, "Gott, wie dein Name" is a straightforward fugue.
"Patrem omnipotentem" appears to be something else: Bach has covered the

counterpoint with such a thick blanket of chordal material that the music no longer resembles a fugue; rather, it takes on the appearance of an imitative ritornello. In this way, Bach disguises the fact that he has strung together two fugues for the "Credo" and "Patrem," one *antico* and one *moderno*.

The "Credo" proclamations, repeated in the second fugal exposition (mm. 39–52), also serve to unite the "Patrem" with the "Credo." In using a "Credo" refrain, Bach was paying homage to the so-called "Credo Mass," in which the words "Credo, Credo" or "Credo in unum Deum" are reiterated among the various articles of the Creed. Credo Masses were common fare in Dresden in Bach's time[13]—Caldara's *Missa dicta reformata*[14] (Example 4–6), performed by Zelenka, illustrates the style—and they became even more popular in Italy, Austria, and Southern Germany as the century progressed. Mozart's *Missa brevis* in F Major, K. 192, of 1774, and *Missa* in C Major, K. 257, of 1776, and Beethoven's *Missa solemnis*, completed in 1823, attest to the strength of the tradition.[15] Still, the *P 180* autograph of the B-Minor Mass shows that the Credo refrain of the "Patrem" was a fortuitous second thought.[16] Bach initially included no chords whatsoever in the chorus parts (in mm. 1–12 the rests in the soprano, alto, and tenor are still visible). He then added the chords to the upper voices in mm. 1–3 but used the words "Patrem omnipotentem." Finally, perhaps realizing that the phrase "Credo in unum Deum" would fit the notes just as well, he altered the "Patrem" in mm. 1–3 and filled in the notes and definitive text in mm. 4–12. By the time he reached the second exposition, he incorporated the "Credo" phrase without hesitation. (Thirty-five years later, C. P. E. Bach was so impressed with the effect that he adulterated his father's score to produce a third appearance of the refrain in mm. 65–71 in the bass voice; see Plate 6–1 in Chapter 6.) These and other changes[17] create the effect of a new composition.

Together with the "Credo," the "Patrem" forms a *stile antico-stile moderno* pair that is balanced at the end of the *Symbolum* by the "Confiteor" and "Et expecto." If the "Credo" represents the immutability of Christian belief, the "Patrem" symbolizes the realization of that belief in the world of humankind. The close connection between the church and the secular domain is reflected in the meters of the two pieces: ₵ for the "Credo" and ₵ for the "Patrem" (the *Bach-Gesamtausgabe* incorrectly gives ₵ for both movements). Technically, each meter denotes *allabreve* time. But in Bach's day, the ₵ signature was more commonly associated with church music and the ₵ signature with chamber music (see the discussion in Chapter 7). By pointedly using the two different meter signatures, Bach was able to underscore the dual nature of Christian faith.

Example 4–6. Caldara: "Patrem omnipotentem" from *Missa dicta reformata*.

Example 4–6 *(continued).*

"*Et in unum Dominum*"

Et in unum Dominum, Jesum Christum, Filium Dei unigenitum. Et ex
Patre natum ante omnia secula. Deum de Deo, lumen de lumine, Deum
verum de Deo vero. Genitum, non factum, consubstantialem Patri, per
quem omnia facta sunt. Qui propter nos homines, et propter nostram
salutem descendit de coelis. (And in one Lord Jesus Christ, the only-
begotten Son of God. And born of the Father before all ages. God of
God, Light of Light, True God of True God. Begotten, not made, being
of one substance with the Father, by whom all things were made. Who
for us men, and for our salvation, came down from heaven.)

Duet: soprano 1 and alto, 2 oboes (d'amore), strings, continuo.

In Luther's Trinitarian interpretation of the Creed, the "Et in unum
Dominum" marks the beginning of the Second Article, "Of Redemption,"
which concerns the incarnation, sacrifice, and grace of Christ. It may be
that by returning to the intimate aria style associated with the Son in the
Missa, Bach signified the shift of focus from God (the topic of the First
Article) to Christ. Here, as in the "Christe eleison" and "Domine Deus," he

utilizes the idiom of the love duet. There can be no doubt that the "Et in unum Dominum" music is amorous in nature, for at one time Bach considered using it for the love duet "Ich bin deine, du bist meine" ("I am yours, you are mine") of the "Hercules" Cantata, BWV 213—a parody issue to which we will return in a moment.

Another sign of the movement's secular ties is its Neapolitan scoring—strings with oboe doubling in the ritornello sections. The combination was used ubiquitously in Italy and adopted abroad by opera-oriented musicians such as Hasse in Dresden and Handel in London. It was an ideal scoring for composers in a hurry: the oboes add a pleasing element of timbral contrast, yet they do not require separate lines in the score but can be indicated in the violin parts with a few words such as "tutti," "violini soli," etc. Bach followed this notational convention in the "Et in unum Dominum" (though this fact is obscured in modern editions by editors who give the oboes separate staves).[18] Bach employed this progressive type of aria instrumentation rather sparingly in his works, and then chiefly in late pieces (we find it in the bass aria "Rühmet Gottes Güt und Treu" from Cantata 195, performed twice in the 1740s, for instance).[19] His contrapuntal inclinations led him more naturally to independent oboe parts. He may have used the doubling oboes in the "Et in unum Dominum" to demonstrate, in his encyclopedic Mass, yet another approach to aria scoring.

Musically, the oboes add an element of unity to the ritornello segments. A similar effect is created by the imitative mimicry of the opening theme (Example 4–7), which Spitta and many commentators since have viewed as a symbol for the relationship of God and Christ. The unison imitation (m. 1) followed by imitation at the fourth (m. 2) is seen as representing the oneness

Example 4–7. "Et in unum Dominum," mm. 1–2.

as well as the separate existence of the Father and Son. This symbolism is underlined by the mixed articulation of the initial motive: the detached falling second of the first voice is followed by a slurred falling second in the second voice. While this varied articulation may represent no more than a simulated echo, common in love duets, it does seem to suggest a certain "distinction of Persons within the Unity," as Spitta put it.[20] The constant reversal of roles (in the instruments as well as the voices) and the abundance of consonant thirds and sixths in the voices add to the sensation. The *andante* walking bass of the continuo lends cohesion to the whole.

Structurally, the "Et in unum Dominum" is a modified da capo design. The A section, framed by ritornello segments, begins in the tonic and concludes in the dominant. The B section, which begins at m. 34 with the second line of the text ("Et ex Patre"), touches on the mediant, B minor, and the submediant, E minor. The A section, greatly modified, returns with the reappearance of the tonic at m. 63 and encompasses the last line of the text ("Qui propter"). The ritornello is one of the most classically proportioned in the B-Minor Mass: in its first appearance, in mm. 1–8, it is a perfectly balanced periodic phrase, with a four-bar antecedent answered by a four-bar consequent. As if to compensate for this symmetry, Bach never repeats the ritornello in the same form. After the opening, it appears in constantly varied guises, though its return is always marked by the sounding of the head motive and the reentry of the oboes. This type of "developing variation," so favored by Brahms in a later era, furthers the effect of diversity within unity.

When Bach revised the "Et in unum Dominum" in conjunction with adding the "Et incarnatus" movement to the Credo (the "Et incarnatus" text originally appeared within the "Et in unum Dominum" music; see Chapter 2), he retained the instrumental material without change but revised the vocal parts, removing the "Et incarnatus" phrase of the Latin text and redistributing the remaining lines more sparsely among the vocal segments as follows:

SECTION	INITIAL VERSION	REVISED VERSION
A (mm. 1–34)	"Et in unum Dominum . . ."	"Et in unum Dominum . . ."
B (mm. 34–62)	"Deum de Deo . . ."	"Et ex Patre . . . "
	"Qui propter . . ."	"Deum de Deo . . . "
A' (mm. 63–80)	"Et incarnatus . . ."	"Qui propter . . . "

Most of the musical alterations in the vocal parts concern matters of declamation: Bach reshaped motives here and there to accommodate the new text. When editing the *Neue Bach-Ausgabe,* Friedrich Smend argued passionately on behalf of Bach's initial concept and printed it in the main text of his edition, even though the "Et incarnatus" phrase then appeared twice in the *Symbolum,* once in the "Et in unum Dominum," and once in the "Et incarnatus" proper.[21] Smend viewed the text of the first version as falling into two halves: the first dealt with Christ's heavenly glory, a concept Bach portrayed, Smend believed, by having the soprano, as heavenly representative, enter before the alto. The second half focused on Christ's earthly accomplishments, which Bach painted by having the alto enter before the soprano (no mention is made of the fact that the soprano again leads in m. 74). To Smend, Bach's retexting destroyed this balanced division.

While one can reject the heaven-earth analysis as overly subjective, other points Smend made in favor of the first version are less easily dismissed. In the first version, the sudden appearance of sharply descending motives in the strings and the voices in mm. 59–62 accompanies the phrase "descendit de coelis" ("came down from heaven"); in the revised version, the falling figures are lost on the words "per quem omnia facta sunt" ("by whom all things were made"; Example 4–8). In the first version, the unusual modulation through E♭ major, C minor, and G minor in mm. 69–76, one of the few times in the entire B-Minor Mass that Bach enters the flat-key terrain (the "Et expecto" bridge and the "Agnus Dei" being the others), is accompanied by the allusion to the incarnation ("Et incarnatus . . ."), the most miraculous mystery of Christianity. (The use of "dark" flat-key coloring for the phrase "Et incarnatus" can be seen in other works of the time such as Zelenka's Credo in D Major, Z. 201, mentioned above, in which the "Et incarnatus" is set in G minor, framed by movements in D major.) But in the revised version, the concept of the incarnation is only implied during the flat-key excursion ("Who for us men, and for our salvation, came down from heaven"). That Bach jettisoned such marvelous imagery is difficult to accept. It is sobering evidence of his willingness to sacrifice local, pictorial details for the larger, structural effect of having of an independent "Et incarnatus" chorus.[22]

But one wonders whether referential details were not already sacrificed in the first version. There is little doubt that the "Et in unum Dominum" is a parody. The clean look of the text in the *P 180* manuscript and the abundance of performance indications point in that direction. So, too, does the appearance of the first four measures of the "Et in unum Dominum" violin 1 line, written in C major, in the autograph score of Cantata 213. Bach apparently considered using the music, which must have existed in another source, for movement 13 of Cantata 213, the duet "Ich bin deine." But after

Example 4–8. "Et in unum Dominum," mm. 59–62, original (a) and revised (b).

writing out the incipit, he crossed it out and abandoned the idea in favor of a new composition.[23] Efforts by Klaus Häfner to pinpoint the model of "Et in unum Dominum" are not convincing,[24] and it is likely that we will never know the precise context in which the music was first conceived. Nevertheless, one suspects that the unusual descending portamento figures in mm. 21–22 and m. 66 once highlighted an appropriate phrase in a now-lost text, just as the falling figures in mm. 58–59 once highlighted "descen-dit de coelis." Sometimes glimpses of Bach's creative process can be as unsettling as they are insightful.

"Et incarnatus"

Et incarnatus est de Spiritu Sancto ex Maria virgine, et homo factus est.
(And was incarnate by the Holy Ghost of the Virgin Mary, and was
made man.)
Chorus: five-part choir (SSATB), violins in unison, continuo.

The "Et incarnatus" is the shortest, yet one of the most expressive, chorus movements of the B-Minor Mass. Bach uses three distinct elements to
create an atmosphere of anticipation—anticipation of the crucifixion that
was made possible through Christ's incarnation. The first is the pulsating
continuo bass, which begins as an extended pedal point in the tonic before
moving sequentially to the dominant (m. 20), where the pedal point and
sequences are repeated. We find similar bass-line gestures in the opening
choruses of the St. John and St. Matthew Passions, which also deal with the
drama preceding Christ's death. While the scale of the "Et incarnatus" is
much smaller, the unmistakable motivic links with the continuo lines of the
"Qui tollis" (in which expiation is sought) and the "Crucifixus" (in which
expiation is gained) broaden the allegorical time frame considerably.

The second expressive element in the "Et incarnatus" is the jagged,
syncopated instrumental line played by the violins. This, too, has its roots
in Passion music: similarly "thorny" unison string figures appear in a variety of arias touching on Christ's suffering: "Können Tränen meiner Wangen"
("Can the tears of my cheeks") from the St. Matthew Passion or "Die Armut,
so Gott auf sich nimmt" ("The weakness which God assumed") from
Cantata 91, for instance. Wolff has proposed another possible model for the
"Et incarnatus" violin line: the unison violin ostinato of the "Quis est
homo" from Pergolesi's *Stabat mater* (Example 4–9).[25] Bach arranged the
Stabat mater as a German motet, *Tilge, Höchster, meine Sünden,* BWV
1083, for performance in the Leipzig worship service around 1746–1747—
that is, just a year or two before he wrote the "Et incarnatus."

Walter Blankenburg and Helmut Rilling have seen the "Et incarnatus"
violin figure as a cross motive (Example 4–10a).[26] Bach unquestionably
associated jagged melodic ideas with Christ's crucifixion, but whether or
not he was thinking specifically in terms of a visual *chiasmus,* or cross, is
less clear. Other rhetorical symbols in the line are more firmly grounded in
Baroque custom: the slurred seconds represent the sigh motive that is associated with supplication in "Kyrie" I, the "Qui tollis," and the "Agnus Dei,"
and the downward movement of the line paints the descent of Christ to earth
to assume the form of man, much as the falling string motive portrayed the

Example 4–9. "Quis est homo" from Pergolesi's *Stabat mater.*

words "came down from heaven" in the first version of the "Et in unum Dominum." Most importantly, the violin figure outlines the falling triads of the vocal parts (Example 4–10b) and consequently serves as a type of *Vorimitation,* or "preimitation," of the voices.

The third expressive element of the "Et incarnatus" is the vocal material itself, which begins with a series of imitative entries before shifting to a homophonic texture with the move to the dominant and the words "ex Maria virgine." Bach reaches the dominant and these critical words of the Ordinary through a German augmented sixth chord (m. 12), which appears at two other mystical moments in the *Symbolum:* the modulation to G major

Example 4–10. "Et incarnatus," opening motive.

at the end of the "Crucifixus" and the final resolution of the *adagio* bridge that leads to the concluding "Et expecto." Theologically, the three passages mark momentous transformations: Christ's incarnation, Christ's resurrection, and the resurrection of the dead. Musically, Bach links these miraculous events with miraculous harmonizations.

The chorus in the "Et incarnatus" seems to "float" above the instrumental parts: one has the feeling that if the instruments were removed, the result would be a fully sufficient, highly expressive *a cappella* vocal motet. In this sense, the "Et incarnatus" resembles a number of Mozart's late church pieces—the *Ave verum corpus* or the "Lacrymosa" of the Requiem, for instance—in which the composer stressed the primacy of voices over instruments. The autograph manuscript of the "Lacrymosa" shows that Mozart wrote the vocal parts first, leaving the instruments to be filled in during a second stage of composition.[27] Bach normally composed vocal and instrumental parts more or less simultaneously, and there is no reason to suppose that that is not the case here. Still, one has the *impression* that the vocal material was conceived first, and the instruments, instead of being part of a tightly integrated contrapuntal web, provide an atmospheric backdrop. For this reason, the "Et incarnatus" resembles the music of Pergolesi and Mozart and is thus one of the most forward-looking movements of the B-Minor Mass.[28]

Why did Bach excise the "Et incarnatus" text from the "Et in unum Dominum" and set it as a separate movement? Several reasons seem obvious. In B minor, ending on a picardy third, the new "Et incarnatus" provides a more compelling harmonic transition from the G major of the "Et in unum Dominum" to the E minor of the "Crucifixus." Metrically, too, the "Et incarnatus" supplies a smoother shift, from $\frac{4}{4}$ to $\frac{3}{4}$ to $\frac{3}{2}$ time, and it establishes the quarter-note bass motion of the "Crucifixus." The descending figures and sigh motives look back to the "Et in unum Dominum"; the pulsating bass, repetitive text treatment, and marked descent of the voices at the end point forward to the "Crucifixus." Bach may also have wished to show his skill at writing a progressive choral piece, even at the expense of retexting the "Et in unum Dominum."

It is possible, too, that at the eleventh hour Bach decided to bow to contemporary convention. In Dresden Masses, the "Et incarnatus" was traditionally set as a separate movement or section, usually a slow, emotionally wrought minor-mode chorus or aria. In the *Missa Circumcisionis*,[29] Z. 11, for instance, Zelenka cast the "Et incarnatus" as a mournful *andante* trio in B minor (Example 4–11) followed by the "Crucifixus" in the same key. The B minor contrasts sharply with the bright D major of the Credo's remaining movements ("Credo in unum Deum," "Et resurrexit," and "Et vitam ven-

Example 4–11. Zelenka: "Et incarnatus" from *Missa Circumcisionis*.

turi") and serves to highlight the "Et incarnatus" and "Crucifixus" as central events in the Creed.

The generally tidy appearance of the "Et incarnatus" in the autograph manuscript of the B-Minor Mass and the abundance of performance indications (slurs and detachment dots) have led several writers to consider the movement a revision of earlier music. Speaking against parody is the five-part vocal texture: it seems to be a part of the original conception and would appear to rule out a cantata origin. Wolff, assuming the "Et incarnatus" to be a completely new composition, has speculated that the movement might be Bach's last original work.[30] The progressive style of the music lends credence to that attractive idea.

"Crucifixus"

Crucifixus etiam pro nobis sub Pontio Pilato, passus et sepultus est. (And was crucified also for us under Pontius Pilate. He suffered and was buried.)

Chorus: four-part choir (S2, ATB), 2 flutes, 2 oboes, strings, continuo.

The music of the "Crucifixus" is derived from the opening chorus of Cantata 12, *Weinen, Klagen, Sorgen, Zagen,* a work composed in Weimar for Jubilate Sunday 1714. Cantata 12 held special significance for Bach, for it was one of the first cantatas he penned after being named *Konzertmeister* at the Weimar Court. The new position, which he held simultaneously with his old post of organist, presented the opportunity to write sacred vocal music for Duke Wilhelm Ernst's professional ensemble. Bach's initial efforts—Cantatas 21, 12, 182, and 172—show him working for the first time in the progressive Italian idiom of the Neumeister cantata, with madrigal texts and full-scale aria and recitative movements.[31] Like the large organ works from the Weimar years, Bach's early Neumeister-style cantatas are adventurous and expansive and display stunning stylistic amalgamations. Cantata 12 is no exception.

The text of *Weinen, Klagen, Sorgen, Zagen* (most probably written by Weimar Court poet Salomo Franck) focuses on the Gospel for Jubilate Sunday, John 16:16–23, which describes Christ comforting the Apostles before his trial and crucifixion:

A little while, and ye shall not see me: and again, a little while, and ye shall see me, because I go to the Father. . . .

> Verily, verily I say unto you, That ye shall weep and lament, but the
> world shall rejoice; and ye shall be sorrowful, but your sorrow shall be
> turned into joy. . . .

The cantata libretto depicts a Christian's journey from despair to stead-
fast faith. The opening chorus is a lament (one of Franck's specialties) that
paints with unbridled Pietistic fervor a baleful picture of woe:

Weinen, Klagen,	Weeping, wailing,
Sorgen, Zagen,	Grieving, fearing,
Angst und Not	Dread and need
Sind der Christen Tränenbrot,	Are the Christians' tearful bread,
Die das Zeichen Jesu tragen.	Those who carry the sign of Jesus.

Bach set the text as a stylistically eclectic da capo chorus: the A section,
covering the first four lines, is an Italian ground-bass lament in the dark
key of F minor. The modulatory B section, covering the last line, contains
free imitation reminiscent of the seventeenth-century German church
motet. The "Crucifixus" music is drawn from the A-section lament.

The poetry of the "Weinen, Klagen" chorus begins with an asyndeton, a
series of phrases or words from which the conjunctions have been removed.[32]
In Bach's music, the hypnotic, accentual repetition of the asyndeton—"Wéi-
nen," "Klá-gen," "Sór-gen," "Zá-gen"—is enhanced by the steady reiteration of the ground bass. The bass outlines the traditional *lamento* pattern
much beloved by seventeenth-century Baroque composers from Monteverdi
to Purcell: the descending tetrachord, which moves gradually downward
from the tonic note to the dominant (Example 4–12a). In the "Weinen,
Klagen" music Bach fills in the descending intervals chromatically, creating
the pungent rhetorical figure of the *passus duriusculus,* or dissonant step
(Example 4–12b). The chromatic additions delay the arrival of the principal
notes until the second beat of the measure, which gives the theme a sara-
bande-like quality appropriate for a mourning ode. Over the ground Bach
weaves a set of twelve variations. As in the famous Passacaglia in C Minor,
BWV 582, from the Weimar years, the variations are arranged in pairs.

While Bach was undoubtedly attracted to the "Weinen, Klagen" music
because its *Affekt* was so appropriate for the "Crucifixus," he may also have
been aware that other composers had used ground basses for the
"Crucifixus" portion of the Ordinary. In Conti's *Missa con trombe* in C
Major,[33] for instance, a work presented in Dresden by Zelenka, the

Example 4–12. "Crucifixus": ground bass origins.

"Crucifixus" is set as a ground bass *adagio* in G minor (Example 4–13). Here, too, the bass pattern is that of the descending tetrachord.

Bach made critical alterations in the "Weinen, Klagen" score as he adapted it for the "Crucifixus." He began by transposing the music from F minor to E minor—a more appropriate key for the sharp-key context of the B-Minor Mass—and assigning the uppermost vocal part to soprano 2. He prefaced the music with a four-bar instrumental introduction, intended perhaps to serve as a prelude (in Cantata 12 the "Weinen, Klagen" chorus is preceded by a short *adagio assai* sinfonia) and to set forth the ground-bass theme more clearly. The autograph score reveals that the introduction was a second thought, squeezed into free space at the end of the "Et in unum Dominum."

Bach animated the ground by changing the half notes to slurred quarter notes (Example 4–12c, above). At the same time, he revised the instrumental scoring, reducing the string parts from five to four and adding a pair of flutes. In the "Weinen, Klagen" chorus, the strings play chords that fall on beats one and three, the traditional strong accents of $\frac{3}{2}$ meter. In the "Crucifixus," the rewritten strings perform the same role. The flutes, however, play chords that fall on beats two and three (Example 4–14), which establishes a second set of accents that reinforce the sarabande nature of the *lamento* bass. This not only produces a more interesting and complex rhythmic pattern but also gives the "Crucifixus" an additional layer of mourning symbolism. Both the strings and the flutes play on the downbeat of the bass theme each time it recurs, to mark the reiteration of the pattern.

To accommodate the Latin text, Bach refashioned the vocal parts, improving the voice-leading and intensifying the chromaticism. To cite two examples: in the cantata, the opening asyndeton is set as a series of imitative entries in which each line ends with a prolonged suspension that

Example 4–13. Conti: "Crucifixus" from *Missa con trombe* in C Major.

resolves downward. In the "Crucifixus," the four words of the asyndeton are replaced with just one word, "Crucifixus," and the musical lines are reshaped into anticipations and downbeat appoggiaturas. The appoggiaturas take on the guise of the sigh motive seen elsewhere in the B-Minor Mass: the slurred, falling second (Example 4–15a). Or in m. 13, Bach substituted an expressive augmented second in the soprano 2 and alto for the blander major second of the Weimar score (Example 4–15b). The *P 180* manuscript shows that this, too, was a second thought.

Finally, Bach added a new and extraordinary concluding variation at m. 49. The instruments drop out and the voices, now singing *piano,* descend to their lowest register for the words "sepultus est, sepultus est" ("and was buried, and was buried"). The harmony veers off course, away from E minor, and a magical augmented sixth chord leads to a cadence in G major, in anticipation of the "Et resurrexit" that follows directly. Ground basses should not modulate, of course, and one suspects that Bach broke with convention to emphasize the unconventionality of Christ's resurrection, an

Example 4–14. "Crucifixus": accompanimental rhythmic patterns.

event that released humankind from the seemingly inexorable pattern of weeping and death. The close is a remarkable addition to the original music; Smend saw it as the "slumbering seed of the cantata movement awakened."[34] Indeed, Bach may have chosen the early score because of its potential for revision and expansion.

If the "Credo" and "Confiteor" of the *Symbolum* serve as homages to the music traditions of the sixteenth century, the "Crucifixus" is a tribute to the music traditions of the seventeenth century. After Bach's death, the "Crucifixus" found greater favor with nineteenth-century musicians than any other movement of the B-Minor Mass (See Chapter 6). While the Romantics may have been inordinately attracted to the passionate tone of the "Crucifixus," who today can argue with Schumann's observation, made

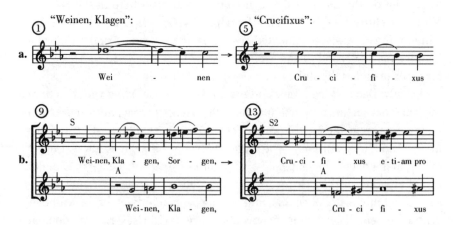

Example 4–15. "Crucifixus" motives.

after hearing the movement performed by Mendelssohn in 1841 in the Leipzig Gewandhaus:

> Perhaps the "Crucifixus" made the greatest impression. It is a piece that is to be compared only with other works by Bach. Before it all masters of other ages must bow in reverence.[35]

"Et resurrexit"

Et resurrexit tertia die, secundum scripturas. Et ascendit in coelum: sedet ad dexteram Dei Patris. Et iterum venturus est cum gloria judicare vivos et mortuos: cujus regni non erit finis. (And on the third day He rose again according to the Scriptures. And He ascended into heaven, and sitteth at the right hand of God the Father. And He shall come again with glory to judge both the living and the dead. Of his kingdom there shall be no end.)

Chorus: five-part choir (SSATB), 3 trumpets & timpani, 2 flutes, 2 oboes, strings, continuo.

The "Et resurrexit" erupts from the hushed close of the "Crucifixus" with a burst of D-major, diatonic, trumpets-and-drums jubilation. It is difficult to imagine a piece of music that would more forcefully, and irrevocably, dispel the chromatic gloom of the E-minor lament.

Bach created this stunning metamorphosis by drawing on the most persuasive resources of late-Baroque instrumental style. The balanced phrases, the triple meter, the emphatic downbeats, and the delicate detachments of the "Et resurrexit" evoke the spirit of a celebratory dance. But it is a celebratory dance with a courtly countenance: the $\frac{3}{4}$ meter suggests a more regal pace and weighty articulation than the music of the "Gloria" or "Osanna," both in $\frac{3}{8}$ time, and the single triplet in the ritornello theme and the *bassetto* interludes—that is, the passages in which the viola, rather than the continuo, serves as bass (mm. 40–47 and 111–119)—impart a special air of elegant grace. Häfner has pointed to the resemblance between the "Et resurrexit" and the *Réjouissance* of Orchestral Suite No. 4 in D Major, BWV 1069, a dance with a similar phrase structure, $\frac{3}{4}$ meter (also with an upbeat of three eighth notes), and *bassetto* interludes.[36] As a dance type, the *réjouissance* was classified among the *Galanterien,* the lighter, homophonic, courtly dances that represented the latest in *galant* style. In BWV 1069, Bach used the *réjouissance* to bring the suite to an exuberant conclusion. In the B-Minor Mass, he employed the *réjouissance*-like music of the "Et resurrexit" in a similar way, to round out the Second Article of the Creed.

The mood of elation is also produced by a number of rising or elevated figures. The phrases "Et resurrexit" ("and He rose again") and "Et ascendit in coelum" ("And He ascended into heaven") are set to the upward-arching theme of the ritornello; elsewhere the word "ascendit" is set to an upward-leaping octave (Example 4–16). These climbing, *anabasis* figures, which represent the very antithesis of the falling, *catabasis* figures of the "Et incarnatus" and "Crucifixus," are reinforced by broader gestures: the compelling upward movement of the supporting parts in the ritornello incipit, the chromatic rise of the bass progression that leads to the principal cadences (mm. 28–34; 60–66; 105–111; 125–131), and the very "highness" of the *bassetto* interludes (which contrasts with the dark, soprano 2 scoring of the "Crucifixus"). Even the dynamics escalate upward: crescendos are created by additive orchestration and by imitative vocal passages in which the voices enter bottom to top.

Bach's contemporary, the theorist Johann Mattheson, comparing vocal and instrumental styles, explained that instrumental melodies have more "fire and freedom" than vocal melodies. Unlike vocal melodies, which must be fashioned "with the nature of breathing in mind," instrumental melodies can include "many-beamed notes, arpeggios, and all sorts of broken figuration."[37] It is by assigning free, fiery instrumental figures to the voices, occasionally without regard for the convenience of breathing, that Bach produces the breathless ebullience of the "Et resurrexit." One suspects that the Enlightenment philosopher and occasional composer Jean-Jacques Rousseau would have cringed at the unnatural vocal demands of the extended melisma on the words "et resurrexit" or the coloratura writing in the "Et iterum ventu-

Example 4–16. "Et resurrexit": ascending melodic figures.

rus" section. But the switch from the primarily vocal idiom of the "Et incarnatus" and "Crucifixus" to the unabashed instrumental style in the "Et resurrexit" helps to produce the miraculous effect of euphoric awakening.

The instrumental nature of the "Et resurrexit" is evident, too, in the abundance of material for instruments alone: over one third of the measures (55 of 131) are devoted to voiceless instrumental ritornello segments. In addition, the "Et resurrexit" is the first movement of the Credo to use the full instrumental ensemble, including flutes.[38] Structurally, the "Et resurrexit" is a modified da capo form, with an initial A section that begins in the tonic and ends with a ritornello in the dominant (much in the fashion of the "Laudamus te"), a B section that touches on the submediant (B minor) and mediant (E minor), and a concluding A' that reestablishes the tonic. While a number of commentators have assailed Bach for squeezing the through-composed "Et resurrexit" text into a rounded A B A' form, the plan works quite well, given the overall division of the movement into four vocal sections—that is, one for each phrase of the text—separated by ritornello segments:

A	mm. 1–9	Ritornello segment (with vocal proclamation; D major)
	mm. 9–34	"Et resurrexit"
	mm. 34–50	Ritornello (A major)
B	mm. 50–66	"Et ascendit"
	mm. 66–74	Ritornello segment (B minor)
	mm. 74–86	"Et iterum venturus"
A'	mm. 86–92	Ritornello segment (with vocal proclamation; D major)
	mm. 92–111	"Cujus regni"
	mm. 111–131	Ritornello segment (D major)

Bach puts the dark, minor-mode shadings of the middle B section to good use to underline the vindictive third line of the text, "And He shall come again with glory to judge both the living and the dead." The passage, sometimes called the "Vox Christi" because it is sung by the iconographical representative of Christ, the bass voice, is probably intended as a solo even though there is no indication to that effect in the original score (the instruments are marked *piano* in the autograph manuscript, which suggests a solo, but the indications are not original: they were added by C. P. E. Bach for his 1786 Hamburg performance). Bach commonly omitted solo markings in his composition scores, inserting them into the performance parts at a later point. Hence the absence of a solo indication in the original score does not rule out a vocal solo in the "Et iterum venturus." Both the light instrumental accompaniment and the coloratura nature of the vocal line point to a bass solo.[39]

Because the vocal parts of the "Et resurrexit" show much more revision than the instrumental parts in the original manuscript, writers have long speculated that the movement is a parody of an earlier piece. Smend, pointing to the music's instrumental character, proposed that the music was drawn from a now-lost instrumental concerto.[40] The unambiguous da capo form of the movement, however, points more strongly to vocal music and a cantata model. Häfner has suggested that the "Et resurrexit" stems from the chorus "Entfernet euch, ihr heitern Sterne!" from the cantata of the same name, BWV Anh. 9.[41] Written for the birthday of Elector Friedrich August I and performed outdoors in front of the Leipzig Town Hall on May 12, 1727, the work survives in the form of a printed text only. Häfner's main arguments are convincing: that the elegant triplet figure of the "Et resurrexit" music (a type of *circulatio* or circle figure) reflects the imagery of the word "Stern," "star"; that the rising melodic figures of the music reflect the rise of August described metaphorically in the cantata text ("Disperse, you fair stars! The reigning sun is rising before us"); that certain lines of the cantata text fit the "Et resurrexit" vocal lines extremely well. But since the original score of the "Et resurrexit" shows that the vocal parts have been reworked, we may not be looking at the vocal material in its original form. That would seem to invalidate many of Häfner's comparisons. Still, the "Et resurrexit" appears to be a parody of some sort. The music probably began with a full ritornello that Bach abridged and overlaid with voices to create a more immediate link with the "Crucifixus."[42]

"Et in Spiritum Sanctum"

Et in Spiritum Sanctum, Dominum et vivificantem, qui ex Patre Filioque
procedit, qui cum Patre et Filio simul adoratur et conglorificatur, qui
locutus est per Prophetas. Et unam sanctam catholicam et apostolicam
Ecclesiam. (And I believe in the Holy Ghost, the Lord and giver of
life, who proceedeth from the Father and the Son. Who together with
the Father and Son is worshipped and glorified. Who spake by the
Prophets. And I believe in one holy catholic and apostolic church.)

Aria: bass, 2 oboes d'amore, continuo.

In the "Et in Spiritum," Bach returns to the intimate aria style of the "Laudamus te" and "Qui sedes." Here he portrays the Holy Ghost with music that has many characteristics of a pastoral: $\frac{6}{8}$ meter, symmetrical phrases, gently rocking triplets, consonant parallel thirds and sixths, and dulcet woodwind tones. Even the key, A major, which serves as a compelling bridge between the D major of the "Et resurrexit" and the F-sharp minor of the "Confiteor," is one of the widely used tonalities for pastoral music (the others being C major, F major, and G major). While the vocal lines of the "Laudamus te" and "Qui sedes" display bravura runs and leaps, the bass part of the "Et in Spiritum" is gently lilting. The initial entrance, derived from the instrumental ritornello, is almost fully conjunct, with a beguiling repetition of m. 2 in m. 3 and a touch of increased note-motion in the penultimate measure, to paint the word "vivificantem" ("giver of life"; Example 4–17).

The instrumental ritornello, too, is seemingly unassuming, showing the tripartite design of the classical Vivaldian mold: opening segment ending on the dominant (r1; mm. 1–5), sequential segment (r2; mm. 5–9), and closing segment (r3; mm. 10–13). Bach creates a pleasing sequence of events in the three segments. In the first (r1), the oboes sound in alluring parallel thirds. In the second (r2), the oboes move in gentle imitation, reminiscent of the texture of the opening movement of Bach's organ Pastorella, BWV 590. And in the third segment (r3), the imitation of the second is resolved as the oboes join together in a unison line with light embellishments for the cadence. The result is a logical progression moving toward euphonious agreement: consonant dialogue (r1) ⟶ debate (r2) ⟶ unanimity (r3).

The pastoral-dance character of the "Et in Spiritum" ritornello is muted in many modern scores by articulation marks that reflect C. P. E. Bach's "legato-ization" of his father's text. For his 1786 Hamburg performance of the *Symbolum* (see Chapter 6), Emanuel edited the "Et in Spiritum" in the autograph manuscript, obliterating the subtle detachment marks in m. 11 of the ritornello theme, lengthening many slurs, and adding still others. *P 23*, a copy of the *P 180* autograph produced between 1750 and 1768—that is, before Emanuel altered the text—shows slurs in mm. 1–4 and 10–12 that encompass two eighth notes rather than three and detachment markings in m. 11 (Example 4–18). This appears to be the original notation of the theme. The two-note slurs produce a more lilting articulation than the three-note slurs shown in both the *Bach-Gesamtausgabe* and the *Neue Bach-Ausgabe*.

Et   in   Spi-ri-tum Sanc - tum Do - mi-num et vi - vi - fi-can   -   -   tem,

Example 4–17. "Et in Spiritum Sanctum": principal vocal theme.

Example 4–18. "Et in Spiritum Sanctum": articulation of the ritornello theme in
the manuscript *P 23*.

In terms of design, the "Et in Spiritum" is a modified da capo form, A
B A', with the bass solo taking segments of the ritornello in the A and A'
sections:

	mm. 1–13	Instrumental ritornello (r1, r2, r3), I⟶V
	mm. 13–18	Vocal ritornello (r1)
A	mm. 18–25	Instrumental ritornello (r2, r3), V⟶I
	mm. 25–49	Vocal material, beginning with r1 segment and ending with r3 segment
	mm. 49–61	Instrumental ritornello (r1, r2', r3), V—V
	mm. 61–75	Vocal material
B	mm. 75–79	Instrumental ritornello (r1), vi⟶V/vi
	mm. 79–93	Vocal material
	mm. 93–96	Vocal ritornello (r1)
	mm. 97–105	Instrumental ritornello (r2, r3), V⟶I
A'	mm. 105–132	Vocal material, beginning with r1 segment and ending with r3 segment
	mm. 132–144	Instrumental ritornello (r1, r2, r3), I—I

Why did Bach turn to pastoral-like music for the Holy Ghost? One
explanation can be found in Luther's gloss of the "Et in Spiritum Sanctum"
in the Small Catechism, in which he portrays the Holy Ghost as a shepherd
who gathers and guides Christians into Christ's fold:

> What does this mean? [The Third Article of the Creed, beginning with
> the "Et in Spiritum"]
>
> I believe that neither from my own reason or strength can I believe in
> Jesus Christ or come to him,

Rather the Holy Ghost has called me through the Gospel, illuminating it
with his gifts, and has sanctified and preserved me,

Just as he has called, gathered, enlightened, and sanctified Christendom
throughout the earth, and held it to Jesus Christ in the true and united
faith.[43]

This commentary, which Bach would have known well, puts the Holy
Ghost on a similar footing with Christ, insofar as music is concerned: as a
mediator for humankind, the Holy Ghost would also seem to call for an intimate aria rather than a large, formal chorus. In the "Et in Spiritum," Bach
may have intended the pastoral idiom and the convergence of melodic lines
to convey the shepherding qualities that Luther attributed to the Holy Ghost.

At the same time, however, Bach seems to have been more concerned
with covering the lengthy text than with giving each point a particularly indi-
vidualized musical interpretation. The lack of detailed imagery, the dispari-
ty between music and text image in the B section (where the words "Who
together with the Father and Son is worshipped and glorified" are set in F-
sharp minor), and the relatively tidy appearance of the aria in the *P 180*
manuscript all suggest that Bach appropriated the music from an earlier
source. Parody or not, it is a marvelous aria. Donald Francis Tovey may have
put it best: "Who could have thought that the jangle of such Latin as *unam
Catholicam et Apostolicam Ecclesiam* could have produced such music?"[44]

"Confiteor"

Confiteor unum baptisma in remissionem peccatorum. (I acknowledge one
Baptism for the remission of sins.)

Chorus: five-part choir (SSATB), continuo; *colla parte* instrumental doubling? (see Chapter 7).

The Credo concludes as it began, with a pair of choruses in contrasting
stile antico-stile moderno styles. The "Confiteor" and "Et expecto" match the
"Credo" and "Patrem omnipotentem," and Bach's desire to mirror the opening movements is nowhere more apparent than in the "Confiteor," whose
allabreve meter, white-note notation, dense vocal polyphony, and plainsong
cantus firmus directly reflect the idiom of the "Credo." Similar, too, is the
presence of a quarter-note walking bass. As in the "Credo," Bach uses the
formal, majestic *stile antico* as a backdrop for ecclesiastical oath: Palestrina's
vocal idiom, the bulwark of church polyphony, complements the confession of
baptism for the forgiveness of sins, the bulwark of church doctrine.

In terms of procedure, however, the "Confiteor" is a very different piece from the "Credo." Bach divides the text of the "Confiteor" into two phrases, assigns each to a musical theme, and uses the themes as the basis for a complex double fugue. Both subjects are derived from the "Confiteor" portion of the "Credo" chant as it appears in the Vopelius Hymnbook of 1682 (which, as we mentioned with regard to the "Credo," seems to have been Bach's source for the Gregorian melody; Example 4–19a). The first theme (Example 4–19b) forms a gradually rising arch that reflects the general shape of the first two-thirds of the chant (both lines ascend to the 4th degree of the scale). The *P 180* manuscript shows that Bach first considered a slightly different reading of theme 1, with E instead of D for the third note (Example 4–19c), a shape that mimicked more precisely the initial ascending third of the chant. In its revised form the theme mirrors the "Confiteor" chant less faithfully. On the other hand, it harmonizes more satisfactorily with the continuo, forms a repeated-note link with the second theme, and works more successfully in later contrapuntal combinations. The second theme (Example 4–19d) forms a complementary falling arch, one that mirrors the "in remissionem peccatorum" portion of the chant.

Bach shows great sensitivity to Latin declamation in both themes, setting the longest syllables—the "-fi-" of "confíteor," the "-o-" of "in remissiónem," and the "-to-" of "peccatórum"—with the longest notes. This contrasts greatly with the more makeshift text underlay of the "Dona nobis pacem" (see Chapter 5) and may reflect the difference between an original

Example 4–19. "Confiteor" themes.

composition (the "Confiteor") and a parody (the "Dona nobis"). As Wolff has shown, the arched shapes, text-oriented rhythms, and suspensions of the "Confiteor" are hallmarks of *stile antico* vocal lines.[45] On the other hand, the repeated notes and accented, triadic, quarter-note leaps are instrumental in nature and represent Baroque modifications of Renaissance style.

The dense imitative web of the "Confiteor" unfolds in five expositions:

Exposition 1 (mm. 1–16) is devoted to theme 1, which is presented in a single point of imitation. The five voices enter with the theme one by one, in descending order, from soprano 1 to bass. The soprano 1 and 2 entries form an overlapping tonic-dominant pair, as do the alto and tenor entries. The bass concludes the point of imitation with a tonic entry. Two deceptive cadences in the continuo (mm. 5 and 8) propel the music forward and help to sustain the linear motion of the vocal counterpoint. Exposition 1 concludes with a half cadence, somewhat in the manner of the first segment of a ritornello.

Exposition 2 (mm. 16–32) is devoted to theme 2, which is also presented in a single point of imitation. The five voices enter with the theme one by one, mostly in ascending order, tenor to soprano 1, then bass. The harmonic structure of exposition 2 is quite different from that of exposition 1: rather than appearing in tonic-dominant pairs, the thematic entrances occur in a circle-of-fifths sequence, f♯, B, E, A, D, which gives the exposition a certain episodic character. Exposition 2 concludes with a cadence in B minor.

Exposition 3 (mm. 31–73), which begins one measure before the end of exposition 2, is devoted to contrapuntal combinations of themes 1 and 2: theme 1 is combined simultaneously with theme 2 (mm. 31, 34, and 37); theme 1 appears in stretto with itself (mm. 40–45 and 54–60); theme 2 appears in stretto with itself (mm. 62–73); and the two themes appear in various overlapping forms (mm. 45–50 and 57–60). The imitation is extremely intense: there are thirty-one thematic (or pseudo-thematic) entries in forty-two measures. These proceedings come to an end on a four-measure dominant pedal (mm. 69–72), which resolves (deceptively) into exposition 4. As Tovey noted, the double counterpoint of exposition 3 has theological implications: baptism is the means to the remission of sins. In the "Confiteor," Bach assigns each element its own theme and then shows that the two are fully realized only in combination.[46] (This metaphor can be extended to the linear nature of the themes as well, since the upward arch initiated by theme 1 is resolved only by the downward arch of theme 2.)

In exposition 4 (mm. 73–92) Bach introduces the "Confiteor" chant as a *cantus firmus,* in a canon at the fifth between the bass and the alto. He surrounds the four phrases of the *cantus* with entries of themes 1 and 2, which often appear in permutated forms that accommodate the harmony of the moment. Exposition 4 ends with a stretto of theme 2 in the soprano and bass, sounding over the last phrase of the "Confiteor" chant in the alto (mm. 88–92). A full cadence in the tonic (F♯ minor) ushers in the final exposition.

In exposition 5 (mm. 92–123) Bach presents the "Confiteor" chant in full once again, but now in augmentation in the tenor, the traditional *cantus firmus* voice in Renaissance music. As in exposition 4, the plainchant melody is wrapped in a thick blanket of thematic entries. The "Confiteor" chant comes to an end in m. 117 on the note D, and the harmony turns toward D major, the key of the "Et expecto." After a short sequence, the music slows to *adagio* and concludes on a D-major chord on the downbeat of m. 123.

Wolff has noted a similarity between expositions 1 through 3 of the "Confiteor" and the "Et misericordia" from the Magnificat in C Major, BWV Anh. II 30, an anonymous work that Bach copied out and performed in Leipzig around 1742.[47] Written in Renaissance vocal style, the "Et misericordia" also has two themes, developed separately and then together, in three expositions. Although Bach had composed *allabreve* fugues of this nature long before the 1740s (the Weimar Organ Fugue in F major, BWV 540/2, for instance), the Latin-texted "Et misericordia" may well have influenced his approach in the similarly styled "Confiteor." Expositions 4 and 5 go beyond any model, however. Exposition 5 in particular is not only a contrapuntal *tour de force* but the *raison d'être* of the movement, since the "Confiteor" chant now appears at the correct pitch (beginning on C♯), in the correct note values (whole notes), and in the correct voice (tenor) to match the "Credo" chant as it appears in the opening measures (mm. 1–4) of the "Credo" movement. In the fifth exposition Bach completes the Credo plainsong, forming a melodic bridge that spans the entire Creed and symbolically unites its contents.

While the "Confiteor" shares many *stile antico* qualities with the "Credo," it is nevertheless a more "Baroque" movement. In the "Credo," cadences are generally elided, in the manner of a Renaissance motet. In the "Confiteor," cadences serve to set off the structural divisions of the music, in the fashion of an Italian concerto. Not only the incisive rhythms and triadic leaps of the themes, but rapid harmonic rhythm and the small *allabreve* measures (₵ with a semibreve, or whole note, per measure) show a certain *rapprochement* with instrumental style. Distinctly Baroque, too, is the expressive chromaticism that accompanies the word "peccatorum" ("sins"), both at its first appearance (mm. 16–19) and just before the climactic entry of the chant as *cantus firmus* in exposition 4 (mm. 65–69).

It is unlikely that the "Confiteor" is a parody of a German-texted movement: the music's dependence on the Credo plainchant appears to rule out the possibility of a cantata model. The chief question scholars have raised is whether Bach composed the "Confiteor" directly into the *P 180* manuscript or worked from sketches or a preliminary draft.[48] It is also possible, of course, that the "Confiteor" existed beforehand as an interpolation, like the "Credo in unum Deum." That would explain the clean appearance of the score (despite the intricacy of the counterpoint).

"Et expecto" bridge

Et expecto resurrectionem mortuorum. (And I look for the resurrection of the dead.)

Chorus: five-part choir (SSATB), continuo. *Colla parte* instrumental doubling? (see Chapter 7).

The twenty-four-measure *adagio* bridge that joins the "Confiteor" with the "Et expecto" proper is one of the most extraordinary passages in the entire B-Minor Mass and merits its own discussion.

As the "Confiteor" *cantus firmus* comes to an end in m. 118, the imitative counterpoint dissolves into homophony, and the music moves toward G major, the key of the expectant close of the "Crucifixus." Three measures later, the sudden appearance of the "Crucifixus" bass motive (slurred, repeated quarter notes) and the return of the "Crucifixus" tempo (*adagio,* which Bach often used interchangeably with *lento*—see Chapter 7) leave no room for doubt: Bach wishes to underscore the pivotal role of the crucifixion in baptism and eternal life. Baptism leads to eternal life, but it is the crucifixion that stands at the center of both.

The "Confiteor" formally concludes in m. 123 on a root-position D-major chord. The function of this chord, however, is ambiguous: Is it the dominant of the just-flirted-with G major, or is it a new tonic? Within two measures, this slight uncertainty yields to major harmonic upheaval, with the appearance of the word "expecto" ("I look for"). The harmony lurches off course and descends precipitously into the dark region of E♭ minor, a key seldom used in Baroque music because of its incompatibility with contemporary tuning systems. The eighteenth-century theorist C. F. D. Schubart described E♭ minor as the key of "deepest distress, of brooding despair, of blackest depression, of the most gloomy condition of the soul."[49] The music of the bridge flirts with this "gloomy condition" but does not reach it, for the i$^6_4$ chord (m. 125) does not resolve to a root position tonic. Instead, the bass descends chromatically downward, past a B♭-major chord (the dominant of E♭ minor), and then toward D major, coming to a halt on the dominant of that key (m. 137).

There is more. Soprano 1, singing alone, presents a motive that appears to be in the key of G minor—the last reference to the flat-key area touched upon in the first part of the bridge. Then comes the most transcendent moment of all: a held C♮ is transformed enharmonically into a B♯, which leads, quickly and miraculously, back to the realm of sharp keys (G♯ major, C♯ major, and F♯ minor). A German augmented sixth chord (m. 145) serves as a springboard to D major, which is finally reached unequivocally in m. 147, via an emphatic downward scale in the continuo line. The "Et expecto" proper erupts, *vivace e allegro,* with the same trumpet-and-drums exhilaration as the "Et resurrexit."

The autograph score (Plate 4–1) shows that Bach did not achieve the remarkable harmonies of the second section of the bridge without considerable labor: the text is littered with erasures, and the cross-outs are so thick at the enharmonic pivot that one needs to turn to the secondary manuscripts made under C. P. E. Bach's supervision to confirm a definitive reading.

The unstable, mystical harmonies of the "Et expecto" bridge remind one of Gesualdo's chromatic madrigals. By contrast, the delay of triumphant D major and the enharmonic modulation that finally leads to its arrival remind one of the symphonic odysseys of Beethoven. But there is no Beethoven-

Plate 4–1. "Et expecto" bridge, mm. 132–141, in the autograph manuscript *P 180* (Berlin State Library).

like struggle in the bridge. Instead, the first section (mm. 123–137) paints the darkness of the crucifixion and the uncertainty that precedes the resurrection. Together with the "Agnus Dei" and the "et homo factus est" passage from the first version of the "Et in unum Dominum," it is one of the few flat-key episodes in the B-Minor Mass. Wilfrid Mellers sees this section's harmonic instability as Bach's way of portraying the doubt and inner questioning that even deeply committed Christians experience when faced with the mystery of eternal life.[50] Will the resurrection—of Christ *and* humankind—come to pass?

The second section (mm. 137–147) resolves the harmonic instability of the first through enharmonic change. Eric Chafe, viewing the passage from a theological standpoint, sees the harmonic transmogrification as a metaphor for the transformation of the Christian soul through Christ's death and resurrection (hence the musical reference to the "Crucifixus" earlier in the bridge).[51] For Christians, this event is reenacted in baptism, the prefiguring of an individual's own death and resurrection. Chafe reasons persuasively that Bach turned to the full Baroque resources of sharp-flat conflict to portray this eschatological event:

> Baptism was the key to the afterlife, and Bach's joining of the "Confiteor" and the "et resurrectionem" makes the fact unmistakably clear. The tonal sense, or key, is suspended in the enharmonic passage, probably as an allegory of the timeless state of the sleep of death articulated within Lutheran eschatological thought. Enharmonicism is a form of tonal style that is defined in terms of sharp/flat conflict. Werckmeister, for example, describes an enharmonic modulation from E major to F minor as a "great metamorphosis in the harmony," a place where "in an instant one passes from one genus to another." . . . His language recalls St. Paul's famous description of resurrection, of transformation in an instant.[52]

Within Bach's bridge, the harmonic questioning of the first section makes the miraculous resolution of the second all the more vivid.

"Et expecto"

Et expecto resurrectionem mortuorum et vitam venturi seculi. Amen. (And I look for the resurrection of the dead and the life of the world to come. Amen.)

Chorus: five-part choir (SSATB), 3 trumpets & timpani, 2 flutes, 2 oboes, strings, continuo.

In the "Et expecto" proper, which begins with the *Vivace e allegro* indication in m. 147, Bach casts aside the E♭-minor darkness and the tonal vagaries of the bridge with music of unabashed brightness and transparency. The contrast is extreme: pure D-major triads sound for ten measures, followed by material that never wavers from the diatonic realm of the tonic and dominant. The fanfare figures and pure harmonies of the "Et expecto" recall the judgment-day trumpet calls and incorruptible happiness of the resurrection as described by St. Paul:

> Behold, I shew you a mystery; We shall not all sleep, but we shall all be changed.
> In a moment, in the twinkling of an eye, at the last trump: for the trumpet shall sound, and the dead shall be raised incorruptible, and we shall be changed. (Corinthians I, 15:51–52)

In Bach's score, the "twinkling of an eye" seems to take place in m. 146, where the four notes of the continuo instantly transport us from the hushed augmented sixth chord of m. 145 to the D-major, trumpet and drums eruption of m. 147.

Bach derived the music of the "Et expecto" from the da capo chorus "Jauchzet, ihr erfreuten Stimmen" of Cantata 120, *Gott, man lobet dich in der Stille,* a work dating from around 1728. He so altered the surface gestures of the cantata score that the borrowing escaped the notice of commentators until Smend's penetrating look at the genesis of the B-Minor Mass in 1937.[53] The "Et expecto" represents the A section of the "Jauchzet" chorus, for which the text runs: "Jauchzet, ihr erfreuten Stimmen, Steiget bis zum Himmel nauf!" ("Exalt, ye joyful voices, climb up to heaven, rise!"). To produce a suitable *allabreve* partner for the "Confiteor" (and to match the "Credo"-"Patrem" *allabreve* pair at the beginning of the *Symbolum*), Bach doubled the note values of the cantata music and changed its meter from **C** to **¢**. In addition, he increased the vocal texture from four parts to five by adding a second soprano part.

The A section of the "Jauchzet" chorus is built upon two main ideas, both wonderfully appropriate for the "Et expecto." The first is the rising fanfare motive, presented in the opening ritornello and used for the "Jauchzet, ihr erfreuten Stimmen" portion of the text. This Bach adopted for the words "resurrectionem mortuorum" (and later, "venturi seculi"): the shouts of rejoicing in the cantata become exclamations of eternal life in the Mass movement (Example 4–20a). The second idea is the twisting, mirthful, ascending figure, used for a fugato on the words "Steiget bis zum Himmel nauf!" This Bach adopted for the words "resurrectionem mortuorum," once again (and later, "Amen"): the climbing of voices to heaven in the cantata becomes, in the Mass movement, the rising up of humankind at the Last Trump (Example 4–20b). To these Bach adds a new motive, a sustained, upward-leaping figure that is used in a point of imitation on the words "Expecto" (and later, "Et vitam venturi"; Example 4–20c).

The A section of the "Jauchzet" chorus has a distinctly symmetrical structure:

Instrumental ritornello (tonic)
    "Jauchzet" fanfare
    "Steiget" fugato

Instrumental interlude (dominant)
    "Jauchzet" fanfare
    "Steiget" fugato

Instrumental ritornello (tonic)

Example 4–20. "Et expecto" themes.

Working directly on the pages of the *P 180* manuscript, Bach made critical changes in this design. He abridged the ritornello and overlaid the
opening measures with the vocal exclamation, "Et expecto resurrectionem
mortuorum." He inserted new, imitative material before the two fanfare passages. And he dropped the concluding ritornello. The resulting form looks
like this:

Ritornello (tonic; abridged, with "Et expecto" overlay in mm. 1–9)
    "Et expecto" imitation (new)
    "Et expecto" fanfare (from the "Jauchzet" fanfare)
    "Resurrectionem" fugato (from the "Steiget" fugato)

Ritornello interlude (dominant)
    "Et vitam venturi" imitation (new)
    "Et vitam venturi" fanfare (from the "Jauchzet" fanfare)
    "Amen" fugato (from the "Steiget" fugato)

As Smend has pointed out, the "Jauchzet" chorus has a balanced, chiastic structure. The "Et expecto," by contrast, has an open-ended, developmental design.[54] By shortening the ritornello and omitting it altogether at
the end of the movement, Bach streamlined the music so that it seems to
hurl forward, almost impetuously, from the "Et expecto" start to the "Amen"
conclusion.

Many factors contribute to the jubilation: the unusual timpani solo that
sounds with the voices during the "Et expecto" fanfare;[55] the *vivace e allegro*
instruction, which denotes a very different performance from the Renaissance
gravitas of the "Confiteor"; the bourrée-like nature of the music, created by
the parallel thirds and sixths and the new ¢ meter; the sense of acceleration
stemming from the progressively faster note-motion of the three main vocal
motives, ♩ → ♪ → ♬; the effect of upward movement produced by the ascending shape of the motives and the ascending order of melodic entries; and the
feeling of crescendo, brought about by the additive instrumentation of each
vocal segment and the instrumental doubling of the second fugato.

Thanks to Bach's pruning, insertion, and revision, the "Jauchzet" music
itself is reborn: in the "Et expecto" it appears anew as an expression of the
exuberant bliss of the resurrection.

SUMMARY

Completed some fifteen years after the Kyrie and Gloria, the Credo shows
new directions in Bach's writing. Like the *Missa*, the *Symbolum* is an encyclopedic compendium. Its stylistic contrasts are more extreme, however. The

movements in Renaissance vocal style, the "Credo" and the "Confiteor," are based directly on chant melodies and show unusually close ties with six-teenth-century modal techniques. One suspects that Bach was attracted to the different possibilities of part writing and harmony offered by Palestrina's antique idiom. The "Credo" and "Confiteor" also seem to reflect his desire, in his only *Missa tota* setting, to pay homage to the musical monuments of the early Catholic Church.

At the opposite end of the spectrum, the concerted movements of the Credo are often more progressive than those of the Kyrie and Gloria. The "Et in unum Dominum" and the "Et incarnatus" display the type of simpli-fied Italianate scoring (oboe-violin doubling in the former, unison violins and continuo in the latter) that Bach normally left to more *galant*-oriented colleagues. In the "Et expecto," the tonic-dominant polarity of the harmon-ic scheme is close to the Preclassical harmonic plans of Bach's son Johann Christian. And in the "Et expecto" bridge, the enharmonic modulation points even further ahead, to Beethoven and later Romantics.

In the Kyrie and Gloria, chorus and aria are almost in equal balance; in the Credo, chorus writing predominates. This change seems to signal a shift in Bach's interest, from the matters of coloristic and virtuosic detail that are inherent in aria writing to the broader issues of balance and unification that accompany choral style. The "Credo" chords in the "Patrem omnipoten-tem," the insertion of the "Et incarnatus" and consequent retexting of the "Et in unum Dominum," the instrumental introduction and concluding modulation to G major of the "Crucifixus," the foreshadowing of the "Crucifixus" bass in the "Et incarnatus" and its reappearance in the "Et expecto" bridge, and the inclusion of the bridge itself all point to Bach's determination to produce a highly balanced and unified work, one with compelling transitions and cyclical allusions. The original manuscript shows that many of these effects were second thoughts, made only after the Credo was assembled in its fundamental form. Robert L. Marshall, who has examined the compositional process in Bach's Leipzig vocal works in numerous studies, has pointed out that the late changes in the Credo are unprecedented:

> The conscious—even self-conscious—preoccupation with issues of large-scale formal design that is manifested in the changes and cor-rections of the *Credo* autograph is unique for Bach. Such fundamental changes affecting the number, genre, succession, and interconnection of movements are hardly ever encountered in earlier manuscripts of the composer—certainly not in such concentration.[56]

Bach's desire for cyclical unity separates the *Symbolum* from the *Missa*. The *Missa* is an extraordinary display piece; the *Symbolum* is a profoundly integrated work. The retexting of the "Et in unum Dominum" attests to Bach's willingness to sacrifice compositional details in order to achieve this integration.

The revised Credo, with the "Et incarnatus" movement in place, has a distinctly symmetrical structure:

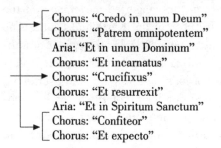

As Smend first demonstrated, by inserting the "Et incarnatus," Bach created a perfect chiastic design: the crucifixion, the central event of Christianity, stands at the center of the form, with choruses and arias radiating out from it in the manner of a palindrome.[57] The "Credo"-"Patrem" and "Confiteor"-"Et expecto," both *stile antico-stile moderno* pairs, act as doctrinal pillars, framing the whole. God's mercy is represented in a hierarchical order, both leading up to Christ's death on the cross and emanating from it. Bach was much enamored of symmetrical structures, of course, using them often in his compositions, both sacred (Cantata 140, *Wachet auf, ruft uns die Stimme*, for example) and secular (the Sonata in G Major for Violin and Harpsichord, BWV 1019, for instance).[58] The fondness for mirroring elements was a fundamental premise of the late-Baroque aesthetic, dominating the visual arts as well as music. One need look no further than Georg Werner's 1732 facade for the renovated Thomasschule (Plate 4–2) to find similar principles at work. The facade's projected central section, crowned with a dominating gable, and symmetrically arranged flanking elements—columns, windows, doors, and medallions—works in the same way as the "Crucifixus" and the axial movements of the Credo.[59]

But the Credo can also be viewed as a developmental form, one that unfolds in three phases that coincide with the three articles of Luther's Trinitarian division of the Creed. The first phase, covering Luther's First Article, "Of Creation," begins with the "Credo" and climaxes with the "Patrem omnipotentem." The second phase, covering the Second Article,

Plate 4–2. The renovated St. Thomas School of 1732 (engraving by Johann Gottfried Krügner Sr.).

"Of Redemption," begins with the "Et in unum Dominum" and climaxes with the "Et resurrexit." And the third phrase, covering the Third Article, "Of Sanctification," begins with the "Et in Spiritum Sanctus" and climaxes with the "Et expecto":

Chorus: "Credo in unum Deum"	A mixolydian
Chorus: "Patrem omnipotentem"	D major
Aria: "Et in unum Dominum"	G major
Chorus: "Et incarnatus"	B minor
Chorus: "Crucifixus"	E minor
Chorus: "Et resurrexit"	D major
Aria: "Et in Spiritum Sanctum"	A major
Chorus: "Confiteor"	F♯ minor
Chorus: "Et expecto"	D major

Viewed this way, each segment of the Credo builds toward a triumphant, trumpet-and-drums concerted movement in D major. The abstract dogma of the First Article "becomes flesh" in the Second, which deals with the life of Christ. And the eschatological events of the Second Article, that is, Christ's death and resurrection, are reenacted symbolically, through baptism, in the Third. The use of Gregorian chant in the "Credo" and "Confiteor" serves to unite the church dogma of the First and Third Articles. The "Et expecto" bridge no longer appears as an interruption, upsetting the balance of the "Credo"-"Patrem" and "Confiteor"-"Et expecto" pairs. It functions instead as a final unfolding of events, a recollection of the "Crucifixus"-"Et resurrexit" sequence in the Second Article that leads naturally to the "Et expecto" conclusion of the Third. That Bach was thinking along Lutheran lines in the Credo is verified by his label for the "Et in unum Dominum" insert: "Duo Voces Articuli 2": "The two vocal parts of Article 2."[60]

The dual interpretations reflect the new organizational logic at work in the Credo. In the Kyrie and Gloria, Bach took an approach that dominates many of the cantatas. Certain movements—the "Gloria" and "Et in terra pax," the "Domine Deus" and "Qui tollis," and the "Quoniam tu solus" and "Cum sancto"—are joined by segues, in the manner of recitative-aria pairs. But on the whole, the music proceeds from movement to movement, from aria to chorus and chorus to aria, without an overriding architectonic plan. The emphasis is on contrasting genres and instrumental colors. In the Credo, Bach focused more sharply on matters of large-scale design, creating a plan that can be interpreted in more than one way. It is the same interest that surfaces in printed collections of the late 1730s and 1740s. One can view the "Goldberg" Variations, for instance, as having either a symmetrical structure, with the aria at the beginning and end and a French overture (Variation 16) in the middle, or a progressive structure, with a series of canons at ever-widening intervals.[61] This corresponds to the symmetrical and developmental aspects of the Credo's design.

The architectonic dualism, the cyclical unifying elements, and the unusual drama of the Credo give it a special dimension and make it one of Bach's most magnificent late creations. One can well understand why C. P. E. Bach and other early admirers of the B-Minor Mass extracted the Credo from the whole and performed it separately—a possibility suggested, of course, by the structure and titling of the original manuscript, as we observed in Chapter 2. It is a practice worthy of revival today.

Chapter 5

THE SANCTUS AND AGNUS DEI

GENERAL CONSIDERATIONS

*F*or Bach, the Sanctus and Agnus Dei may have been the most challenging part of the B-Minor Mass project, for his own experience with the concluding portions of the Ordinary was limited. By the late 1740s he had copied and performed numerous Kyrie-Gloria pairs and had written at least five settings of his own. In addition, he had revised the Credo movements from Bassani's *Acroama missale* and composed two "Credo in unum Deum" interpolations. He had little working knowledge of the Sanctus and Agnus Dei, however. To be sure, he had arranged and composed Sanctus settings, but only in the truncated "Sanctus"/"Pleni sunt coeli" form used in the Lutheran worship service in Leipzig.

Moreover, Bach had few models for reference. From what we can discern of his personal library, he had only two examples of Catholic Sanctus and Agnus Dei music in his possession: the concerted Bassani Masses, which ended with "Osanna" I, and Palestrina's *Missa sine nomine,* which contained the Sanctus and Agnus Dei in full form, though in sixteenth-century *a cappella* style. Even if Bach's music collection was much more extensive than the surviving sources indicate (as it probably was), it is difficult to say where he would have found Sanctus and Agnus Dei music on a scale that would have matched the Kyrie, Gloria, and Credo of his emerging *Missa tota.* As we noted earlier, the most inspiring models for the B-Minor Mass, the Neapolitan-oriented works of Durante, Mancini, Sarri, and others, normally encompassed the Kyrie and Gloria only. Bach undoubtedly heard and examined complete settings of the Ordinary in Dresden, and his adherence in the B-Minor Mass to conventions such as setting the "Pleni sunt coeli" and "Osanna" to similar music or assigning the phrase "Dona nobis pacem" to a closing chorus shows that he was familiar with local Sanctus and Agnus Dei traditions. In Dresden Ordinaries the Sanctus and Agnus Dei were treated in a very modest way, however. No matter what the style of the earlier portions—Venetian/Viennese or Neapolitan—the Sanctus and Agnus Dei were normally cast as small sectional settings, with a dozen or so measures sufficing for each subsection.[1] There was no tradition of large, multi-movement Sanctus or Agnus Dei settings. To write music that matched the five-voice Kyrie, Gloria, and Credo, Bach had to forge his own solutions.

As we observed earlier, in the *P 180* manuscript of the B-Minor Mass Bach partitioned the Sanctus and Agnus Dei in a liturgically unorthodox way, setting off the "Sanctus" (with "Pleni sunt coeli") as No. 3 and the "Osanna" to "Dona nobis pacem" movements as No. 4. The division reflects the separate origins of the segments as well as the change in performance forces, which Bach duly noted on the title pages. Compared with the Kyrie, Gloria, and Credo, the "Sanctus" requires a second alto (to make a six-part chorus, SSAATB) and a third oboe, but no flutes; the "Osanna" to "Dona nobis pacem" movements call for the same instrumental ensemble as the Kyrie, Gloria, and Credo but need an additional alto, tenor, and bass (to make two SATB choruses).

In the *P 180* autograph the text of the "Sanctus" is untidy and error-ridden even though it is largely taken over from the earlier version of the piece, and the "Dona nobis pacem" is notated in a shorthand way (choruses 1 and 2 are written together, on one four-staff system, even though a second four-staff system was ruled but not used). Moreover, the "Dona nobis pacem," which reprises the music of the "Gratias," seems to call for adjustments in scoring and text underlay that Bach did not make. And everywhere there is an obvious reliance on parody. These aspects strongly suggest that Bach assembled the Sanctus and Agnus Dei with unusual dispatch, a circumstance that makes the extraordinary music of these final portions all the more remarkable.

THE MUSIC OF THE SANCTUS

"Sanctus"

Sanctus, sanctus, sanctus, Dominus Deus Sabaoth. Pleni sunt coeli et terra gloria eius. (Holy, holy, holy, Lord God of hosts. Heaven and earth are full of his glory.)

Chorus: six-part choir (SSAATB), 3 trumpets & timpani, 3 oboes, strings, continuo.

By the time Bach began work on the final portions of his *Missa tota* in the late 1740s, he had assembled a collection of at least six "Sanctus"/"Pleni sunt coeli" settings for practical use in Leipzig: the eight-voice polychoral setting in D Major, BWV 241, arranged from Kerll's *Missa superba;* the six-voice setting in D major, BWV 232[III], of 1724; and four four-voice settings in C major, D major, D minor, and G major, BWV 237–240, which are most probably arrangements of works by other composers.[2] All six works contain the Lutheran variant of the Latin text: "gloria eius" ("*his* glory") rather than the Roman Catholic "gloria tua" ("*thy* glory").

From these Bach chose the six-voice setting, BWV 232[III], to refashion into the Sanctus of the B-Minor Mass. He may have decided on this piece not only because it was the most sophisticated "Sanctus" in his library, but also because it may have been the only setting that was completely his own. In adapting the 1724 music, Bach retained the third oboe: although it represented a departure from the two-oboe scoring of the *Missa* and *Symbolum,* it was indispensable for the four-part oboe choir (oboes 1–3 and basso continuo, which presumably included a bassoon, a "bass oboe" of sorts) that plays a critical role in the German-oriented polychoral instrumentation of the movement. On the other hand, he converted the soprano 3 line into an alto by lowering slightly the range of the part, from b–g" (soprano 3 in the 1724 "Sanctus") to b–e" (alto 1 in the revised version). Aside from this, he adopted the music with little modification.

Liturgically, the Sanctus is part of the preparation for the Eucharist in both the Lutheran and Roman Catholic rites. It emerges from the Proper Preface, an intoned versicle that begins with seasonal exhortations and concludes with a set proclamation. The proclamation varied somewhat from place to place in Bach's time, but it commonly ran:

> Et ideo cum Angelis et Archangelis, cum Thronis et Dominationibus, cumque omni militia coelestis exercitus, hymnum gloriae tuae canimus, sine fine dicentes: (Therefore with Angels and Archangels, with the Enthroned and Those in Power, and with the Company of Heaven, we laud and magnify Thy glorious Name, evermore praising Thee, and saying:)[3]

The Sanctus followed immediately.

In the appropriated six-voice setting, Bach presents the first line of the Sanctus text, "Sanctus, sanctus, sanctus, Dominus Deus Sabaoth," as a stately polychoral piece in $\frac{4}{4}$ meter, and the second line, "Pleni sunt coeli et terra gloria eius," as a vivacious fugue in $\frac{3}{8}$ time. The overall effect is that of a large prelude and fugue. In the "Sanctus" prelude, Bach divides the performing forces into five contrasting groups—a string choir, an oboe choir, a brass choir (with timpani), and two vocal choirs of constantly changing composition. All five are supported by a single basso continuo.

Dominating the music is the phrase "Sanctus, sanctus, sanctus," which Bach sets forth in a number of remarkable guises. In the opening measures, he presents it as an emphatic four-bar invocation establishing the tonic: a choir of high voices (soprano 1 and 2, alto 1), accompanied by the strings, intones the phrase melismatically (Example 5–1a),[4] while a choir of lower voices (alto 2, tenor, bass), accompanied by the oboes and brass, adds downbeat punctuation (Example 5–1b). This is followed by a two-measure modulatory bridge with a bass motive derived from the rhythm of the words "Sanctus, Dominus Deus Sabaoth" (Example 5–1c).

The bridge leads to the dominant, where Bach repeats the "Sanctus" invocation with a new scoring. A choir of middle voices (alto 1 and 2, tenor), accompanied by the oboes, sings the melismatic line, and a choir of high and low voices (soprano 1 and 2, bass), accompanied by the strings and brass, performs the downbeat punctuation. The bridge material returns and takes us back to the tonic, where Bach presents the invocation a final time, shuffling the forces once again (and inverting the triplets of the melismatic line for good measure). The use of strongly variegated vocal and instrumental choirs reflects the coloristic approach to Venetian polychoral style favored by German composers since the beginning of the seventeenth century, when Michael Praetorius outlined a host of contrasting possibilities in his *Syntagma Musicum* of 1618. The energetic regrouping of forces in the "Sanctus"—the five choirs are rearranged three times in the first sixteen measures—represents Bach's ambitious reinterpretation of this long-standing German tradition.

In terms of form, the four-bar "Sanctus" invocation sounds and functions like a ritornello, firmly defining stable key areas amidst modulatory episodes. At the same time, the threefold appearance of the segment—in the tonic, in the dominant, and in the tonic—carries the threefold "Sanctus, sanctus, sanctus" cry to a higher organizational level. Bach transforms the hypnotic thematic element into a forceful structural element.

The remainder of the "Sanctus" prelude is sequential. Having established the "Sanctus" invocation as a dominating gesture, Bach proceeds to develop it in a series of inventive permutations. In one, the five upper voices

Example 5–1. Motives from the "Sanctus."

intone "Sanctus, sanctus, sanctus" in augmentation as the bass reiterates the "Sanctus, Dominus Deus Sabaoth" motive below (mm. 17–22 and 35–40). In another, the material of the opening measures is compressed and the melismatic triplet figure inverted (mm. 25–27 and 41–43). These passages represent long and short variants of the invocation. In measures 29 to 32 Bach even hints at a fugue before bringing the "Sanctus" to a close with a sudden, dark modulation to F♯ minor. This proves to be a harmonic tease, however, for no sooner is F♯ reached than the "Pleni" bursts forth in bright D major, sounding all the more brilliant for the brief excursion to the relative minor. The 1724 composition score reveals that Bach plotted this surprise quite carefully, sketching the modulatory bass and initial "Pleni" statement in advance.[5]

The "Pleni" is an extensive fugue whose structure can be outlined as follows:

A (mm. 48–78)   I — I   Vocal fugue, accompanied by continuo only
                                   (until the final entry, in the bass).

B (mm. 78–119)   I — I   Free imitation, divided into three sections
                                   (mm. 78–93, 93–104, 104–119), each
                                   concluded by a hemiola cadence and the
                                   appearance of the fugue theme.

A (mm. 119–137)   I → IV   Vocal fugue, with doubling instruments.

B (mm. 137–168)   IV → I   Free imitation, divided into two sections
                                   (mm. 137–153, 153–168), each concluded
                                   by a hemiola cadence and the appearance of
                                   the fugue theme.

The fugue theme (Example 5–2) is especially rich in Baroque imagery. The word "coeli" ("heaven") is marked by an *anabasis* figure, an upward leap of a sixth; the word "terra" ("earth"), by a *catabasis* figure, a downward leap of a fifth. And the word "gloria" is set with an appropriately florid melisma. The fugue theme concludes with an arresting hemiola cadence— that is, a momentary (and delightful) metrical shift from the three-beat units expected in $\frac{3}{8}$ time to smaller two-beat units that are syncopated over the bar line (marked with brackets in Example 5–2). The hemiola is even clearer in Bach's notation, which shows the ♫ figure as a slurred grouping straddling the measure (see Example 5–2). As the above summary of the fugue indicates, Bach transfers the hemiola cadence of the theme to a larger structural level, using it to mark off the principal sections of the movement. The almost heady interruption of the dactylic pulse at these points serves both to clarify the structure and to enhance the playful character of the music.

Example 5–2. Fugue theme from the "Pleni sunt coeli."

A second sketch in the 1724 "Sanctus" score shows that Bach initially envisioned the "coeli" leap as an octave—an interval that would have linked the theme more closely with the octaves of the "Sanctus" prelude.[6] But as Robert L. Marshall has noted, the sixth of the final version is "sharper" than the octave (that is, it is less stable) and provides a better pivot from the F♯-minor conclusion of the "Sanctus" to the D-major beginning of the "Pleni."[7] Both sketches show that Bach first considered notating the "Pleni" in $\frac{3}{4}$ meter. The final meter, $\frac{3}{8}$, implies a lighter articulation and somewhat faster tempo (see Chapter 7). It makes the hemiola cadences all the more striking and gives the music an ebullient yet elegant passepied quality. Bach shaped the subject and its countersubject (a more extensive "gloria" melisma) so that both can be combined simultaneously in parallel thirds or sixths (Example 5–3), a contrapuntal possibility that is realized three times, at mm. 66, 75, and 125. This not only helps to compress the fugal expositions but adds greatly to the exuberant nature of the counterpoint, making the polyphonic web, like the heaven and earth of the text, all the more "full."

In the B sections, Bach embellishes motives derived from the fugue subject and countersubject and the continuo line of the A section. The use of the fugue theme to conclude each segment of free imitation reminds one of the "Wedge" Fugue in E Minor for organ, BWV 548/2, in which the subject returns, almost like an *idée fixe*, at the end of each free episode. It is significant that the "Wedge" Fugue dates from the same period as the "Sanctus"— Bach's early Leipzig years. As the music of the "Pleni" progresses, the figural play in the B sections becomes increasingly elaborate until Bach finally presents, with unison trumpets and seemingly tongue-in-cheek, a simplified version of the triadic bass motive that began the section (Example 5–4). Some twenty-five years later, he picked up this fanfare-like motive in the "Osanna."

In the "Sanctus," as in the "Et in terra pax" of the Gloria, Bach may have wished to capture the specific imagery of the Biblical passage from which the Latin text was derived. It was Philipp Spitta who first suggested that Bach's decision to use a six-voice chorus, the only such instance in his sacred works, was influenced by the number six mentioned in Isaiah 6:1–3, the Old Testament source of the Sanctus:[8]

Example 5–3. Subject and countersubject in the "Pleni sunt coeli."

Example 5–4. Fanfare-like motive in the "Pleni sunt coeli."

In the year that King Uzziah died I saw also the Lord sitting upon a throne, high and lifted up, and his train filled the temple.

Above it stood the seraphim: each one had six wings; with twain he covered his face, and with twain he covered his feet, and with twain he did fly.

And one cried unto another, and said, Holy, holy, holy is the Lord of hosts: the whole earth is full of his glory.

Vopelius's New Leipzig Hymnal of 1682 includes a short six-voice setting of the "Sanctus"/"Pleni," and there may have been a tradition of viewing six-part vocal texture as ideal for Sanctus movements (although in Dresden, four-voice settings, SATB, seem to have been the norm). The Isaiah text may have inspired other aspects of Bach's "Sanctus" as well: the use of three sopranos (the least practical voice, since the part was sung by the youngest boys) in the 1724 version to stress the "highness" of the angels and the throne of the Lord; the use of undulating triplets (often in contrary motion) and the ongoing sequences (after m. 16) to paint the movement of the angels' wings; and the use of imitation and rising crescendos in the "Pleni" to portray the animated dispersal of the angelic proclamation. Comparable imagery appears in Baroque paintings of the *Hymnus seraphicus*, ("Hymn of the Seraphim"), as Luther and other theologians termed the Sanctus, and it is not inconceivable that Bach wished to portray a similar scene in his ambitious score.

For those wishing to compare the original and revised versions of the "Sanctus," the *Neue Bach-Ausgabe* is of little help. The 1724 version is not included in volume II/2, "Bach's Lutheran Masses and Mass Movements," where one would expect to find it, and the "Sanctus" given in volume II/1, Friedrich Smend's edition of the B-Minor Mass, is a compilation of the early and revised versions (the notes represent the revised version, but most of the performance indications, especially the slurs, are taken from the score and performance parts of the 1724 version). To see the texts of each version, one must turn to the *Bach-Gesamtausgabe*, where the situation is confusing nonetheless: the 1724 "Sanctus" (with three sopranos and one alto) appears in the original edition of volume 6 (1856), within the context of the B-Minor Mass, on pages 243–269; the revised version (with two sopranos and two altos) appears in the second edition of volume 6 (sometimes numbered "6¹"; 1857), on the same pages.[9]

"Osanna" I

Osanna in excelsis. (Hosanna in the highest.)

Chorus: choir 1 (SATB), choir 2 (SATB), 3 trumpets & timpani, 2 flutes,
2 oboes, strings, continuo.

The jubilation of the "Pleni" continues in the "Osanna in excelsis," a
lively polychoral chorus for two four-part choirs and instruments. That the
"Osanna" represents the A section—minus opening instrumental ritornello—of a preexistent da capo movement there can be little doubt: the
music appears in full form in the opening chorus, "Preise dein Glücke," of
Cantata 215, a work Bach fashioned for the election-anniversary celebration of Friedrich August II in Leipzig on October 5, 1734. There has been
some question as to how the Mass and cantata music are related, however.
Arnold Schering, writing before the precise chronology of the B-Minor Mass
was known, proposed that the "Osanna" was written first and "Preise dein
Glücke" derived from it. Smend, reiterating Spitta's premise that Bach
always parodied in the direction secular to sacred, believed the order to be
the opposite, with the cantata serving as the model for the Mass movement.
Werner Neumann seems to have set the matter straight by demonstrating
that both pieces were derived from a third work, the chorus "Es lebe der
König, der Vater im Lande" from the secular cantata of the same name,
BWV Anh. 11, written for the name day of Friedrich August I on August 3,
1732.[10]

Although *Es lebe der König* survives as a printed libretto only, the music
of the opening chorus can be reconstructed sufficiently to see why it was
ideal for the "Osanna." As the Picander text reveals, the general character
of the A section of the opening chorus, praise and jubilation, was marvelously appropriate for the Mass movement, even though the acclaim was
directed to a secular rather than a sacred king:

Es lebe der König, der Vater im Lande,
Der weise, der milde, der tapfer August!

Long live the King, the father of our country,
The wise, the gentle, the valiant August!

Equally advantageous was the fact that the rhythmic pattern instigated
by the "Es lebe" text, dactylic with an upbeat (⌣ | ⁄ ⌣ ⌣ | ⁄ ⌣ ⌣), was a

perfect match for the declamation of the "Osanna." Even the choral echo passages could be maintained with little or no change (Example 5–5; the elision of the word "Osanna" appears in the *P 180* autograph).[11]

Example 5–5. Text underlay in "Es lebe der König" and the "Osanna."

The "Osanna" parody of the "Es lebe" music proved to be ideal for Bach's growing Mass Ordinary. The orchestral forces—trumpets and timpani, two oboes, two flutes, strings, and continuo—matched those of the Kyrie, Gloria, and Credo. The vocal scoring, while calling for eight voices (SATB + SATB), represented a logical expansion of the polychoral writing of the "Sanctus." And the music displayed organic links with the "Pleni": D-major tonality, $\frac{3}{8}$ meter, and a number of similar melodic motives (Example 5–6). To judge from the parallel parody "Preise dein Glücke," these connections were already present in the "Es lebe" prototype. In fact, so uncanny are the thematic ties between the "Osanna" and the "Pleni" that Walter Blankenburg once speculated—and not entirely in jest—that Bach might have already envisioned the "Osanna" music when he wrote the "Sanctus" in 1724![12] The "Es lebe der König" chorus had not yet been written, of course, and the links stem from the fact that the motives are the common vocabulary of D-major, $\frac{3}{8}$ meter, dance-derived music (and of the passepied in particular). Nevertheless, we can imagine that Bach was delighted to create a piece through parody procedure that matched the "Pleni" so well, especially since it allowed him to pay homage to the Dresden convention of setting (on a much smaller scale) the "Osanna" to the same music as the "Pleni." In many of Zelenka's and Caldara's Masses,

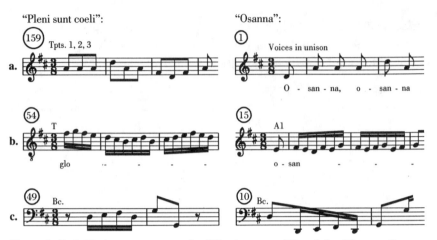

Example 5–6. Motives common to the "Pleni sunt coeli" and the "Osanna."

the "Pleni" and "Osanna" texts follow one another without pause, as part of a single section (in Zelenka's *Missa Circumcisionis* or Caldara's *Missa dicta Reformata,* for instance); "Osanna" II is then set to the same or new music.

The omission of the instrumental ritornello at the beginning of the "Osanna" music tightened further the bond with the "Pleni" and brought the music closer still to Catholic practice. In the Mass Ordinary, the words "Osanna in excelsis Deo" follow the "Pleni" (and on repetition, the "Benedictus") directly. By dropping the opening ritornello of the "Es lebe der König," Bach eliminated the instrumental interruption.

Es lebe der König was a *drama per musica,* performed out-of-doors in Zimmermann's Coffee Garden by the Collegium Musicum. It is not hard to imagine the purpose of the polychoral writing of the opening chorus: it would have simulated the overlapping and gradually rising shouts of praise for the Saxon Elector. In its "Preise dein Glücke" form in Cantata 215, the chorus was performed by torchlight on the immense market square in Leipzig, where the antiphonal acclamations would have been even more impressive. (Unhappily, Bach's prize trumpeter, Gottfried Reiche, overcome with smoke inhalation and perhaps the demands of the first trumpet part as well, hemorrhaged and died the day after the performance.[13])

In its "Osanna" form, the music produces a remarkably joyful effect. After an initial "Osanna" acclamation, in unison, with a fanfare-like motive (Example 5–6a, above) and a quick echo affirmation, chorus 1 launches into an imitative sequence (mm. 15–38) that grows in intensity as chorus 2 reiterates the fanfare motive over it three times (mm. 27–37). After a cadence in E minor, the sequence is repeated (mm. 38–62) with the forces reversed: chorus 2 presents the imitative material and chorus 1 sounds the fanfare motive. After a cadence in B minor, both choruses join in the imitative sequence. D major is restored at m. 81 with an exchange of the fanfare motive, followed by new contrapuntal combinations involving both choruses. Over the vocal material the instruments present the last three-quarters of the deleted thirty-two-measure opening ritornello (mm. 81–104), which cadences in D major at m. 104. A short, echo-filled coda (the *piano* and *forte* marks appear in the original score; the earlier analogous passage, mm. 10–15, displays no such indications, however) leads to the full ritornello, played by the instruments alone. Bach's form makes wonderful logic: brief introduction, point of imitation for choir 1, point of imitation for choir 2, point of imitation for both choirs, reiteration of various vocal motives with the instrumental ritornello, instrumental ritornello close. The plan creates the sensation of increasing bliss, of growing ecstasy.

The ecstasy is greatly reinforced by the passepied dance idiom, which we also noted in the "Pleni." In the "Osanna," passepied style is especially apparent in the presence of the characteristic rhythm ♪|♫♫|♫♫♫|♫♫|♩. and the symmetrical melodic units (the imitative entries and "Osanna" fanfares occur at regular two-measure intervals, the ritornello is divided into phrases of 8 + 12 + 12 measures, etc.). As John Butt has observed, the balanced phrasing of the dance idiom nicely accommodates the polychoral writing, since the two choirs can exchange motives within the repeated patterns of the music.[14] The balanced phrasing also produces a very different type of polychoral piece from the "Sanctus": the "Osanna" is more *galant,* its textures more transparent (despite the use of larger vocal forces). The brisk tempo and light passepied articulation create an air of graceful exuberance. Once again, Bach uses worldly means to accomplish sacred ends.

"Benedictus"

Benedictus qui venit in nomine Domini. (Blessed is he that cometh in the
   name of the Lord.)

Aria: tenor, flute or violin, continuo.

The "Benedictus" poses questions of setting, origin, and style. With regard to the first, it is unclear what instrument should play the obbligato instrumental line. The part is not labeled in the autograph manuscript (Plate 5–1), and the treble clef allows three possibilities: violin, flute, or

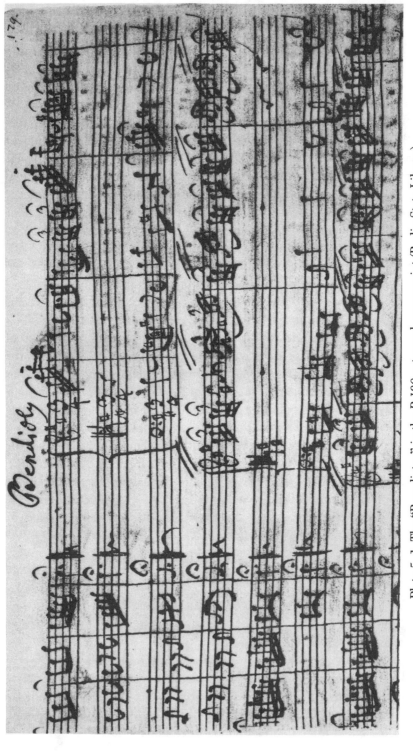

Plate 5–1. The "Benedictus" in the *P 180* autograph manuscript (Berlin State Library).

oboe. Julius Rietz, editor of the *Bach-Gesamtausgabe*, opted for the violin. As Smend demonstrated in his commentary for the *Neue Bach-Ausgabe*, Rietz's decision, made in the mid-nineteenth century in the wake of Spontini's famous pairing of the B-Minor Mass with the *Missa solemnis* (see Chapter 6), was probably influenced by the scoring of Beethoven's "Benedictus," which features solo violin.[15] Smend also pointed out that the range of the instrumental line in Bach's "Benedictus"—d' to f♯'''—is more typical of a transverse flute than a violin (when writing for the violin, Bach normally took advantage of the G string and composed below d'). In addition, Smend asserted that the figurations in the "Benedictus" are "flute-like" and that Bach would not have used an obbligato string sound in two consecutive arias, the "Benedictus" and the "Agnus Dei."[16] It is noteworthy, too, that the key of the "Benedictus," B minor, was one of Bach's favorite for the flauto traverso. Taking these factors into consideration, Smend reassigned the line to transverse flute in the *Neue Bach-Ausgabe*, and most recent recordings follow his recommendation.

While Smend's reasoning makes sense, the issue is not so easily settled. Normally, Bach did indeed utilize the range d' to f♯''' when writing for flute. When writing for oboe and violin, however, he used different tessituras: c' to b'' (or occasionally c''') for oboe, and g to e''' (though sometimes as high as a''', as in the "Laudamus te," for instance) for the violin. The high notes in the "Benedictus" eliminate the oboe from consideration. But the violin cannot be discounted completely. The distinction between idiomatic flute writing and idiomatic violin writing is often very fine in Bach's music. The obbligato instrumental line of the aria "Seele, deine Spezereien" from the Easter Oratorio, BWV 249, for instance, contains figurations quite similar to those of the "Benedictus": upward leaping appoggiaturas, groups of triplets as well as sixteenth notes, and so forth (Example 5–7). The line has a "flute range," d♯' to d''', and in the performance parts, it is assigned to a transverse flute. In the original score, however, Bach indicated an option: "Travers. o Violino Solo." In the tenor aria "Handle nicht nach deinen Rechten" from Cantata 101, Bach initially assigned the obbligato instrumental line (range: d'–g''') to the transverse flute but subsequently transferred it to the violin.

It is possible, then, that the absence of a label on the solo instrumental line of the "Benedictus" reflects not carelessness on Bach's part (the scoring of the "Agnus Dei," by contrast, is clearly marked), but indecision (perhaps he had not yet made up his mind which instrument to use, flute or violin) or indifference (as in the Easter Oratorio aria). Although it was

Example 5–7.   a. Obbligato instrumental line of the "Benedictus."
b. "Travers. o Violino Solo" line of the aria "Seele, deine Spezereien" from
the Easter Oratorio, BWV 249.

Bach's habit to vary the instrumentation of arias, it would not have been
outside the realm of Mass convention to score the "Benedictus" and "Agnus
Dei" similarly. In Dresden Masses, the "Benedictus" and "Agnus Dei" were
sometimes set to the same music (in Zelenka's Sanctus and Agnus Dei for
Durante's *Missa Modestiae*, for instance).

The concise form of the "Benedictus"—ritornello in B minor, vocal material, ritornello in D major, vocal material, ritornello in B minor—and the
errorless text of Bach's score both point to parody, a possibility first raised by
Spitta and repeated by most commentators since. It would seem that the
music represents the A section of a lost da capo aria. In the *P 180* manuscript it appears that Bach, after completing the "Osanna," started to write
out the "Benedictus" on a new fascicle, the gathering of pages that now holds
the "Agnus Dei" (the "Bend" of "Bendictus"—Bach's elided title—can be
perceived under the "Agnus" of "Agnus Dei").[17] He then realized that he
could squeeze the aria onto the page and a half of empty staves left over from
"Osanna" (see Plate 5–1, above, where the end of the "Osanna" is visible to
the left). Such economic usage of space is common in Bach's fair-copy manuscripts, in which he knew precisely how long pieces would run. This circumstance, too, suggests that he had a model in front of him as he sat down
to write out the "Benedictus." As we noted in Chapter 2, Yoshitake
Kobayashi claims that Bach sketched out parts of the "Benedictus" in light

ink before tracing over it in dark. That may be, but it would still not rule out parody: Bach may have been revising earlier music directly on the page.

Parody or not, the "Benedictus" is unquestionably progressive in style. The obbligato instrumental line, with its rich variety of figurations (six-teenth- and thirty-second note groups, as well as triplets), resembles the writing found in a number of other forward-looking pieces from the 1730s and 1740s: the first movement of the B-Minor Flute Sonata, BWV 1030, or the Andante of the Trio Sonata from the Musical Offering (Example 5–8), for example. In such music, Bach seems to have been consciously moving away from the more mechanistic idiom of Vivaldi, with its angular motives and motoric rhythms, toward the more pliant, flexible idiom of the emerging *empfindsamer Stil,* the "sensitive style," with its rapidly changing note val-ues, circumscribed phrases, and sigh-like motives. That eighteenth-century composers commonly associated the "sensitive style" with the breathy, dul-cet tones of the transverse flute may once again speak for the use of the instrument in the "Benedictus."

The tenor line of the "Benedictus," like the melodic line of the Andante from the Musical Offering, is discontinuous—that is, the melody consists of short phrases separated by rests (compare, for example, the much longer vocal phrases of the "Laudamus te" or the "Qui sedes"). What is most unusu-al is the way in which the tenor echoes the solo instrument in an inexact way, more in the manner of a reminiscence than a precise repetition. The principal notes are often the same (though commonly displaced by an octave), but the melodic gestures are constantly reinterpreted. In the initial theme, for instance, the upbeat note D is approached in the solo instrument by an

Example 5–8.   a. Flute Sonata in B Minor, BWV 1030.   b. Trio Sonata from the Musical Offering, BWV 1079.

ascending appoggiatura, in the voice, by a turn; or the note E is reached in the
instrument by a falling sixth, in the voice, by a downward detour to F♯
(Example 5–9). This broken, calculatedly circumspect style is quite different
from any other aria writing in the B-Minor Mass. Unlike the straightforward
instrumental-vocal mimicry of, say, the "Et in Spiritum Sanctum," it creates a
faintly halting effect. Bach may have desired this for purely expressive reasons, to illustrate the *con affetto* emotionalism of the *empfindsamer Stil.*

Example 5–9. Opening theme of the "Benedictus."

The discontinuity may also have had an allegorical purpose, however. In
its Biblical context (Matthew 21:9) the Benedictus text has a triumphant tone:
it is the greeting shouted by the multitudes to Christ as he enters Jerusalem.
In the Ordinary, it takes on a more somber shade, acting as part of the Preface
for the Eucharist, the reenactment of Christ's Communion with the Apostles.
Helmut Rilling has pointed to the remarkable juxtaposition of the "Osanna,"
with the largest forces in the B-Minor Mass, and the "Benedictus," with the
smallest.[18] His observation is well taken: Bach seems to have gone out of his
way to contrast the public shouts of the "Osanna" with the private professions
of the "Benedictus." In late-Baroque Masses it was common practice to set
the "Osanna" as a tutti chorus and the "Benedictus" as a solo aria. But Bach's
approach seems extreme. Wilfrid Mellers' rhapsodic interpretation of the
"Benedictus" describes the contrast well:

> Once more Bach sings from his apprehension of mortality: he has dis-
> covered what bliss and mercy mean, and makes from that knowledge a
> music purged. . . . In a sense, the whole of the Benedictus's purgator-
> ical meditation is a "middle section" to the worldly hubbub of the
> "Hosanna": a moment outside time that man may occasionally discov-
> er or rediscover.[19]

Mellers is right. The "Benedictus," framed by the dance-like "Osanna,"
creates a very different world, one of solitary, almost mystical reflection.

"Osanna" II

Osanna in excelsis. (Hosanna in the highest.)

Chorus: choir 1 (SATB), choir 2 (SATB), 3 trumpets & timpani, 2 flutes, 2
   oboes, strings, continuo.

In many Dresden Mass settings, the "Benedictus" is followed by new
"Osanna" music. In others, the first "Osanna" is reprised. Bach follows the
second course in the B-Minor Mass, indicating at the end of the
"Benedictus," "Osanna repetat."—"The Hosanna is repeated."

THE MUSIC OF THE AGNUS DEI

As we discussed in Chapter 1, within the liturgy of the Mass, the Agnus Dei
is a threefold supplication that is sung just before the distribution of the
eucharistic bread and wine:

   Agnus Dei, qui tollis peccata mundi, miserere nobis.
   Agnus Dei, qui tollis peccata mundi, miserere nobis.
   Agnus Dei, qui tollis peccata mundi, dona nobis pacem.

In Dresden, composers set the three phrases in a variety of ways, as one,
two, or three movements. More often than not, they allotted the final plea,
"Dona nobis pacem," its own music in the form of a concluding chorus.
When Bach divided the final portion of the Ordinary into an "Agnus Dei"
aria and a "Dona nobis pacem" chorus, he was thus following a well-established custom.

"Agnus Dei"

Agnus Dei, qui tollis peccata mundi, miserere nobis. (Lamb of God, who
   takest away the sins of the world, have mercy upon us.)

Aria: alto, violins 1 & 2 in unison, continuo.

With the "Agnus Dei" Bach returns a final time to the intimate aria style.
The text is a plea for Christ's mercy, somewhat like that of the "Christe eleison," and the use of the same instrumentation in both movements—unison
violins and continuo[20]—may be a calculated cross-reference.

It has been known since the nineteenth century that the "Agnus Dei" is
a parody, for the same music appears, albeit in a more expansive form, in the

aria "Ach, bleibe doch, mein liebstes Leben" ("Oh stay with me, my dearest life") from the Ascension Oratorio, BWV 11, of 1735. But as was true of the "Osanna," the relationship between Mass movement and supposed model has been clarified only in recent times. Smend, writing in 1950, demonstrated that "Ach, bleibe doch" was derived from a still earlier piece, the aria "Entfernet euch, ihr kalten Herzen" ("Withdraw, you cold hearts") of the wedding serenade *Auf! Süßentzückende Gewalt* of 1725.[21] Although the music for the serenade is lost, Gottsched's printed libretto is enough to show that "Entfernet euch" most certainly served as the model for "Ach, bleibe doch" (the poetic structure, the rhyme scheme, and the general *Affekt* of the texts are quite the same). More recently, Alfred Dürr refined Smend's thesis by showing that the "Agnus Dei" stems directly from "Entfernet euch" rather than from "Ach, bleibe doch."[22] Therefore the "Agnus Dei" and "Ach, bleibe doch" are sister parodies, rather than parody and model.

In the opening ritornello of the "Agnus Dei" Bach utilizes three emotionally charged rhetorical figures to create an appropriate atmosphere of mourning for Christ, the "Lamb of God" sacrificed to assuage the sins of humanity. The first is the fragmented, leaping motive that appears in the first and third ritornello segments (mm. 1–2 and 5–8; Example 5–10, x).

Example 5–10. "Agnus Dei," opening ritornello.

Formed from highly dissonant intervals such as the minor seventh, the diminished seventh, and the tritone, the motive resembles the jagged figures that appear in the St. John and St. Matthew Passions as Christ approaches the crucifixion.[23] Baroque theorists termed this type of melodic idea a *saltus duriusculus:* a "harsh leap" (from the Latin "durus," "hard" or "harsh," and "saltus," to "dance" or "leap," as in the Renaissance "saltarello," a dance calling for a "little hop"). In "Ach, bleibe doch" (and most probably in "Entfernet euch" as well), Bach used the *saltus duriusculus* to underscore the meaning of the word "Schmerz" ("pain").[24] In the "Agnus Dei," he employs it to produce a "Schmerz"-like *Affekt,* linking it in the vocal sections with the words "miserere" ("have mercy") and "peccata" ("sins"). The second expressive figure is the lamentation motive, the slurred, conjunct note-pairs that we have seen elsewhere in minor-mode movements dealing with Christ's passion and mercy: "Kyrie" I, "Qui tollis," "Et incarnatus," and "Crucifixus." In the "Agnus Dei," the lamentation motive appears in the second segment of the ritornello (mm. 3–4; Example 5–10, y). In the vocal portions of the aria Bach uses it to impart a sense of weeping to the words "Agnus Dei" ("Lamb of God"; Example 5–11, below). The dissonant leap and the lamentation motive are united by the third

Example 5–11. Opening vocal material in (a) "Ach, bleibe doch, mein liebstes Leben" and (b) "Agnus Dei."

expressive idea: the punctuated eighth notes of the continuo (Example 5–10, z, above). Bach and his contemporaries would have viewed this line, broken by intermittent respirations, as a *suspiratio,* a passionate sigh. The three plaintive figures, combined in a dense contrapuntal web, make for music that is awash in rhetorical angst.

The compressed form of the "Agnus Dei" also contributes to the emotional intensity. The music is a modified da capo design, with an opening A section of modest proportions (mm. 1–27), a very short B section (mm. 27–31), and an abridged A' section (mm. 31–49), which is delineated by the return of the "Agnus Dei" vocal theme in the tonic. The proceedings of the A' section are interrupted by a fermata in m. 34, and the pause heightens all the more the hesitant, anxious quality of the music. A comparison of the "Agnus Dei" with "Ach, bleibe doch" (which most certainly reflects more closely the music of the lost "Entfernet euch" aria) shows that the concise form and fermata pause are the result of calculated revisions: Bach dropped some thirty measures of the original music, mostly from the lengthy B section, and fully refashioned the initial measures of the vocal material, setting the words "Agnus Dei" to the lamentation motive rather than the leaping motive, which was used to open the vocal segment in "Ach, bleibe doch" (Example 5–11).[25] Christoph Wolff sees the strict counterpoint of the new "Agnus Dei" theme (it appears in canon at the fifth with the unison violins) as a "deliberate aesthetic *rapprochement*" with the severe contrapuntal writing of the *Symbolum Nicenum.*[26] This is quite true. But canon also mirrors the motivic imitation that already existed in the parody model.

Bach also transposed the music from A minor to G minor. The choice of G minor is striking, for it renders the "Agnus Dei" the only flat-key movement in the entire B-Minor Mass. The G minor nicely complements the B minor of the "Benedictus" and adds variety to the Sanctus and Agnus Dei portions, which are otherwise dominated by D-major choruses:

"Sanctus"	D major
"Osanna" I	D major
"Benedictus"	B minor
"Osanna" II	D major
"Agnus Dei"	G minor
"Dona nobis"	D major

Bach may also have wished G minor to serve as a reference to the flat-key writing that accompanied the words "et propter nostram salutem descendit de coelis" ("and for our salvation descended from heaven") in the revised "Et in unum Dominum" (presumably now in place in the *Symbolum*) and the flat-key digression that darkened the first segment of the "Et expecto" bridge. Both passages focus on the salvation that results from Christ's assumption of human form to become the sacrificial lamb.

In lowering the music a whole step, from A minor to G minor, Bach was forced to transpose measures 5 and 6 of the opening instrumental line an octave higher (unchanged, the line would have descended below the lowest note of the violin, g). He seems to have turned this necessary alteration into an inventive compositional procedure, displacing portions of the line elsewhere where transposition was not required in order to make the leaps even more wrenching. In m. 41, for instance, the violins jump upward a fourteenth rather than a seventh on the word "miserere," producing a very "harsh leap" indeed. The new displacement is especially evident in the final ritornello. In "Ach, bleibe doch," the violin line is repeated as it appeared in the opening; in the "Agnus Dei," it is greatly altered, displaying unpredictable, jarring leaps (Example 5–12). The leaps are counterbalanced by a new, continuous bass line, which adds urgency to the final measures and sets the stage for the steady tactus of the "Dona nobis." The final cadential figure of the "Agnus Dei" foreshadows the D–E–F♯–G opening of the "Dona nobis."[27] At the same time, it echoes the end of the "Benedictus," which closes with a similar motive in the solo instrumental line.

In the "Agnus Dei," then, Bach appears to have greatly transformed the music of his model, "Entfernet euch." Would it not have been easier to write a new piece altogether? As was true of the "Crucifixus and "Et expecto," so it is here: Bach probably considered the revision as an opportunity to improve an earlier score, to make the counterpoint and imagery richer. While the "Dona nobis" that follows is a straightforward parody, the "Agnus Dei" borders on being a new piece. As Wolff has pointed out, together with the progressive "Et incarnatus," the "Agnus Dei" may have been one of Bach's last compositional efforts.[28]

"Dona nobis pacem"

Dona nobis pacem. (Grant us peace.)

Chorus: choir 1 (SATB) and choir 2 (SATB) in unison, 3 trumpets and timpani, continuo; other instruments (2 flutes, 2 oboes, and strings) *colla parte.*

Example 5–12. Closing ritornello in (a) "Ach, bleibe doch, mein liebstes Leben" and (b) "Agnus Dei."

In the "Dona nobis pacem" Bach recapitulates the music of the "Gratias agimus tibi." This type of inner borrowing was common in Mass settings performed in Dresden, in which the "Dona nobis" was often derived from a segment of the Kyrie or Gloria. In Francesco Durante's *Missa Modestiae* and Antonio Caldara's *Missa Intende in adjutorium meum*, the "Dona nobis" recapitulates "Kyrie" I, and in Caldara's *Missa Divi Xaverii* the "Dona nobis" recapitulates music from the Gloria "Amen," to cite but three examples.[29] Aesthetically, such repetition served as a unifying device, relating the opening Kyrie and Gloria sections, performed at the beginning of the service, to the Sanctus and Agnus Dei, which sounded much later, during the Eucharist. In Dresden in particular, the return to earlier material in the "Dona nobis" (and other portions of the Credo, Sanctus, and Agnus Dei as well) often reflected a more pragmatic concern—the expeditious expansion of a two-part *Missa* into a five-part *Missa tota*. It is possible that Bach had both goals in mind as he concluded the B-Minor Mass. The use of the "Gratias" music in the "Dona nobis" helped to unite the 1733 *Missa* with the new movements from the late 1740s. Yet the borrowing may also have provided Bach with a practical means of completing his Mass Ordinary project as his eyesight began to fail.

The matching of the "Dona nobis" text to the "Gratias" music seems to have posed a number of problems. As we saw in Chapter 3, the "Gratias" music is a double fugue, and in double fugues Bach normally allotted each subject a different portion of the text. For the "Dona nobis" there was insufficient text to go around: Bach had only three words to work with, and consequently he had to employ the phrase "Dona nobis pacem" for both subjects. For the first he used the full "Dona nobis pacem" but repeated the word "pacem" to fill out the phrase (Example 5–13a). This works acceptably well, creating a type of hypnotic invocation—"pacem, pacem"—much like the reiteration of the same word (in the nominative case), "pax," on long notes in the "Et in terra pax" of the Gloria. For the second subject, however, Bach reversed the word order—"pacem dona nobis" (Example 5–13b)—with the result that "dona" lands, not ideally, on the long melisma that more suitably highlights the word "gloriam" ("glory") in the "Gratias."

Example 5–13. Themes from the "Dona nobis pacem": a. First theme. b. Second theme. c. Second theme, hypothetical text underlay without inverted word order. d. Second theme, using music from "Wir danken dir, Gott," BWV 29/2.

It is obvious why Bach inverted the words: if he had not, the result would have been worse, with "pacem" ("peace") coming out under the long melisma (Example 5–13c). Such an underlay would have worked against the meaning of the word "pacem." But the inverted word order has the quality of a makeshift solution, the "product of a pronounced predicament" as Smend put it.[30] Bach might have gained slightly better results with the second theme, at least, if he had gone back to the music of the "Wir danken dir, Gott" chorus on which the "Gratias" is based: word repetition still would have been required, and one would have faced a small melisma on "pacem" (Example 5–13d). Word inversion could have been avoided, however. Bach turned to the "Gratias" nevertheless.[31] Whether motivated by design (to make the connection with the "Gratias" absolutely clear) or by necessity (time was running out), he did not fashion the type of artful revisions in deriving the "Dona nobis" from the "Gratias" that he made when adapting the "Gratias" from the "Wir danken dir" chorus.

The *P 180* manuscript of the B-Minor Mass clarifies several issues regarding the "Dona nobis" while at the same time reinforcing the impression that not all was in order. In terms of scoring, the autograph shows that flutes 1 and 2 should double oboe 1 and that the vocal parts are to be taken by choruses 1 and 2—a clear reference to the vocal forces of the "Osanna" and an effort on Bach's part to link the tutti movements of "No. 4." Both points are muddled in the *Bach-Gesamtausgabe* and its various reprints, which show flute 2 doubling oboe 2 and omit mention of two choruses. In the autograph, the "Dona nobis" begins on the last page of the "Agnus Dei" and then continues alone for six additional pages. On all but the first page, Bach ruled systems of eighteen staves. He used only the top fourteen, however, leaving the bottom four empty. This is the only such miscalculation in the B-Minor Mass, and it has raised interesting debate. The most obvious explanation for the empty staves is that Bach intended to write out chorus 1 and chorus 2. Although this would have been an unusual procedure (in Cantata 215, for instance, when the two choruses of the first movement consolidate in the last, Bach used a single four-staff system), one requiring extra work, it would have emphasized the organizational link between the "Dona nobis" and the polychoral "Osanna" all the more strongly. Having decided against this, however, Bach realized that by doubling the choruses notationally, he could save space and begin the text underneath the "Agnus Dei" (much in the same fashion that he wrote out the "Benedictus" on the empty "Osanna" pages, apparently as an afterthought).

There are two more provocative possibilities. Arthur Mendel seems to have been the first to suggest that Bach might have intended to write other

De - o   di - ca - mus   gra - ti - as.

Example 5–14. The chant "Deo dicamus gratias."

music altogether, perhaps a chorus in which the two choirs acted independently of one another.[32] The second idea, raised by Butt, is that Bach intended to write still more music, perhaps an "Agnus Dei" II aria, in the manner of many Dresden settings.[33] The notation of movements in extra space is not at all uncommon in Bach's scores (as the "Benedictus" attests), and an "Agnus Dei" II written below the "Dona nobis" could have been inserted after the "Agnus Dei" I with a siglum, much like the "Et incarnatus" after the "Et in unum Dominum." Both theories may strike one as highly speculative. Yet the layout of the autograph manuscript and the music of the "Dona nobis" show signs of haste, and Bach may have been forced to curtail plans that were even more ambitious than the ones he carried out.

In the end, we must accept Bach's judgment that the general appropriateness of the "Gratias" music outweighs matters of compositional detail. The noble grace, the steady tactus (whose serenity is increased through the virtual elimination of the subdivisional strokes used in the "Gratias"), and the climactic brilliance of the double fugue bring the B-Minor Mass to a dignified end. Bach's turn to Renaissance vocal style certainly seems to be a more fitting conclusion for a large setting of the Ordinary than the $\frac{6}{8}$-meter dances that close many Viennese Masses of the time. Wolff has raised the possibility that the first fugue subject of "Wir danken dir"—and hence of the "Gratias" and "Dona nobis" as well—is based on the concluding phrase, "Deo dicamus gratias" ("Let us give thanks to God"), of the *Benedicamus dominicale* chant that was sung at the end of Leipzig worship service each Sunday (Example 5–14).[34] If that is true, the link would have made the use of the "Wir danken dir" music all the more suitable.

SUMMARY

While the "Sanctus" has received unanimous praise since its rediscovery in the nineteenth century, the "Osanna," "Benedictus," "Agnus Dei," and "Dona nobis" have been judged harshly at times. Criticism of the music following the "Sanctus" began with Spitta, who was uneasy about the role of the four pieces in the Lutheran worship service. As far as Spitta could discern, the movements could have served but one function: Communion music, played during the distribution of the Eucharistic bread and wine. The separate title pages for the "Sanctus" and the "Osanna" to "Dona nobis" seemed to substantiate this conclusion:

> Thus Bach performed both sections in the course of one service, so that the preface ended with the *Sanctus*, then the Sacramental words were recited, and afterwards, during the distribution of the Lord's Supper the *Osanna, Benedictus, Agnus,* and *Dona* were sung as a consecutive whole.[35]

Spitta believed it was for this reason that the "Osanna" had the character of an introductory chorus rather than a finale (the music's function as both in *Es lebe der König*, in which the opening chorus is repeated at the close, was unknown at the time), and the lack of an opening sinfonia for the movement would have been remedied in the worship service by an organ prelude. Bach's heavy reliance on parody in the "Osanna" to "Dona nobis" portion was thus explained: since the music was performed "sub communione," it was not as important as the other sections of the B-Minor Mass, and as a consequence, Bach dispatched it, in Spitta's words, "with no great effort."

Smend voiced similar reservations. In the Critical Report for the *Neue Bach-Ausgabe,* he proclaimed the music after the "Sanctus" "distinctly inferior to what comes before" and suggested that the artistic gulf between the "Osanna" to "Dona nobis" movements and the rest of the Mass is visible even in Bach's notation: the unused staves in the "Dona nobis" reflected, he felt, a certain indifference on Bach's part.[36] Nowhere else, aside from the inserts for the "Et incarnatus" and the revised "Et in unum Dominum" (which Smend viewed as not entirely convincing), does one find such a notational lapse. With the "Gratias" model in front of him, Bach should have been able to calculate the staves needed for the "Dona nobis." Going further, Smend expanded Spitta's *sub communione* thesis, pointing out (correctly) that while the text of "Hauptmusik" was normally printed and distributed to the Leipzig congregation, that of Communion music was not, presumably because people were not paying much attention as they came forward for the Eucharist.[37] Smend also cited statements from Bach's time saying that when Latin-texted music was performed, the laity could not comprehend the words. Played as background music without a printed text sheet, sung in an antiquated language, the "Osanna" to "Dona nobis" movements were understandably of secondary importance, Smend reasoned.

The issues raised by Spitta and Smend are "problems," of course, only if one attempts to fit the B-Minor Mass into the context of a Lutheran service. If the work is viewed as a setting of the Catholic Ordinary and the "Osanna" and "Benedictus" are not wrenched from the "Sanctus," Bach's music and organization plan make a great deal of sense, as Dadelsen and others have pointed out more recently. While the texts of the Sanctus and Agnus Dei do not lend themselves quite as readily to the same type of grand architectonic schemes as the tripartite supplications of the Kyrie and the extended phrases of the Gloria and Credo, they nevertheless provide opportunities for musical continuity. Within the Catholic rite, the Sanctus sequence—"Sanctus," "Pleni sunt coeli," "Osanna," "Benedictus," "Osanna"—is performed without pause. The same is true of the Agnus Dei sequence, which follows shortly thereafter in the Eucharist. Spitta and Smend overlooked Bach's conscious efforts to unite the final movements in a variety of ways: the direct union of the "Sanctus" and "Pleni," the metrical and motivic links between the "Pleni" and "Osanna," the willful elimination of the sinfonia in the "Osanna" music to tighten the connection with the "Pleni," the revised final cadence of the "Agnus Dei" that echoes the final cadence of the "Benedictus" and presages the opening of the "Dona nobis," the unified vocal and instrumental scoring of the "Osanna" and the "Dona nobis," and the use of polychoral techniques in both the "Sanctus" and the "Osanna." The presence of so many coalescent features can hardly be coincidental. In Dresden, court composers commonly created a *Missa tota* by manufacturing *ad hoc* Credo, Sanctus, and Agnus Dei movements from the Kyrie and Gloria music of a *Missa*. Bach's concept of the Ordinary obviously went far beyond the Dresden makeshift approach.

In performance, the change of forces first in the "Sanctus" and then in the "Osanna" to "Dona nobis" would have necessitated a change of vocal and instrumental parts. As we discussed in Chapter 2, the title pages for each segment seem to anticipate this practical concern, since they are most probably the remnants of wrappers that Bach typically used to store the score and performance parts of individual works. In addition, the fascicle structure of the *P 180* manuscript shows Bach thinking in terms of liturgical groupings: the "Sanctus" is set forth in one gathering; the "Osanna" and "Benedictus," which would be performed with the "Sanctus" in the Catholic Mass, are set forth in another; and the "Agnus Dei" and "Dona nobis," which would be performed together as a separate group, are set forth in yet another.[38]

The final portions of the B-Minor Mass admittedly contain little new music. Spitta realized that four movements were parodies and suspected that the "Benedictus" music was borrowed as well. To Spitta and Smend, the reliance on old scores stood as a sign that Bach was less interested in the final movements. In the last thirty years scholars have come to suspect that most movements of the Kyrie, Gloria, and Credo, too, are derivative rather than original and to realize that while the "Sanctus" and "Dona nobis" of the closing section are straightforward adaptations, the "Agnus Dei" displays almost as much invention as a new composition. The degree of reworking in the "Osanna" and "Benedictus" cannot be judged fully, since the models (if one indeed existed for the "Benedictus") are not longer extant.

One thing is certain. In the music of the Sanctus and Agnus Dei, Bach shows the same concern for stylistic diversity seen in the Kyrie, Gloria, and Credo. In the arias, he considers the ritornello form ("Benedictus") and the da capo form ("Agnus Dei") once again. In both movements he proposes new and unusually concise designs. In the choruses he covers the Baroque *stile moderno* ("Sanctus" and "Osanna") as well as the Renaissance *a cappella* style ("Dona nobis"). Indeed, the desire to include *a cappella* style in the final portion may be yet another reason that he reached back to the "Gratias." Most significantly, in the concluding sections Bach introduces the one style not found in the Kyrie, Gloria, and Credo: the polychoral chorus. Here, too, he sets forth diverse possibilities. The "Sanctus," with its heterogeneous scoring of string, woodwind, brass, and varying vocal choirs, and its dense "Pleni" fugue, illustrates the seventeenth-century Germanic approach to polychoral writing. The "Osanna," with two equal choirs and a single tutti band, and a more homophonic texture, illustrates the more straightforward eighteenth-century Italian approach, complete with Venetian *piano-forte* echoes.

These factors refute the reservations of Spitta and Smend—as do the pieces themselves. Is it possible to listen to the contrapuntal interplay of the "Osanna" or the intricate *Affekts* of the "Agnus Dei" and say that the music represents a decline in interest on the composer's part? Far from being the products of indifference, or "a sort of catch-all," as Joshua Rifkin once put it,[39] the Sanctus and Agnus Dei emerge as equal partners with the Kyrie, Gloria, and Credo. They represent a unique solution to the problem of creating substantial settings for the final portions of the Mass Ordinary. Following the Kyrie, Gloria, and Credo, they bring Bach's "Great Catholic Mass" to a weighty and dignified close.

Chapter 6

THE B-MINOR MASS AFTER BACH'S DEATH: SURVIVAL, REVIVAL, AND REINTERPRETATION

THE SURVIVAL OF THE MANUSCRIPT MATERIALS

The B-Minor Mass was not published during Bach's lifetime, and it was of little practical use to contemporary musicians. Thus we are fortunate that it survived the half-century following Bach's death, a period when his vocal music attracted little interest. Fate smiled favorably on the manuscript materials of the B-Minor Mass—the Dresden performance parts of the *Missa* and the composite score of the entire work. Were it not for good fortune, we might know little more of the B-Minor Mass than we do of the St. Mark Passion, an equally monumental piece that was lost sometime after 1754.[1]

The *Missa* parts and the score of the B-Minor Mass took very different routes to their present homes. The *Missa* parts, which Bach had presented to Elector Friedrich August II in 1733, stayed in Dresden as part of the Royal Music Collection. There they remained unnoticed until the 1830s, when they were spotted by the Bach enthusiast and manuscript collector Franz Hauser.[2] Hauser shared his discovery with Felix Mendelssohn, who viewed the parts in 1846 and used them to correct his personal copy of the Nägeli edition of the Kyrie and Gloria. Hard at work on his own vocal masterpiece, *Elijah*, Mendelssohn reported to his friend Carl Klingemann:

I obtained from Dresden the parts to the Bach B-Minor Mass (do you recall our Fridays with Zelter?) and from these, which Bach mostly wrote himself and dedicated to the Elector of the time ("To His Most Royal Highness and Elector . . . whose grace shines on Saxony, please accept the enclosed Mass as a sign of . . . the abject devotion of its author J. S. Bach"), I little by little freed my own score from its host of printing errors, which I had noticed, of course, but never had the opportunity to rectify properly.[3]

The Royal Music Collection was transferred to the Saxon State Library in 1896. The *Missa* parts were given their present-day call number, *Mus. 2405–D–21*, in conjunction with the move.

During World War II the *Missa* parts were evacuated from Dresden and consequently survived the Allied bombing raids of February 1945. After the war they were returned to the Saxon State Library, where they remain today. A facsimile edition was issued by Hänssler Verlag in 1983.[4] Bach's dedicatory letter to the Elector was stored separately during the war and perished. It is known today through prewar transcriptions and photographs.[5]

The autograph score of the B-Minor Mass traveled a much more circuitous path to its present location. The score's destiny—and probably its ultimate survival—was determined in the fall of 1750, when Bach's musical estate was divided among his heirs. Although the bulk of the sacred vocal works went to Wilhelm Friedemann, who as organist of the Liebfrauenkirche in Halle had the most use for church pieces, the B-Minor Mass went to Carl Philipp Emanuel. Friedemann was later forced to sell most of his inheritance (including the now-lost scores of the chorale cantatas and the score and parts of the St. Mark Passion). Emanuel, by contrast, made every effort to preserve the manuscripts he received from his father's estate. Characteristically, he retained the B-Minor Mass score to the end of his life. If the manuscript had gone to Friedemann, we would probably have only the Dresden *Missa* portion today.

At first, even Emanuel may not have comprehended the extraordinary nature of the B-Minor Mass. He made no special mention of it in the lengthy Obituary of his father that he helped to prepare in 1754. There we read only of a large body of unpublished miscellaneous vocal compositions: "Many oratorios, Masses, Magnificats, single Sanctus settings, secular cantatas, serenades, cantatas for birthdays, name days, and funerals, wedding cantatas, and several comic vocal pieces."[6] Sometime between 1750 and 1768, however, Emanuel had one of his Berlin scribes (known in modern Bach schol-

arship as Anonymous 300) write out a copy of the autograph score, a copy
that he then revised and appears to have sold or given away (it was no longer
in his possession at the time of his death). The manuscript survives today in
the Berlin State Library as the three-part complex *P 572 (Missa)/P 23
(Symbolum Nicenum)/P 14* ("Sanctus" to "Dona nobis pacem").

Emanuel left Berlin in 1768 to assume the position of Town Kantor and
Music Director in Hamburg. The next year he produced another copy of the
B-Minor Mass from the autograph score, this time for his father's former stu-
dent Johann Philipp Kirnberger, who was serving as court composer and
music advisor for Frederick the Great's sister Anna Amalia in Berlin.
Emanuel's letter to Kirnberger of July 21, 1769, describes the transaction:

> I had a few leaves of the Mass copied, but they were full of errors. So
> I tore them up and am sending you the original. Do take care and don't
> write in it, and send it back to me after you have made a copy. The
> beginning is somewhat torn, but the remainder is fine. No fee is
> required for the return, for I have prepaid the postage. Perhaps you
> would like to show the Mass to our Princess.[7]

Kirnberger's copy seems to be the Berlin State Library manuscript
Am.B. 3, which was made by a professional scribe working at Amalia's
court. A second Berlin manuscript, *Am.B. 1-Am.B. 2*, also penned by a
court amanuensis, may represent a further copy made specifically for the
Princess. Through these manuscripts the B-Minor Mass gained an early toehold in Berlin.

In 1786 Emanuel presented the *Symbolum Nicenum* of the B-Minor
Mass in a Hamburg benefit concert for the Medical Institute for the Poor.
For the performance (to which we will return in the next section), he edited
and revised the music of the Credo portion, writing changes directly into his
father's autograph. While this strikes us today as an unforgivable sin, it was
not at all unusual in the eighteenth century, when music manuscripts were
viewed as working tools (this attitude obtained even in the first half of the
nineteenth century: when Friedrich Conrad Griepenkerl edited Bach's
organ works for the Peters edition in the 1840s, he sometimes jotted down
variant readings in the manuscripts themselves). Since Emanuel's alterations in the Credo occasionally obscure his father's text, the *P 23, Am.B.
3*, and *Am.B. 1-Am.B. 2* manuscripts, copied before the changes were made,
are of great importance for deciphering the original readings of the autograph score (see Plate 6–1).

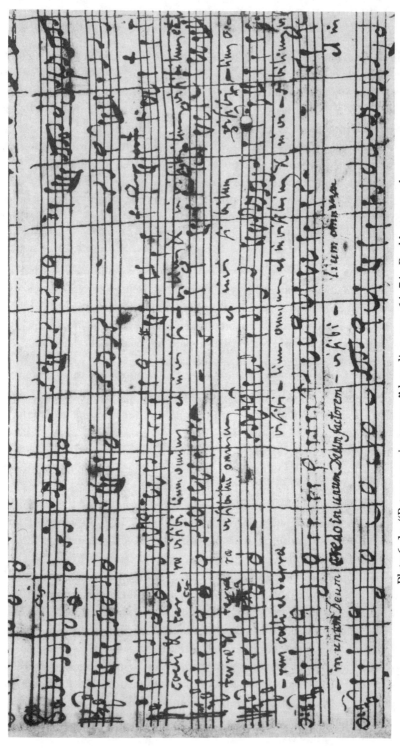

Plate 6–1a. "Patrem omnipotentem," bass line, mm. 64–74: Bach's autograph, with C. P. E. Bach's "Credo in unum Deum" revision of 1786 (Berlin State Library, *P 180*).

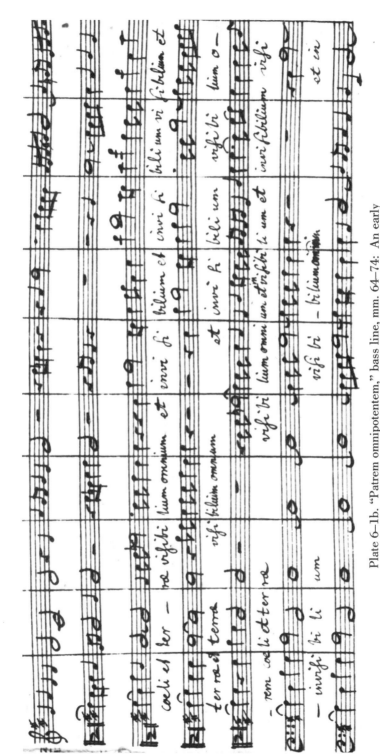

Plate 6–1b. "Patrem omnipotentem," bass line, mm. 64–74: An early Berlin copy of the autograph, showing the original text (Berlin State Library, *P 23*).

Shortly after Emanuel's death in 1788 the autograph score of the B-Minor Mass was offered for sale. In the 1790 catalogue of his estate, we find the work listed as "Die große catholische Messe"—"The Great Catholic Mass"—consisting of four manuscripts: *Missa, Symbolum Nicaenum, Sanctus,* and *Osanna.* Each manuscript is described as an "eigenhändige Partitur"—"a score in the composer's hand." Thus the original B-Minor Mass "score" was probably a group of four discrete manuscripts, each enclosed in a folder of which only the front portion, with the title and required forces, survives. This idea was first posed by Arnold Schering in 1936 and has been reiterated more recently by Georg von Dadelsen.[8] Bach stored most of his works in folders as unbound leaves, a format that greatly facilitated performance and copying. The binding that once enclosed the manuscript of the B-Minor Mass probably stemmed from the nineteenth century.[9]

There were no takers for the B-Minor Mass manuscript in 1790, and with the death of Emanuel's last heir in 1804, his daughter Anna Carolina Philippina, it was put up for sale a second time. In the auction catalogue of 1805 the manuscript is listed once again as "The Great Catholic Mass," giving some weight to the notion that the epithet reflects an oral tradition within the Bach family.

This time the score met with a buyer, the Swiss music publisher Hans Georg Nägeli. In 1818 Nägeli announced his intention to issue the B-Minor Mass in a printed edition at the Leipzig Easter Fair the following year (we will return to his announcement shortly), but for want of subscribers the project was postponed indefinitely. It was not until 1833 that he succeeded in releasing Part I, the Kyrie and Gloria, "engraved from the autograph." Nägeli kept the autograph under close wraps, and after his death in 1836 his son Hermann did the same. Hermann completed the publication of the B-Minor Mass in 1845, releasing the second and final part, Credo, Sanctus, and Agnus Dei, again "engraved from the autograph." But in 1850, when the newly formed Bach-Gesellschaft wished to inaugurate their scholarly edition of Bach's complete works with the B-Minor Mass, Nägeli refused to let them see the autograph manuscript. The Bach-Gesellschaft postponed publication of the Mass for a number of years, until Julius Rietz finally edited the piece from the Dresden parts and secondary manuscripts. His edition appeared in 1856 as volume 6 of the *Bach-Gesamtausgabe.* By this time, however, the Nägeli firm was running into financial difficulties, and in 1857 Hermann sold the B-Minor Mass score to Arnold Wehner, Kapellmeister at the Royal Court in Hanover, under the mistaken impression that Wehner was acting on behalf of King George V.[10]

Wehner's true backer was the famous Handel scholar Friedrich Chrysander, who immediately turned the manuscript over to the Bach-Gesellschaft for use in reediting volume 6 of the *Bach-Gesamtausgabe*. A revised edition, with a new preface by Rietz, was issued in 1857. With the editing work completed, the Bach-Gesellschaft sold the B-Minor Mass manuscript in 1861 to the Royal Library in Berlin, predecessor of the Berlin State Library. There, ironically, it was reunited with the bulk of Emanuel Bach's estate, which had entered the library twenty years earlier with the purchase of Georg Poelchau's large collection of Bach manuscripts. The autograph was assigned its modern call number *Mus.ms.Bach P 180,* or *P 180* for short.

In 1895 thirty-six pages of the autograph score appeared in facsimile in volume 44 of the *Bach-Gesamtausgabe* ("Johann Sebastian Bach's Handwriting in Chronologically Arranged Reproductions").[11] In 1924 Insel-Verlag issued a facsimile of the complete score.[12] In the 1930s the manuscript was thoroughly restored, and pages suffering from *Tintenfraß* (the acidic action of the ink on the paper) were laminated with thin sheets of silk gauze. During World War II the manuscript was evacuated from Berlin to the Beuron Monastery on the Danube for safekeeping. After a stay in the Music Library of Tübingen University, it was returned to the Preussischer Kulturbesitz division of the Berlin State Library in 1967. It is now part of the reunited State Library collection. In 1965 Bärenreiter issued a new facsimile edition, using plates from the Insel facsimile for a number of pages that were in poor condition.[13] At present the manuscript is again in a perilous state and unavailable to scholars. It is scheduled for further restoration.

A CURIOSITY FOR CONNOISSEURS (1750–1800)

While Bach's keyboard works enjoyed wide circulation and performance in the second half of the eighteenth century, his vocal pieces generally sat in oblivion on cabinet shelves. Such was the fate of the B-Minor Mass: between 1750 and 1800 it was little more than an historical curiosity, known only to a small group of connoisseurs who were devoted to preserving and studying Bach's compositions as precious relics. We can document only one performance of music from the B-Minor Mass during this time. Yet through word of mouth and circulation of manuscript copies, knowledge of the work spread slowly but steadily from Bach circles in Berlin and Hamburg to more distant regions, preparing the way for the full-scale resurrection that was to take place in the nineteenth century.

Christoph Nichelmann, a composer and theorist who attended the St. Thomas School from 1730 to 1733, seems to have been the first to mention the B-Minor Mass in print. In his 1755 treatise, *Die Melodie nach ihrem Wesen sowohl, als nach ihren Eigenschaften* ("Melody According to its Nature as well as its Properties"), he printed the *adagio* introduction to "Kyrie" I as a masterful example of harmonization, one in which "the natural *Affekt* of the melodic line is fully realized through the use of strong, expressive, appropriate chords."[14] As second harpsichordist at the court of Frederick the Great, Nichelmann undoubtedly learned of the work from Frederick's first harpsichordist, C. P. E. Bach, who, as we have seen, owned the original manuscript of the work between 1750 and 1788.

Some twenty years passed before the B-Minor Mass was again mentioned in print. Kirnberger, who had come to know the piece through the copy procured from C. P. E. Bach, cited it twice in *Die Kunst des reinen Satzes* ("The Art of Strict Musical Composition"). In the discussion of ostinato technique, he presented the ground bass from the "Crucifixus," describing it as "a tenvoice example . . . from a Mass by J. S. Bach, full of invention, imitation, canon, counterpoint, and beautiful melody"; in the chapter on meters, he referred to the "Credo in unum Deum" as a rare example of $\frac{2}{1}$ time: "I know of only one Credo by the elder Bach in the large alla breve of two beats, which he designated, however, with $\mathbf{C}$ to show that the rests have the same value as in ordinary alla breve."[15] Around the same time, another Bach student, Johann Friedrich Agricola, also pointed to the "Credo" in a discussion of $\frac{2}{1}$ meter: "From the modern age the reviewer has in hand a piece of this very type on the words *Credo in unum Deum,* from a great Mass by the late J. S. Bach with eight obbligato voices, namely five vocal parts, two violins, and general bass."[16] And in an Amalia Library manuscript from the 1780s that probably represents the draft of an unrealized treatise by Kirnberger, we find the "Kyrie" I fugue subject and answer quoted in a discussion of fugue-writing techniques.[17]

To Nichelmann, Kirnberger, Agricola, and others, the B-Minor Mass represented an *exemplum classicum*—a classical model to be studied and revered. The work was of particular attraction from a theoretical standpoint because it illustrated musical arts that were rapidly vanishing from the scene. It was the *antico* and fugal movements that were of interest; the *moderno* sections were hopelessly out of date. Performing the B-Minor Mass did not come into question, and hence it is no surprise that the work circulated not in parts, the form desired by practical musicians, but in score, the form ideal for contemplation.

Viewed in this light, C. P. E. Bach's decision to present the complete *Symbolum Nicenum* at a benefit concert for Hamburg's Medical Institute for the Poor in the spring of 1786 appears as a bold stroke. Emanuel's program was a *potpourri* of the type much loved by middle-class audiences in the late eighteenth and early nineteenth centuries. It was a *potpourri* with an unusual, retrospective slant, however, one that foreshadowed by a half-century Mendelssohn's famous "historical concerts" at the Leipzig Gewandhaus (which were also to include music from the B-Minor Mass). With the exception of the Introduction and possibly the unidentified Sinfonie, the music was "old"—a rare occurrence in concerts of the time:

Introduction by Herr Kapellmeister Bach [H. 848]

Credo, or Nicene Creed, by the late Herr Johann Sebastian Bach

Aria, "I know that my redeemer liveth," by Handel

"Hallelujah" by Handel

Sinfonie by Herr Kapellmeister Bach [unspecified]

Magnificat, or Mary's Hymn of Praise, by Herr Kapellmeister Bach [H. 772, 1749]

Heilig, for Double Chorus, by Herr Kapellmeister Bach [H. 778, c.1776]

The presence of music from *Messiah* suggests that Emanuel knew of the highly popular revivals of Handel's large-scale choral works—and of *Messiah*, in particular—that were taking place in England, Germany, and Vienna. His decision to attempt the Credo may, in fact, have been influenced by the success of the Handel concerts.

Emanuel arranged the Credo score especially for the Hamburg program, fashioning what we would call today a "practical edition." Extant materials from the event—a set of performance parts, *St 118,* and a score, *P 22,* both in the Berlin State Library—allow us to follow his changes in detail. He began by prefacing the *Symbolum* with a twenty-eight-measure Introduction of his own composition. Written for four-part strings in the style of a *Vorimitation* organ chorale prelude (a prelude in which each phrase of the chorale melody is foreshadowed by a series of imitative entries), the music is based on the German Gloria hymn, *Allein Gott in der höh sei Ehr,* which appears in long notes in the bottom voice as a *cantus firmus* (Example 6–1).[18] The Introduction is set in A mixolydian and leads directly into the "Credo in unum Deum" movement, in the same key.

Within the *Symbolum,* Emanuel altered the instrumentation here and there. Like Mendelssohn some forty years later, he had to work around the problem of the oboe d'amore, the alto instrument much beloved by Saxon composers of his father's generation but now obsolete. For the St. Matthew Passion, Mendelssohn simply substituted clarinets. For the Credo, Emanuel

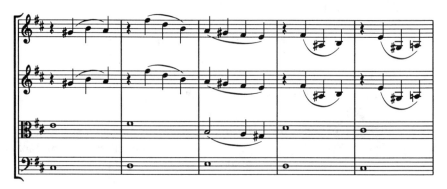

Example 6–1. C. P. E. Bach: Introduction to the Credo.

took a varied approach: in the aria "Et in unum Dominum" he replaced the oboes d'amore with normal oboes, rewriting the parts where necessary to bring them into a higher range. In the aria "Et in Spiritum Sanctum," where the oboe d'amore lines are fully obbligato and not easily revised, he replaced the instruments altogether with violins.

Other changes of instrumentation seem to have been motivated by aesthetic considerations. In the "Crucifixus" Emanuel substituted oboes for the flutes, perhaps to create a darker timbre (one thinks of Mozart's Requiem score of 1791, which calls for sombre reeds rather than flutes). In the "Patrem omnipotentem" Emanuel altered the notes and Latin text of the bass voice toward the end (mm. 69–72), introducing the words "Credo in unum Deum" once again to heighten the "Credo Mass" effect and further strengthen the ties between the "Patrem" and the "Credo" (Plate 6–1, above).

These changes reflect practical circumstances and Emanuel's personal tastes. Other alterations, such as *colla parte* instrumentation in the "Credo in unum Deum" (Plate 6–2) and the "Confiteor," paired violin slurrings in the "Et in unum Dominum," and *tasto solo* indications in the continuo part of several movements, may be closer to his father's style than generally assumed and cannot be summarily dismissed as *Empfindsamkeit* updatings. We will return to these matters in Chapter 7.

The care with which Emanuel arranged the Credo underscores his dedication to his father's masterpiece (and the tremorous appearance of his handwriting reminds us that the reworking was no easy task for the seventy-two-year-old—see Plate 6–2). To judge from a contemporary review in the Hamburg *Correspondent*, the *Symbolum* was favorably received:

> Hamburg. Among the things that were performed with great approbation at the four concerts given this year for the Medical Institute for the Poor were funeral music and a coronation anthem by Handel, *Armide* by Salieri, *Alceste* by Gluck, *Magnificat* and *Heilig* by C. P. E. Bach, and a Credo by Johann Sebastian Bach. Here one had the opportunity to observe different artifices in the works of the famous, above-named composers and the effect created by the performance of their compositions. Especially admirable was the five-voice Credo of the immortal Sebastian Bach, which is one of the most outstanding musical works that has ever been heard. The vocal parts must be sufficiently manned if it is to achieve its full effect, however. Once again our gallant singers displayed their well-known skill both in meeting and executing the most difficult passages, especially in the Credo. And in all four concerts several female dilettantes ["Liebhaberinnen"] caused the liveliest pleasure through their fine voices and tasteful execution.[19]

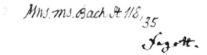

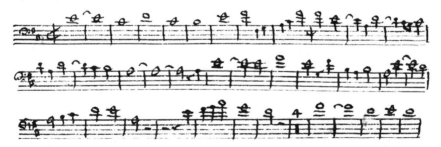

Plate 6–2. C. P. E. Bach's 1786 *colla parte* bassoon part for the "Credo" (Berlin State Library, *St 118*).

The *St 118* performance materials include just one part per voice and instrument,[20] which points to modest forces closer in nature to the Dresden *Missa* ensemble of 1733 than to the choral-society groups of the nineteenth century. Did Emanuel wish to use such forces, or was he compelled to do so by financial considerations? For church performances in Hamburg he normally employed a small professional group consisting of twelve to fifteen instrumentalists and eight to ten singers.[21] The Credo ensemble of 1786, which seems to have been along the same lines, may thus reflect a Baroque approach that was still normal practice. We will return to this matter, too, in Chapter 7.

Historians have long hailed Emanuel's concert as the initial step in the posthumous rise of the B-Minor Mass. True, it demonstrated the work's potential as a concert piece, played outside the worship service before a paying, public audience. But it also marked the emergence of what we might call a "Credo cult." Emanuel's selection of the Credo rather than the Kyrie, Gloria, Sanctus, or Agnus Dei was surely not just a practical matter. With its tightly organized form and its inner drama—qualities we examined in Chapter 4—the Credo stands as the most transcendent segment of the Mass. No other portion displays such a wide range of styles, such rich chromaticism, such stunning transitions. Emanuel's choice of the Credo may well have represented an artistic judgment on his part, that this portion of the B-Minor Mass most fully represented his father's late aesthetic ideals.

The numerous early manuscript copies of the Credo alone—there are at least seven[22]—also point to an unusual interest in the segment. No other section was circulated independently to such a great degree. Three of the Credo copies can be connected with England and most probably stem from the famous English traveler, music historian, and *homme des lettres* Charles Burney. Writing in 1789 in his *General History of Music,* Burney reported:

> Sebastian Bach set innumerable cantatas for the church, besides the Sanctus three times, with accompaniments, excellent in harmony and expression; *Kyrie cum Gloria* six times, all for four voices with instruments; with a *Credo* for five voices with accompaniments, of which I am in possession of the score, which is one of the most clear, correct, and masterly, I have ever seen.[23]

Burney almost certainly procured his Credo score directly from C. P. E. Bach, whom he visited in Hamburg in 1772, a full fourteen years before the Medical Institute performance. *P 1212,* a copy of the *Symbolum* in the

Berlin State Library with an English connection,[24] shows the music in its "unsullied," pre-1786 form and suggests that Emanuel was championing the Credo long before the Hamburg concert.

The 1786 performance, then, most likely represents the culmination of an extended—if low-key—campaign by C. P. E. Bach to promote the music of the Credo. His efforts even extended beyond the grave: after his death, the poet Christoph Daniel Ebeling, who had been present at the 1786 performance, recalled the Credo and christened it "the masterpiece of the greatest of all harmonists" in his memorial tribute to Emanuel.[25] And when Gaspare Spontini gave the premiere of music from the B-Minor Mass in his landmark Berlin concert of 1828 (to which we will turn shortly), he not only chose Emanuel's Credo arrangement but even used the 1786 Hamburg performance parts. Many other early concerts of B-Minor Mass music featured the Credo alone. C. P. E. Bach himself appears to have been the founder of this Credo cult.

Finally, the B-Minor Mass also gained a toehold in Vienna in the second half of the eighteenth century. Baron Gottfried van Swieten, the Austrian diplomat who introduced Haydn, Mozart, and Beethoven to Bach's keyboard music, owned a copy of the B-Minor Mass, according to the catalogue of his estate. Van Swieten served as ambassador to Berlin during the years 1770 to 1777 and was in close contact with C. P. E. Bach, Kirnberger, and Princess Amalia. It is likely that he obtained the B-Minor Mass at that time.[26]

A Second *Missa solemnis* for Choral Societies (The Nineteenth Century)

The transformation of the B-Minor Mass from historical curiosity to mainstay of the choral repertory began with the Bach Revival. Historians generally agree that this movement, which canonized Bach as a cultural hero and led to the resurrection of his "great choral works," was officially launched in 1802 with the publication of Johann Nikolaus Forkel's biography, *Über Johann Sebastian Bachs Leben, Kunst und Kunstwerke* ("On Johann Sebastian Bach's Life, Art, and Works"). Working with information supplied some thirty years earlier by Wilhelm Friedemann and Carl Philipp Emanuel Bach, Forkel sketched a concise but vivid portrait of Sebastian Bach as an industrious and highly skilled performer, composer, and teacher. Forkel focused mainly on Bach's accomplishments as a keyboard virtuoso and mentioned the vocal works only in passing, making no reference whatsoever to the St. John Passion, the St. Matthew Passion, or the B-Minor Mass. Nevertheless, by discussing Bach's lineage and moral character, by emphasizing his regimen of steady self-improvement, and by delineating his triumphs as a musician of modest roots working amidst unappreciative aristocratic employers, Forkel laid the groundwork for viewing Bach as a Romantic genius, a *Davidsbündler*-like figure battling for the cause of art against philistine forces. It would not be long before the "Crucifixus" of the B-Minor Mass would be granted a psychological dimension and taken to epitomize Bach's personal struggle, much as the Fifth Symphony was taken to represent Beethoven's.

Forkel also presented Bach as an object of nationalistic pride, dedicating *Über Johann Sebastian Bachs Leben, Kunst und Kunstwerke* to "Patriotic admirers of true musical art" and admonishing those admirers to emulate the composer's accomplishments:

> Only through the union of the greatest genius with the most indefatigable study was Johann Sebastian Bach able to extend, no matter which way he turned, the bounds of his art so greatly that his successors have never once been in the position to expand this enlarged domain in its whole extent. This alone enabled him to produce such numerous and such perfect works, all of which are and will forever remain true ideals and imperishable models of art.
>
> And this man, the greatest musical poet and the greatest musical orator that ever existed, and probably ever will exist, was a German. Let our country be proud of him. Let it be proud, but, at the same time, worthy of him![27]

It was precisely this type of nationalistic temperament that spurred the rescuers of the B-Minor Mass.

In the first decade of the nineteenth century, however, those wishing to follow in Bach's footsteps and emulate his "imperishable models" had difficulty doing so, at least in the case of the B-Minor Mass. Available in manuscript only, the work was painfully inaccessible. Haydn, according to his estate catalogue, owned a manuscript copy and was thus among the privileged few to know the piece in its entirety. Beethoven, by contrast, attempted without success to procure the B-Minor Mass score. On October 15, 1810, he wrote from Vienna to the music-publishing house of Breitkopf &

Härtel in Leipzig, requesting a copy of the work and quoting, most probably from Kirnberger's *Die Kunst des reinen Satzes,*[28] the ground bass from the "Crucifixus" "which it is said to contain." Breitkopf & Härtel was a good bet for obtaining the work, since the firm maintained a large manuscript inventory of Bach vocal works and produced handwritten copies of individual pieces on demand. Unfortunately, Breitkopf's stock did not include the B-Minor Mass.[29] On September 9, 1824, apparently still without a copy, Beethoven made a second attempt to get one, writing directly to Nägeli in Zurich, who, as we have seen, was then in possession of Bach's autograph. This effort, too, appears to have been fruitless, for there is no evidence of the Bach work in Beethoven's estate at the time of his death. Thus Beethoven composed the *Missa solemnis,* op. 123, without first-hand knowledge of the B-Minor Mass. It was left to Romantic performers and critics to place the two grand vocal works side by side.

If Beethoven had resided in Berlin, matters might have been different. There the Bach tradition was more vigorous than it was in Vienna and the B-Minor Mass more readily available. In 1811, just one year after Beethoven's request to Breitkopf, the Berlin *Singakademie* began to read through Bach's "Great Mass." Founded by the conductor and composer Carl Friedrich Fasch in 1791, the *Singakademie* gathered weekly to study masterpieces of the choral repertory. Germany's first bourgeois choral society, it was a world apart from Emanuel's *Symbolum* ensemble of 1786. Composed mainly of enthusiastic amateurs, it grew steadily in size, from thirty-seven members its first year to almost 200 by the second decade of the nineteenth century (Mendelssohn's famous *Singakademie* performance of the St. Matthew Passion in 1829 featured 158 singers plus a large instrumental ensemble drawn chiefly from the membership).[30] Fasch led readings from the piano—a tradition continued by his successors—and for difficult works held pre-rehearsals with a smaller group. The *Singakademie* repertory included Bach's music almost from the start. In 1794 Fasch introduced the motets one by one, spending half a year on *Komm, Jesu, Komm,* BWV 229, before moving on to *Fürchte dich nicht,* BWV 228, and *Singet dem Herrn ein neues Lied,* BWV 225. With a large, unwieldy group of nonprofessionals, progress was slow.

When Fasch died in 1800, the *Singakademie* directorship fell to his student Carl Friedrich Zelter, one of the most important early proponents of Bach's vocal music. Zelter continued the systematic study of the motets but in 1807 began to read through Bach's instrumental pieces with a small group of ten *Singakademie* members. From there he turned to the concerted vocal works: cantatas, passions, and oratorios. According to the weekly register, Zelter introduced the B-Minor Mass on October 25, 1811, and by November had led the group through the three movements of the Kyrie portion. He then set the music aside until September 1813, when he guided his singers through the entire Mass over the course of three sessions. During the winter of 1814–1815 Zelter returned to the work, reading selected choruses and arias. Although the B-Minor Mass does not reappear in the register, Zelter must have picked it up again, for, as we have seen, Mendelssohn, who joined the *Singakademie* in 1820 as an eleven-year-old alto with his fifteen-year-old sister Fanny (Zelter assessed both as "usable"), later recalled reading through it at the weekly meetings.

We can only speculate on the details of Zelter's approach to the B-Minor Mass, since his *Singakademie* score was lost in World War II.[31] Georg Schünemann, who examined Zelter's manuscript in the 1920s, states that in the "Quoniam tu solus Sanctus" Zelter suggested that the corne da caccia be replaced with a flute, and the bassoons with basset horns or muted cellos. In addition, the text displayed changes and simplifications, especially in the solo sections.[32] In the St. John Passion and other vocal works, Zelter did not hesitate to modify Bach's lines in order to tone down what he considered to be overly ornate extravagances.[33] There is no reason to doubt that he followed the same procedure in the B-Minor Mass.

To Zelter and his contemporaries, Bach's aria writing was too florid, too complicated, too *Baroque*. It was the choruses, with their dense textures, rich chromatic harmonies, and more straightforward vocal writing, that deeply touched Romantic sensibilities. Like Beethoven, Zelter was drawn to the "Crucifixus." As he wrote to Goethe:

> A "passus et sepultus" leads to the last pulse of the silent Might, a "resurrexit" or "In gloria dei patris" to the eternal regions of blessed death compared with the hollowness of the earthly endeavors. It is as if this feeling were indivisible, and it would be difficult to present it as a melody or something tangible.[34]

With Zelter's *Singakademie* readings, and with the growing interest in Bach's choral works in general, enthusiasm for the B-Minor Mass increased, so much so that during the years 1816–1818 three attempts were made to bring the work to print. In February 1816 Samuel Wesley, champion of Bach's music in England, proposed the idea of publishing the Credo to demonstrate Bach's skill in vocal composition. For want of sufficient subscribers, the project came to naught. In June 1818 in the Leipzig *Allgemeine musikalische Zeitung* Nägeli announced his intention to print the complete Mass, and one month later the journal reported that Georg Poelchau (who had joined the *Singakademie* in 1814) planned to undertake the same endeavor. Of these two, it was Nägeli who finally succeeded, though not for some time. His 1818 solicitation, in which he proclaimed Bach's composition "the greatest musical art-work of all times and all people," is a remarkable document, highlighting in print for the first time the transcendent qualities of the Mass. Once again we find the Credo portion singled out for high praise:

> In technical regards the work contains, in twenty-seven lengthy move-
> ments, all kinds of contrapuntal and canonic art, in which one can
> observe Bach's continuous and admirable perfection. The instrumen-
> tation, too, especially the art of interludes, is astonishingly well car-
> ried out. With respect to aesthetics, it is sufficient to cite the Credo,
> which Ebeling in his "Lobgesang auf die Harmonie" . . . described in
> verse as "the masterpiece of the greatest of all harmonists." This
> Credo (in itself the first extensive movement on the words "Credo in
> unum deum" alone) is probably the most wonderful musical art-work
> in existence. The difficult task, often discussed by the judges of music
> in his time and our own, of how the Credo is to be handled by church
> composers, stands here resolved in an eternal model. In it, the
> strength of faith is revived through the strength of art.[35]

Nägeli concluded by claiming that study of the B-Minor Mass was as salutary for musicians as a trip to Rome for artists. In spite of great expec-tations, his words fell on deaf ears, and the project lay dormant for the next decade.

The year 1828 witnessed the first public performances of music from the B-Minor Mass in the nineteenth century, in Frankfurt on March 10 and in Berlin on April 30. Both featured the *Symbolum Nicenum* alone.

The March performance was given by the *Cäcilien-Verein*, the Society of St. Cecilia, under the direction of its founder, Johann Nepomuk Schelble. Like the *Singakademie*, the *Cäcilien-Verein* was an amateur choral associa-tion, with a membership of about 200. Schelble himself described the preparations and performance of the *Symbolum:* the members of the *Verein* were initially biased against Bach's work because of its extreme difficulties, and in the first rehearsal chaos reigned. But Schelble persevered, working through the movements little by little, and by the first orchestral rehearsal, all confessed that they had never encountered anything "richer or more elevated."[36] Some two hundred musicians took part in the March performance, with an orchestra that included 18 violins, 4 violas, 4 cellos, and 2 double basses. Performance indications in the conducting score show that Schelble augmented the instrumentation with bassoons, clarinets, and horns, which he used to double vocal as well as instrumental lines in the choruses. Crescendo, diminuendo, ritardando, and other expressive markings point to a heavily Romantic interpretation (Plate 6–3).

Adolf Bernhard Marx, the eminent theorist, critic, and early advocate of Bach's music, reviewed the concert and, in general, praised the performance.[37] But he raised a larger issue: to understand the Credo truly, one had to hear it preceded by the "Cum sancto" of the Gloria and followed by the "Sanctus" and "Osanna." Proceeding further along these lines, Marx advocated a performance of the entire work. Three years later, in January 1831, the *Cäcilien-Verein* performed the Kyrie and Gloria portions; in April of the same year, the Kyrie, Gloria, and Credo; and in November, with Mendelssohn in attendance, the Credo once again. Two years later it presented the Gloria and the "Et incarnatus" and "Crucifixus" from the Credo. While the complete performance desired by Marx did not take place until 1861, the 1828–1833 concerts were critical in placing the music of the B-Minor Mass before the public. The *Cäcilien-Verein* pattern was soon to be repeated elsewhere in Germany, and in England, too: initial consternation over the technical difficulties of Bach's score, followed by a resolute struggle to master the music, followed by a triumphant public performance.

Associating the B-Minor Mass with the Romantic concept of struggle and triumph was even clearer in the April 1828 performance of the *Symbolum Nicenum* given in the Berlin Opera House by opera director Gaspare Spontini. Like C. P. E. Bach's Medical Institute concert of 1786, the Berlin program was a miscellany:

Beethoven: Fifth Symphony
Beethoven: Kyrie and Gloria from the *Missa solemnis*

Beethoven: Coriolanus Overture
J. S. Bach: *Symbolum Nicenum* from the B-Minor Mass [from "Credo in unum Deum" to "Et resurrexit" only]
C. P. E. Bach: *Heilig*

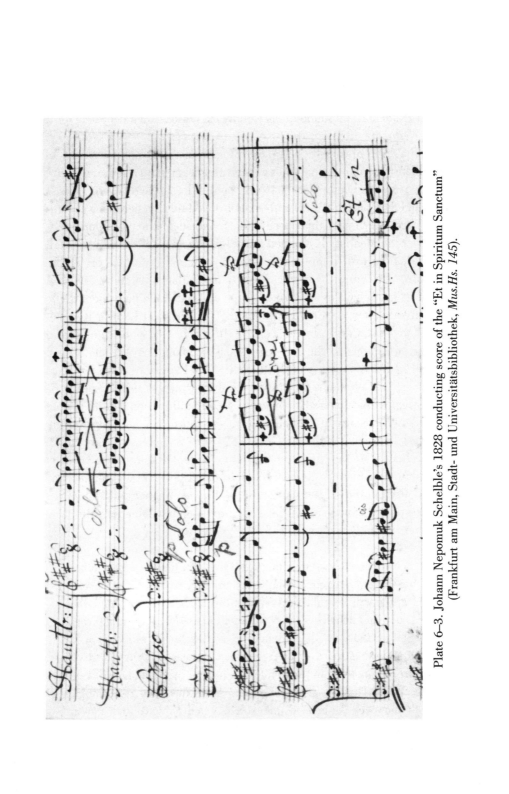

Plate 6–3. Johann Nepomuk Schelble's 1828 conducting score of the "Et in Spiritum Sanctum" (Frankfurt am Main, Stadt- und Universitätsbibliothek, *Mus.Hs. 145*).

Indeed, there was a direct connection with the 1786 concert, since Spontini used Emanuel's arrangement of the Credo (complete with the newly composed instrumental introduction) as well as his performance materials for it and the *Heilig*.[38]

But Spontini obviously had new programmatic goals in mind. As Gerhard Herz has noted, Spontini's concert represented, in a sense, a gigantic composite "concert Mass"—Kyrie and Gloria (Beethoven), Credo (Bach), and Sanctus (C. P. E. Bach)—that bridged three generations of composers.[39] Marx, reviewing this concert, too, found such a juxtaposition offensive.[40] Ever the idealist, he claimed that such a "mélange" would work well in Paris, "par curiosité," but not in Germany, where it would be preferable to perform the entire B-Minor Mass alone. Marx distinctly disliked Emanuel's "hurdy-gurdy-like" introduction and found the placement of the *Heilig* directly after the Credo "ridiculous." By contrast, Ludwig Rellstab and an anonymous critic in the Leipzig *Allgemeine musikalische Zeitung* raised no objections to the heterogeneous programming.[41] What is most important is that the joining of Beethoven's Fifth Symphony, with its victorious finale, the Coriolanus Overture, with its portrayal of the Roman patrician's struggles, and Bach's Credo, with its Latin affirmation of faith and its redemptive "Et resurrexit" conclusion (in the Berlin version), blurred the boundaries between secular and sacred to an even greater degree than Emanuel Bach's Medical Institute concerts. It pointed toward the creation of a secular, humanistic, universal religious experience of the type that was to be espoused in the second half of the century by Wagner and Mahler.

The spirit of the moment was best captured by Fanny Mendelssohn, who reported emotionally two weeks before the concert:

> Whether or not we want to admit it, we live in a time in which unbelievable things are being accomplished in every regard, including art. The Passion will be published without fail by Schlesinger before the year is out, and Schelble performed a part of the Mass in Frankfurt to great approbation. In all corners it is stirring, in all branches it is rustling, one has to cover one's ears not to hear it! Long-deceased Phoenix does nothing but search for his funeral pyre, and he will certainly find it. The time is not far off—we will experience great things. I don't know why I'm in such an historical mood and have such a great desire to measure everything by centuries and nations. Would it be because Spontini is going to present the first half of Beethoven's Mass and the second half of Bach's on Repentance Day?[42]

Spontini's pairing of the B-Minor Mass with the *Missa solemnis* had far-reaching consequences: it led to the linking of the two works by critics and audiences.[43] It undoubtedly influenced Nägeli and Simrock's decision to change the title of Bach's piece from simply "Messe" to "Die hohe Messe" for their 1845 print of part II, in parallel to Beethoven's "Grosse Messe" (as it was commonly termed at the time). And it most probably determined Julius Rietz's decision, in the *Bach-Gesamtausgabe,* to assign a violin to the unlabeled obbligato instrumental line of the "Benedictus," in imitation of Beethoven's scoring for the same section.[44] But even more fundamentally, it marked the B-Minor Mass as a grand choral masterpiece, a work to be presented in the secular arena of the concert hall, with immense vocal and instrumental forces, in the monumental style of the *Missa solemnis* or the Ninth Symphony.

The performance parts used by Spontini for the Credo attest to this monumentality. We find that C. P. E. Bach's Hamburg materials were augmented with fifteen new chorus parts[45] and then combined with an entirely new set of materials[46] that utterly transformed the nature of the piece: seventy-five additional choral parts, thirty additional string parts, and seven new wind parts (calling for two clarinets, two bassoons, and three "corni" [which despite their "horn" label double the trumpet parts at pitch]). Assuming that the vocal and string parts of both sets were shared by two performers each, as was common practice (see Chapter 7), this would have resulted in an ensemble of Bruckneresque proportions and character: 190 singers, 68 string players (18 first violins, 18 second violins, 12 violas, 12 cellos, and 8 double basses), two flutes, two oboes, two clarinets, two bassoons, three trumpets, three horns (or brass instruments of some sort), and timpani.[47]

If Marx criticized Spontini's programming, he nevertheless praised the performance of the "Crucifixus," which he viewed as the emotional center of the Credo:

> The Crucifixus can be named as the sanctuary of this most holy Mass, in whose tonal dance one perceives the wonder, the unending pain, the deepest compassion—the full extent of the purpose of consecration in death leading to the redemption of mankind. Here no line can be altered without damage and sacrilege to the whole, either in the voices or in the orchestra, which presents the following figure in the strings and winds over the basso ostinato [measures 1 to 4 given here]. These soft exhalations, these sighs of the lamenting flutes were strengthened with clarinets and oboes.[48]

The oboes in the "Crucifixus" performance were a carry-over from Emanuel's Hamburg arrangement, of course. But Spontini's addition of clarinets and, as the parts indicate, bassoons (doubling the vocal bass and continuo) enhanced even further the plaintive, tragic nature of the "Crucifixus" for nineteenth-century listeners. The new instruments brought the reed group into line with typical early nineteenth-century wind bands, such as those used by Beethoven in the *Marcia funebre* of the "Eroica" Symphony and the *Allegretto* of the Seventh Symphony, two pieces whose cataclysmic journeys caught the imagination of Romantic audiences. Spontini's Berlin performance, with its massive chorus, operatically schooled soloists (evaluated in detail by the Leipzig *Allgemeine musikalische Zeitung* reviewer), and large, Romanticized orchestra helped even more than Schelble's concert to set the course of the B-Minor Mass as a choral-society colossus, a second *Missa solemnis*. The extensive doubling and the dominating choral forces (which now outweighed the instrumentalists almost three to one) transmogrified Bach's score, obscuring the details of counterpoint and creating, as Nikolaus Harnoncourt has nicely put it, a "magnificently harmonized, monumental sound," a "chordal Bach."[49]

The full-scale revival of Bach's large vocal works followed soon thereafter. On March 11, 1829, Mendelssohn led the *Singakademie* in the first public performance of the St. Matthew Passion. During the next two years, the St. Matthew and St. John Passions were published in full score and piano-vocal reductions. In 1833, Nägeli, together with Simrock of Bonn, issued the full score of the Kyrie and Gloria of the B-Minor Mass. A year later the two firms released vocal parts and a piano-vocal score (arranged by Marx) of the entire Mass. The second part of the full score, containing the Credo, Sanctus, and Agnus Dei, did not appear until 1845. The printed piano-vocal reductions and vocal parts, especially, greatly facilitated large-scale choral-society performances.

In 1834 Zelter's successor, Karl Friedrich Rungenhagen, led the Berlin *Singakademie* in a public performance of the Kyrie, Gloria, and Credo sections of the B-Minor Mass. A reviewer for the Leipzig *Allgemeine musikalische Zeitung* singled out the "Crucifixus" once again for special praise but also extended sympathy toward the solo instrumentalists, who were "forced to fight with the strangeness of the figurations, especially in terms of range and divisions."[50] In Braunschweig the same year, Konrad Friedrich Griepenkerl, editor of the complete Bach organ works for C. F. Peters, performed the "Sanctus." Here, too, we encounter the element of gigantism: Griepenkerl used the combined vocal forces of the local Gymnasium chorus and the Braunschweig *Singakademie* and a large orchestra with more than seventy string players.[51]

After 1834, performances of music from the B-Minor Mass proliferated: Rungenhagen with the Berlin *Singakademie* in 1835 (Kyrie to Osanna); the Choral Harmonists' Society of London in 1838 (Credo); Mendelssohn in a "historical retrospective" in the Leipzig Gewandhaus in 1841 ("Crucifixus"-"Et resurrexit" sequence and the "Sanctus"); Mendelssohn, again, at the inauguration ceremonies for the Bach monument in Leipzig in 1843 ("Sanctus"). The B-Minor Mass was not performed in its entirety until after the mid-century mark. The first complete performance—albeit in German—appears to have been given by Karl Riedel and the *Riedel-Verein* in Leipzig in 1859, with Liszt in attendance. Other early complete performances include Christian Carl Müller conducting the *Cäcilien-Verein* in Frankfurt in 1861; Otto Goldschmidt, the Bach Choir in London in 1876 (with Jenny Lind singing the soprano arias); Alessandro Costa, a mixed choir in Rome in 1885;[52] Frederick Wolle, the Bethlehem Bach Choir in 1900; and Frank Damrosch, the Oratorio Society of New York, also in 1900. During this time, the vocal forces continued to grow in size. By the end of the century, a chorus of 200 singers was passé—still larger forces were desired. Damrosch's greatly applauded Oratorio Society, for instance, featured 500 singers.

During the course of the nineteenth century, then, the B-Minor Mass went from an obscure work, unmentioned by Forkel, to a staple of the choral repertory. Philipp Spitta devoted thirty pages to the B-Minor Mass in his epic *Johann Sebastian Bach* of 1873–1880. Carl Hermann Bitter gave it a full chapter in the 1881 revised edition of his similarly named biography. The Mass had finally come to life again, but it was reborn in new clothes: it was no longer a Baroque work. In 1786 C. P. E. Bach altered the instrumentation here and there, but preserved the size of the forces and the balance between chorus and orchestra. In the nineteenth century, the chorus grew to the point where it overwhelmed the orchestra, obscuring the details of the scoring. It was as if Bach, like Beethoven with the *Missa solemnis* or Brahms with the German Requiem, had written a work specifically to exhibit the capabilities of a new and mighty instrument, the mixed chorus. In performance, the lines of the B-Minor Mass were agglutinized, through the use of heavier voices (older men, rather than young, for the tenors and basses; women, rather than boys, for the sopranos and altos), more mellifluous instruments (horns, trombones, clarinets), and excessive numbers of performers on both vocal and instrumental parts. In the Romantic quest for overall effect, the Latin text could even be discarded as long as the harmony and melodic lines were preserved: Mendelssohn's solo organ arrangements of "Kyrie eleison" II and the "Gratias agimus tibi"[53] result in a "Mass without Words" of sorts.

To nineteenth-century ears, the massive sound of the choruses was overwhelming. The anonymous reviewer of Rungenhagen's 1834 *Singakademie* performance of the Kyrie, Gloria, and Credo found the "Crucifixus" and "Et resurrexit" "especially gripping" and the "Confiteor" "of extraordinary harmonic magnitude." He ranked the arias, however, as "relatively less appealing,"[54] undoubtedly because they did not match the thick textures, the dynamic extremes, the very *Gesamt*ness of the choruses. Spitta expressed the nineteenth-century viewpoint well:

> The arias stand among the choruses like isolated valleys between gigantic peaks, serving to relieve the eye that tries to take in the whole composition. The choruses, indeed, are of a caliber and grandeur that almost crush the small and restless generation of the present day. Throughout the entire work the most essential portions are given to them, and they are best understood by a general consideration of the whole.[55]

The "gigantic peaks" of the choruses, scaled surefootedly by European and American choral societies by the end of the nineteenth century, would not be forgotten easily in the twentieth century. In the "original forces" movement, it was the concept of the B-Minor Mass as a large choral work that would be most difficult to set aside.

THE GROWING ISSUE OF ORIGINAL FORCES (THE TWENTIETH CENTURY)

Just as the nineteenth-century choral-society tradition was reaching its peak in the form of Mahler's Eighth Symphony (the "Symphony of a Thousand," composed in 1906 and premiered in 1910), the use of gigantic forces for Bach's music began to be questioned. Albert Schweitzer was one of the first to take up the issue. Writing in the revised edition of his influential *J. S. Bach, le musicien-poète,* Schweitzer complained that the sound of women's voices was foreign to Bach's music and expressed the hope that the time would come when more attention would be given to the advantages of boy sopranos and altos.[56] To Schweitzer, Bach's church works were "a type of sacred chamber music," and the desire to hear them "with original equipment" was fully justified. While Schweitzer did not go so far as to reject a large-scale performance of the B-Minor Mass, he at least urged a reduction in the size of the chorus:

> Bach indeed never dreamed of a performance of the "Gloria," the "Et resurrexit," and the "Osanna" of his B-Minor Mass by three or four hundred singers; nevertheless we may venture to perform them in this way, and it has been done successfully. We ought to recognize, however, that it is all a matter of chance. Even with a choir of a hundred and fifty voices there is a danger of lines of the vocal polyphony coming out too thickly and heavily in a way directly opposed to the nature of Bach's music.[57]

Others writing about Bach's music were moving in the same direction. In an article appearing in 1904 in the first issue of the *Bach-Jahrbuch*, Arnold Schering pointed to the loss of Baroque traditions and reasoned that their passing made it difficult—if not impossible—to re-create Bach's performance practices.[58] The rise of middle-class music making, the advent of the public concert, the training of musicians in the Classical and Romantic schools, and the disappearance of many Baroque instruments created an immense gulf between Bach's time and the twentieth century. Schering doubted that a return to Bach's performance style was possible.

Nevertheless, the picture of Bach's performance conditions soon became much clearer, thanks to archival studies. In an article appearing in the 1912 *Bach-Jahrbuch*, Schering examined the practices of Bach's Thomaskantor predecessors.[59] Charles Sanford Terry explored in remarkable detail Bach's instrumental players and their instruments in *Bach's Orchestra* (1932). Schering presented a broad portrait of Leipzig music making in the second volume of *Musikgeschichte Leipzigs* (1926) and in *Johann Sebastian Bachs Leipziger Kirchenmusik* (1936), and in his highly influential article in the 1936 *Bach-Jahrbuch* argued that Bach performed the *Missa* of the B-Minor Mass in Leipzig on April 21, 1733, as an homage and coronation piece for Friedrich August II.[60] As we noted in Chapter 2, most scholars now agree that if the *Missa* was performed at all in 1733, it most probably was given in Dresden, not Leipzig. But Schering's thesis was persuasive when first presented, and its implications for performance were clear: it removed the B-Minor Mass from the lavish, professional circles of Dresden and placed it squarely in Leipzig, where Bach's resources—described in the carefully documented investigations of Terry and Schering himself—were unquestionably modest.

Finally, Smend, in a probing 1937 essay on the genesis, transmission, and meaning of the B-Minor Mass, underscored in a clinical way the imbalance inherent in choral-society performances.[61] In discussing Bach's transformation of the chorus "Jauchzet, ihr erfreuten Stimmen" of Cantata 120 into the "Et expecto" of the Mass, Smend noted that in mm. 25–26 of the "Et expecto," thematic material carried by soprano, alto, and bass in the cantata was reassigned to two flutes and a bass (Example 6–2).

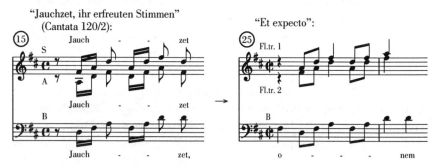

Example 6–2. "Et expecto" rescoring.

In terms of scoring, this meant, logically, that Bach viewed the flute lines as the dynamic equivalent of soprano and alto lines. Such equality was irreparably distorted in choral-society performances:

> In the Passions or the B-Minor Mass, at least, every vocal part is assigned to a large, strongly manned chorus. If we are not already convinced, for various reasons, that the strong manning of the vocal parts must have as its consequence a falsification of the timbral picture, then passages like this must win us over. The flutes of the Mass are the equivalent of the vocal parts of the cantata. If the chorus is not of the very smallest type, then the threefold harmony between the vocal part and the two flutes is destroyed. One will hear only the vocal part. Bach was, as Schering has set before our eyes in a lively manner, an eminently practical musician—something confirmed by his scores. He created his works with a view to the performance forces that he had at hand.[62]

Smend's argument was convincing indeed, and as performers began to move toward the idea of using "original forces" for Bach's vocal music, the restoration of balance between chorus and orchestra was among their high-est priorities. The Bach Cantata Club of London, formed in 1926 by Hubert Foss, E. Stanley Roper, and Charles Kennedy Scott to perform Bach's choral music with a new degree of authenticity, was one of the first groups to spurn the choral-society tradition. With the active encouragement of Schweitzer, Terry, and others, the Club performed Bach's vocal works with small forces. In 1929, it presented the B-Minor Mass with a choir of thirty-six voices. This was still almost twice as many singers as Bach normally used (as we shall see in Chapter 7), and the Club employed a mixed group of men and women and modern instruments. Nevertheless, it was a decisive step away from nineteenth-century practices.

In New York, the Cantata Singers, directed from 1936 to 1953 by Arthur Mendel, moved in the same direction, performing Bach cantatas with a small chorus and a chamber ensemble (of modern instruments, for the most part). In a paper entitled "Problems in the Performance of Bach's Choral Music," presented in New York in 1941, Mendel argued that modern per-formers were using the "alleged inadequacy of performances in Bach's time" as an excuse to ignore the character of his ensemble.[63] Mendel appraised the historical documents regarding Bach's singers and instru-mentalists—documents that were soon to be made widely accessible to English-reading audiences through *The Bach Reader*—and discussed the practical problems of trying to re-create eighteenth-century conditions with a mixed chorus and modern instruments. The greatest obstacle to restoring Bach's sound, Mendel felt, was the Romantic training of modern performers and listeners—the very problem mentioned by Schering back in 1904.

In Germany, Wilhelm Ehmann helped to revive interest in Baroque vocal practices through his work at the Hochschule für Kirchenmusik in Münster in the 1950s and 1960s and his concerts and recordings with the Westfälische Kantorei. Equally influential, especially with regard to the B-Minor Mass, was Ehmann's series of articles on the role of concertists and ripienists in Bach's choir, published in 1960.[64] Pointing to accounts by Praetorius, Schütz, Demantius, Walther, and others, Ehmann demonstrated that the use of a small choir divided into soloist and tutti groups, outlined by Bach in his "Short but Necessary Draft" of 1730, was a Baroque con-vention of long standing. Ehmann proposed that the practice be applied to the B-Minor Mass and enumerated passages in the choruses that could be taken by the solo group. Although Ehmann's specific suggestions were flawed in a number of regards (we shall return to this in Chapter 7), the gist of his argument was both accurate and convincing: Bach's choir was as small and as flexible as his instrumental group.

Ehmann's theory was quickly put into practice in Robert Shaw's 1961 recording of the B-Minor Mass, which featured a chorus of thirty-three select professional singers and an orchestra of twenty-nine players. "Apparently, Bach was used to an equal numerical and auditory balance between singers and instrumentalists," Shaw stated in the liner notes.[65] "We have granted to this present chorus a slight numerical advantage, perhaps justified by the greater sonority of today's instruments." Shaw divided his chorus into concertists and ripienists and used the concertists for arias and solo passages in the choruses, in Baroque fashion. His streamlined performance demonstrated for the first time in a recording the merits of a scaled-down approach to the B-Minor Mass, albeit with a mixed chorus and modern instruments.

The leap to boys' chorus and original instruments was taken by Nikolaus Harnoncourt in 1968, in a recording of the B-Minor Mass with the *Concentus Musicus Wien* and the *Wiener Sängerknaben* and *Chorus Viennensis*.[66] Harnoncourt noted that Bach's major works were conceived more or less as chamber music in terms of forces, the 150-year-old Romantic tradition notwithstanding. In his opinion, reducing the size of the ensemble was not enough to recapture the balance of Bach's delicate scoring—it was also necessary to use boys' voices and period instruments, with their lighter, more transparent timbre. Echoing Smend, Harnoncourt reasoned:

> When a choral part is played in thirds or in sixths with *one* instrument, it makes musical sense only if the number of singers is very small, or if multiple wind instruments are used. There are many such passages in the B-Minor Mass: for example, in the "Kyrie," measures 35–36, or "Et expecto," measures 27, 29, 31, 69, 71, 73. Similar problems of balance arise also in the "Et resurrexit," where two flutes are played for long stretches quite independently and must remain audible against both the chorus and the orchestra. Also the reinforcement of the trumpets by the flutes in mm. 101–105 is only plausible if the flutes are not drowned out by the trumpets. From these few randomly chosen examples it is evident that the distribution of the voices and instruments, weighed most subtly by Bach, loses its meaning completely if even one link is changed in this complicated chain.[67]

Harnoncourt also employed what he considered to be Baroque performance techniques—lighter, meter-oriented articulations, faster tempos, softer dynamic levels, the use of a conductorless ensemble, etc.—which he had refined with *Concentus Musicus* in the fifteen-year period preceding the recording.

Reaction to Harnoncourt's approach was mixed. Rudolf Klein, writing in the *Österreichische Musikzeitschrift,* voiced unreserved enthusiasm for the recording, praising both the clarity and balance of the orchestra and chorus and the elegant, "fatless" nature of the overall interpretation.[68] *High Fidelity Magazine,* posing the question "Bach's B-Minor Mass: Does the Concentus Musicus' Authenticity Make Musical Sense?" presented positive and negative views side by side.[69] Clifford F. Gilmore, speaking for the "Yes" camp, lauded the extraordinary clarity of the "new" instrumental ensemble and smaller chorus and found that the generally fast tempos and short, distinct articulations made the work "come alive" in an unprecedented fashion. Certainly the tempos *were* much faster than those taken in previous recordings. Even Shaw's 1961 performance runs two hours and thirteen minutes; Harnoncourt's, at one hour and forty-five minutes, is almost half an hour shorter. Paul Henry Lang, writing for the "No" camp, labeled Harnoncourt's recording "an example of overzealous antiquarianism; long on well-meant but naïve musicology, and short on plain musicianship." High on Lang's list of complaints was the very nature of early instruments and boys' voices:

> When the baroque flute descends to its lower regions, what we hear mostly is the *pft-pft* of the player blowing into it; the baroque horn is afraid of its own shadow; and the baroque bassoons haven't even a shadow—the "Quoniam" is really funny. Only the baroque oboes sound pleasant with their plaintive, slightly nasal tone . . . The choral treble and alto are sung by boys, the famed Vienna Choir Boys, who do a good job. But of course boys cannot do justice to this kind of music, and a mixed chorus is infinitely preferable to the combination of men, falsettists, and boys.[70]

Sharply rejecting the notion that early forces might offer certain advantages over modern, Lang sided with the nineteenth-century practitioners and expressed the conviction that the B-Minor Mass was inarguably a large choral work: "Whatever the historical data, the B minor Mass is not chamber music; we must not confuse economic history with musical actuality." He concluded by admitting that while the Bethlehem Bach Choir and the Boston Handel and Haydn Society might give one "inflated Bach,"

Harnoncourt was offering up "deflated Bach." Despite Lang's rebuke, within six months *High Fidelity* awarded the Harnoncourt recording the Gold Prize in its "Best Records of the Year" competition.[71] "Deflated Bach" was moving into the mainstream.

Part of Harnoncourt's goal was to trim down the forces used for the B-Minor Mass and eliminate the extreme contrast between chorus and aria that had been created by the Romantic tradition. His performance nevertheless displays certain aspects of the choral-society approach that he wished to overthrow. To judge from the liner materials, his chorus contained approximately thirty boys and men—still a much larger group than Bach's in either Leipzig or Dresden (see Chapter 7). Harnoncourt reasoned[72] that boy sopranos and altos are younger and smaller in modern times than they were in Bach's day (in the eighteenth century, boys normally reached puberty three or four years later than they do now),[73] and hence more are needed to achieve the same amount of sound. Harnoncourt also used professional soloists—men and women—for the arias, on the assumption that Bach performed the *Missa* in Dresden, where opera singers were available.

The performing forces were reduced still further by Joshua Rifkin in his 1982 recording of the B-Minor Mass made with the Bach Ensemble.[74] Proceeding on the premise that Bach's resources in Leipzig were extremely limited, and that his "chorus" normally consisted of no more than a quartet of voices, Rifkin presented the Mass with an ensemble of twenty instrumentalists (including 2 first violins, 2 second violins, 1 viola, 1 cello, 1 violone, and 1 bassoon) and eight professional singers (men and women), with no more than one singer per part in each portion of the work. To many, Rifkin's one-on-a-part choral approach, which we will examine more closely in Chapter 7, seems extreme. But without question, it endows the choruses of the B-Minor Mass with an unprecedented degree of clarity and detail. The choral "peaks" so admired by Spitta in the nineteenth century are brought to the same level as the arias, and the Mass is unveiled as a work in which monumentality is created mostly by changes in texture, rather than changes in forces. Rikfin's B-Minor Mass is Schweitzer's "sacred chamber music" indeed.

Whether or not Rifkin's approach will gain wide acceptance remains to be seen. Some have dismissed it as an aberration, as "Baroque Minimalism." Others have embraced Rifkin's thesis, at least in part. Recent recordings by John Eliot Gardiner and Andrew Parrott feature the use of one voice per part in selected chorus passages[75] (though not necessarily along the same lines as Ehmann's complex concertist-ripienist schemes). And still more recently, Harnoncourt has made a second recording of the B-Minor Mass, one in which he retreats somewhat from the "original forces" concept by combining an enlarged *Concentus Musikus Wien* ensemble of early instruments (including 6 first violins, 6 second violins, 3 violas, 2 cellos, 2 violones, and 2 bassoons) with the *Arnold Schönberg Chor*, a mixed choir of men and women. In an interview, Harnoncourt explained his decision not to use a boys' choir:

> We take the view that women's voices are just as accurate, that they reproduce the rhythmic structures and coloratura just as clearly, but that they also contribute the sensuous flair of adults to the music. As far as I am concerned—and probably today's listener—this is an essential element in the work and it is no longer all that important whether the ideal, historically accurate rendering is by a boys' choir or a mixed choir.[76]

This approach seems to represent the beginning of a new, "post-original forces" stage, in which performers knowingly—and unabashedly—seek a middle ground between Bach's conventions and modern tastes.

Chapter 7

ISSUES OF PERFORMANCE PRACTICE

———————————— ✣ ————————————

*A*ny discussion of B-Minor Mass performance practices will be unavoidably speculative, for two reasons. First, it is unclear which particular ensemble—if any—Bach had in mind when he composed the work. Since the B-Minor Mass in its collected form does not seem to have been performed during the composer's lifetime, we cannot link it with a specific group of players. We can obtain an idea of Bach's highest performance expectations, perhaps, by looking at the Dresden court ensemble of Friedrich August II, recipient of the 1733 *Missa*. But Leipzig groups, too, must be considered since large portions of the music (the models of eight movements and the parodies of three others) were fashioned for Leipzig and performed there. Thus for the B-Minor Mass we can hope for no more than a general picture of performance conditions, and this is best obtained by appraising both Leipzig and Dresden practices.

Second, the B-Minor Mass is an unfinished piece, a fact that becomes obvious if we consider the composer's working habits. When writing music for ensemble, Bach normally carried out his task in two stages. He began by penning a full score, which contained the musical text and intermittent instructions for performance. He then produced performance parts, usually with the aid of students or family members (or both). In the parts, he commonly clarified the way the work was to be performed by inserting supplementary tempo markings and more specific articulation indications, by adding figures to the keyboard continuo part, or by delineating more precisely the role of the continuo players and doubling instruments, even to the point of creating new instrumental lines (such as the flute and bassoon parts in the *Missa*). Not infrequently, Bach also revised details of the musical text itself: he often improved the underlay of words, sharpened rhythms, enriched part-writing, or recomposed melodic lines. We might say that Bach treated a score like an undraped body, which in the process of making performance parts was clothed and coiffured in a manner appropriate to the occasion at hand. When Bach produced performance materials, he often elevated the music to a higher level of refinement. In the case of the B-Minor Mass, the lack of parts for the Credo, Sanctus, and Agnus Dei portions renders the work "unfinished." It prevents us from seeing the more detailed level to which the composer surely would have carried the music had he been able to bring it to performance.

Keeping these limiting factors in mind, let us explore a number of the most interesting performance issues.

INSTRUMENTAL AND VOCAL FORCES

The *P 180* manuscript score indicates, with a few exceptions, the kinds of voices and instruments that are required for performing the B-Minor Mass, and the Dresden *Missa* parts (*Mus. 2405-D-21* in the Saxon State Library) further clarify matters of scoring here and there for the Kyrie and Gloria in particular. Two larger matters are not fully resolved by these materials, however: the size of the string body and choir, and the makeup of the continuo group.

In both instances the Dresden performance parts are the best place to begin. The individual parts, with Bach's titling, are as follows:

Soprano I
Soprano II
Alto
Tenore
Basso
Clarino 1 [Trumpet 1]
Clarino 2 [Trumpet 2]
Principale [Trumpet 3]

Tympana [Timpani]

Corne da Caccia [Horn]

Traversiere 1 [Transverse flute 1]

Traversiere 2 [Transverse flute 2]

Hautbois d'Amour 1 [Oboe d'amore and Oboe 1]

Hautbois d'Amour 2 [Oboe d'amore and Oboe 2]

Violino 1 [principal Violin 1, with "Laudamus te" solo part]

Violino 1 [second Violin 1, with "Laudamus te" *ripieno* part]

Violino 2

Viola

Violoncello

Basson [Bassoon; from "Quoniam tu solus" to the end: Bassoon 1 and 2]

Continuo [at pitch, figured]

The set of parts points to a small chamber ensemble. But *how* small?

The most radical interpretation is that of Joshua Rifkin (see Chapter 6), who proposed some fifteen years ago that one take the Dresden materials at face value and assume that each part was used by no more than one singer or player (with the exception of the bassoon part, which included the music for bassoons 1 and 2).[1] The result is a chorus of five and an orchestra of seventeen or eighteen (if the continuo part served both a keyboard player and a violinist). Although this idea may seem extreme, Rifkin has pointed out rightly that C. P. E. Bach's materials for the 1786 performance of the *Symbolum Nicenum* in Hamburg also include just one part per voice and instrument.[2] Could J. S. Bach's B-Minor Mass ensemble have been no larger than Rifkin's figure?

Let us consider the instrumental forces first. Here, additional factors come into play. For cantata performances in Leipzig, Bach normally prepared a set of parts that included a number of duplicates: an extra violin 1 part, an extra violin 2 part, and one or two extra continuo parts. When he lent the performance parts for the "Sanctus" (in its original 1724 form) to Count Sporck in Bohemia, he retained the duplicates and later used them as the basis for a new set of performance materials when Sporck failed to return the originals.[3] Hans-Joachim Schulze has reasoned that Bach may have done the same with the *Missa,* carrying back to Leipzig a duplicate violin 2 part, one or two continuo parts, and possibly a viola part as well.[4] If that were true, the Dresden materials would have been more encompassing than they now appear to be.

In addition, it was common practice in Bach's day for several performers to read from one part, a procedure that saved time and labor in an age of handwritten materials. Even with printed music, which was expensive in the first half of the eighteenth century, sharing parts was a practical means of stretching available texts. Giovanni Lorenzo Gregori's remark in the preface to his concerti grossi of 1698 is typical:

> So as not to multiply the number of partbooks, I have written down this opus as best I could in the concertini parts. Those who play in the concerto grosso will please be careful to remain silent and count wherever it is written "Soli," and re-enter immediately where it is written "Tutti."[5]

Bach's Weimar colleague Johann Gottfried Walther complained in his old age that his eyes were greatly weakened from years of straining to read shared parts.[6] Within the Dresden *Missa* materials, the indication "solo" in the principal violin part at the beginning of the "Laudamus te" suggests that two players were reading off the page (only one of whom was to play the obbligato line), and the indication "pizzicato" in the continuo part at the beginning of the "Domine Deus" reveals that a string player—presumably a violonist (since there is a separate cello part)—was reading over the shoulder of the keyboard player.

Taking into account the possibility of missing duplicate parts, the sharing of parts, and the presence of the violone, we get the following ranges for the strings and continuo instruments for the Dresden *Missa:*

Upper strings:	Violin 1	2 to 4 players
	Violin 2	1 to 4 players
	Viola	1 to 4 players
Continuo group:	Cello	1 to 2 players
	Violone	1 to 2 players
	Bassoon	2 players

An additional piece of evidence concerning the continuo group comes from the *Missa*'s twin (as far as setting is concerned), the D-Major Magnificat, BWV 243. In the Magnificat, as in the *Missa,* the violone is not specifically indicated at the top of the score. But the remark "Cont. e Violoncelli senza Violono è Bassoni" before the "Suscepit Israel" verifies

the violone's presence and at the same time hints at a specific makeup of
the continuo group: organ (the continuo line is labeled "Organo"), two cellos, one violone, and two bassoons. That would seem to be an appropriate
continuo body for the B-Minor Mass as well (and as we noted in Chapter 2,
the revised version of the Magnificat dates from the same period as the
Missa and may also have been intended for performance in Dresden).

These figures are very close to those given by Bach in his oft-cited
"Short but Most Necessary Draft for a Well-Appointed Church Music."[7] In
the Draft, submitted during the summer of 1730 to the Leipzig Town
Council, he outlined in detail the basic requirements for a church ensemble. The instrumentalists were to include:

Violino 1	2 or even 3 players
Violino 2	2 or 3 players
Viola 1	2 players
Viola 2	2 players
Violoncello	2 players
Violone	1 player
Oboe	2, or, if the piece requires, 3 players
Flutes	2 players
Bassoon	1, or even 2 players
Trumpets	3 players
Kettledrums	1 player

As Bach makes clear elsewhere in the memorandum, the instrumentalists in his Leipzig ensemble left much to be desired. Only eight—the Town
Pipers and Art Fiddlers—were professional musicians, and Bach held their
skills in contempt ("Modesty forbids me to speak at all truthfully of their
qualities and musical knowledge. Nevertheless it must be remembered that
they are partly *emeriti* and partly not at all in such *exercitio* as they should
be").[8] The remaining players were amateurs—students from the University
and boys from the St. Thomas School. The group was surely no better than
an average college chamber orchestra today.

Conditions were far better in Dresden, of course, for Friedrich August I
and then Friedrich August II, especially, assembled one of the largest and
finest groups of musicians in Europe. The personnel roster of the Court
Capella for 1738 lists twelve violinists, four violists, five cellists, two con-
trabassists, five oboists, three flautists, five bassoonists, two corno da caccia players, two organists, and one lutenist.[9] Trumpet and timpani were
manned by the Court Trumpeters, an independent guild. Not all of the

instrumentalists seem to have been used in church performances, however. After an extensive study of performance parts from the Hofkirche, Wolfgang Horn has estimated that during the tenures of Heinichen and Zelenka—that is, between 1720 and 1745—the string, oboe, and continuo forces used for sacred pieces commonly included:[10]

Upper parts:	Oboes	2 to 4 players
	Violin 1	4 to 6 players
	Violin 2	4 to 6 players
	Viola	2 to 4 players
Continuo group:	Cello	2 to 4 players
	Violone	2 players
	Bassoon	2 to 3 players
	Organ	1 player
	Theorbo	1 player

The Dresden ensemble was not only large but was composed of virtuoso players, musicians "relieved of all concern for their living, free from *chagrin* [emphasis original], and obliged each to master but a single instrument," as Bach mentioned with envy to the Leipzig Town Council in the "Short but Most Necessary Draft." Concertmaster Johann Georg Pisendel, flautist Pierre-Gabriel Buffardin, oboist Johann Christian Richter, lutenist Silvius Weiss, and others enjoyed international renown. Weiss's annual salary in 1719 was 1,000 taler, 300 taler more than Bach received as Kantor of St. Thomas four years later. Scholars have been quick to link the virtuoso instrumental writing in the *Missa* with the Dresden ensemble, associating the solo violin part of the "Laudamus te" with Pisendel, the flute solo of the "Domine Deus" with Buffardin, and so forth. But as we have seen in Chapter 2, there are reasons to question whether the *Missa* was actually performed in the Hofkirche im Theater, and by the Court Capella. Whatever the case, Bach cited the Dresden group as his ideal, and one is surely on firm ground to take its size and quality as models for a performance of the B-Minor Mass.

Turning to the vocal forces, we find that the Dresden *Missa* materials contain a single set of vocal parts, like most of Bach's Leipzig cantatas. Here, too, Rifkin has argued for a restricted interpretation, saying that the cantatas were performed with no more than a vocal quartet. In the "Short but Most Necessary Draft" Bach described a larger group, however:

Every musical choir should contain at least 3 sopranos, 3 altos, 3 tenors, and as many basses, so that even if one happens to fall ill (as very often happens, particularly at this time of year [August 23], as the prescriptions written by the school physician for the apothecary must show) at least a double-chorus motet may be sung. (N.B. Though it would be still better if the classes were such that one could have 4 singers on each part and thus could form every chorus with 16 persons).[11]

Earlier in the Draft, Bach explained that a choir is divided into two groups, concertists (the best singers, who serve as the soloists in arias, recitatives, and choruses) and ripienists (who assist in chorus movements, where they double the concertists to create a thicker, tutti texture). The concertists are four in number (one for each part), he said, and the ripienists must be "at least 8, namely two for each part." Hence Bach stated, and restated, that a choir should have three to four singers on each part. Rifkin has argued that the figures in the Draft are an exaggeration, that between illness and the use of St. Thomas School students as instrumentalists, the choir membership was so depleted that only a quartet remained. But the use of a choir with ripienists as well as concertists was a well-established tradition in Leipzig. One finds mention of a "pool" of vocalists, enough to provide two, three, or four singers per part in each choir, in St. Thomas School documents from the seventeenth century,[12] and one can observe the use of solo-tutti vocal effects in church works of Sebastian Knüpfer, Thomaskantor from 1657 to 1676, and Johann Kuhnau, Bach's immediate predecessor. The solo-tutti indications in the opening chorus of Christoph Graupner's Magnificat in C Major,[13] submitted to the Town Council as a test piece for the St. Thomas cantorate in 1723, imply that the availability of ripienists in Leipzig was taken as a given. And a number of Bach's Leipzig vocal works contain extra ripieno vocal parts among the performance materials: Cantata 21 (in its revised form), Cantata 29 (the parody model for the "Gratias agimus tibi" and the "Dona nobis pacem" of the B-Minor Mass), Cantata 110, and others. In Cantata 24 solo and tutti indications are given in the soprano, alto, and tenor parts,[14] showing not only that the Leipzig choir was more than a quartet, but also verifying that single parts were shared by several singers.

Other facts support the use, in Leipzig, of a choir with several singers to a part. There is the stipulation in the 1723 St. Thomas School Regulations that when the choirboys were called to the music stands to sing during *Hauptgottesdienst,* they were to place themselves "in front of the stands in such a way that each can see the text on the stand without hindering the singing of the others."[15] There is the manuscript discant part of Johann Walter's *Choralpassionen* from the New Church that contains a penciled remark noting the Third Choir personnel for 1731. The list includes the names of two discantists (sopranos), two altos, two tenors, and four basses.[16] While these figures do not quite match the total suggested by Bach— twelve—the group is clearly not a quartet. And of course this was the Third Choir. The First and Second Choirs, which performed the cantatas each week, were presumably larger. Finally, if one takes the minimum and maximum forces mentioned by Bach in his Draft—nineteen to twenty-five instrumentalists (including the unmentioned but surely present continuo keyboard player) and twelve to sixteen singers—one gets a total of thirty-one to fortyone performers. It is a striking coincidence that the two eyewitnesses to Bach performances in Leipzig who cite figures give numbers remarkably close to those of the Draft. Rector Johann Matthias Gesner, writing in 1738, described Bach struggling on Sunday mornings to hold together an ensemble of "thirty or even forty musicians,"[17] and J. C. Trömer, writing in 1745, described Bach leading "over forty musicians" in the 1727 performance of *Entfernet euch, ihr heitern Sterne*, BWV Anh. 9[18] (probably the parody model for the "Et resurrexit" of the B-Minor Mass). If Bach had been using a choir of four singers only, these numbers would have been much smaller.

In sum, Bach's Leipzig choir appears to have been close to what he described in his Draft: twelve singers or so, and ideally, as many as sixteen.

At the Dresden court, choral forces seem to have been about the same size. The chief difference may have been the quality of the solo singers. It appears that Dresden composers could draw on two resources for sacred works. First, there were the *Kapellknaben*, or Chapel Boys, a choir of approximately twenty boys, men, and castratos trained in Catholic ritual at the "Historia Missionis," the institute attached to the Hofkirche. The *Kapellknaben* seem to have been analogous to Bach's First Choir at the St. Thomas School, though the group may have been more talented, since its members were often actively recruited from Prague, where Catholic practices were more firmly rooted than in Dresden.[19] Second, one could turn to the vocal soloists from the Court Capella, which, as we observed in Chapter 1, included some of the most famous opera singers in Europe: soprano Faustina Bordoni), castrato Giovanni Bindi, alto Margherita Ermini, countertenor Nicolo Pozzi, bass Cosimo Ermini, and others.

Performance materials at the Court Church commonly include one set of parts for the soloists (who participated in the chorus movements as well as arias) and two for the ripienists. Renaissance-style works lacking solos are transmitted with only two sets of vocal parts per voice.[20] All this suggests that the court soloists joined the Hofkirche ensemble only when solo singing was required in the arias and concertino interludes of concerted works. The Dresden vocal parts for the 1733 *Missa* contain the word "solo" twice (in the alto before the "Qui sedes" and in the bass before the "Quoniam tu solus") and the word "Duetto" once (in the tenor before the "Domine Deus"). This points to the use of aria soloists drawn from the choir.

The type of ensemble that Bach was accustomed to in Leipzig and Dresden, then, was a modest-sized chamber group, consisting of roughly thirty to forty players and singers (or perhaps a few more in Dresden). Such an ensemble would have produced a transparent, balanced sound, with the strings in approximate proportion to the woodwinds and brass and the instrumentalists in approximate proportion to the vocalists. For the 1786 performance of the Credo, C. P. E. Bach embellished the vocal parts of the "Et incarnatus" and other choruses with cadential trills, putting the voices on the same plane as the instruments. The equality of instrumental and vocal forces was clearly the norm for both J. S. Bach and his son Emanuel, and it would seem to be especially appropriate for the B-Minor Mass, a work in which motives are set forth in an egalitarian manner by player and singer alike. It is sometimes difficult for listeners raised on the sounds of choral-society performances to imagine the B-Minor Mass as an intimate chamber work, with instrumental band and chorus on an even footing. That was unquestionably Bach's standard, however.

THE USE OF CONCERTISTS AND
RIPIENISTS IN CHORUS MOVEMENTS

If we thus assume that Bach had at his disposal a modest-sized choir divided into concertists (or soloists) and ripienists (or tutti singers), to what extent might he have used the former to create solo effects in the chorus movements of the B-Minor Mass? As early as 1855 Wilhelm Rust pointed out that on occasion Bach began vocal fugues with the concertists alone and added the ripienists with the entrance of the orchestral tutti.[21] Seventy years later, Arnold Schering suggested applying the solo fugue-incipit approach widely in Bach's vocal works, even in pieces such as the B-Minor Mass that lack any original indication of a concertist-ripienist division.[22] More recently, Wilhelm Ehmann proposed the extensive use of solo-tutti effects in the choruses of the B-Minor Mass, not just for fugues, but for Venetian *piano-forte* effects as well.[23] Alfred Dürr was quick to criticize many of Ehmann's schemes as being overly complicated.[24] Dürr reasoned that Bach may indeed have carried out solo-tutti vocal effects in the choruses of his con-certed vocal works on an *ad hoc* basis and not taken time to put indications in scores or parts. But if that were the case, the schemes would have been, by necessity, relatively straightforward—something that could be conveyed through a hand signal or verbal instruction in a rehearsal or performance.

The picture presented by the original materials of Bach's vocal composi-tions is far from clear. Written-out ripienist parts have been handed down for only nine works: Cantatas 21, 29, 63, 71, 76, 110, 195, and 201 and the St. John Passion, and solo-tutti indications appear in the single set of vocal parts for Cantata 24 and in the scores of Cantata 75 and the Mass in A Major. That is not much to go on. In some chorus movements the ripienists create well-worked-out solo-tutti contrasts (Cantatas 21, 24, 71, 75, 76, and 110 and the Mass in A Major). But in others, the ripienists simply double the concertists throughout, without differentiation (Cantatas 29, 63, and 201, and the St. John Passion), even when a lightly-orchestrated fugue exposition (such as mm. 13–19 of the closing chorus "Höchster, schau in Gnaden an" of Cantata 63) would seem to call for concertists only. Dürr has suggested that Bach may have arrived in Leipzig eager to take advantage of solo-tutti vocal effects. After using them in his initial works (Cantatas 75, 76, 21, and 24), however, he may have realized that producing ripieno parts or even marking solo and tutti in parts shared by concertists and ripienists required too much time.[25] From then on, Bach may have used the procedure without writing it down (until the last two decades of his life, when he had time to be more specific, in Cantata 195 or the Mass in A Major, for instance).

Without question, chorus contrasts were a fundamental part of Baroque concerted style, and they were used by Bach's Leipzig predecessors (Knüpfer and Kuhnau, for instance) and Dresden contemporaries (Heini-chen, Zelenka, Hasse, and others). If one wants to apply them to the B-Minor Mass, it would seem logical to model them after Bach's procedure in other works. What patterns can we see?

First, the highlighting of chorus passages with concertists alone appears to have been, for Bach, a performance option, a shading to be used or not used according to circumstances. The ripienist parts for Cantatas 21, 110, and 195 were fashioned after the first performance. Thus the choruses in these works may have been performed "straight" initially and then "solo-tutti" at a later point, when a larger choir or time for the writing of addi-tional parts was available. Second, solo-tutti differentiation was not made in

Renaissance-style movements: in the chorus "Wir danken dir, Gott" from Cantata 29, the parody model of the "Gratias" and the "Dona nobis pacem," the ripienists double the concertists throughout. Third, Bach used concertists in choruses in two obvious places. He employed them in initial fugal expositions, accompanied either by the continuo alone (Cantata 21/11, Cantata 24/3, Cantata 71/7, etc.) or by continuo and detached instrumental chords (Cantata 195/1), as Rust correctly pointed out. There are three such passages in the B-Minor Mass, and by analogy they might be performed with concertists only:

"Et in terra pax"—mm. 120–138 (first fugal exposition)

"Cum Sancto Spiritu"—mm. 37–64 (first fugal exposition)

"Pleni sunt coeli" of the "Sanctus"—mm. 48–72 (first imitative exposition)

In each case, the second exposition, with instrumental doubling, would seem to call for the participation of the ripienists, in accordance with Bach's own practice.

Another type of chorus passage taken by concertists is a lightly scored solo episode (Cantata 110/1, Cantata 195/1). In the B-Minor Mass, the "Vox Christi" episode ("Et iterum venturus est") of the "Et resurrexit"— mm. 74–86—belongs to this category. As we noted in Chapter 4, the fact that the bass is not marked "solo" in the *P 180* manuscript does not eliminate the passage from consideration: the solos in Cantata 110 are not marked in the score either but emerge only in the parts fashioned for the second performance.

Other, more complicated uses of concertists cannot be ruled out, and Bach's delineation of solo and tutti in the choruses of Cantata 195 and the Mass in A Major is indeed almost as complex as some of Ehmann's schemes. It is difficult to formulate generalizations beyond the two practices we have just discussed, however.

CONTINUO PRACTICES

The continuo group was the heart of Bach's ensemble. For the B-Minor Mass, we need to consider two central issues: which instruments were included in the continuo, and what was the role of each? The continuo instruments fall into two categories: chordal—organ, harpsichord, and lute—and melodic— cello, violone, and bassoon.[26] Let us examine each in turn.

There can be little doubt, based on surviving continuo parts, that Bach viewed the organ as the principal chordal continuo instrument for church pieces. In Leipzig, the organs in the main churches were tuned in *Chorton,* or choir pitch, a major second above local wind instruments. As a consequence, the organ part was transposed down a major second in church works to match the fixed pitch of the winds. The consistent presence of a transposed continuo part in the performance materials of the Leipzig cantatas, passions, and Latin-texted pieces substantiates the central function of the organ in the continuo group.

As Laurence Dreyfus has recently demonstrated, however, the harpsichord also played a significant role in Bach's church music.[27] The presence in the Leipzig performance materials of a good number of figured, untransposed continuo parts, many labeled "Cembalo," along with receipts for harpsichord regulation and repair, reveals that Bach often used the harpsichord in the continuo group, sometimes to supplement the organ and sometimes to replace it (either for musical reasons, to obtain a different timbre, or for circumstantial reasons, to serve as a substitute when the organ was not playable). Moreover, harpsichord parts for Palestrina's *Missa sine nomine,* Peranda's Kyrie in C Major, and the Sanctus (BWV 241) arranged from Kerll's *Missa superba* show that on some occasions, at least, Bach used the harpsichord in Latin-texted church works. In the Peranda Kyrie, the harpsichord seems to have been a later replacement for the organ. In the Palestrina *Missa* and the Kerll Sanctus, the harpsichord sounded simultaneously with the organ, producing a "mixed" chordal sound.

Now and then Bach also included the lute in the continuo group, mainly for special effects in arias such as "Betrachte, meine Seel'" from the St. John Passion or "Wie starb die Heldin so vergnügt" and "Der Ewigkeit saphirnes Haus zieht" from Cantata 198 (the "Trauer-Ode"). In Cantata 198, the lute is used further as a continuo instrument in an accompagnato recitative (movement 4) and three choruses (movements 1, 7, and 10). Although Dreyfus feels that the lute played a very limited role in Bach's continuo group,[28] one needs to keep in mind that the composer wrote solo works for the lute in the 1730s and 1740s, that there was a lute in his estate (possibly a theorbo, or bass lute, judging from the high value at which it was appraised), and that there were a number of lute players in his immediate circle (St. Thomas School students Johann Ludwig Krebs, Maximilian Nagel, and Rudolph Straube, and possibly Town Piper Johann Caspar Gleditsch). The unlabeled, figured, at-pitch continuo parts could have served a lutenist just as easily as a harpsichordist (though a lutenist could have retuned his instrument and played from a transposed organ part, too).

The *P 180* manuscript of the B-Minor Mass does not specify the chordal instrument—or instruments—to be used: the continuo line is labeled "Continuo" and no more. In the Dresden *Missa* materials, the continuo part, also labeled "Continuo," is figured and untransposed (see Plate 2–1 in Chapter 2). In Leipzig that would point to the harpsichord. In Dresden, however, the organs in both the Hofkirche and the Sophienkirche—the two possible venues for the *Missa* performance—were tuned in *Kammerton,* or chamber pitch, making transposition unnecessary (as we observed in Chapter 2). Thus if the *Missa* portion of the B-Minor Mass was performed in Dresden, as all signs indicate, the continuo figures could have been realized on the organ, even though the part is not specifically labeled "Organo."

Scattered bits of information reinforce the idea that the organ should be the primary chordal instrument for the B-Minor Mass. First, the Leipzig performance materials for the 1724 version of the Sanctus include a transposed continuo part. Second, in the score of the D-Major Magnificat, the sister work of the B-Minor Mass, the continuo line is specifically labeled "Organo." Finally, at the Dresden Court Heinichen and Zelenka used the organ as a continuo instrument for Latin-texted sacred settings as a matter of course.

We cannot rule out the use of the harpsichord, however. Since there is only one extant figured continuo part for the *Missa,* it is unlikely that both organ and harpsichord would have been employed in a Dresden performance. But Bach clearly considered the tone of the harpsichord appropriate for some of the music. The "Osanna," "Agnus Dei," and probably the "Domine Deus" were carved from secular models that would have been accompanied by harpsichord continuo. The prototype for the "Gratias" and the "Dona nobis pacem," the chorus "Wir danken Dir, Gott" from Cantata 21, were performed in Leipzig with the dual accompaniment of organ and harpsichord.[29] And the Leipzig parts to Palestrina's *Missa sine nomine* show that Bach did not object to harpsichord timbre even in *stile antico* scores.

The lute, too, cannot be summarily dismissed. One is tempted to view it as an old-fashioned, seventeenth-century-oriented continuo instrument, appropriate only for Bach's highly colorful scores of the 1710s and 1720s, such as the St. John Passion or Cantata 198. Yet in Dresden, the theorbo was a regular member of the Hofkirche continuo group, as the surviving instrumental parts attest. Heinichen and Zelenka undoubtedly wished to capitalize on the talents of Silvius Weiss, whose achievements in "Tiorba" and general-bass accompaniment were singled out for praise by Johann Gottfried Walther.[30] Since the theorbo was regularly combined with the organ in Dresden for Latin church works, a similarly mixed sound would not seem to be inappropriate for the B-Minor Mass.

What would be the role of the harpsichord and lute, if they were used with the organ? In choruses, they would lend additional color and rhythmic incisiveness to the tutti ensemble. In arias, one or the other might substitute for the organ on occasion. For example, in the "Domine Deus," with its pizzicato strings, either the lute or the harpsichord with lute stop would blend very nicely with the overall timbre. The fact that Bach himself used three different instruments—organ, harpsichord, and lute—for "Betrachte meine Seel" on three different occasions shows that his view of the continuo group was quite flexible and that he did not always write music with a preconceived continuo sound in mind.[31]

Like most Bach scores, the *P 180* manuscript of the B-Minor Mass is generally devoid of continuo figures. The figures that appear in the *Missa* portion in modern editions are taken from the Dresden continuo part, which was copied from the score by Anonymous 20 and Bach and then figured by Bach alone. A number of other movements of the Mass can be figured from secondary sources. For the "Dona nobis pacem," one can turn to the figures of the "Gratias agimus tibi," obviously. For the Credo portion one can use the figures from C. P. E. Bach's 1786 Hamburg performance, entered in part into the text of the *P 180* autograph (from the "Credo in unum Deum" through m. 66 of the "Patrem omnipotentem") and in full into the score and continuo part of the 1786 Hamburg materials.[32] Although the Credo figures are not the composer's, they at least emanate from someone extremely well versed in his practices. For the "Credo" movement alone one can also use the figures in the recently discovered G-mixolydian version (see Plate 2–2 in Chapter 2)—figures that may well have stemmed from J. S. Bach himself.[33]

Emanuel's continuo part for the Credo portion also contains *tasto solo* markings. "Tasto solo," or "one key alone," was used in Baroque continuo parts to indicate that only the written-out continuo line should sound, without chords, until figures reappear. Like continuo figures, *tasto solo* markings were generally not included in the scores of works but rather added to the continuo line during the production of performance parts. Emanuel's markings merit study, for they add delicate touches to the Credo score. For instance, in the "Crucifixus" the continuo is marked *tasto solo* in mm. 49–53, the final repetition of the ground bass (Plate 7–1). It is a marvelous, hushed moment, during which the ground veers away from E minor and modulates unexpectedly to G major, in anticipation of the "Et resurrexit"

Plate 7–1. The continuo part for the 1786 Hamburg performance of the Credo, with C. P. E. Bach's figures, dynamics, and *tasto solo* marks at the conclusion of the "Crucifixus" (Berlin State Library, *St. 118*).

that follows. The *tasto solo* underscores the silence of the upper instruments and the *piano* of the vocal parts.

Turning to the melodic continuo instruments, we find that there is no specific mention of the cello or violone in the original score of the B-Minor Mass. The Dresden *Missa* materials include a separate cello part, which doubles the continuo line throughout the Kyrie and Gloria with one notable exception: in the "Qui tollis," the cello plays repeated quarter notes, to be performed "col arco e staccato." The other continuo instruments, presumably organ and violone, are to play the downbeat only, with normal articulation (Example 7–1).

This effect is correctly rendered in the *Bach-Gesamtausgabe.* In the *Neue Bach-Ausgabe,* however, both parts are marked "col arco e staccato," diminishing the intended contrast between the lines. As we observed in Chapter 3, the differentiated bass of the "Qui tollis" was a third thought,

Example 7–1. The differentiated bass line of the "Qui tollis," as per the Dresden parts.

incorporated into the music after Bach adopted it from Cantata 46. We can see a similar process in the St. John Passion: Bach added a differentiated bass to the opening chorus, "Herr, unser Herrscher," only in the third version of the work, represented by the 1739 revision score. The *ad hoc* nature of the differentiated bass opens the possibility that Bach eventually might have used it in another movement of the B-Minor Mass, the "Et incarnatus est." The pulsating, repeated-quarter-note bass of the "Et incarnatus" closely resembles that of the "Qui tollis" and "Herr, unser Herrscher." A differentiated bass would give the "Et incarnatus" music a similarly accented, throbbing sound (Example 7–2). While this can be no more than a conjecture, it is in line with Bach's procedures elsewhere.

Example 7–2. Hypothetical differentiated bass for the "Et incarnatus."

We have already made a case for the presence of the violone in the Dresden *Missa*. By extension, the violone would have appeared in the other portions of the B-Minor Mass as well, adding a 16' foundation to the score. The more difficult issue is deciding the extent to which the instrument should be used. Should it sound in the choruses only, or in the arias as well? For the Leipzig cantatas, Bach rarely prepared a separate violone part. Instead, the violone player seems to have read from an unfigured, "generic" continuo part, one that normally contained all the movements of the work at hand. The violone player was probably informed by word of mouth when to play and when to be silent. Dreyfus has shown that the few parts specifically labeled "Violone" give a contradictory picture.[34] In Cantatas 100 and 210, which are passed down with violone parts, the instrument takes a varied role in arias, sometimes playing throughout a movement, sometimes playing in the instrumental ritornellos only, and sometimes not playing at all. In Cantatas 195 and 214, by contrast, the violone plays from start to finish, in all movements, even secco recitatives.

In the choruses of the B-Minor Mass, the violone probably should double the continuo line throughout. Although one might be tempted to drop the violone during *concertino* episodes of the concerted choruses, such as

mm. 37–64 of the "Cum Sancto Spiritu" or mm. 74–86 of the "Et resurrexit" (the "Et iterum venturus est" section), the extant violone parts in
cantatas from the Leipzig years do not show Bach making such distinctions.[35] In the arias, the violone would also be a useful presence, especially in performances in large spaces. It is noteworthy that in the original
score of the D-Major Magnificat the violone is mentioned only once, in the
"Suscepit Israel," a *bassetto* aria, or aria with a bass in the tenor or alto
range. There Bach indicated "Cont. e Violoncelli senza Violone è
Bassoni." Could that mean that the violone is to play in *all* other movements, both choruses and arias? It may, and that might hold relevance for
the B-Minor Mass, a piece with the same grand scoring as the Magnificat
and Cantatas 195 and 214.

With the bassoon we are on firmer ground than with the violone, since we
can turn to the Dresden bassoon part of the *Missa* for guidance. Like other
bassoon parts written out by Bach himself, the Dresden part differs significantly from the continuo line of the score.[36] First, Bach marked the bassoon
tacet during all arias except the "Quoniam tu solus," in which the two bassoons have obbligato roles. This implies that the bassoon would have been
silent during the arias of the Credo, Sanctus, and Agnus Dei as well, even
during the "Et in unum Dominum" and the "Et in Spiritum Sanctum," which
like the "Qui sedes" have obbligato oboe.[37] Second, in the *antico* movements,
"Kyrie eleison" II and "Gratias agimus tibi," the bassoon doubles the vocal
bass rather than the continuo line. That would appear to be its role, then, in
the "Dona nobis pacem" and in the "Credo in unum Deum" and "Confiteor,"
as well, if one decides to use *colla parte* doubling (see discussion below).
Third, in the concerted choruses, the bassoon plays a considerably more
complex role. In the "Gloria in excelsis Deo," it doubles the continuo part
but drops out during *concertino* episodes (mm. 25–29, 41–44, and 67–75). In
the "Cum Sancto Spiritu," it does much the same: it doubles the continuo
(except at mm. 100–104) but drops out for the two vocal fugatos (mm. 37–64
and 82–100). In "Kyrie eleison" I and "Et in terra pax" the bassoon follows
a threefold path: sometimes it doubles the continuo bass line, especially
when the voices are silent; at other points, it doubles the vocal bass line; and
at still other times, it either rests or goes its own way. The role of the bassoon
in "Kyrie eleison" I can be summarized as follows:

    mm. 1–4 (introduction)—doubles the vocal bass

    mm. 5–30 (orchestral exposition)—doubles the continuo

    mm. 30–58 (vocal exposition)—doubles the vocal bass

mm. 58–62 (vocal episode)—doubles the continuo

mm. 62–72 (vocal exposition)—doubles the vocal bass

mm. 72–81 (instrumental interlude)—partly doubles the continuo, partly
   rests

mm. 81–126 (final vocal exposition)—partly doubles the continuo, partly
   doubles the vocal bass, partly independent

As Dreyfus rightly observes, the inventive schemes of "Kyrie eleison" I
and "Et in terra pax" show Bach reconciling in a highly sophisticated way
the two historical roles of the bassoon, that of choral bassist and that of
modern continuo player.[38] For the remaining concerted, *stile moderno* choruses of the B-Minor Mass, we can extrapolate the function of the bassoon
from the *Missa* movements. To take three examples:

"Patrem omnipotentem": bassoon doubles continuo throughout (= the
   "Gloria in excelsis" scheme, aside from the vocal-fugue expositions)

"Et incarnatus est": bassoon tacet (= the "Qui tollis" scheme)

"Et resurrexit": bassoon doubles continuo, except during vocal-fugue
   expositions and vocal solos (= the Cantata 110/1 scheme and the
   "Gloria in excelsis Deo," including the vocal-fugue expositions):

mm. 1–9	doubles continuo line
mm. 9–14	tacet (vocal fugue exposition)
mm. 14–50	doubles continuo line
mm. 50–56	tacet (vocal fugue exposition)
mm. 56–74	doubles continuo line
mm. 74–86	tacet (bass solo)
mm. 86–93	doubles continuo line
mm. 93–97	tacet (vocal fugue exposition)
mm. 97–131	doubles continuo line

In the "Crucifixus," the bassoon would probably have doubled the continuo
throughout, possibly dropping out with the flutes and upper strings for the
final reiteration of the ground bass in mm. 49–53.[39]

   All of these suggestions are speculative, obviously. What is clear from
the *Missa* is that Bach wished the bassoon to do more than simply double
the continuo line in choruses. In the Credo, Sanctus, and Agnus Dei the
best we can do is try to recreate his sophisticated approach, using the
refined Dresden bassoon part as a guide.

   In Dresden, continuo practices at the Hofkirche seem to have been more
straightforward than Bach's. For sacred works, Zelenka normally divided
the continuo into two groups: "Organo," which included the organ, theorbo,

and cellos, and "Ripieno," which included the violones and bassoons.[40] The "Organo" players performed throughout the arias and choruses and the "Ripieno" players performed throughout the choruses only.

COLLA PARTE SCORING IN THE "CREDO" AND "CONFITEOR"

When C. P. E. Bach presented the *Symbolum Nicenum* in 1786, he augmented the scoring of the "Credo in unum Deum" and "Confiteor" movements by having instruments double the vocal lines. Such *colla parte* scoring—the instrumentalists were instructed to play "with the part" of the appropriate voice—was common in Germany in Bach's time for pieces written in Renaissance motet style. *Colla parte* scoring provided the singers with support, it broadened and enriched the sound, and, in an age when most churches and court chapels had instrumental ensembles, it gave the instrumental players something to do in pieces that otherwise would not have required their services. In the B-Minor Mass, Bach used *colla parte* scoring in three movements, all written in Palestrina vocal style: "Kyrie eleison" II, "Gratias agimus tibi," and "Dona nobis pacem." Did he also intend *colla parte* instrumentation for the stylistically similar "Credo in unum Deum" and "Confiteor" even though it is not indicated in the *P 180* manuscript?

This is a question of long standing, at least for the "Confiteor." Pointing to Emanuel's Hamburg performance and Bach's normal practice, Albert Schweitzer first raised the possibility of fleshing out the "Confiteor" almost a century ago.[41] More recently the issue has been posed by Helmut Rilling as well as Hans-Joachim Schulze and Christoph Wolff.[42] The "Credo," by contrast, has not been deemed a serious candidate because it contains two independent violin parts, which seem to lift it out of the realm of normal *a cappella*-style practice.[43] Like continuo matters, the *colla parte* issue could be resolved definitively if we had original performance parts for the Credo portion, since they would show the precise role of instruments in the "Confiteor" and "Credo" and tell us whether Emanuel was following a long-established *colla parte* convention or altering the instrumentation to fit circumstances unique to his performance.

Secondary evidence suggests that he was following tradition. There can be little question that north of the Alps, music written in the Palestrina mode was commonly performed with *colla parte* instrumental support. In *Gradus ad Parnassum*, Fux reviewed the two possible types of performance for this repertory—*a cappella* and *colla parte*—and tied each to stylistic considerations.[44] *A cappella* performance was appropriate for diatonic pieces that avoided chromaticism and transposition (Fux cited the Kyrie from Palestrina's *Missa vicissitudinus* as an example). *Colla parte* performance "with organ and other instruments" was appropriate for freer works, with more chromaticism and modulation. Fux's distinction stemmed chiefly from practical considerations: in more difficult chromatic pieces, instrumental doubling buttressed the voices. As we observed in our earlier discussions of Palestrina style, Bach owned a copy of *Gradus ad Parnassum* and thus was probably acquainted with Fux's views.

The dual practice outlined by Fux and presumably used by him in Vienna does not seem to have been employed in Bach's circles, however. In Middle Germany, *colla parte* reinforcement appears to have been the standard method of performance for Renaissance *a cappella*-style works, no matter what degree of chromaticism and modulation they displayed. As we noted in Chapter 1, in Dresden, where Palestrina's music formed an integral part of the Hofkirche repertory, instrumental doubling was standard procedure. Extant performance materials of Palestrina Masses and motets presented by Heinichen and Zelenka show the constant use of *colla parte* reinforcement.[45] When Bach, aided by an assistant, wrote out a set of parts to Palestrina's *Missa sine nomine* around 1742, he added *colla parte* cornetti and trombones to the Kyrie and Gloria, the portions that were usable in the Leipzig worship service. The Credo-to-Agnus Dei sections, which were unsuitable for Leipzig, appear in the score without instruments, as do the Kyrie and Gloria—a fact not irrelevant to the "Confiteor" and "Credo," since it suggests that *colla parte* doubling was realized only when pieces were brought to performance. So established was *colla parte* practice in Middle Germany that Walther, writing in 1732, defined *a cappella* not as a performance by unaccompanied choir, as we do today, but rather as "when vocal and instrumental parts are executed together at the same time, and indeed in such a way that the latter are heard to be the same as the former."[46]

From an aesthetic standpoint, *colla parte* doubling allowed German composers to indulge in their deep-seated love for instruments—a penchant already visible in the instrument-oriented ensemble combinations suggested for polychoral music in *Syntagma Musicum* by Praetorius (who, of course, was drawing on the practice of Giovanni Gabrieli). For Praetorius and succeeding generations of German composers, unaccompanied vocal music appears to have been, as Wilhelm Heinse has nicely put it, "the equivalent of a naked figure in art,"[47] one which required some sort of instrumental clothing. This was especially true for Bach, who used *colla parte* instruments ubiquitously to flesh out purely vocal scoring in motets and harmonized chorales, as well as in Palestrina-style movements in cantatas. Instrumental parts to *Der Geist hilft unser Schwachheit auf,* BWV 226, *Fürchte dich nicht,* BWV 228, and Sebastian Knüpfer's *Erforsche mich Gott* (presented under Bach's direction around 1746)[48] reveal that Bach performed polychoral motets *colla parte* whenever instruments were available. Mozart's comment on his manuscript score of *Singet dem Herrn ein neues Lied,* BWV 225—"Nota Bene: a complete orchestra must be added to this piece"[49]—demonstrates the extension of the *colla parte* tradition into the second half of the eighteenth century. Bach always used *colla parte* scoring for the harmonized chorales of his sacred vocal works, doubling the voice parts with whatever instruments were available in the ensemble at hand.

Most telling, however, is Bach's consistent use of instrumental doubling in vocal choruses written in Palestrina style:

"Ach Gott, vom Himmel sieh darein" from Cantata 2
"Nun lob, mein Seel, den Herren" from Cantata 28
"Wir danken dir, Gott, wir danken dir" from Cantata 29
"Aus tiefer Not schrei ich zu dir" from Cantata 38
"Christum wir sollen loben schon" from Cantata 121
"Nimm, was dein ist, und gehe hin" from Cantata 144
"Siehe zu, daß deine Gottesfurcht nicht Heuchelei sei" from Cantata 179
"Kyrie eleison" II from the B-Minor Mass
"Gratias agimus tibi" from the B-Minor Mass
"Dona nobis pacem" from the B-Minor Mass
"Kyrie eleison" I from Mass in F Major, BWV 233
"Kyrie eleison" I from Mass in G Major, BWV 236

Aside from the "Credo in unum Deum" and "Confiteor," there are only four Palestrina-style movements that seem to lack *colla parte* doubling:

"Kyrie eleison, Christe du Lamm Gottes," BWV 233a
"Sicut locutus est" from Magnificat in D Major, BWV 243
"Credo in unum Deum," BWV 1081, for Bassani's Mass in F Major
"Suscepit Israel," BWV 1082, arrangement for Caldara's Magnificat in
     C Major

What is striking about the exceptions is that, like the "Credo" and "Confiteor," they are pieces for which we have original scores (or early copies) but no performance parts.

This brings us to the issue of notation. For a number of *colla parte* movements, such as the "Gratias agimus tibi" or the "Dona nobis pacem," Bach wrote out a full score, allotting each instrument and voice a separate line. However, for other Palestrina-style pieces, such as the "Kyrie eleison" II (Plate 7–2), he wrote out the vocal parts and continuo line only, forming a simpler score that appropriately conveyed the vocal nature of the Renaissance *a cappella* style. In these scores, Bach indicated *colla parte* doubling through designations such as "Stromenti in unisono" ("Instruments in unison"), "Violino 1 col soprano" ("Violin 1 with the soprano"), and so forth. Modern editions, including the *Neue Bach-Ausgabe*, normally allot each instrumental part a separate line no matter what Bach's original score looks like. For the "Kyrie eleison" II and other pieces, this creates an erroneous picture of Bach's notational practice.

Critical to the "Credo" and "Confiteor" is the fact that Bach commonly omitted *colla parte* indications altogether in his scores. As it is well known, the scores of the motets *Der Geist hilft* and *Fürchte dich nicht* carry no suggestion of instrumental doubling; the doubling was carried out, without comment in the score, during the production of performance parts. The same is true of harmonized chorales: Bach's scores typically contain no indication whatsoever of instruments *colla parte*. Doubling seems to have been so taken for granted that mention of it in the score was unnecessary. Our modern perception of the "Credo" and "Confiteor" as vocal movements with continuo accompaniment only, a perception derived from the *P 180* manuscript, is surely distorted. One suspects that Bach would have verified the need for *colla parte* doubling during the production of performance parts—as he did in so many other cases.

Fux associated the "Styl a Capella" with "the full chorus,"[50] and in Palestrina-style organ works such as *Kyrie, Gott heiliger Geist*, BWV 671, or *Aus tiefer Not, schrei ich zu dir*, BWV 686, Bach calls for full-organ registrations: "Cum Organo pleno," "In Organo pleno," etc. As the doublings in the motets, harmonized chorales, and Palestrina-style movements show, Bach did not waste instrumentalists when a tutti sound was called for: he normally assigned every possible player a part.[51] Would he have allowed instrumentalists to sit idly during the "Credo" and "Confiteor," movements for "the full chorus"? His other *a cappella* pieces suggest that he would have drawn them into play.

Within the *Symbolum* the "Credo" is joined with the "Patrem omnipotentem," and the "Confiteor" with the "Et expecto," to form two *stile antico-stile moderno* pairs. Bach's creation of balanced pairs in both cases implies that the *stile antico* is on an even footing with the *stile moderno*. Otherwise, theologically, the church dogma of the *antico* movements would seem less

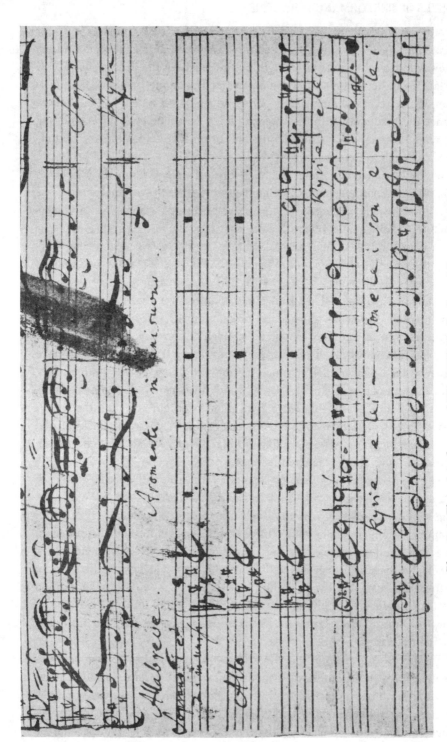

Plate 7–2. The original score of "Kyrie" II (Berlin State Library, *P 180*).

important than the apotheosis of the *moderno* movements. The traditional performance with undoubled chorus renders the *antico* music less weighty dynamically and creates a nineteenth-century-oriented crescendo. A performance with *colla parte* doubling, on the other hand, produces a symmetrical *plenum* sound closer to Baroque convention. Wolff has viewed the scoring of the "Credo" and "Confiteor" as a sign of Bach's desire to return to the pure, classical, undoubled *a cappella* style of Palestrina.[52] But one is hard-pressed to find evidence of such a style in Bach's other works or in the performances of Palestrina's music in Leipzig and Dresden.

If we accept a *colla parte* performance of the "Credo" and "Confiteor," we need to consider just how it would have been carried out. The doubling used by Emanuel Bach for the Hamburg performance is unorthodox, at least by his father's standards:

VOICE	"CREDO" DOUBLING	"CONFITEOR" DOUBLING
soprano 1	oboe 1	violin 1, oboe 1
soprano 2	oboe 2	violin 2, oboe 2
alto	viola	viola
tenor	bassoon	bassoon
bass	cello	cello

While the doubling for the sopranos and alto is conventional, the assignment of the bassoon to the tenor and the cello to the bass is odd. Although it is not an unprecedented *colla parte* scoring (Handel used it), it does not appear in any of J. S. Bach's works. For a more conventional doubling, we can turn to the standard *colla parte* scoring used for five-voice works in Dresden:

VOICE	DOUBLING
soprano 1	violin 1, oboe 1
soprano 2	violin 2, oboe 2
alto	viola 1
tenor	viola 2
bass	continuo

Bach used split violas in Weimar cantatas scored in the French manner with five-part strings. Suddenly dividing the violas for the "Credo" and "Confiteor" of the B-Minor Mass, a work with an Italianate four-part string body, would be an unusual step. But we need to look no farther than the

"Quoniam tu solus" to find license for such a measure. The bassoons divide for that movement alone. Why can't the violas similarly divide just for the "Credo" and "Confiteor"?

The Dresden *colla parte* scheme calls for adjustment in light of Bach's procedure in "Kyrie eleison" II, "Gratias agimus tibi," and "Dona nobis pacem": flute 1 and flute 2 should double soprano 1 (not soprano 1 and soprano 2, respectively, because the notes b and c♯' in soprano 2 were unplayable on the Baroque flute), oboes d'amore should be used in the "Confiteor" (because of the low range of soprano 2), and the bassoon should double the vocal bass, leaving the cello and violone free to play the independent continuo line. In addition, since the violins are occupied with independent lines in the "Credo," the sopranos should be doubled by the flutes and oboes only in that segment. These modifications lead to the following *colla parte* plan:

VOICE	"CREDO" DOUBLING	"CONFITEOR" DOUBLING
soprano 1	oboe 1, flute 1 & 2	violin 1, oboe d'amore 1, flute 1 & 2
soprano 2	oboe 2	violin 2, oboe d'amore 2
alto	viola 1	viola 1
tenor	viola 2	viola 2
bass	bassoon	bassoon
continuo	cello, violone	cello, violone

Finally, in the *P 180* manuscript the "Et expecto" proper—that is, the *vivace e allegro* at m. 147—is prefaced by five measures of rests in the upper instruments, rests that begin with the turn to page 140. That does not eliminate the possibility of *colla parte* scoring, since the rests could be viewed as a compositional indication, referring to the beginning of the obbligato writing. It is conceivable that Bach would have made *colla parte* adjustments as parts were written out, just as he clarified in the Dresden parts that one flute rather than two in unison should be used for the "Domine Deus" (see Chapter 3).

There is a second, more intriguing possibility: that the instrumental doubling would have been dropped at the "Et expecto" bridge, on the final syllable of the "Confiteor" text (the "-rum" of "peccatorum") that falls on a conclusive, downbeat, D-major chord in m. 123. From there on, in the bridge to the "Et expecto" proper, Bach composed in a style that is closer to the Renaissance madrigal than to the Palestrina Mass or motet. The rests in the original manuscript may indicate that the *colla parte* doubling stopped on the previous page (page 139), at the *adagio,* and that in the "Et expecto" bridge, the voices should indeed be accompanied by the continuo only.[53] That would create a highly unusual effect (though one finds it in the Credo of Zelenka's *Missa Circumcisionis*, Z. 11, where the instruments suddenly drop out for the word "mortuorum").[54] But it is precisely the effect produced in the final measures of the "Crucifixus," when the upper instruments become silent, leaving the voices to sing alone with the continuo, in hushed expectation of the "Et resurrexit" that follows. The musical allusion in the "Et expecto" bridge to the bass of the "Crucifixus" only strengthens the parallel between the two passages.

TEMPO MATTERS

In Bach's German circles, tempo was indicated less by Italian or French designations than by the basic notation with which a piece was written down. The first and foremost indicator of tempo was the time signature, which stipulated the number of underlying pulses in each measure, no matter how fast or slow the pace. The time signature also carried with it an expected subdivision of the beat into smaller units. Considered together, the meter and the smallest note value pointed to an appropriate tempo. Johann Philipp Kirnberger, who, as we have seen, was close to Bach and frequently cited his works in theoretical discussions, called this appropriate tempo the *tempo giusto:*

> [A composer] must acquire a correct feeling for the natural tempo of every meter, or for what is called *tempo giusto.* This is attained by diligent study of all kinds of dance pieces. Every dance has its definite tempo, determined by the meter and the note values that are employed in it.[55]

To take an example: in $\frac{3}{4}$ time, the smallest note value would normally be the sixteenth note. A piece notated in $\frac{3}{4}$ with sixteenth-note subdivisions would be played at a neutral "allegro" tempo, with the quarter note roughly equal to a heartbeat (the most frequently cited measure), $\quarternote$ = 72 or so.[56] But if the smallest subdivision is the eighth note, as in a minuet, the quarter note would be taken somewhat faster. Conversely, if the smallest subdivision is the thirty-second note, as in a sarabande, the quarter note would be taken a bit more slowly than an *allegro* tempo. In all three cases, however, the overall pulse of three beats per measure would be preserved. The minuet would not be played so quickly that the sense of three was lost to one large beat, and the sarabande would not be played so slowly that a sense of three was obscured by subdivisions. In straightforward $\frac{3}{4}$ meter or $\frac{4}{4}$ meter, extremes of tempo seem to have been avoided, unless a tempo word such as *prestissimo* or *adagio assai* indicated otherwise.

In addition, meters were arranged in hierarchical orders: those with larger denominators (that is, with larger note values, such as the half note) suggested a slower tempo and "heavier" performance than those with smaller ones. For instance, among simple triple-time signatures, $\frac{3}{2}$ meter was the slowest and heaviest, $\frac{3}{4}$ meter was faster and lighter, $\frac{3}{8}$ meter was faster and lighter still, and $\frac{3}{16}$ was the fastest and lightest of all. Kirnberger gave a more general example:

> Regarding meter, those having larger values, like alla breve, $\frac{3}{2}$, and $\frac{6}{4}$ meter, have a heavier and slower tempo than those of smaller values, like $\frac{2}{4}$, $\frac{3}{4}$, and $\frac{6}{8}$ meter, and these in turn are less lively than $\frac{3}{8}$ or $\frac{6}{16}$ meter.[57]

The fact that meters implied a type of articulation as well as a tempo is also critical to performance, and we will explore this issue in greater detail in the next section.

Tempo words, which often pointed to an *Affekt* or character as much as to a specific pace, served to modify the pace and articulation suggested by the meter. The time signature $\frac{3}{8}$, for example, normally pointed to a fast and light performance—as in the "Pleni sunt coeli" or "Osanna in excelsis" of the B-Minor Mass. This could be modified, however, by the addition of a tempo word. The designation *Un poco allegro* in the third movement of the Trio Sonata in E Minor for organ, BWV 528, mitigates the effect of the $\frac{3}{8}$ time signature and calls for a slightly slower and less lightly articulated performance. To quote Kirnberger once again:

> Thus the *tempo giusto* is determined by the meter and by the longer and shorter note values of a composition. Once the young composer has a feeling for this, he will soon understand to what degree the adjectives *largo, adagio, andante, allegro, presto,* and their modifications *larghetto, andantino, allegretto,* and *prestissimo* add to or take away from the fast or slow motion of the natural tempo. He will soon be able not only to write in every type of tempo, but also in such a way that this tempo is captured quickly and correctly by the performers.[58]

For Bach, meter and note value seem to have been the principal indicators of tempo, with French and Italian designations playing a supplementary role. In Italian-derived instrumental works—sonatas, trios, and concertos—tempo designations were expected, as a convention, and Bach used them in such pieces as a matter of course (except in first movements, where the neutral *allegro* tempo of $\frac{4}{4}$ or $\frac{3}{4}$ meter was the understood norm and usually required no comment). But in keyboard and vocal music, he was noticeably frugal with tempo markings, often adding them only at a later point, after the score was finished. We can observe these patterns in the B-Minor Mass. Of the twenty-six movements, only six have tempo words in the *P 180* manuscript:

"Kyrie eleison" I, fugue (m. 5)	*largo*
"Kyrie eleison" II	*allabreve*
"Gratias"	*allabreve*
"Cum Sancto Spiritu"	*vivace*
"Et expecto" bridge ("Confiteor," m. 121)	*adagio*
"Et expecto"	*vivace e allegro*

In the Dresden *Missa* parts, Bach added indications to the "Kyrie eleison" I introduction and to the "Gloria" and "Qui tollis" movements. But his markings are both incomplete and inconsistent, as can be seen in the following summary:

PART	"KYRIE ELEISON" I, INTRODUCTION (M. 1)	"GLORIA"	"QUI TOLLIS"
Trumpets and timpani		—	
Flutes 1 & 2	*adagio*	—	—
Oboes 1 & 2	—	—	
Violin 1 (two parts)	*adagio*	*vivace*	*adagio*
Violin 2	*adagio*	—	—
Viola	*adagio*	—	—
Violoncello	*molt' adagio*	*vivace*	*lente*
Bassoon	—	—	
Continuo	*adagio*	—	*lente*
Soprano 1	—	—	
Soprano 2	—	—	—
Alto	—	—	*lente*
Tenor	—	—	—
Bass	—	—	—

This suggests, obviously, that Bach was working in haste. First, he appears to have marked only the most essential parts. In the introduction to "Kyrie eleison" I, indications appear in most of the instrumental parts but in none of the vocal—a pattern that can be observed in the performance materials of many Leipzig cantatas. In the "Gloria" the vocal parts are again neglected (though here the instrumental introduction provides the chorus with the tempo), and among the instrumental parts, only the first violin and continuo, the traditional leaders of the Baroque ensemble, are marked. And in the "Qui tollis," indications appear solely in the first violin, continuo, and cello—critical tempo setters, once again—and in the only vocal part to sound on the downbeat, the alto. Thus while Bach's markings are incomplete by today's standards, they probably got the job done: they alerted the most important participants.

Second, Bach seems to have been working so quickly, without checking one part against another, that he put down different indications for the same movement. Thus for the "Kyrie eleison" I introduction, seven parts (including the second violin 1 part and both flutes) have *adagio,* but the cello is marked *molt' adagio;* for the "Qui tollis" the violin 1 parts are marked *adagio,* the remainder, *lente.* Such discrepancies are not uncommon in Bach performance materials, especially those of the Leipzig cantatas, which were frequently written out under considerable time pressure.[59] Bach therefore seems to have viewed a number of terms as roughly synonymous, which implies that his interpretation of tempo or *Affekt* terms was anything but rigid. With these circumstances in mind, let us survey the individual movements of the B-Minor Mass and explore the tempo precepts that might obtain in each. We will draw heavily on the contemporary observations of Kirnberger and Walther, both of whom worked with Bach and were closely attuned to Middle German practice.

"Kyrie eleison" I. The indication *adagio,* found in m. 1, is generally used in two ways in Bach's works: as a mid-movement or concluding indication of ritardando (as in the "Qui sedes," m. 73) or as a more encompassing mark of tempo or *Affekt* for an entire movement or passage. The latter is its use here. Walther defined *adagio* as "leisurely, slowly."[60] "Leisurely" implies a certain amount of expressive freedom. In vocal works, Bach commonly used *adagio* for emotionally charged passages with plaintive or beseeching texts, especially in recitatives (such as the climactic moment in the St. Matthew Passion when Christ cries out from the cross, "My God, my God, why hast thou forsaken me?").[61] In the introduction to "Kyrie" I, *adagio* suggests an expressive, perhaps even recitative-like performance.

Pointing even more strongly in that direction is the *molt' adagio* of the cello part, a designation found in the aria "Es ist vollbracht" ("It is finished") from the St. John Passion.

Whether the *largo* used for the fugue at m. 5 means a faster or slower tempo is not easily determined. Walther allowed for both possibilities: he first defined *largo* as "very slowly"—that is, slower than *adagio.* But he then went on to say that "certain authors view it as a faster tempo than *adagio,* because *adagio* is often found at the end of *largo* pieces, to mark a ritard."[62] Kirnberger seems to place *largo* on the slower side of *adagio* (in the quotation on *tempo giusto,* above). To Bach, the two terms must have been fairly close in meaning: in the parts to the aria "Wo Zwei und Drei versammlet sind" from Cantata 42, he used *adagio* and *largo* simultaneously. In "Kyrie" I the move from *adagio* to *largo* may mark a change in rhythmic strictness rather than pace, with *adagio* indicating an expressive, recitative-like opening and *largo* indicating a more measured gait for the fugue. A similar passage occurs in the third section of Cantata 131, *Aus der Tiefen rufe ich, Herr, zu dir,* in which a short, declamatory introduction with recitative-like flourishes, marked *adagio,* is followed by a vocal fugue, marked *largo.*

"Christe eleison." In $\frac{4}{4}$ time with the sixteenth note as the smallest note value and lacking any mitigating tempo or *Affekt* indication, the "Christe" seems to call for a straightforward, neutral *allegro.* For such pieces many composers (most notably Handel) used the term *tempo ordinario,* which Walther described as "designated with a **C** , which means that all notes should be performed in their natural and normal value."[63]

A second, more likely possibility is that the "Christe" is a walking-bass *andante,* similar to the "Et in unum Dominum" or the first movement of the B-Minor Flute Sonata, BWV 1030. *Andante* implied not just a slower tempo than *allegro* (Kirnberger placed it between *adagio* and *allegro* in the *tempo giusto* discussion) but a very steady pace, especially in the bass. Walther described *andante* as "derived from the Italian verb *andare*" (to walk, to go) and "somewhat faster than *adagio.*" Pieces marked *andante,* he went on, display "a fair amount of movement" and are performed "so that all notes are nicely even and equal."[64] In the "Christe" Bach may have viewed the designation *andante* as superfluous, since the unceasing, steady, eighth-note motion of the bass would have suggested a walking-bass aria to contemporary players.

"Kyrie eleison" II. As we noted in earlier chapters, the term *allabreve* implied Renaissance motet style. Walther's full definition is instructive:

Allabreve, or *a la Breve* (ital.) was used by the old Italians to designate that meter, in which a breve, or a note with two slashes ◨, is realized half in the downbeat and half in the upbeat or, in its place, two semibreves, or four minims (that is, *intactu aequali*). This meter always concludes on the beat (*"cum Tempore"*), that is, with a breve, or a still longer note, which begins with the lowering of the hand and ends with the lifting of the hand, and not in tempo. A half circle with a line through it designates this meter, which is beat very quickly and occurs only in motets. . . . Compositions set in this meter were full of syncopations, ties, and points of imitation, and had no smaller notes than quarters, which were used sparingly at that.[65]

In the B-Minor Mass, the "Kyrie eleison" II, "Gratias agimus tibi," "Credo in unum Deum," and "Gratias agimus tibi" are notated in the true *allabreve* time described by Walther—that is, $\frac{2}{1}$ time with two whole notes (semibreves) per measure. During the Baroque, $\frac{2}{1}$-meter *allabreve* was gradually replaced by an *allabreve* with reduced values: $\frac{2}{2}$ meter with two half notes per measure (making it, in a sense, "alla semibreve"). In the B-Minor Mass, the "Confiteor" and "Patrem omnipotentem" movements are notated in the reduced-value *allabreve*. Kirnberger called $\frac{2}{2}$ time "large *allabreve*" and claimed in 1776 that it was no longer in use.[66] Johann Friedrich Agricola, writing four years later, also stated that $\frac{2}{1}$ meter was seldom if ever encountered, especially in its pure form, and cited the "Credo" from the B-Minor Mass as an example.[67]

According to Agricola, large *allabreve* meter requires a special gravity and "heavy" mode of performance. Kirnberger, too, connected it with a very serious and emphatic performing style, one in which the notes are closely connected and given their full value—a point of articulation to which we will return in the next section. But he also pointed out that the serious nature of *allabreve* does not mean slow: the tempo should be twice as fast as the note values indicate. That parallels Walther's view of *allabreve* as "beat very quickly."

"Gloria in excelsis." The *vivace* in the first violin and cello parts most probably points more to an *Affekt* than to a specific tempo. As we have seen, Kirnberger omitted *vivace* from his overview of *tempo giusto* modifiers. Walther defined it simply as "lively," and in Bach's music overall there is a remarkably high correspondence between the use of *vivace* and the appearance of detachment dots. Another reason to suspect that *vivace* is chiefly a character is Bach's occasional use of the phrase *vivace e allegro* (in Cantata

24/3, Cantata 201/1, and "Et expecto" of the B-Minor Mass). In that expression, *allegro* seems to indicate the tempo—fast—and *vivace* the intended mode of performance: light, springy, spirited, with detached articulation. Occurring mainly in Italian-derived instrumental idioms, *vivace* might be viewed as the antithesis of heavier, motet-related *allabreve*, as far as *Affekt* is concerned. In the B-Minor Mass, Bach appears to have exploited the dichotomy of the two, contrasting *vivace stile-moderno* movements ("Gloria," "Cum Sancto Spiritu," "Et expecto") with *allabreve stile-antico* movements ("Kyrie" II, "Credo," "Confiteor").

In terms of tempo, the $\frac{3}{8}$ meter (faster and lighter than $\frac{3}{4}$ time, on Kirnberger's scale) and the giga idiom, with its balanced phrases, place the "Gloria" in the brisk category. This view is supported by the macro-beat notation used by Bach in the bassoon part: | ♫♫ ı ♫♫ | .

"Et in terra pax." This appears to be a neutral *tempo ordinario* modified somewhat toward a slower pace by the affective paired slurrings of the principal motive.

Arthur Mendel proposed a proportional tempo relationship between the "Gloria" and the "Et in terra pax" in which the quarter note of the hemiola cadence of the "Gloria" equals the quarter note of the "Et in terra pax":[68]

$$\frac{3}{8}\ \overline{♫♫}\ |\ \overline{♫♫} \rightarrow \mathbf{c}\ ♩\ ♩\ ♩$$

While this idea is attractive because it systematizes the connection between the "Gloria" and the "Et in terra pax," it seems to have no foundation in eighteenth-century practice. Proportional relationships might obtain in a Renaissance-oriented *a cappella*-style piece, but it is unlikely that they would be in effect in a Baroque-oriented *stile moderno* work, in which metrical considerations were determined by dance and instrumental conventions rather than mensural principles.

"Laudamus te." The "Laudamus te" seems to require a straightforward *tempo ordinario,* modified somewhat toward the slower side of the scale by the thirty-second-note figuration in the principal violin, the paired sixteenth-note slurrings in the strings, and the sixteenth-note trills in the soprano solo.

"Gratias agimus tibi." The "Gratias" is another *allabreve* movement; see the discussion under "Kyrie eleison" II.

"Domine Deus." Like the "Christe eleison," this appears to be a walking-bass *andante.*

"Qui tollis." The *adagio* in the two violin 1 parts and the *lente* in the violoncello, continuo, and alto parts imply that the "Qui tollis" should be taken slowly. As we have seen with "Kyrie eleison" I, *adagio* also suggests a certain expressive freedom. Walther defined *lento* (or *lent* or *lentement*) as "slowly"—no more, no less.

"Qui sedes." The $\frac{6}{8}$ meter and abundance of symmetrical phrases suggest that the "Qui sedes" is dance-derived. John Butt has associated it with the polonaise,[69] but Bach always notated polonaises in simple triple meter ($\frac{3}{4}$ or $\frac{3}{8}$). A more likely candidate is the Italian giga, often notated in $\frac{6}{8}$ time, with an active sixteenth-note melody and homophonic accompaniment. Either way, the $\frac{6}{8}$ meter, unmodified by a tempo word, would point to a lively tempo and articulation. Kirnberger categorized $\frac{6}{8}$ meter as a "light" theater and chamber meter. He also warned, however, that it was not as fast or light as $\frac{6}{16}$ time.[70] In his hierarchy of meters, it stood midway between $\frac{6}{4}$ and $\frac{6}{16}$.

"Quoniam tu solus." A neutral *allegro*, with the quarter notes in the *tempo ordinario* range, seems to be the appropriate tempo here.

"Cum Sancto Spiritu." As in the "Gloria in excelsis," the *vivace* probably points to a lively articulation rather than to a fast tempo. In the *P 180* manuscript, the musical text flows directly from the "Quoniam" into the "Cum Sancto": there is no double bar or new meter sign. This may indicate that the neutral *allegro* of the "Quoniam" is to be continued in the "Cum Sancto," but that the articulation should change to *vivace*—that is, it should be lighter and more spirited.

"Credo in unum Deum." The "Credo" is a brisk *allabreve*, performed twice as fast as the note values indicate; see the discussion under "Kyrie eleison" II.

"Patrem omnipotentem." This is an example of the Baroque "reduced value" $\frac{2}{2}$-meter *allabreve*, mentioned in the discussion of "Kyrie eleison" I. Presumably its tempo matches that of the "Credo," but with one whole-note beat per measure rather than two. In the *P 180* manuscript, the "Patrem" is notated with a ₵ meter sign (not ₵, as given in the *Bach-Gesamtausgabe*). Kirnberger stated that for pieces in "small *allabreve*" time, or $\frac{2}{2}$ meter, one could use either a ₵ or a ₵ signature. Works in $\frac{2}{1}$, however, required ₵.[71]

"Et in unum Dominum." This is a walking-bass aria. The *andante* implies a tempo between *adagio* and *allegro* and an even, steady pace.

"Et incarnatus." The text, the B-minor mode, and expressive slurring in the instruments point to a tempo slower than is suggested by $\frac{3}{4}$ meter, with the eighth note as the smallest value. The *adagio* or *lente* of the "Qui tollis," which has similar slurring in the strings as well as a pulsating, repeated-note bass, would seem to be appropriate here.

"Crucifixus." The passacaglia, *lamento*-bass nature of the "Crucifixus" dictates a moderate, steady tempo. Walther viewed the passacaglia as "slower than the chaconne in most cases, the melody more subdued or caressing, and the expression less lively" and hence "always in the minor mode."[72] Bach marked the ground-bass lament of the *Capriccio on the Departure of a Most Beloved Brother,* BWV 992, *adagiosissimo.* More importantly, he marked the A section of the Cantata 12 chorus "Weinen, Klagen, Sorgen, Zagen," on which the "Crucifixus" is based, *lente.* That appears to be an appropriate tempo for the revised music.

"Et resurrexit." As was true of the "Qui sedes," so here: the periodic nature of the music suggests a dance idiom. Klaus Häfner has pointed to similarities with the *Réjouissance* of the Overture in D Major, BWV 1069, a movement also in $\frac{3}{4}$ meter with the sixteenth note as the smallest value.[73] The *Réjouissance* is a plausible match, especially if the "Et resurrexit" is derived from the chorus "Entfernet euch, ihr heitern Sterne" from the secular celebratory cantata BWV Anh. 9, as Häfner has proposed (see Chapter 4). Another possible dance model is the minuet, which sometimes displays triplet flourishes as part of its *galant* figurations.

Whatever the case, the tempo of the "Et resurrexit" is probably close to a neutral *allegro.* The music should not be as fast or lightly articulated as the dance-like movements in $\frac{3}{8}$ meter (the "Gloria in excelsis," "Pleni sunt coeli," and "Osanna").

"Et in Spiritum Sanctum." The "Et in Spiritum" is more certainly a dance than the "Et resurrexit." As pointed out in Chapter 4, it is most probably a pastoral, which would call for a moderate, lilting tempo. Like the giga, to which it is related as a slower cousin, the pastoral calls for a well-articulated performance.[74]

"Confiteor." This is another *allabreve* movement, this time in $\frac{2}{2}$ meter, with reduced values, like the "Patrem omnipotentem."

"Et expecto" bridge. The *adagio* that marks the beginning of the bridge to the "Et expecto" (m. 121 of the "Confiteor") signifies a change of *Affekt*—from the neutral, rhythmically straightforward *allabreve* of the "Confiteor" to a more expressive, rhythmically freer mode—as much as a change of tempo. The adventurous chromatic progressions and the modulation to extremely distant key areas (E♭ minor at m. 125) point in that direction. The approach is analogous to that taken in the *adagio* introduction of "Kyrie eleison" I: slowly and with expression.

"Et expecto." The *"allegro"* of *vivace e allegro* for the "Et expecto" proper probably signals a return to the brisk *allabreve* tempo of the "Confiteor." In its original form, in the chorus "Jauchzet, ihr erfreuten Stimmen" from Cantata 120, the music of the "Et expecto" was notated in $\frac{4}{4}$ meter with the note values twice as small (c ♪ [musical notation] rather than ¢ [musical notation]). This, too, points toward a neutral, *tempo-ordinario allegro.*

The *"vivace"* calls for a change in the manner of performance, from the connected Renaissance-motet style of the "Confiteor" to a more lively and detached instrumental style.

"Sanctus." With no tempo indication, how fast should the "Sanctus" go? Is it a *tempo ordinario*-range *allegro*, or do the triplet subdivisions point to a slower pace? A hint comes from the original materials of the 1724 version. The score and most of the parts (seventeen of twenty-two) carry a ₵ meter signature. The practice of using an *allabreve* sign in a piece notated in normal $\frac{4}{4}$ meter with four quarter notes per measure and the sixteenth note as the smallest note value is sometimes called "corrupt ₵." It occurs commonly in the original scores and performance materials of Bach's works, and the ₵ indication is often interspersed with the "correct" C meter. Alfred Dürr has speculated that Bach used an improper ₵ to indicate to his players that the music should be performed at a brisk *allegro.*[75] In a number of movements in "corrupt ₵" meter Bach added tempo words indicating a pace faster than *allegro.* For example, in the aria "Ach bleib bei uns, Herr Jesu Christ" from Cantata 6, a movement later transcribed for organ as one of the Schübler chorales, he used corrupt ₵ meter and added, in pencil, the designation *allegro assai* to the solo violoncello piccolo part. This points to a velocity that may approach ₵ time—that is, two beats per measure. The ₵ meter in the 1724 "Sanctus," then, may indicate an *allegro assai*-type tempo.

As we noted in Chapter 5, when Bach composed the original version of the "Sanctus," he initially sketched the "Pleni sunt coeli" theme in $\frac{3}{4}$ meter but changed the time signature to $\frac{3}{8}$ when writing out the music in full. Some have viewed this change as a sign that Bach wished to notate a proportional relationship between the "Sanctus" and the "Pleni," in which either the ♩[76] or ♩.[77] of the "Pleni" is equal to the ♩ of the "Sanctus." What seems to hold true for the "Gloria"-"Et in terra pax" transition seems to apply here: both the "Sanctus" and "Pleni" are in Baroque concerted style, and it is unlikely that the two would be connected by means of a Renaissance proportional relationship. More probably Bach changed the meter of the "Pleni" to $\frac{3}{8}$ because he wanted a faster tempo and lighter articulation than $\frac{3}{4}$ time would suggest. Kirnberger described $\frac{3}{8}$ meter as having the "lively tempo of a passepied." He added that it appears "chiefly in chamber and theatrical music" (and thus has a purely Baroque—that is, non-mensural—origin) and calls for a "light but not entirely playful manner."[78] An "entirely playful" piece, presumably, would be notated in $\frac{3}{16}$.

"Osanna in excelsis." In $\frac{3}{8}$ meter with no modifying term, the "Osanna" should be performed in the same fashion as the "Pleni sunt coeli."

"Benedictus." The triplet and thirty-second-note subdivisions point to a slower tempo than $\frac{3}{4}$ meter would normally dictate.

"Agnus Dei." Certainly *tempo ordinario* would not seem to apply to this highly emotional piece. Several factors point to a slower, *affettuoso* tempo: the allusions to anguish and sin in the text, the expressive slurring in the violin and vocal parts, the halting fermata at m. 34, and the omnipresent dissonant leaps. The aria "Seufzer, Tränen, Kummer, Not" from Cantata 21 is quite similar to the "Agnus Dei" in these regards, and it is marked *molt' adagio.*[79] *Molt' adagio,* very slowly and expressively, would seem to be an appropriate tempo and *Affekt* for the "Agnus Dei" as well.

"Dona nobis pacem." This movement has the same neutral *allabreve* tempo and performance as the "Gratias."

ARTICULATION

Compared to many of Bach's scores, the *P 180* manuscript of the B-Minor Mass displays an abundance of articulation markings—that is, slurs and detachment dots. This can be explained in part by the high degree of parody: when Bach reworked earlier material, he customarily refined and amplified the articulation indications directly in the revised score. In fact, as we have noted in earlier chapters, the presence of so much articulation in movements such as the "Benedictus," for which no model is extant, is taken as a sign of a parody origin. But the presence of copious markings is also characteristic of Bach's scores from the 1730s and 1740s, a period when he was no longer pressed with weekly cantata production and better able to devote more time to each project. The autograph scores of the Six Trio Sonatas for Organ (c. 1728–1732), the Christmas Oratorio (1734–1735), the St. Matthew Passion (c. 1736), and the B-Minor Flute Sonata (c. 1740) show the same high level of articulatory detail as *P 180*.

While the articulation marks in the B-Minor Mass are far from complete or consistent, they nevertheless point to a number of trends that help us to understand Bach's practices.[80]

First, in Bach's time, slurs generally demarcated a small motivic unit, usually consisting of the arpeggiation of a single harmony or the embellishment of a single note. This is quite different from the later Classical and Romantic concept of "phrasing," in which slurs set off a melodic unit that often extended over several beats or measures. In Baroque music, detachment dots were often used in conjunction with slurs to single out a particular note (in the "Qui sedes," for instance), to mark a shift of a rhythmic accent (in the "Agnus Dei"), or to clarify the extent of a slur (in the "Laudamus te"). Many Baroque writers describe slurring and detachment dots as a type of embellishment, a decoration adding color to a florid line.[81] In the *P 180* autograph of the B-Minor Mass, two-note slurs outnumber other types, appearing in music in major mode (where the small groupings portray a sense of excitement and joy, in the "Et in terra pax" and "Et resurrexit") as well as in minor mode (where they create a sense of mystery or melancholy, in the "Et incarnatus" and "Qui tollis"). Butt, armed with statistical analysis, has demonstrated that Bach used the two-note slur more than any other articulatory unit.[82] Thus in movements like the "Cum Sancto Spiritu," where one finds four-note and two-note slurs appearing with the same motive (in mm. 21–23, for instance), it is probably the two-note slur that should prevail. The prominence of two-note slurs reinforces the notion that Bach was thinking in terms of small motivic units rather than melodic phrases. It also raises the possibility that the two-note slurrings used in the "Et in unum Dominum" by C. P. E. Bach for the 1786 Hamburg performance, markings traditionally rejected as a foreign *galant* element,[83] may be appropriate after all (Example 7–3).

Second, within Bach's compositions one can observe a hierarchy of instrumental articulation. Strings are the most heavily marked, not only because stringed instruments represent the foundation of Bach's ensemble but also because slurring is intimately bound with the realities of bowing. With string instruments, articulation markings are more than a musical nicety—they are often a mechanical necessity, showing the player how to negotiate a figure within the confines of the bow. Woodwind instruments—flutes, oboes, and bassoons (when used in an obbligato role, as in the "Quoniam tu solus")—rank next, frequently showing copious but less complete indications. And brass instruments, with lines that tend to be more straightforward (especially in the case of second and third players), carry the fewest indica-

Example 7–3. C. P. E. Bach's slurrings for the "Et in unum Dominum."

tions of all. In vocal parts, slurs normally clarify matters of text underlay, somewhat in the fashion of ligatures in Medieval and Renaissance notation.

Bach commonly employed slurs and detachment dots in a very abbreviated way. In many instances he marked a figure fastidiously at its first appearance but only sporadically thereafter. The ritornello theme of the "Et resurrexit," for instance, is carefully marked with detachment dots in mm. 1–7 (Example 7–4). After that, the dots are rarely present. This incomplete notation parallels Bach's method of indicating tempo refinements and lombardic rhythm. The marks gave the players a notion of how the figure should be articulated elsewhere in the movement.

Third, the degree of articulation often mirrors the style of a piece. In the B-Minor Mass, movements written in Renaissance vocal style contain almost no articulation markings. Slurs are found here and there in the vocal parts to clarify text underlay, and in the *Missa* these slurs were sometimes carried over to the *colla parte* instruments when performance parts were copied from the vocal lines of the score (as in "Kyrie eleison" II). The neutral style of the *a cappella* movements points to a neutral mode of perfor-

Example 7–4. The opening theme of the "Et resurrexit," as marked in its first appearance in trumpet 1 in the *P 180* manuscript.

mance, in which affective slurrings and detachments have little role. The steady beat of the tactus, the rise and fall of the mostly conjunct vocal lines, and the calculated preparation and resolution of dissonance—these "horizontal" elements predominate and render small-scale articulatory interruptions inappropriate. As we have seen in the discussion of tempo, Kirnberger and Agricola associated the *allabreve* meter of Palestrina-style music with a "very serious and emphatic" or "heavy" performance—that is, the notes are to be played in a more connected, legato manner than in *moderno* pieces.

The concerted movements, with independent instrumental parts, are quite different. Instead of a connected performance, they call for articulated playing to delineate motivic patterns of diminution, embellishment, and *Affekt*. Articulation highlights figural detail, which is as fundamental to Baroque *stile moderno* writing as linear suspensions are to Renaissance *stile antico* writing. But even in the concerted movements, articulation marks are restricted, on the whole, to the instrumental parts. In the vocal parts, the text serves as a guide to articulation, and the few slurrings that appear there normally clarify matters of text underlay.

The most heavily marked concerted movements are the arias with obbligato solo instruments: the "Laudamus te," "Domine Deus," "Benedictus," and others. As might be expected, concerted choruses exhibit fewer indications, since Bach was painting with a broader brush. Nevertheless, it is clear from detachment dots, markings such as *vivace*, and the abundance of instrumental figurations that these movements, too, should be well articulated.

LOMBARD RHYTHM IN THE "DOMINE DEUS"

In the Dresden *Missa* parts, Bach indicated the use of lombard rhythm in the main theme of the "Domine Deus." His method of notation and the way it is to be interpreted have caused considerable controversy over the years, so much so that it is worth considering the issue in some detail here.

When Julius Rietz edited the *Bach-Gesamtausgabe* in 1856, he correctly observed in the Critical Commentary that in the Dresden parts, Bach indicated lombard rhythm in the first measure of the flauto traverso solo (Example 7–5a). Since the figure appeared solely in this measure in the flute, and not at all in violin 1, Rietz decided that it was insignificant and published the flute line, and the rest of the "Domine Deus" text, with even sixteenth notes (Example 7–5b). Rietz's examination of Bach's autograph

Example 7–5. The opening motive of the "Domine Deus" as it appears in the flute part (a) in the Dresden parts, and (b) in the *P 180* manuscript.

score one year later for the revised *Bach-Gesamtausgabe* only strengthened his view, for in the *P 180* manuscript there is no hint of lombard rhythm whatsoever in the "Domine Deus." Therefore, Rietz retained the even sixteenth notes, and it is this version that is passed down in the *Bach-Gesamtausgabe* and the other editions based on its text.

The matter was further complicated by Smend's *Neue Bach-Ausgabe* edition. As we have seen, Smend viewed the Dresden parts with a certain disdain, and for the "Domine Deus" he ignored the lombard measure altogether: he printed the even sixteenth-note reading in the *Neue Bach-Ausgabe* text and omitted all reference to the Dresden variant in his Critical Report. Dadelsen, in his memorable review of the edition, took Smend to task for the omission and voiced the opinion that Bach wanted the lombard reading not only in the flute, but in the strings as well, when they carried the theme.[84]

Dadelsen's view received vindication in 1974 from Gerhard Herz, who examined the Dresden parts in detail and discovered, much to everyone's astonishment, that the lombard notation can be found in the violin 2 and viola parts, too.[85] In both cases it appears at m. 27, where the second violin and viola take up the main theme for the first time. As in the flute part, the lombard rhythm is notated for just one bar. Herz viewed the three incipits as a type of shorthand notation, in which Bach, pressed for time, wished to make clear as succinctly as possible (perhaps for future performances under someone else's direction) that the slurred pairs of falling sixteenth notes are to be played with lombard rhythm throughout the piece. Herz pointed out that it was not necessary for Bach to notate the rhythm in the first violin part, since the players of that instrument performed the theme immediately after the flute, in m. 2, and could judge by ear how it was to be played. In Baroque ensembles, such spontaneous adjustments appear to have been common practice. As we have seen, Bach used precisely this sort of incomplete notation to mark tempo and articulation.

Why use lombard rhythm at all? Johann Joachim Quantz claimed that short-long figures came into special vogue around 1722, through the music of Lombard violinists.[86] While noting that the rhythm was related to Scottish music (hence the modern synonym "Scotch snap") and that it had been used earlier from time to time by German composers, Quantz credited Vivaldi in particular with making it a festive gesture associated with fash- ionable, *galant* music. According to Herz's research, Bach adopted lom- bardic figures with particular intensity between 1732 and 1735, in the Ascension Oratorio (1735), the Christmas Oratorio (1734–1735), and a good number of progressive celebratory works written for the Leipzig Town Council, the Saxon Elector, and other secular patrons.[87] It remained a com- mon element of Bach's style in the 1730s (as the large setting of *Vater unser im Himmelreich* in *Clavierübung* III of 1739 attests) but appears less and less frequently in works written in the 1740s.

One can observe a similar trend at the Dresden Court, where there appears to have been a "lombard-rhythm craze" in the 1730s, perhaps insti- gated by Vivaldi's student and champion Johann Georg Pisendel, who upon the death of Volumier in 1728 had taken over the concertmaster duties. In sacred works performed in the Hofkirche im Theater, lombard figures com- monly appear in *galant* movements of the Mass dealing with Christ's inti- mate relationship with humankind. The "Christe eleison" from Zelenka's *Missa Eucharistica*,[88] Z. 15, of 1733, is typical (Example 7–6). In light of this convention, it would seem that Bach was currying favor by using lombard rhythm in the 1733 performance of the "Domine Deus" in Dresden. The text of the "Domine Deus," which dwells on Christ the "only-begotten son" and "Lamb of God," would have been an ideal candidate for the gesture.

As to the performance of lombardic figures, we find varying instructions. C. P. E. Bach suggested an imprecise, gentle execution:

> The first note [of this figure], because it is slurred, should not be dis- patched too quickly, especially when the tempo is moderate or slow, for otherwise too much time would remain. This first note is to be played with gentle pressure, and not marked with a short jolt or too quick a jerk.[89]

This makes for a soft rhythmic interpretation, somewhat akin to *notes inégales* in reverse. Quantz recommended a much sharper performance: "The shorter one makes the first note, the more spirited and saucy (*frecher*) the expression."[90] That interpretation seems to fit the exuberant quality of

Example 7–6. The "Christe eleison" from Zelenka's *Missa Eucharistica.*

the "Domine Deus." But it depends on tempo, of course. If the "Domine
Deus" is interpreted as a walking-bass *andante* rather than a *tempo-ordinario allegro,* then Emanuel Bach's mode of performance might be more
appropriate than Quantz's.

In the "Domine Deus" it is the slurred pairs of falling sixteenth notes
that are to be given lombardic rhythm. Either manner of interpretation, soft
(C. P. E. Bach) or sharp (Quantz), is challenging for singers. The sharp
interpretation, associated with a fast tempo, is especially difficult. Thus if
the "Domine Deus" is taken at a fast pace, the lombardic rhythm is probably restricted to the instruments alone. The lack of slurs or written-out indications of lombardic rhythm in the soprano 1 and tenor parts points in this
direction, as does the fact that the pairs of sixteenth notes in the vocal parts

are mostly ascending, making them somewhat less likely candidates for short-long rhythm (as Herz's statistics demonstrate). One other snippet of evidence for a nonlombardic interpretation in the voices comes from Quantz's discussion of *notes inégales*. After describing the instances in which notes should be performed unequally, Quantz points out the exceptions, which include:

> Fast passages made by singers, especially when such passages are not slurred, for in this kind of singing every note must be made clear and well marked, through a gentle push of air from the chest. Inequality has no place here.[91]

In the "Domine Deus," it may be that the voices are to sing even sixteenth notes while the instruments use lombard rhythm for the slurred pairs.

Should a lombardic interpretation be applied to slurred pairs of notes found in other movements in the B-Minor Mass? The absence of any notational indication in the Dresden parts of movements such as the "Et in terra pax" or the "Quoniam tu solus sanctus" speaks against it. In addition, no section of the Mass contains such an abundance of slurred, falling seconds as the "Domine Deus." It is noteworthy that when Bach later rearranged the "Domine Deus" as the "Gloria Patri" of Cantata 191 around 1745, he adopted the even rhythm of the *P 180* manuscript, omitting all reference to a lombardic interpretation. It may be that he indicated lombardic rhythm in the parts of Cantata 191, which are lost, or that he requested it verbally in rehearsal. But it may also be that by 1745 his passion for lombardic figures had cooled. As his other works from the 1740s seem to indicate, he may have felt that lombard rhythm was no longer *de rigueur*. Could that mean, ironically, that a lombardic interpretation was no longer necessary for the "Domine Deus"?

PRONUNCIATION OF THE LATIN TEXT

As we have observed, the text of the B-Minor Mass contains a number of "Germanisms" and local variants that diverge from the standard Latin of the Roman Catholic Ordinary:

> "Domine Deus":
>> "Jesu Christe altissime, Domine Deus" instead of "Jesu Christe, Domine Deus"

"Qui sedes":
> "dextram" instead of "dexteram"

"Et resurrexit":
> "ad dexteram Dei Patris" instead of "ad dexteram Patris"

"Sanctus":
> "gloria eius" instead of "gloria tua"

These differences imply that Bach approached the text from a Germanic standpoint and probably envisioned a Germanic pronunciation of the Latin (or Greek, for the Kyrie). That means, for instance, that the letter "c" in "coeli" would have been treated as "ts" (followed by an umlauted o: tsö-li), the "g" in "Agnus" as a hard "g," and the "y" of "Kyrie" as a German y.[92]

At the Dresden Court, a more Italianate approach prevailed. Both Friedrich August I and Friedrich August II were Catholics, and Friedrich August II, at least, was demonstrably an Italophile. In church matters the two rulers emulated Roman practice.[93] Most of the court singers and many of the composers were born and raised in Italy or trained there, and church works from the Hofkirche collection show a much stricter adherence to the Latin text of the Roman Catholic Ordinary ("ad dexteram Patris" not "ad dexteram Dei Patris"; "gloria tua" not "gloria eius," etc.). In Dresden it is likely that the Latin of the Ordinary was pronounced in a more Italianate way. That means that the "c" in "coeli" and "g" in "Agnus" would have been softened in the Italian manner and the letter "y" of "Kyrie" treated as an Italian "i" (which is sometimes likened to the i in "police"), and so forth. If the *Missa* sounded at the Dresden Court in 1733, it may well have been performed with an Italianized pronunciation.

If Bach had been extremely sensitive to the Italianate habits of the Dresden Court, he might have altered the text of the *Missa* to bring it precisely into line with the Roman Ordinary that was used there. But he submitted the *Missa* with its Germanisms intact, and he continued to use a Germanic approach in the Credo, Sanctus, and Agnus Dei some fifteen years later. From this we may conclude either that he desired a Germanic pronunciation or that he did not consider the matter to be of critical importance in the performance of the work.

Chapter 8

"THE GREAT CATHOLIC MASS"

The Work as a Whole:
Style, Structure, and Unity

For Baroque composers concerned with creating unified musical settings, the Mass Ordinary presented a special challenge. Unlike the libretto of a cantata, oratorio, or Passion, the text of the Ordinary was a literary miscellany, a compilation of liturgical supplications, hymns, and professions expressed at different moments in the worship service. Since recitative, the most effective Baroque tool for producing narrative continuity, was avoided in Mass settings, composers had to find other means of welding the diverse portions of the text into a cohesive musical whole.

The B-Minor Mass in particular posed unusual problems of unification. Bach began not from scratch but rather with the 1733 *Missa*. He then proceeded to fill in the remaining portions with music derived largely—if not entirely—from other preexistent compositions. In terms of genesis, the B-Minor Mass fit solidly into the Dresden tradition of the pragmatic pastiche. But in terms of architectural congruity, it posed unprecedented challenges, for it was an unprecedented work. Up to this point, no one had composed a "numbers" Mass of comparable length. How did Bach manage to create a unified *Missa tota* from a such a vast array of seemingly disparate textual and musical elements?

In Dresden Mass settings, composers commonly joined contiguous sections through leading cadences. Bach used this procedure numerous times in the B-Minor Mass to connect two movements, by ending the first on the dominant of the second ("Laudamus te"→"Gratias agimus tibi," "Qui tollis"→"Qui sedes," and "Et incarnatus"→"Crucifixus"), by ending the first on the tonic of the second ("Pleni sunt coeli"→"Osanna in excelsis"), or even by beginning the second movement on its dominant in order to match the final chord of the first ("Credo"→"Patrem omnipotentem"). It is noteworthy that he employed similar intermovement cadential links in the *Clavierübung* III collection of 1739 and the first version of the Art of Fugue of c. 1740, though on a more tentative basis.[1] Elsewhere in the B-Minor Mass Bach joined movements through elided cadences ("Gloria"→"Et in terra pax," "Domine Deus"→"Qui tollis," "Quoniam tu Solus Sanctus"→ "Cum sancto spiritu," and "Sanctus"→"Pleni sunt coeli") or, in one instance, a transitional bridge ("Confiteor"→"Et expecto").

In some cases Bach strengthened the bond between two movements by eliminating an instrumental interlude that otherwise would have separated the pieces. He achieved this by adding vocal parts to what was originally instrumental material (the conclusion of the "Crucifixus," the opening of the "Et expecto," and probably the opening of the "Et in terra pax") or by deleting a preexistent instrumental sinfonia or ritornello (the openings of the "Qui tollis" and "Osanna," and probably of the "Et resurrexit" and "Cum Sancto Spiritu"). He also used thematic references to link movements, such as the $\frac{3}{8}$-meter motives that appear in both the "Pleni sunt coeli" and "Osanna," the descending B-minor triad that emerges near the end of the "Domine Deus" to foreshadow the "Qui tollis," and the slurred bass figure that appears in the "Et incarnatus," the "Crucifixus," and the "Et expecto" bridge. In the opening of the Credo, he joined the "Patrem omnipotentem" with the "Credo in unum Deum" by using a superimposed motto in the manner of a "Credo Mass." John Butt has pointed out that the connection is also motivic: the top line of the motto motive in the "Patrem" echoes the chant theme of the "Credo."[2]

Equally effective is the way Bach used the "torsos" of earlier compositions to structural advantage. As we noted in the central chapters, there appear to be at least seven such torsos in the B-Minor Mass: the "Domine Deus" (which lacks its A' section), the "Qui tollis" (which lacks its opening sinfonia), the "Et expecto" (which lacks its closing sinfonia), the "Crucifixus" (the A section of a da capo chorus), the "Osanna" (the A section of a da capo chorus), the "Benedictus" (probably the A section of a da capo aria), and the "Agnus Dei" (a da capo aria from which most of the B section has been deleted).[3] Bach used the torsos as contemplative interludes between tutti movements to create new "A B A" structures (the "Osanna"→"Benedictus"→"Osanna" or the "Osanna"→"Agnus Dei"→"Dona nobis pacem" sequences, for example), or he combined the torsos with other movements to form innovative units (for example, the "Qui tollis" functions as the A' section of the da capo "Domine Deus,"[4] or the "Sanctus"→"Pleni sunt coeli"→"Osanna" stands as an unusual tripartite tutti group).

The carefully calculated sequence of choruses and arias also contributes to the cohesiveness of each portion of the B-Minor Mass. The subtle alternation of chorus and aria, the use of chorus as framing element, and the balancing of movement pairs make the progression of the music both logical and forceful. In the Credo, the insertion of the "Et incarnatus" and subsequent revision of the "Et in unum Dominum" shows that Bach was willing, in his last years, to sacrifice compositional detail for structural goals. One suspects that of the five portions of the Ordinary, it is the Credo, created toward the end of the 1740s, seemingly at a more leisurely pace than the Sanctus and Agnus Dei, that comes closest to Bach's ideal. Its balanced, symmetrical plan, outlined in Chapter 4, brings to full realization organizational principles that the aging Kantor of St. Thomas had been refining in his keyboard publications for over twenty years.

Looking at the unification of the B-Minor Mass as a whole, we find a number of overarching factors at work. Most obviously, the return to the "Gratias" music in the "Dona nobis pacem" connects the Gloria and Agnus Dei portions and organically bridges the music from 1733 with the music from 1748–1749. Bach may have intended the unison violins that appear in the "Christe eleison" and the "Agnus Dei" to act as a theological marker, underlining the belief that the plea voiced in the Kyrie finds its answer in the redemptive sacrifice of the Agnus Dei. The instrumental band, which remains the same except in the "Sanctus," also lends cohesiveness to the entire Ordinary, especially since it sounds in the tutti choruses that close each portion (the Kyrie and Gloria forming one unit in performance). The use of varying vocal forces, while unusual in a concerted Mass, is not unprecedented. In Antonio Lotti's *Missa* in G Minor, a work Bach wrote out sometime between 1732 and 1735, the vocal forces fluctuate several times, from four to five to six voices in varying combinations. Bach inscribed the manuscript "Missa a 4, 5 et 6 Voci." By analogy, the B-Minor Mass might be viewed as "Missa a 5, 6 et 8 Voci."

Also uniting the B-Minor Mass is the very intensity of Bach's idiom. The constant blending of styles, the encyclopedic exploration of genres, the omnipresent use of imitative counterpoint, and the rich harmonic vocabulary give the music a distinctive, highly personal stamp. Bach's determination to imbue the music with detail is evident even in the progressive "Et incarnatus": in the final measures, the unison violins divide to produce a new imitative line for the concluding cadence. The inherent integrity of the score, especially evident in such passages, allowed Bach to "cut and paste" sections of the B-Minor Mass, to bind together movements drawn from earlier, unrelated scores.

Certain rhetorical figures return from portion to portion, almost in the manner of nineteenth-century leitmotifs. The lamentation motive, slurred pairs of descending seconds in minor mode, is used to express beseeching and lament in the "Domine Deus" (in the "Domine Deus, Agnus Dei" section), the "Qui tollis," the "Crucifixus," and the "Agnus Dei." In major mode, the same slurred-note pairs appear as a symbol of joy and exultation in the "Et in terra pax," the "Laudamus te," the "Domine Deus" (in the "Domine Deus, Rex coelestis" section), and the "Et in unum Dominum."

Bach created other allegorical cross-references by using particular keys to symbolize particular emotional states. D major appears not only in laudatory tutti choruses, but also in arias concerning Christ's omnipotence ("Christe eleison" and "Quoniam tu solus sanctus"). B minor is linked with supplication ("Kyrie I" and "Qui tollis"), incarnation ("Et incarnatus"), and beneficence ("Benedictus"). A major is tied to praise ("Laudamus te" and "Et in Spiritum Sanctum") and F♯ minor to declaration ("Kyrie" II and "Confiteor"). G major and G minor are related to Christ's reign ("Domine Deus" and "Et in unum Dominum") and suffering ("Agnus Dei" and mm. 73–76 of "Et in unum Dominum"). Contrasting with the multiple appearances of these keys is the uniqueness of E minor, often associated in Baroque works with suffering, sorrow, and the Passion. It occurs but once in the B-Minor Mass, in the "Crucifixus," whose text deals with the central event of Christianity: Christ's suffering and death on the cross to redeem the sins of humankind.

The key scheme of the B-Minor Mass is more conservative than those of the most comparable large-scale vocal works by Bach, the St. John and St. Matthew Passions. As Friedrich Smend and more recently Eric Chafe have shown,[5] the two Passions traverse a broad, allegorical tonal terrain, beginning in the area of sharp keys and moving gradually to the darker sphere of flat keys as the crucifixion approaches (in the St. Matthew Passion, the music progresses from E minor in the opening chorus to A♭ minor for Christ's final words on the cross). The B-Minor Mass exhibits no such evolutionary tonal plan. Instead, Bach employed a single central key, D major, and with the sole exception of the "Agnus Dei," set in G minor, he never stepped outside the five closely related keys of D major in the Baroque spectrum: B minor, A major, F♯ minor, G major, and E minor. As we noted in Chapter 5, the G minor of the "Agnus Dei" has associations with Christ's incarnation mentioned in the "Et in unum Dominum"; but tonally, it can be viewed as a harmonic coloration of the subdominant, G major, just as the transposed mixolydian of the "Credo" can be viewed as a harmonic coloration of the dominant, A major.

The absence of recitative, often a vehicle for far-flung modulations, and the presence of trumpets, which required the use of D major whenever the full instrumental ensemble entered into play, placed limitations on Bach's choice of keys. The most striking feature of the tonal scheme of the B-Minor Mass is the pervasive presence, in each portion, of D major, the Baroque key of exultation and victory:

Kyrie:	b ⟶ D ⟶ f♯
Gloria:	D ⟶ D ⟶ A ⟶ D ⟶ G ⟶ b ⟶ b ⟶ D ⟶ D
Credo:	A ⟶ D ⟶ G ⟶ b ⟶ e ⟶ D ⟶ A ⟶ f♯ ⟶ D
Sanctus:	D ⟶ D ⟶ D ⟶ b ⟶ D
Agnus Dei:	g ⟶ D

During the course of the Ordinary the move to D major becomes more concentrated and urgent, a tendency especially apparent in the Sanctus and Agnus Dei. Theologically, Bach may have used the continual reiteration of D major to underline the eschatological triumph of faith, a triumph that results equally from supplication (Kyrie and Agnus Dei), praise (Gloria and Sanctus), and declaration of faith (Credo). The gratuitous use of D major in the "Christe" and the "Quoniam tu solus," two movements that lack trumpets and could have been set in other keys, also points to D major as the key of Christ victorious. In the aria "Es ist vollbracht" from the St. John Passion, Bach jumps abruptly from B minor to D major to paint the contrast between the expired Christ on the cross ("It is finished") and the triumphant Christ who defeats Satan ("The hero from Judea conquers with might"). So it is in his *Missa tota*. Harmonically, it is not the somber minor modes that prevail, but the bright vanquishing tone of D major. The title "Mass in B Minor," coined in the nineteenth century, is thus especially inappropriate, for B minor is not the principal key of the work, either literally or symbolically. D major serves as the foundation of the setting. The title handed down in C. P. E. Bach's circle, "The Great Catholic Mass," is far more fitting, for it best summarizes the work's nature and unique status. It has been adopted as a subtitle in the *Bach Compendium*, and one can hope that it will be used more extensively in the future.

WHY A MASS ORDINARY?

When the B-Minor Mass was rediscovered in the first decades of the nineteenth century, little consideration was given to its original purpose. To Hans Georg Nägeli, Johann Nepomuk Schelble, Gaspare Spontini, and other early champions, the B-Minor Mass was an art-work "for all people," conceived in the same spirit of universal religion as Beethoven's *Missa solemnis*. The concert hall, rather than the church, was the appropriate venue for performance, and it was there that Bach's masterpiece was revived.

It was only after the midcentury mark, with the emergence of the first extensive Bach biographies, that the function of the work became an issue. As C. L. Hilgenfeldt, Carl Hermann Bitter, and Philipp Spitta labored to portray Bach as devout Lutheran and productive St. Thomas Kantor, they were forced to consider how the B-Minor Mass fit into the picture they were painting. The "Sanctus" and the *Missa* (despite its Dresden dedication) had Lutheran roots, but the *Symbolum Nicenum* and "Osanna" to "Dona nobis pacem" portions were more difficult to account for. What motivated Bach to write such a suspiciously Catholic work?

Bitter, for instance, seemed flabbergasted by the prospect of Bach composing a Catholic Mass Ordinary: "How the plan to set a 'High Catholic Mass' could have arisen and matured in the mind of a master so completely filled with the evangelical consciousness of Protestantism will perhaps remain unclear forever."[6] Spitta, a more objective scholar, acknowledged that Bach adhered to the Catholic practice of eschewing recitative. On the whole, however, he viewed the B-Minor Mass as a Protestant creation, "more inseparable from the Protestant Church of Bach's time than even the cantatas and Passion music" and, because of its excessive length, "unfit for use in the Catholic Church."[7] Spitta proposed instead that Bach performed the various sections in the Lutheran rite in Leipzig: the "Sanctus" and the *Missa* (in its shortened form, as the Latin work *Gloria in excelsis Deo*) in *Hauptgottesdienst*, the Credo as a special piece on Trinity Sunday or a Saint's Day, and the "Osanna" to "Dona nobis pacem" as Communion music.

The desire to keep the B-Minor Mass in the Lutheran realm continued
in the first part of the twentieth century. Arnold Schering's theory that the
Missa was initially composed for a special homage service in the St. Nikolai
Church in Leipzig met with wide acceptance, even though his suggestion
that the Kyrie was performed before the sermon as a memorial to Friedrich
August I, and the Gloria after the sermon as a tribute to the new ruler,
Friedrich August II, made little liturgical sense.[8] Smend's hypothesis, presented in the *Neue Bach-Ausgabe,* was still more elaborate. Pointing to the
fact that the *Leipziger Kirchenandachten* of 1694 includes the texts of the
Kyrie, Gloria, Credo, and Sanctus (without the "Osanna" and "Benedictus"), he claimed that Bach intended these portions of the B-Minor Mass
(Nos. 1–3 of the *P 180* manuscript) for performance in the Leipzig liturgy
and the "Osanna" to "Dona nobis pacem" segment (No. 4 of the manuscript) as Communion music, just as Spitta had suggested three quarters of
a century earlier.[9] Smend, who descended from a long line of Lutheran theologians, found the entire notion of Bach composing music for a Catholic
ruler so odious that he excluded the text of the 1733 *Missa* petition to
Friedrich August II from the Critical Report of the *Neue Bach-Ausgabe.*

The new Bach chronology, which revealed the full extent of Bach's dis-
illusionment with the Thomaskantor post and his broad interest in Latin-
texted church music in the 1730s and 1740s, opened the door to new
interpretations. Georg von Dadelsen, the first to demonstrate the shortcomings of Smend's edition, set forth the idea that the B-Minor Mass was not,
functionally speaking, a church work at all but rather Bach's last and most
ambitious personal project:

> As a whole, this Mass has no place in the Lutheran worship service,
> and at the same time it is unlikely that it was expressly written for a
> particular Catholic rite. . . . Bach probably wished to compose in a
> field that represented the highest achievement since the time of
> Josquin and Palestrina, who elevated the Mass to an independent work
> of art. Bach took it outside the realm of the liturgy, as an expression of
> his personal mastery.[10]

Dadelsen grouped the B-Minor Mass with the Musical Offering and the Art
of Fugue, classifying it as an abstract composition that appeared to transcend performance.

Christoph Wolff took Dadelsen's idea a step further. Pointing to Bach's
late preoccupation with the *stile antico* and his study of seemingly unper-

formed pieces such as Bassani's Mass settings, Wolff proposed that the B-Minor Mass might have been compiled as a type of extraordinary "specimen book," a volume in which the composer demonstrated through parody reworkings his own historical contribution to the realm of church music:

> More traditions attach to the Mass than to any other form of vocal music, and it has indeed been regarded since the fourteenth-century as the central genre of sacred vocal music, so it is not surprising if Bach wanted to write his own contribution to this particular chapter of the history of music.[11]

The notion of the B-Minor Mass as an abstract composition, assembled for posterity alone, has Romantic appeal. Indeed, it takes the Mass back to the nineteenth century, when it was associated with Beethoven and the *Missa solemnis*. It is attractive to imagine Bach breaking the bonds of Baroque pragmatism, wrapping himself in the mantle of Beethoven (even before Beethoven's time), and writing a work for future generations. But would the composer have assembled a 188-page *Missa tota* for that purpose?

Both the "abstract work" and the "written-for-posterity" theories have their shortcomings. Most obviously, it is difficult to classify movements such as the "Et resurrexit," the "Et in Spiritum Sanctum," or the "Osanna" as "abstract." On the contrary, they seem calculatedly extroverted, as if tailored to appeal to an audience of the composer's time. Unlike Schütz's late Passion settings or Stravinsky's Mass, the B-Minor Mass is an exuberant, outgoing work. Furthermore, as Yoshitake Kobayashi's recent study has shown, Bach was working on a variety of projects during his final years, and not all of them were of an abstract, theoretical nature like the Musical Offering and Art of Fugue. One finds the composer also performing, revising, and composing pieces such as the effervescent wedding cantata *Dem Gerechten muß das Licht immer wieder aufgehen,* BWV 195, the *galant* Sonata in E♭ Major for flute, BWV 1031, and the progressive sonatas for violin and harpsichord, BWV 1014–1019.[12] These do not appear to be creations of a composer retreating from the world.

Moreover, several aspects of the *P 180* autograph of the B-Minor Mass point more to performance than to contemplation. The structure of the manuscript, loose gatherings, is typical of Bach's performance scores. Although there is no evidence that performance parts were prepared during Bach's lifetime, the four title pages that list the necessary forces for each section and that surely functioned at one time as folder covers point only to performance. If Bach viewed the B-Minor Mass as an impractical, abstract work, why did he fashion liturgically incorrect title pages? The title pages make sense *only* in terms of performance.

Then, too, there are the missing details in the manuscript that we noted earlier: the labeling of the instrumental solo in the "Benedictus"; the bassoon part in the Credo, Sanctus, and Agnus Dei; the possible *colla parte* scoring in the "Credo" and "Confiteor"; the tempo indications in various movements; and many critical articulation marks. These matters would have been resolved only when the Mass was "completed" through the process of making performance parts. Finally, if Bach viewed the Mass in B-Minor as an abstract work, why did he bother to revise the 1724 "Sanctus" at all? Why bring its vocal parts more closely into line with those of the other sections? The adjustment of the chorus from SSSATB to SSAATB makes sense, once again, only if one is concerned about performance. All this strongly suggests that Bach viewed his work as a potentially performable Catholic Mass Ordinary.

But performance in what venue? The five-voice setting, the ambitious dimensions, and other Neapolitan traits point, of course, to Dresden, where Bach had promised in his petition of 1733 to show the Elector his "untiring zeal in the composition of music for the church as well as for the orchestra." That the *Missa*, at least, could have been used within the Catholic service in Dresden is clear: as we have seen, certain *Missa* settings by Francesco Mancini, Domenico Sarri, Antonio Lotti, and others performed in the Hofkirche match the forty-five-minute duration of Bach's work. Johann David Heinichen, Kapellmeister to the Court from 1717 to 1729, claimed that the first five *Missa* settings he composed for Dresden were forty-five to fifty minutes in length (after that, he seems to have settled on half an hour as the ideal).[13] Bach's expansion of the Kyrie and Gloria into a full Ordinary seems to have lifted the B-Minor Mass out of the normal Dresden rite, however, for there are no *Missa tota* settings of comparable length in the Court inventory.[14]

But is it possible that Bach wrote the B-Minor Mass for a special event in Dresden? Wolfgang Osthoff has suggested that the work may have been intended for the inauguration of the new Hofkirche, the magnificent edifice designed by the Roman architect Gaetano Chiaveri as a replacement for the makeshift Hofkirche im Theater.[15] The cornerstone of the Hofkirche was laid in 1739, and the building was completed and dedicated in 1751, a year after Bach's death. Bernardo Bellotto's landscape painting of 1748 shows the exterior of the Hofkirche almost finished except for the west tower, which is encompassed by scaffolding (Plate 8–1). One could envision Bach

Plate 8–1. Bernardo Bellotto, known as Canaletto the Younger: Dresden from the right bank of the Elbe (1748; Dresden, Gemäldegalerie Alte Meister, Staatliche Kunstsammlungen).

working on the B-Minor Mass as the Hofkirche moved toward completion, with the idea of presenting the composition as part of the dedication festivities. As Osthoff points out, the work performed at the inauguration, Johann Adolf Hasse's Mass in D Minor, displays a number of gestures anticipated in the B-Minor Mass: the setting of the "Christe eleison" as a duet and the "Kyrie" II as a Renaissance-style chorus, the presentation of the Kyrie-Christe-Kyrie segment in minor mode and the remaining portions in major, the use of chant over a walking bass in the Credo, and so forth. Despite this kinship, Hasse's work is less than half the length of the Mass in B-Minor. It is certainly conceivable that Bach aimed at the same event and cast his work in the same general mold as Hasse. But as was his habit, Bach was much more ambitious.

A second Dresden festivity that might have accommodated the B-Minor Mass is the St. Cecilia's Day celebration, an annual event that seems to have featured special music and lasted nearly three hours. According to the log of the *Historia Missionis,* the Italian opera singers who were soon to perform regularly in the Hofkirche made their first appearance at the St. Cecilia's Day service in 1717:

And here the Italian artists, which were sent from Venice to Dresden by his ever-knowing Elector Prince, inspired our church, as they brought praise to St. Cecilia on her feast day through a sung service that lasted almost three hours, and embellished it with astoundingly accomplished polish with voices as well as instruments, the likes of which one has never seen in Dresden before.[16]

Here also might have been an occasion for the B-Minor Mass.

Then, too, the work could have been Bach's response to a private commission from a Catholic patron. Count Sporck, the borrower of the "Sanctus" parts in the 1720s, cannot be considered, for he died in 1738. But Bach had other acquaintances—Friedrich Ludwig von Haugwitz in Silesia and Count Johann Adam von Questenberg in Moravia—who might have been interested in a monumental Catholic church work. Bach reportedly corresponded with Questenberg in the spring of 1749 about a commission or project.[17] Unfortunately, nothing is known of its nature.

Without question certain portions of the B-Minor Mass could have been performed as independent segments in church: the *Missa,* the *Symbolum,* the Sanctus, and the Agnus Dei in the Catholic service, and the *Missa* and the "Sanctus" movement in the Lutheran service. The unorthodox division of the *P 180* manuscript undoubtedly reflects Bach's desire to preserve such options. But was it possible that the entire work, with its great length, could have been used within a Catholic Mass celebration, even a special one? There is at least one comparable case: Nicolò Jommelli's *Missa concertata* of 1769 equals the B-Minor Mass in size and was performed in Lisbon in the spring of 1770 for the "Festa de nossa Senhora do Cabo."[18] Under the right circumstances, and with the right patron, then, it appears that the B-Minor Mass could have been performed within the church, either as part of the liturgy or extra-liturgically—at least in theory.

If Bach was aiming at Dresden circles, however, he seems to have been moving against the forces of history. Hasse's Mass in D, as we have noted, is markedly shorter than the B-Minor Mass, and after Hasse's departure from Dresden in 1763, Court composers began to move in the direction of *Missa brevissima* settings, occasionally writing pieces of remarkably diminutive proportions. As Wolfgang Horn has shown, Georg Reutter, Jr. (1708–1772) was able to squeeze the entire Gloria into nine measures of music through the use of polytextuality.[19] Although the Reutter is an extreme case, and there is evidence that other composers working at the Dresden Court in the second half of the eighteenth century penned a number of very large Ordinary settings,[20] the general trend in Mass writing seems to have been in the direction of concision—as it clearly was in Vienna.

Thus whether Bach wrote the B-Minor Mass for himself, for posterity, for a Dresden event, or for a private commission, it was posterity, in the nineteenth century, that would first accept, and welcome, the work's monumental scale.

THE UNIVERSALITY OF THE B-MINOR MASS

Although we may not be able to pinpoint Bach's specific reason for writing a *Missa tota*, we can be reasonably sure that in turning to the Latin Ordinary for his last large-scale project, he wished to devote his final energies to music that would transcend the parochialism of his German-texted vocal pieces. As Bach must have realized toward the end of his life, his German-texted vocal works were local fare, based on libretti by town poets and aimed at area rites and celebrations. Removed from their original contexts, the pieces lost much of their meaning. In 1753 Caspar Ruetz, Kantor of the Marienkirche in Lübeck, described how a huge pile of church music he had inherited from his predecessors had been diminished by half from its use for stove fires and scrap paper. "Who will give anything for it," he lamented, "other than someone who needs scrap paper, since nothing is more useless than old music."[21] Surely Bach was aware that vast quantities of music suffered this fate, especially vocal works with circumscribed utility. One can imagine him sitting in his study in the late 1740s, sullenly scrutinizing the 350 or so German-texted vocal pieces he had labored so diligently to produce and realizing that the entire lot might be consigned to flames or the scrap paper pile after his death.

The Latin Ordinary offered an alternative. Its text was universal, unbound by day, event, or location. It was a public, not private, proclamation, with Biblical citations removed from their incident-specific contexts and transported to a more generalized realm. The opening lines of the Gloria, connected with Christ's birth in the Book of Luke, are transformed into an esctatic hymn of praise in the Ordinary. The words of the Sanctus, spoken by Isaiah in the Old Testament, become a broad, congregational affirmation. Writing a Mass gave Bach the opportunity to transfer his endeavors from the Lutheran Proper to the Catholic Ordinary, from the specific to the universal. In the half-century following his death, it was the B-Minor Mass that traveled to Vienna and London, not his German-texted cantatas. "The Great Catholic Mass" presented the possibility of geographical and historical transcendence.

The project also allowed Bach to survey his own vocal composition, from the first mature cantatas of Weimar (the "Crucifixus," from Cantata 12), to the five Leipzig church cycles of the 1720s (the "Qui tollis," from Cantata 46 or the "Patrem Omnipotentem," from Cantata 171), to the *galant* Collegium pieces of the 1730s (the "Osanna," from BWV Anh.11), and finally to the Latin-texted studies of the final years (the "Credo"). It also gave him the opportunity to draw on music written for church (Cantatas 46, 171), for bureaucratic rituals (Cantatas 29, 120), and for ceremonial events (Cantatas BWV Anh. 9, BWV Anh. 11, and the wedding serenade *Auf! süß-entzuckende Gewalt*). Whether or not it was the goal of the work, the Mass does represent a Bach "specimen book," as Wolff put it, a highly select sampling of vocal music culled from four decades of sacred and secular composition.

Then, too, the parody procedure gave Bach a final chance to rework and refine his earlier scores. Bach's first biographer, Johann Nikolaus Forkel, expressed delight in the composer's ability to make "little by little, the faulty good, the good better, and the better perfect."[22] In the B-Minor Mass, we find the type of perfection that appears in the skillful parody revisions of the 1730s and 1740s. But there is something else. During the revisional process Bach normally expanded preexisting material, embellishing lines, thickening textures, adding measures, composing new sections. His indefatigable inventiveness seemed to propel him in that direction. The opening movement of the Concerto in A Minor, BWV 1044 (fifty-one measures longer than its harpsichord prelude original), Contrapunctus 10 from the Art of Fugue (twenty-two measures longer than its original), or the parody movement "Sicut erat in principio" from the *Gloria in excelsis Deo* (six measures longer than its "Cum Sancto Spiritu" original) are typical examples of his tendency to enlarge.

In the B-Minor Mass, Bach moved in the opposite direction, toward concision. The "Osanna in excelsis" is thirty-three measures shorter than its model (the "A" section of the chorus "Es lebe der König"), the "Agnus Dei" thirty measures shorter than its model (the aria "Entfernet euch, ihr kalten Herzen"), the "Qui tollis" fifteen measures shorter than its model (the chorus "Schauet doch und sehe, ob irgend ein Schmerz sei"). In many cases, the succinct character of the Latin text and the sectional nature of a Mass setting called for torsos rather than full movements. No matter what the motivation, however, in making abridgments Bach not only rescued some of his best "old music": he also distilled it. The B-Minor Mass is more than a cross-section of Bach's art. It is his art in highly concentrated form.

The synthesis of styles also contributes to the universality of the B-Minor Mass. At the outset of the Baroque Era, Monteverdi effectively demonstrated the potential of stylistic pluralism—the idea that composers could use both the *a cappella* writing of the sixteenth century and the *Affekt*-filled writing of the seventeenth—in the Vespers Collection of 1610. The Vespers Collection is just that, however: a collection of independent liturgical pieces illustrating the various stylistic possibilities of the time. The B-Minor Mass, which might be viewed as Bach's answer to the Vespers of 1610, goes beyond Monteverdi's principles. It is a true "réunion des goûts" (to play on François Couperin's term of 1724), a true joining of tastes, in which ancient and modern; Italian, French, and German; vocal and instrumental are amalgamated in a single continuous work.[23] Styles are sometimes juxtaposed, as in "Credo" or "Confiteor," in which a Renaissance chorus and a Baroque walking bass are combined. Other times they are placed side by side, as in the operatic "Christe eleison" and the Palestrina-style "Kyrie" II. Yet as we have seen, the work has overarching organizational bonds that fuse the movements into a harmonious whole. The inclusive eclecticism of the B-Minor Mass, with its blending of diverse elements, points to the cosmopolitan idiom—and Enlightenment ideals—of the Classical Era.

Furthermore, the B-Minor Mass has a directness that counterbalances the complexity of Bach's writing. The key scheme is unusually straightforward for a large-scale vocal work. The emergence and eventual dominance of D major after the dark B-minor/F♯-minor opening produces a sensation of triumph not unlike the apotheosis that takes place in Beethoven's minor-key symphonies. The instrumental band of the B-Minor Mass has a distinctly modern cast, with a four-part Italian string body and pairs of woodwinds—two flutes, two oboes (aside from the "Sanctus"), and (presumably) two bassoons—that point forward to the late-eighteenth-century public ensemble of Haydn's "London" Symphonies. As we noted in Chapter 3, with the exception of the oboe d'amore, Bach avoided the colorful specialized instruments found in many of his earlier vocal works. The absence of recitative, too, contributes to the broad appeal of the B-Minor Mass. The text and music do not address personalized emotions, the role of recitative in Bach's cantatas. Rather, they speak more generally, in public terms. In place of recitative, the "formless form" of the Baroque, Bach employed strong, unambiguous structures: fugue, da capo, motet, ritornello, ground bass. The architectural clarity of each movement adds to the directness of the whole.

The presence of dance and dance-like idioms further broadens the appeal of the B-Minor Mass. As Doris Finke-Hecklinger has shown, Bach's attraction to dance music began in earnest in the Cöthen years, when *galant* dances first appeared in substantial numbers in his secular cantatas.[24] The B-Minor Mass is permeated with dance: the giga- or gigue-related nature of the "Gloria in excelsis Deo" and "Qui sedes," the passepied qualities of the "Pleni sunt coeli" and "Osanna," the *réjouissance* character of the "Et resurrexit," the passacaglia bass pattern of the "Crucifixus," the pastoral hues of the "Et in Spiritum Sanctum," and the gavotte-like rhythms of the "Et expecto" point to a work that is very much a part of the present world. Bach used the secular to portray the sacred, and in so doing he lifted both to an all-embracing plane. His repeated use of chamber meters—$\frac{3}{8}$ in the "Gloria," "Pleni sunt," and "Osanna" and $\frac{6}{8}$ in the "Qui sedes" and "Et in Spiritum," in particular—shows that he was attuned to the growing appeal of light, *galant* instrumental dances and did not hesitate to draw on their persuasive power.

Indeed, much of the attraction of the B-Minor Mass comes from the instrumental nature of Bach's writing. Thrasybulos Georgiades has reasoned that as Mass settings evolved from the Middle Ages to the Baroque Era, they moved from a literal reiteration of the text to a more ambiguous interpretation. In the Middle Ages, the monophonic lines of plainchant reflected Latin speech patterns. In the Renaissance, chant was retained in polyphonic settings and used as the basis for composition, but it was objectified—that is, placed into a mensural rhythm. With the advent of concerted settings in the Baroque, the text of the Mass Ordinary was further distanced from its speech origins and placed in a fully instrumental context.[25] Taking the "Et incarnatus" from the B-Minor Mass as an example, Georgiades argues that its depth of expression goes far beyond normal Baroque text settings. The "Et incarnatus" expresses the inexpressible because Bach created music that serves as symbol, symbol not specifically tied with speech. The opening instrumental figure not only outlines in advance the general shape of the vocal theme, as we noted in Chapter 4, but establishes the *Affekt* of the entire movement, an *Affekt* of mystery and wonder.[26] Thus the instrumental writing determines the outcome of the setting, even though the setting is highly vocal in nature.

One can easily point to other examples: although the fugue theme of "Kyrie" I reflects the rhythmic declamation of the word "Kyrie" (♩. ♪ ♩), the melody itself is strongly instrumental, with leaps that do not come naturally to the voice. Indeed, the piece initially proceeds for twenty-nine measures in a purely instrumental manner. When the voices enter in m. 30, they add complexity and expressiveness to the movement. But the *Affekt* has been set by the instrumental band. In the "Gloria," the opening instrumental fanfare establishes the atmosphere of triumph before the voices are heard. The instrumental parts in the "Gloria" could well stand alone, a fact which led Smend to propose that the music stemmed from an instrumental concerto, as we noted in Chapter 3. Even in Palestrina-style movements we find that Bach uses instrumental lines to ameliorate the severity of the vocal counterpoint: violin parts and a walking bass in the "Credo," a walking bass in the "Confiteor," a battery of trumpets and timpani in the "Gratias" and "Dona nobis pacem," and an independent continuo part in "Kyrie" II. The *stile antico* preludes of *Clavierübung* III, written ten years earlier, are much more austere. They are more strongly modal and without instrumental additions— "unsympathetically old-fashioned," as Peter Williams has put it.[27] The *a cappella* movements of the B-Minor Mass are different. Bach has enriched the Palestrina idiom with Baroque instrumental counterpoint.

All of this contributes greatly to the Mass's universal appeal. The intense instrumentalization of the score gives the work an attractiveness that goes beyond its text and helps to account for its success in the concert hall as well as the church, before listeners who know no Latin. Wilfrid Mellers credits the remarkable impetus of the music to its linear energy and "rhythmic ecstasy."[28] The forward drive comes from the instrumental character of Bach's writing.

In the B-Minor Mass, Bach realized the full potential of the Neapolitan idiom—the same idiom that gave birth to the enduring instrumental forms of the Classical Era.[29] Surveying the significance of Beethoven's symphonies in 1813, the well-known writer and critic E. T. A. Hoffmann praised instrumental music as the highest art, because "scorning every aid, every admixture of another art (the art of poetry)," it "gives pure expression to music's specific nature."[30] This is a Romantic view, of course, and Hoffmann praised Beethoven's instrumental music most of all because it opened a realm "of the monstrous and the immeasurable." Bach's "Great Catholic Mass," with its strong instrumental foundation, does not open the realm of the monstrous. It does, however, transport the Latin Ordinary to the realm of the immeasurable.

A Word on Modern Editions

The venerable *Bach-Gesamtausgabe* edition of the B-Minor Mass (BG 6), edited by Julius Rietz, appeared in 1856. Initially, Rietz was compelled to edit the text without benefit of Bach's autograph score, which at the time was in the possession of Swiss publisher Hermann Nägeli, whose firm had printed its own edition. When the score became available in 1857, Rietz issued a revisions list for the Kyrie and Gloria and a revised text for the Credo, Sanctus, and Agnus Dei. The original edition was numbered 6 and the revised segments 6^1. In subsequent reprints, the two were combined into a single revised edition, numbered 6.

In the BG, many details of slurring and articulation are normalized or omitted altogether, and the text contains a good number of outright mistakes. For instance: in mm. 1–4 of the "Et in unum Dominum," oboe d'amore 2 doubles violin 1 instead of violin 2, and in the "Benedictus" the obbligato instrumental line is assigned to a violin, whereas Bach failed to specify the solo instrument in the original score. Steuart Wilson has provided a useful summary of the problems with the BG,[1] and users should consult his critique. Despite its flaws, the BG gives a reasonably straightforward reading of the B-Minor Mass text, and in many ways it is more reliable and consistent than the *Neue Bach-Ausgabe.* Considered fully authoritative for many years, it served as the basis for other scores such as the Novello and Eulenburg. In recent times Dover has reprinted the text in an inexpensive paperback edition that is especially handy for study purposes (there are no measure numbers, however). The BG preserves the original C-clef notation of the upper vocal parts.

The *Neue Bach-Ausgabe* edition (NBA II/1), edited by Friedrich Smend, was issued in 1954 (the *Kritischer Bericht,* or Critical Report, appeared in 1956). Smend gave great weight to the *P 180* autograph score and a number of secondary sources derived from it, and he played down the importance of the Dresden performance parts. Mirroring the format of *P 180,* the NBA text is divided into four sections—*Missa, Symbolum Nicenum,* "Sanctus," and "Osanna" to "Dona nobis pacem"—each prefaced by a facsimile of the original title page. Matters of mistaken chronology and misinterpreted sources aside (see Chapter 2), the NBA is a highly personal interpretation of the B-Minor Mass text, one that reflects Smend's desire to present the work as a heterogeneous compilation of independent pieces.

One finds many peculiarities in the NBA: Bach's first version of the "Et in unum Dominum" is presented in the main text (the revised version is consigned to an appendix), with the result that the phrase "Et incarnatus est" appears in two movements; there is no mention, even in the Critical Report, of the lombard rhythm that is found in the instrumental parts of the "Domine Deus" in the Dresden materials. Although the NBA includes many details absent in the BG, the treatment of slurring, articulation, and other matters is highly subjective. To take but one example: in the *Missa* portion, Smend turned to the Dresden materials for the independent bassoon part, but he omitted the tempo indications found there, even though most of the indications are in Bach's hand. To find the *adagio* marking for opening of "Kyrie" I, one needs to refer to the BG. Georg von Dadelsen has provided an excellent summary of the source and text problems of the NBA,[2] and anyone using the edition should consult his review. The NBA is available from Bärenreiter in full score, piano-vocal score, and instrumental parts. The vocal lines are notated in modern clefs.

The new Peters edition (1994), edited by Christoph Wolff, serves a twofold purpose. First, Wolff reevaluates the sources of the B-Minor Mass in light of the new Bach chronology. Using the manuscripts *P 572/P 23/P 14* and *Am.B. 3,* which were copied from *P 180* before it was adulterated by C. P. E. Bach in 1786 (see Chapter 6), he restores many original readings missed by the BG and NBA. The Peters edition thus represents the most accurate text of the B-Minor Mass to date. Second, Wolff fleshes out the scoring, continuo figures, and other performance details in the Credo, Sanctus, and Agnus Dei by widening the range of primary sources to include those of parody models, parodies, and relevant arrangements. Thus in the *Symbolum Nicenum* portion he provides continuo figures from the recently discovered early version of the "Credo in unum Deum" movement and from C. P. E. Bach's 1786 Hamburg arrangement, and in the "Crucifixus" he proposes an independent bassoon part derived from the original music for the movement, the chorus "Weinen, Klagen, Sorgen, Zagen." The new Peters edition combines thorough source work with a pragmatic concern for performance matters, and it goes a long way towards filling in the

gaps in the B-Minor Mass score caused by the lack of performance materials for the Credo, Sanctus (in its revised form), and Agnus Dei. The Peters
edition is available in full score, piano-vocal score, and instrumental parts.
The vocal parts are printed in modern clefs.

Notes

∽

CHAPTER 1
The Late Baroque Church Mass

1. Joseph A. Jungmann, *The Mass of the Roman Rite: Its Origins and Development,* trans. Francis A. Brunner (New York: Benziger, 1959), 225. I have drawn on Jungmann's classic study for much of the present survey.

2. Jungmann, *The Mass of the Roman Rite,* 236.

3. An ancient city of the Byzantine Empire, located at the present site of Iznik in northwest Turkey.

4. François F. Amiot, *The History of the Mass,* trans. Lancelot C. Sheppard (London: Burns and Oates, 1966), 80.

5. Jungmann, *The Mass of the Roman Rite,* 380.

6. Jungmann, *The Mass of the Roman Rite,* 485.

7. Monteverdi, speaking through his brother, issued the statement in the *Scherzi musicali* of 1607. Translations appear in *Source Readings in Music History: The Baroque Era,* ed. Oliver Strunk (New York: W. W. Norton, 1965), 45–52, and *Music in the Western World: A History in Documents,* ed. Piero Weiss and Richard Taruskin (New York: Schirmer Books, 1984), 171–174.

8. Johann Mattheson, *Der vollkommene Capellmeister* (Hamburg, 1739; reprint, Kassel: Bärenreiter, 1954), 73–83.

9. *Claudio Monteverdi: Tutte le opere,* ed. Gian Francesco Malipiero (rev. ed., Asolo, 1954) 15: 117.

10. Saxon State Library, *Mus. 2358-D-33.*

11. Saxon State Library, *Mus. 2170-D-8.*

12. Walther Müller, *Johann Adolf Hasse als Kirchenkomponist: Ein Beitrag zur Geschichte der Neapolitanischen Kirchenmusik* (Leipzig: Breitkopf & Härtel, 1910), 83.

13. Saxon State Library, *Mus. 2397-D-1.*

14. In the *Bach-Werke-Verzeichnis* Schmieder credits the Mass to Johann Ludwig Bach. Recent research has shown Durante to be the author. See *Bach Compendium* 4: 1218–1219 (*E8*).

15. Mizler, founder of the monthly publication *Neu eröffnete musikalische Bibliothek,* served as permanent secretary of the Society of Musical Sciences, which Bach joined in 1747.

16. Christoph Wolff, *Der Stile Antico in der Musik Johann Sebastian Bachs: Studien zu Bachs Spätwerk* (Wiesbaden: Franz Steiner, 1968), 20.

17. Sébastien de Brossard, *Dictionaire de musique* (3rd ed., Amsterdam, c. 1703; reprint, Geneva: Éditions Minkoff, 1992), 59.

18. Wolfgang Horn, *Die Dresdner Hofkirchenmusik 1720–1745* (Kassel: Bärenreiter, 1987), 108–118.

19. Johann Joseph Fux, *Gradus ad Parnassum* (Vienna, 1725; reprint, New York: Broude Brothers, 1966), 183–192. Fux also mentioned that the first style was performed with the voices alone—that is, without organ and other instruments— and the second style was performed with organ and other instruments, to give support to the voices in difficult chromatic passages. In Dresden, at least, performance parts show that both styles were accompanied by instrumental doubling.

20. Martin Luther, *Luther's Works* 53 (*Liturgy and Hymns*), ed. Ulrich S. Leupold (Philadelphia: Fortress Press, 1965), 63.

21. Gottfried Vopelius, *Neu Leipzig Gesangbuch* (Leipzig, 1682); *Agenda: Das ist, Kirchen-Ordnung* (Leipzig, 1712, as well as many other editions, basically unchanged, between 1647 and 1771); *Leipziger Kirchen-Andachten* (Leipzig, 1694); *Leipziger Kirchen-Staat* (Leipzig, 1710); Christoph Ernst Sicul, *Leipziger Jahr-Geschichte 1721* (Leipzig, 1723); and Johann Christoph Rost, *Nachricht, Wie es, in der Kirchen zu St. Thom. alhier . . . pfleget gehalten zu werden* (manuscript, begun in 1716).

22. The music practices are surveyed in Günther Stiller, *Johann Sebastian Bach and Liturgical Life in Leipzig,* ed. Robin A. Leaver (St. Louis: Concordia, 1984), 108–156.

23. There were four choirs in all, composed of pupils from the St. Thomas School. When the First Choir, which contained the most talented singers and was conducted by the Kantor, sang in St. Thomas, the Second Choir, under a prefect's direction, sang in St. Nikolai. The two groups switched churches each week.

24. Stiller, *Johann Sebastian Bach,* 122. The *Agenda* of 1712 and Sicul also report the chanting of the Latin Credo. In addition, the Credo chant, used by Bach in the *Symbolum* of the B-Minor Mass, was printed in Vopelius's hymnal (see Chapter 4).

25. Interestingly enough, this practice closely paralleled that of the Lübeck Marienkirche, where Buxtehude served as organist. There, on high feasts, the Kyrie, Gloria, Credo, and Sanctus were sung in Latin. See Kerala Snyder, *Dieterich Buxtehude: Organist in Lübeck* (New York: Schirmer Books, 1987), 88.

26. It appears, though, that for Kyrie and Gloria settings he initially relied on pieces by other composers, such as Johann Christoph Pez's *Missa* in A Minor. See Wolff, *Der Stile Antico,* 162.

27. One must note, however, that Philipp Spitta and Friedrich Smend have argued otherwise. See the discussion in Chapter 8.

28. Horn, *Die Dresdner Hofkirchenmusik*, 22.

29. Horn, *Die Dresdner Hofkirchenmusik*, 27.

30. Christoph Wolff, review of Wolfgang Horn's *Die Dresdner Hofkirchenmusik*, in *Bach-Jahrbuch* 76 (1990): 95.

31. The training and arrival of the singers is described in Moritz Fürstenau, *Zur Geschichte der Musik und des Theaters am Hofe zu Dresden* (Dresden, 1861; reprint, Leipzig: Edition Peters, 1971) 2:159–165.

32. *The Bach Reader*, 123.

33. Horn, *Die Dresdner Hofkirchenmusik*, 95–189.

34. Horn, *Die Dresdner Hofkirchenmusik*, 95–99.

35. The remark appears in Emanuel's letter of January 13, 1775, to Johann Nikolaus Forkel. See *Bach-Dokumente* 3: no. 803, or *The Bach Reader*, 279.

36. Unfortunately, most of the Hofkirche repertory remains unpublished, and Horn's study contains short excerpts only. To become acquainted with the music one must consult the manuscripts themselves. I am indebted to the Saxon State Library for permitting me to survey its collection, which contains the bulk of the surviving Hofkirche inventory, and for providing microfilms of several dozen works. The Hofkirche excerpts in the present volume have been transcribed from manuscripts in the Saxon State Library collection.

37. Horn, *Die Dresdner Hofkirchenmusik*, 97–99, 150–153.

38. Wolff, *Der Stile Antico*, 21–22.

39. Saxon State Library, *Mus. 2170-D-7*.

40. Saxon State Library, *Mus. 2397-D-10*.

41. See the discussion in Horn, *Die Dresdner Hofkirchenmusik*, 180.

42. Which was, significantly, printed in a separate folder from the ricercars and canons. See Christoph Wolff, "New Research on Bach's *Musical Offering*," *The Musical Quarterly* 57 (1971): 379–408.

43. Saxon State Library, *Mus. 2356-D-1* and *Mus. 2358-D-42*.

44. Saxon State Library, *Mus. 2203-D-1, 2; Mus. 2203-D-1, 1;* and *Mus. 2356-D-2*, respectively.

CHAPTER 2
The Composition of the B-Minor Mass

1. The Obituary is reproduced in *Bach-Dokumente* 3: no. 666, and translated in *The Bach Reader*, 213–224.

2. Most notably Alfred Dürr, "Zur Chronologie der Leipziger Vokalwerke J. S. Bachs," *Bach-Jahrbuch* 44 (1957): 5–162 (rev. ed., *Zur Chronologie der Leipziger Vokalwerke J. S. Bachs* [Kassel: Bärenreiter, 1976]); Georg von Dadelsen, *Beiträge zur Chronologie der Werke Johann Sebastian Bachs* (Trossingen: Hohner, 1958); and the KBs of the NBA.

3. The running debate between William H. Scheide and Alfred Dürr over the existence and nature of the fifth cantata cycle is summed up in Christoph Wolff,

"Wo blieb Bachs fünfter Kantatenjahrgang?" *Bach-Jahrbuch* 68 (1982): 151–152. Wolff suggests that during the first year in Leipzig Bach may have started to compile a double cycle (that is, a cycle with two cantatas for each Sunday—one for performance before the Sermon and one for performance after), completing it during the two-year period 1725–1727. Such a procedure would account for five cycles between 1723 and 1729.

4. *Bach Dokumente* 1: no. 22; translation in *The Bach Reader*, 120–124. See, too, the discussion of the document in Chapter 7.

5. Such as during his visit to Berlin in August 1741, when family secretary Johann Elias Bach wrote to say that Anna Magdalena had been ailing for over a week and that music was expected for the upcoming change of the Town Council.

6. Although this is generally true, one needs to note that at times the text characters of model and parody could be quite different and yet made to work with basically the same music. See Ludwig Finscher, "Zum Parodieproblem bei Bach," in *Bach Interpretationen*, ed. Martin Geck (Göttingen: Vandenhoeck & Ruprecht, 1969), 94–105.

7. Johann Gottfried Walther, *Musicalisches Lexicon* (Leipzig, 1732; reprint, Kassel: Bärenreiter, 1953), 558.

8. Quoted from Hans-Joachim Schulze's survey "The Parody Process in Bach's Music: An Old Problem Reconsidered," *Bach: The Journal of the Riemenschneider Bach Institute* 20/1 (1989): 12.

9. The most straightforward figures are given in Finscher, "Zum Parodieproblem bei Bach," 94.

10. Schulze, "The Parody Process in Bach's Music," 17–18.

11. Schulze, "The Parody Process in Bach's Music," 19.

12. Three factors of the D-Major Magnificat point to Dresden: the watermark of the original manuscript, which is the same as that found in the score of the 1733 *Missa* (no. 121 in NBA IX/1) and suggests chronological proximity of the two works; the removal of the German-texted interpolations, which would not have been appropriate in Dresden; and the transposed notation of the oboes d'amore, which was appropriate for Dresden but not for Leipzig.

13. The Caldara and Bassani arrangements are described in Wolff, *Der Stile Antico*, 21–23 and 62–63, especially; the Kerll arrangement is discussed in Peter Wollny, "Bachs Sanctus BWV 241 und Kerlls 'Missa Superba,'" *Bach-Jahrbuch* 77 (1991): 173–176; and the Pergolesi arrangement is treated in Thomas Kohlhase, "J. S. Bachs Psalm 51. Die Bearbeitung von Pergolesis 'Stabat mater,'" *Bachfest der Neuen Bachgesellschaft. Marburg 1978*, 135–141.

14. These plans are surveyed in Christoph Wolff, "Principles of Design and Order in Bach's Original Editions," in Wolff, *Bach: Essays on His Life and Music* (Cambridge, Mass.: Harvard University Press, 1991), 340–358.

15. Robert L. Marshall, "Johann Sebastian Bach," in *Eighteenth-Century Keyboard Music*, ed. Robert L. Marshall (New York: Schirmer Books, 1994), 68–123.

16. See David Benjamin Levy, *Beethoven: The Ninth Symphony* (New York: Schirmer Books, 1995), 18–46.

17. The sketches, first mentioned by Spitta in 1880, are analyzed by Robert L. Marshall in *The Compositional Process of J. S. Bach: A Study of the Autograph Scores of the Vocal Works* (Princeton, New Jersey: Princeton University Press, 1972), 1:128, 144–145; 2:Sketches 153–155.

18. Alfred Dürr, *Zur Chronologie der Leipziger Vokalwerke J. S. Bachs*, 77, 93, 116.

19. Translation from *The Bach Reader*, 128–129.

20. Arnold Schering, "Die Hohe Messe in h-moll. Eine Huldigungsmusik und Krönungsmesse für Friedrich August II," *Bach-Jahrbuch* 33 (1936): 1–30.

21. The organs in the principal churches in Leipzig were tuned in choir tone, a major second higher than local wind instruments. To bring the two into line, Bach normally wrote out an organ part a step lower than the rest of the ensemble. In Dresden, the organs in the Hofkirche and the Sophienkirche (to which we will turn in a moment) were tuned in chamber tone—the same pitch as the wind instruments—and transposition was unnecessary. On the Dresden organs see the documentation in Werner Müller, *Gottfried Silbermann: Persönlichkeit und Werk* (Frankfurt am Main: Das Musikinstrument, 1982), 161, n. 907; 162, n. 919; and 348, n. 2208.

22. Rausch was first identified by Hans-Joachim Schulze in *Johann Sebastian Bach. Missa h-Moll BWV 232ⁱ. Faksimile nach dem Originalstimmensatz der Sächsischen Landesbibliothek Dresden* (Neuhausen-Stuttgart: Hänssler-Verlag, 1983), Commentary.

23. It is possible that the one additional hand that appears in the Dresden parts, Anonymous 20 (so named in modern Bach research), belongs to Bach's daughter Catharina Dorothea, then twenty-five years old, or son Johann Gottfried Bernhard, then eighteen. Identifiable handwriting samples for the two remain elusive.

24. Detailed scenarios are proposed in Schulze, *Johann Sebastian Bach. Missa h-Moll BWV 232ⁱ*, Commentary, and Joshua Rifkin, Review of B-Minor Mass facsimile editions, *Notes* 44 (1988): 791–794.

25. In Leipzig, at least. Among the few dated scores, Cantata 174 was finished one day before it was performed; Cantata 198 (the "Trauer-Ode"), two days before it was performed. See Alfred Dürr, *Die Kantaten von Johann Sebastian Bach* (rev. ed., Kassel: Bärenreiter Verlag, 1985), 72–73.

26. The autograph score of the *Missa*, contained within the *P 180* manuscript of the B-Minor Mass, is undated (like most Bach manuscripts), and its watermark (No. 121 in NBA IX/1) points only to the general period 1732–1735.

27. The autograph of the final version of the Prelude and Fugue exhibits the same watermark as Bach's letters to the Dresden Council and Schröter. See Hans-Joachim Schulze, *Studien zur Bach-Überlieferung im 18. Jahrhundert* (Leipzig: Edition Peters, 1984), 17, and the remarks under watermark no. 98 in NBA IX/1: 83–84.

28. Robert L. Marshall, "Bach the Progressive: Observations on His Later Works," in Marshall, *The Music of Johann Sebastian Bach: The Sources, the Style, the Significance* (New York: Schirmer Books, 1989), 40–43 or Georg von Dadelsen, "Bachs h-Moll-Messe," in Dadelsen, *Über Bach und anderes* (Laaber: Laaber-Verlag, 1983), 139–143, for instance.

29. See note 21, above.

30. One such event was the dedication of the Silbermann organ in 1720, when Vice-Kapellmeister Pantaleon Hebenstreit led the Capella in a concert of special music. See Müller, *Gottfried Silbermann: Persönlichkeit und Werk*, 168.

31. Horn, *Die Dresdner Hofkirchenmusik*, 65, and my own observations.

32. The settings in A major and G major can be dated from surviving original materials; the settings in F major and G minor are transmitted in secondary copies only.

33. The extant original parts, *St 400* in the Berlin State Library, contain a transposed continuo part.

34. Philipp Spitta, *Johann Sebastian Bach* (Leipzig: Breitkopf & Härtel, 1873–1880); English translation by Clara Bell and J. A. Fuller-Maitland (London: Novello, 1889; reprint, New York: Dover Publications, 1952) 2:30–37.

35. Arnold Schering, especially, was offended by the plentiful borrowing in the short Masses. See Schering, "Die Hohe Messe in h-moll," 28–30.

36. On the dating of BWV 191 see Gregory G. Butler, "Johann Sebastian Bachs Gloria in excelsis Deo BWV 191: Musik für ein Leipziger Dankfest," *Bach-Jahrbuch* 78 (1992): 65–71. Butler has proposed that Bach arranged the *Gloria in excelsis Deo* for the special service that took place in the University Church on December 25, 1745, in celebration of the Peace of Dresden.

37. A detailed comparison of the two works can be found in NBA I/2, KB, 157–164.

38. Peter Wollny, "Ein Quellenfund zur Entstehungsgeschichte der h-Moll-Messe," *Bach-Jahrbuch* 80 (1994): 163–169. The manuscript that contains the early version, *Mus.2° 54c/3* in the Landes- und Forschungsbibliothek in Gotha, was written in Berlin after Bach's death by his student Johann Friedrich Agricola. It gives no clue about the movement's date of composition.

39. Yoshitake Kobayashi, "Zur Chronologie der Spätwerke Johann Sebastian Bachs. Kompositions- und Aufführungstätigkeit von 1736 bis 1750," *Bach-Jahrbuch* 74 (1988): 7–72.

40. Spitta, *Johann Sebastian Bach* 3:279–280.

41. NBA II/1, KB, 191–193 in particular.

42. Heated responses include Hermann Keller, "Gibt es eine h-moll-Messe von Bach?" *Musik und Kirche* 27 (1957): 81–87, and Walter Blankenburg, "'Sogenannte h-moll-Messe' oder nach wie vor 'h-moll-Messe'?" *Musik und Kirche* 27 (1957): 87–94.

43. Georg von Dadelsen, "Exkurs über die h-moll-Messe," in Dadelsen, *Beiträge zur Chronologie,* 143–156, and idem, "Friedrich Smends Ausgabe der h-moll-Messe von J. S. Bach," *Die Musikforschung* 12 (1959): 315–335. The latter has been issued in an English translation by James A. Brokaw II: "Friedrich Smend's Edition of the B-Minor Mass by J. S. Bach," *Bach: The Journal of the Riemenschneider Bach Institute* 20/2 (1989): 49–74.

44. Dadelsen's own *Bemerkungen zur Handschrift Johann Sebastian Bachs, seiner Familie und seines Kreises* (Trossingen: Hohner-Verlag, 1957) and *Beiträge zur Chronologie der Werke Johann Sebastian Bachs* and Dürr's "Zur Chronologie der Leipziger Vokalwerke."

45. The four divider pages of the manuscript display a third watermark (No. 100 in NBA IX/1), one that does not appear elsewhere in Bach's works.

46. Wolff, *Der Stile Antico,* 149–153.

47. Kobayashi, "Zur Chronologie der Spätwerke Johann Sebastian Bachs," 61.

48. Christoph Wolff, "The Compositional History of the Art of Fugue," in Wolff, *Bach: Essays on his Life and Music* (Cambridge, Mass.: Harvard University Press, 1991), 265–281.

49. Marshall, *The Compositional Process of J. S. Bach,* 1:43–68 (66, in particular). According to Marshall, Bach wrote cantatas movement by movement, in order (except for recitatives, which he sometimes left for last).

50. Detlev Kranemann, "Johann Sebastian Bachs Krankheit und Todesursache—Versuch einer Deutung," *Bach-Jahrbuch* 76 (1990): 53–64.

51. In the *P 180* manuscript, the title pages of parts 1 and 2 differ slightly from those of parts 3 and 4 (compare the form of the N of the word "No." in the facsimile edition). This reinforces the idea that Bach completed the *Missa* and *Symbolum* in one stretch and the Sanctus and remaining sections in another.

52. Yoshitake Kobayashi, "Die Universalität in Bachs h-moll-Messe—Ein Beitrag zum Bach-Bild der letzten Lebensjahre," *Musik und Kirche* 57 (1987): 19 (n. 50 in particular).

53. *Bach-Dokumente* 3: no. 957 (p. 495, especially). The description reads: "*No 2. Symbolum Nicaenum (Credo.)* With trumpets, timpani, flutes, oboes, and bassoon. Score in the composer's hand, together with fully written-out parts. An Introduction by C.P.E.B. also belongs to this Credo."

54. Unfortunately, this is precisely what has been done in the Schmieder Catalogue, in which the prelude and fugue, chorale preludes, and duets of *Clavierübung* III are classifed under different genres, as BWV 552, 669–689, and 802–805.

55. See Klaus Häfner, "Über die Herkunft von zwei Sätzen der h-moll-Messe," *Bach-Jahrbuch* 63 (1977): 55–74.

56. The folio structure of the *P 180* manuscript is diagrammed by Alfred Dürr in *Johann Sebastian Bach. Messe in h-Moll, BWV 232. Faksimile der autographen Partitur* (Kassel: Bärenreiter Verlag, 1965 reprint, 1984), Commentary, 14–15.

57. On these points see Robert L. Marshall, "The Mass in B Minor: The Autograph Scores and the Compositional Process," in Marshall, *The Music of Johann Sebastian Bach*, 175–189.

58. Klaus Häfner, *Aspekte des Parodieverfahrens bei Johann Sebastian Bach* (Laaber: Laaber-Verlag, 1977), and Joshua Rifkin, Notes to Nonesuch recording no. 79036 (New York, 1982). Also important are Alfred Dürr, "Zur Parodiefrage in Bachs h-moll-Messe: Eine Bestandsaufnahme," *Musikforschung* 45 (1992): 117–138, and Hans-Joachim Schulze's review of Häfner's book, in *Bach-Jahrbuch* 76 (1990), 92–94.

CHAPTER 3
The Kyrie and the Gloria

1. See the discussion of the large Dresden Kyrie-Gloria settings in Horn, *Die Dresdner Hofkirchenmusik*, 190–194.

2. Horn, *Die Dresdner Hofkirchenmusik*, 150–153.

3. An excellent, detailed, and up-to-date summary of Bach's instruments can be found in Jürgen Eppelsheim's "The Instruments," in *Johann Sebastian Bach: Life, Times, Influence*, ed. Barbara Schwendowius and Wolfgang Dömling (Kassel: Bärenreiter, 1977), 127–142.

4. As Horn notes, in Dresden Mass settings the choruses rather than the arias commonly contain the most virtuosic passages for solo voices and instruments. See *Die Dresdner Hofkirchenmusik*, 190.

5. Schering, "Die Hohe Messe in h-moll," 11–13.

6. Johann Gottfried Walther, *Briefe*, ed. Klaus Beckmann and Hans-Joachim Schulze (Leipzig: VEB Deutscher Verlag für Musik, 1987), 120.

7. Christoph Wolff, "Zur musikalischen Vorgeschichte des Kyrie aus Johann Sebastian Bachs Messe in h-moll," in *Festschrift Bruno Stäblein*, ed. Martin Ruhnke (Kassel: Bärenreiter, 1967), 314–326; English translation: "Origins of the Kyrie of the B Minor Mass," in Wolff, *Bach: Essays on His Life and Music* (Cambridge, Mass.: Harvard University Press, 1991), 141–151.

8. Only a bass part survives. See Alfred Dürr, "Marginalia Bachiana," *Musikforschung* 4 (1951): 374–375, and NBA I/2, KB, 8–9.

9. Saxon State Library, *Mus. 2170-D-7*.

10. Carl Hermann Bitter, *Johann Sebastian Bach* (rev. ed., Berlin, 1881; reprint, Leipzig: Zentralantiquariat der Deutschen Demokratischen Republik, 1978) 3:7.

11. Rita Steblin, *A History of Key Characteristics in the Eighteenth and Early Nineteenth Centuries* (Ann Arbor, Michigan: UMI Research Press, 1983), 306.

12. Though we must note here that the "Kyrie" fugue may have stemmed from a model in C minor (see discussion, below).

13. Rifkin, Notes to Nonesuch recording no. *79036*.

14. A possibility first raised by Marshall in *The Compositional Process of J. S. Bach*, 1:19.

15. John Butt, in *Bach: Mass in B Minor* (Cambridge: Cambridge University Press, 1991), 111–112, notes additional transpositional mistakes in support of Rifkin. On the other hand, Dürr, in "Zur Parodiefrage in Bachs h-moll-Messe," 119–120, questions Rifkin's hypothesis.

16. Walther, for instance, claimed to have written an isolated Kyrie for the installation ceremony of a general superintendent at his church in Weimar. See Walther, *Briefe*, 153. In light of how common slow introductions were in Dresden Masses, it is remarkable to think that Bach's large Kyrie model—if there was one— did not contain an opening *adagio*. The subsequent addition of the introduction might also speak in favor of Bach's growing familiarity with music practices at the Hofkirche in the 1730s.

17. Robert L. Marshall, "Bach the Progressive: Observations on His Later Works," *The Musical Quarterly* 62 (1976): 339–340.

18. Wolff, "Origins of the Kyrie," 412 (n. 33, in particular). Wolff expands on a point made initially by Arnold Schmitz in "Die oratorische Kunst J. S. Bachs— Grundfragen und Grundlagen," *Bericht über den musikwissenschaftlichen Kongreß Lüneburg* (Kassel: Bärenreiter, 1950), 47–48.

19. Wolff, "Origins of the Kyrie," 148–149. The opening measures of the vocal parts of the Wilderer "Christe" are given on p. 149.

20. It is also noteworthy that when Bach composed the "Christe eleison" inter- polation, BWV 242, for Durante's Mass in C Minor he used the same vocal setting (soprano and alto) and a similar chamber style.

21. Walter Blankenburg, *Einführung in Bachs h-moll-Messe* (Kassel: Bärenreiter, 1974), 29.

22. Butt, *Bach: Mass in B Minor*, 45. This slip could just as easily reflect habit on Bach's part: despite firmly assigning the second vocal part to "Sopr. 2" at the beginning of the duet, he may have used the alto clef now and then because he was far more accustomed to writing for soprano and alto than for two sopranos.

23. Dürr, "Zur Parodiefrage," 121.

24. Klaus Häfner, *Aspekte des Parodieverfahrens bei Johann Sebastian Bach* (Laaber: Laaber-Verlag, 1977), 245–246.

25. Wolff, *Der Stile Antico in der Musik Johann Sebastian Bachs: Studien zu Bachs Spätwerk* (Wiesbaden: Fritz Steiner, 1968), 13–16 and 119–129.

26. Johann Mattheson, *Das neu-eröffnete Orchestre* (Hamburg, 1713), 232.

27. Rifkin, Notes to Nonesuch recording no. *79036;* Häfner, *Aspekte des Parodieverfahrens*, 243.

28. Even in the exemplary *stile antico* Kyrie from Fux's *Missa vicissitudines*, printed in *Gradus ad Parnassum*, for instance. See the facsimile in Wolff, *Der Stile Antico*, 227.

29. Schering, "Die Hohe Messe in h-moll," 11–18.

30.   The distinctions between the Italian giga and the French gigue are outlined in Meredith Little and Natalie Jenne, *Dance and the Music of J. S. Bach* (Bloomington, Indiana: Indiana University Press, 1991), 143–184. Bach often used the term gigue for pieces that fall into the giga category, such as the $\frac{3}{8}$-meter pieces cited here.

31.   The organization of the Vivaldi ritornello was first analyzed by Wilhelm Fischer, who proposed the terms *Vordersatz, Fortspinnung,* and *Epilog* for its three parts. See Fischer, "Zur Entwicklungsgeschichte des Wiener klassischen Stils," *Studien zur Musikwissenschaft* 3 (1915): 24–84.

32.   Smend, NBA II/1, KB, 109–112.

33.   Rifkin, Notes to Nonesuch recording no. *79036.*

34.   Butt, *Bach: Mass in B Minor,* 46.

35.   Saxon State Library, *Mus. 2356-D-2.*

36.   Wilfrid Mellers, *Bach and the Dance of God* (New York: Oxford University Press, 1981), 184.

37.   Werner Neumann, *J. S. Bachs Chorfuge: Ein Beitrag zur Kompositionstechnik Bachs* (2nd ed., Leipzig: Breitkopf und Härtel, 1950), 14–52. The present chart is adapted from Neumann's analysis of the "Et in terra" fugue (p. 36).

38.   Marshall, *The Compositional Process of J. S. Bach* 1: 5.

39.   Rifkin, Notes to Nonesuch recording no. *79036.*

40.   Neumann, *J. S. Bachs Chorfuge,* 36.

41.   Walther, *Musicalisches Lexicon,* 246.

42.   This reading was first pointed out by Smend, in NBA II/1, KB, 279.

43.   Marshall, "Bach the Progressive: Observations on His Later Works," 341. Marshall credits the observation to a remark made by Arthur Mendel.

44.   As quoted in Charles Burney, *A General History of Music from the Earliest Ages to the Present* (London, 1776–89), modern edition, ed. Frank Mercer (New York: Harcourt, Brace and Company, 1935) 2:736–737.

45.   Marshall, "The Mass in B Minor: The Autograph Scores and the Compositional Process," 181; Rifkin, Notes to Nonesuch recording no. *79036.*

46.   Alfred Dürr, *Johann Sebastian Bach: Seine Handschrift* (Wiesbaden: Breitkopf und Härtel, 1984), commentary to Plate 48.

47.   Rifkin, Notes to Nonesuch recording no. *79036.*

48.   Wolff, *Der Stile Antico,* 50–52.

49.   Wolff, *Der Stile Antico,* 120–121.

50.   In the figured continuo part of the Dresden materials from 1733, the bass line of the "Domine Deus" is marked "pizzicato"—most certainly an instruction for a violone player reading over the shoulder of the organist. See the discussion of continuo practices in Chapter 7.

51.   Spitta, *Johann Sebastian Bach,* 3:49.

52.   As first noted by Smend in NBA II/1, KB, 291.

53.   Spitta, *Johann Sebastian Bach,* 3:38.

54. Wolff, *Der Stile Antico,* 177, n. 10.

55. Eric Chafe, *Tonal Allegory in the Vocal Music of J. S. Bach* (Berkeley, Calif.: University of California Press, 1991), 152.

56. Häfner, "Über die Herkunft von zwei Sätzen der h-Moll-Messe," 56–64.

57. That the opening choruses of many of Bach's Leipzig cantatas resemble large preludes and fugues was first set forth by Neumann in *J. S. Bachs Chorfuge,* 7–14.

58. Marshall, "The Mass in B Minor," 180.

59. Marshall, "The Mass in B Minor," 171.

60. Smend, NBA II/1, KB, 102.

61. Spitta, *Johann Sebastian Bach,* 3:50.

62. Mattheson, *Der vollkommene Capellmeister,* 228.

63. Häfner, *Aspekte des Parodieverfahrens,* 282.

64. See Dürr, "Zur Parodiefrage," 126.

65. From time to time the question has been raised as to whether the horn should not sound at notated pitch. Peter Damm, in "Zur Ausführung des 'Corne da Caccia' im Quoniam der Missa h-Moll von J. S. Bach," *Bach-Jahrbuch* 70 (1984): 91–105, and Jürgen Eppelsheim, "Beobachtungen zum Instrumentarium und Orchester Bachscher Kompositionen aus den beiden letzten Lebensjahrzehnten," in *Johann Sebastian Bachs Spätwerk und dessen Umfeld,* ed. Christoph Wolff (Kassel: Bärenreiter, 1988), 82, have convincingly demonstrated that it should sound an octave lower than written. One should also note that Heinichen and Zelenka commonly notated the horn in Dresden scores in a manner parallel to Bach's. See Horn, *Die Dresdner Hofkirchenmusik,* 200.

66. See the discussion in Chafe, *Tonal Allegory in the Vocal Music of J. S. Bach,* 342.

67. Helmut Rilling, *Johann Sebastian Bach's B-Minor Mass,* trans. Gordon Paine (Princeton, N.J.: Prestige Publications, 1984), 41.

68. See Laurence Dreyfus, *Bach's Continuo Group: Players and Practices in His Vocal Works* (Cambridge, Mass.: Harvard University Press), 127–131.

69. To judge from the personnel list of 1738 (reproduced in *Bach-Dokumente* 4: no. 490), Rousseau's report of the year 1754 in his *Dictionnaire de Musique* (Paris, 1768; reprint, Hildesheim: G. Olms, 1969), 354, and the biographical entries in Walther's *Musicalisches Lexicon* of 1732.

70. Horn, *Die Dresdner Hofkirchenmusik,* 109 and 194.

71. Saxon State Library, *Mus. 2398-D-14.*

72. Horn, *Die Dresdner Hofkirchenmusik,* 188–189 and 200.

73. The virtuoso horn part from the aria is reproduced in Damm, "Zur Ausführung des 'Corne da Caccia,'" 102.

74. Rifkin, Notes to Nonesuch recording no. *79036.*

75. Häfner, *Aspekte des Parodieverfahrens,* 287; Butt, *Bach: Mass in B Minor,* 49.

76. Spitta, *Johann Sebastian Bach* 3:56.

77. Donald Francis Tovey, *Essays in Musical Analysis* (Oxford: Oxford University Press, 1935–39), 5:34–35. Tovey failed to take into account the fact that Bach normally ended the first segment of a ritornello on the dominant rather than in the tonic, however: in his reconstruction, the tonic cadence in m. 4 produces a premature harmonic closure.

78. Smend, NBA II/1, KB, 105–108; Häfner, *Aspekte des Parodieverfahrens*, 291–292.

79. Rifkin, Notes to Nonesuch recording no. *79036*.

80. These are discussed in Georg von Dadelsen, "Die Crux der Nebensache: Editorische und praktische Bemerkungen zu Bachs Artikulation," *Bach-Jahrbuch* 64 (1978): 110–112.

CHAPTER 4
The Credo

1. *Ms. 15773.*

2. Albert Schweitzer, *J. S. Bach*, trans. Ernest Newman (London: A & C Black, 1923; reprint, Boston: B. Humphries, 1962), 2:317–318.

3. Jaroslav Pelikan, *Bach Among the Theologians* (Philadelphia: Fortress Press, 1986), 123.

4. Peter Wagner, *Publikationen älterer Musik* 5 (Leipzig: Breitkopf & Härtel, 1930): viii.

5. Wolff, *Der Stile Antico*, 102.

6. Wolff, *Der Stile Antico*, 106.

7. Spitta, *Johann Sebastian Bach*, 3:57.

8. Pelikan, *Bach Among the Theologians*, 116–127.

9. The Caldara arrangement is discussed in Wolff, *Der Stile Antico*, 204–209, and it has been published by Bärenreiter (ed. Christoph Wolff, 1969).

10. As Georg von Dadelsen first noted, in "Eine unbekannte Messenbearbeitung Bachs" in *Festschrift Karl Gustav Fellerer*, ed. Heinrich Hüschen (Regensburg: G. Bosse, 1962), 88–94. The Bassani interpolation is also analyzed in Wolff, *Der Stile Antico*, 15–16, 32–33, 64–65, and 69–70.

11. The variant readings are given in Wollny, "Ein Quellenfund zur Entstehungsgeschichte der h-Moll-Messe," 163–169.

12. Rifkin, Notes to Nonesuch recording no. *79036.*

13. See Horn, *Die Dresdner Hofkirchenmusik*, 162.

14. Saxon State Library, *Mus. 2170-D-8.*

15. On Credo Masses see Georg Reichert, "Mozarts 'Credo-Messen' und ihre Vorläufer," *Mozart-Jahrbuch* 6 (1955), 117–144.

16. As first noted by Friedrich Smend, NBA II/1, 134–135.

17. The changes are discussed in detail in Butt, *Bach: Mass in B Minor*, 86–87.

18.   In the autograph score, Bach wrote "Violino e Hautbois" at the beginning of the violin 1 and violin 2 lines, even though the violin 2 line, with a range of a–b", requires an oboe d'amore. When Bach used two oboes he normally employed a matching pair, and he most probably intended two oboes d'amore for the "Et in unum Dominum." In the *Bach-Gesamtausgabe* and editions derived from it, the oboe 2 incorrectly doubles violin 1 in mm. 1–4. Bach's initial oboe indications (those in mm. 1–17) were erased from the *P 180* manuscript sometime after his death, probably with the goal of eliminating the oboes altogether (since oboes d'amore were no longer available). The marks are preserved in early copies of *P 180*, such as *AmB 3* and *P 23* (see Chapter 6).

19.   Interestingly enough, "Rühmet Gottes Güt und Treu" also contains porta-mento figures like those found in mm. 21–22 and m. 66 of the "Et in unum Dominum."

20.   Spitta, *Johann Sebastian Bach* 3:51.

21.   NBA II/1, KB, 147–156.

22.   See, too, Finscher's observations on parody procedure in the Christmas Oratorio, in "Zum Parodieproblem bei Bach," 94–105.

23.   The violin line is not a sketch but a fair copy, as Marshall points out in "The Mass in B Minor: The Autograph Scores and the Compositional Process," 183.

24.   See Hans-Joachim Schulze's review in *Bach-Jahrbuch* 76 (1990): 92–94.

25.   Christoph Wolff, "'Et incarnatus' and 'Crucifixus': The Earliest and the Latest Settings of Bach's B-Minor Mass," in *Eighteenth-Century Music in Theory and Practice: Essays in Honor of Alfred Mann*, ed. Mary Ann Parker (Stuyvesant, N.Y.: Pendragon Press, 1994), 12–13.

26.   Blankenburg, *Einführung in Bachs h-moll-Messe*, 75; Rilling, *Johann Sebastian Bach's B-Minor Mass*, 69.

27.   Christoph Wolff, *Mozart's Requiem: Historical and Analytical Studies, Documents, Score*, trans. Mary Whittal (Berkeley, Calif.: University of California Press, 1994), 104–112.

28.   See the detailed appraisal of the movement's progressive features in Wolff, "'Et incarnatus' and 'Crucifixus': The Earliest and Latest Settings of Bach's B-Minor Mass," 9–17.

29.   Saxon State Library, *Mus. 2358-D-24*.

30.   Christoph Wolff, "The Agnus Dei of the B Minor Mass: Parody and New Composition Reconciled," in Wolff, *Bach: Essays on His Life and Music* (Cambridge, Mass.: Harvard University Press, 1991), 332.

31.   Earlier, in Mühlhausen, Bach had cast his cantatas in the seventeenth-century North-German mold, with texts drawn from Biblical sources and hymns and with sectional, rather than multi-movement, forms. The "Neumeister cantata" was named after Hamburg minister Erdmann Neumeister, who in *Geistliche Cantaten statt einer Kirchen-Music* (Weissenfels, 1700) introduced the concept of modeling sacred pieces after Italian cantatas.

32. The classical roots of the "Weinen, Klagen" verse are discussed in Z. Philip Ambrose, "'Weinen, Klagen, Sorgen, Zagen' und die antike Redekunst," *Bach-Jahrbuch* 66 (1980): 35–45.

33. Saxon State Library, *Mus. 2367-D-1.*

34. Friedrich Smend, "Bachs h-moll-Messe. Entstehung, Überlieferung, Bedeutung," *Bach-Jahrbuch* 34 (1937): 16.

35. Robert Schumann, *Neue Zeitschrift für Musik* 14 (1841): no. 22, 88–89.

36. Häfner, "Über die Herkunft von zwei Sätzen der h-Moll-Messe," 74.

37. Mattheson, *Der vollkommene Capellmeister,* 203–208.

38. One suspects, though, that if Bach had made out performance parts for the Credo, he would have added flutes to the "Patrem," as doubling instruments with the oboes. In that case, the "Et resurrexit" would have been the second movement to use the full ensemble.

39. Nikolaus Harnoncourt, in his ground-breaking 1968 recording of the B-Minor Mass with original forces (Telefunken recording no. *SKH 20/1–3*), assigned the "Et iterum venturus" to a bass solo. When he rerecorded the work in 1986 (Teldec recording no. *8.35716*), however, he used the bass section of the chorus for the same passage.

40. Smend, NBA II/1, KB, 145–147.

41. Häfner, "Über die Herkunft von zwei Sätzen der h-moll-Messe," 65–74.

42. Tovey attempted to recreate the "missing" ritornello segment in *Essays in Musical Analysis,* 5:41–42. The closing ritornello of the "Et resurrexit" is twenty measures long and begins in the subdominant; the original opening ritornello, which surely began in the tonic, presumably would have been somewhat longer. With eighteen measures, Tovey's reconstruction seems too short.

43. Martin Luther, "The Small Catechism," quoted from *Luther's Works: American Edition,* ed. Jaroslav Pelikan and Helmut T. Lehmann (St. Louis: Concordia Publishing House, and Philadelphia: Fortress Press, 1955–86) 51:163

44. Tovey, *Essays in Musical Analysis,* 5:43.

45. Wolff, *Der Stile Antico,* 55–65.

46. Tovey, *Essays in Musical Analysis,* 5:43.

47. Wolff, *Der Stile Antico,* 95.

48. Rifkin, in the Notes to Nonesuch recording no. *79036,* and Butt, in *Bach: The Mass in B Minor,* 56, make the case for direct composition; Dürr, in "Zur Parodiefrage in Bachs h-moll-Messe," 134, makes the case for the use of sketches or a draft.

49. C. F. D. Schubart, *Ideen zu einer Ästhetik der Tonkunst* (c. 1784), quoted in Steblin, *A History of Key Characteristics in the Eighteenth and Early Nineteenth Centuries,* 250.

50. Mellers, *Bach and the Dance of God,* 230.

51. Chafe, *Tonal Allegory in the Vocal Music of J. S. Bach,* 82–83.

52. Chafe, *Tonal Allegory in the Vocal Music of J. S. Bach,* 82.

53. Smend, "Bachs h-moll-Messe. Entstehung, Überlieferung, Bedeutung," 1–58.

54. Smend, "Bachs h-moll-Messe. Entstehung, Überlieferung, Bedeutung," 21–24. In his remarkable analysis of the two movements, Smend also shows how Bach was able to insert a fifth voice into the "Steiget" fugato without adding any measures to the original material.

55. The timpani solo stems from the "Jauchzet" chorus, where there is no allusion to timpani in the text. Rifkin (Notes to Nonesuch recording no. *79036*) has suggested that "Jauchzet" is also a parody, because of the fair-copy nature of the original score. If so, the timpani solo, like that in the opening chorus of Part I of the Christmas Oratorio, "Jauchzet, frohlocket!" could be the remnant of an earlier setting in which timpani are mentioned in the text.

56. Marshall, "The Mass in B Minor: Autograph Scores and the Compositional Process," 185.

57. Smend, "Bachs h-moll-Messe. Entstehung, Überlieferung, Bedeutung," 52.

58. See, *inter alia*, the discussions in Gerhard Herz, ed., *Bach: Cantata No. 4, Christ lag in Todesbanden* (New York: W. W. Norton, 1967), 83–86, and Wolff, "Principles of Design and Order in Bach's Original Editions," in Wolff, *Bach: Essays on his Life and Music* (Cambridge, Mass.: Harvard University Press, 1991), 340–358.

59. The architectural qualities of the St. Thomas School and other buildings in Leipzig are discussed in George B. Stauffer, "The *Thomasschule* and the *Haus 'zum Goldenen Bären'*: A Bach-Breitkopf Architectural Connection" in *Bach Perspectives II: Bach and the Breitkopfs*, ed. George B. Stauffer (Lincoln, Nebraska: University of Nebraska Press, 1996), 181–203.

60. As many commentators have noted, Bach's Latin is incorrect. The feminine case of "vox" ("voice") calls for "Duae Voces." Butt's translation of the phrase (*Bach: Mass in B Minor*, 52) as "Two voices express 2" is misguided; Bach's capitalization of "Articuli" suggests that he was viewing the word as a noun.

61. The design of the "Goldberg" Variations is discussed in detail in David Schulenberg, *The Keyboard Music of J. S. Bach* (New York: Schirmer Books, 1992), 320–322.

CHAPTER 5
The Sanctus and Agnus Dei

1. This is especially evident in cases where Zelenka turned a preexistent Neapolitan Kyrie-Gloria setting into a *Missa tota*. To the large Kyrie and Gloria of Durante's *Missa Modestiae*, for instance, Zelenka added a modest Sanctus and Agnus Dei, mostly by reworking segments of the Kyrie and Gloria. See the discussion of the procedure in Horn, *Die Dresdner Hofkirchenmusik*, 179–180.

2. Schmieder lists the four settings as Bach compositions in the *Bach-Werke-Verzeichnis*, but with the caveat that they are probably arrangements rather than

original works. The *Neue Bach-Ausgabe* and the *Bach Compendium* have dropped the D minor and G major settings from the Bach canon, and it is likely that in time the C major and D major settings will be rejected as well. They seem too *galant* stylistically and too pedestrian harmonically to be original compositions.

3.   It stands thus in the so-called Dresden Songbook, *Neuauffgelegte Dressdnische Gesang-Buch* (Leipzig 1707), and Carl Gottlob Hofmann's *Privilegirtes vollständiges und verbessertes Leipziger Gesangbuch* (Leipzig, 1737), which were used alongside Vopelius's New Leipzig Hymnal in Bach's time. See Walter Blankenburg, *Einführung in Bachs h-moll-Messe*, 90–91.

4.   In the original scores of both versions of the "Sanctus," the sixteenth notes of dotted figures are normally lined up with the last notes of triplets when the two appear together contrapuntally. This alignment, which is reproduced in Example 5–1a, strongly suggests that the dotted figures would have been absorbed into the triplet rhythm.

5.   Robert L. Marshall, in *The Compositional Process of J. S. Bach*, 1:141–147, points out that Bach commonly made such drafts (which Marshall terms "continuation sketches") at the bottom of right-hand pages, apparently to preserve his train of thought as he waited, impatiently, for the ink to dry before turning over the page and continuing on the reverse side.

6.   The sketch was first mentioned by Philipp Spitta in *Johann Sebastian Bach*, 3:278–280.

7.   Marshall, "The Mass in B Minor: The Autograph Scores and the Compositional Process," 186–187. Marshall reproduces the sketch in full.

8.   Spitta, *Johann Sebastian Bach*, 3:60.

9.   The confusion is increased by the Schmieder Catalogue, which does not allot the 1724 "Sanctus" its own BWV number or entry. One must look under the B-Minor Mass, BWV 232, to find information on the 1724 version. The *Bach-Compendium* has moved toward restoring the separate identities of the two pieces, assigning the 1724 "Sanctus" an independent entry (E 12) from the B-Minor Mass version (E 1, movement 22).

10.   All three views are summarized by Neumann in NBA I/37, KB, 70–74.

11.   Example 5–5 is patterned after Neumann, NBA I/37, KB, 73.

12.   Blankenburg, *Einführung in Bachs h-moll-Messe*, 97.

13.   *Bach-Dokumente* 2: no. 352, Commentary.

14.   Butt, *Bach: Mass in B Minor*, 71.

15.   Smend, NBA II/1, KB, 184.

16.   Smend, NBA II/1, KB, 184.

17.   Different writers have seen different things under the "Agnus." Smend believed the overwritten word to be the "Dona" of "Dona nobis pacem" (NBA II/1, KB, 182–183); Christoph Trautmann thought it was "JJ" (for "Jesu Juva") later covered by "Bene" ("'Soll das Werk den Meister loben?' Zur h-moll-Messe von Johann Sebastian Bach," *Bachtage Berlin*, ed. Günther Wagner [Neuhausen-Stuttgart: Hänssler Verlag, 1985], 190–191); and John Butt believed it to be the "Bene" of

"Benedictus" (*Bach: Mass in B Minor*, 18). "Bend" (or "Bene") seems to be the best reading. See the facsimile of the B-Minor Mass, *Johann Sebastian Bach. Messe in h-Moll BWV 232*, 181.

18. Rilling, *Johann Sebastian Bach's B-Minor Mass*, 141.

19. Mellers, *Bach and the Dance of God*, 237–238.

20. Whether the unison line in the "Agnus Dei" should be played by violins 1 and 2 or by violin 1 alone is not altogether clear. In the detailed performance parts of "Ach, bleibe doch" from the Ascension Oratorio, a movement derived from the same music as the "Agnus Dei" (see discussion below), the second violins are tacet. See NBA II/8, KB, 27.

21. Friedrich Smend, "Bachs Himmelfahrts-Oratorium," *Bach-Gedenkschrift 1950* (Leipzig: VEB Deutscher Verlag für Musik, 1950), 42.

22. Alfred Dürr, "'Entfernet euch, ihr kalten Herzen.' Möglichkeiten und Grenzen der Rekonstruktion einer Bach-Arie," *Musikforschung* 39 (1986): 32–36.

23. For example, in the chorus "Kreuzige, kreuzige" or the aria "Eilt, ihr angefochtnen Seelen" (the "Wohin?" query) from the St. John Passion or the chorus "Laß ihn kreuzigen" or the recitative "Erbarm es Gott" from the St. Matthew Passion.

24. The texts of "Ach, bleibe doch" and "Entfernet euch" are given in Smend, "Bachs Himmelsfahrts-Oratorium," 42.

25. These revisions are discussed in detail in Dürr, "'Entfernet euch,'" and in Wolff, "The Agnus Dei of the B Minor Mass," 332–339.

26. Wolff, "The Agnus Dei of the B Minor Mass," 338.

27. Wolff, "The Agnus Dei of the B Minor Mass," 339.

28. Wolff, "The Agnus Dei of the B Minor Mass," 332.

29. Saxon State Library, *Mus. 2397-D-10, Mus. 2170-D-10,* and *Mus. 2170-D-9,* respectively. In all three works works the "Dona" movements appear to be parodies crafted by Zelenka. See Horn, *Die Dresdner Hofkirchenmusik,* 163 and 180.

30. Smend, NBA II/1, KB, 180.

31. As Smend convincingly demonstrated in NBA II/1, KB, 390–395.

32. Marshall, "The Mass in B Minor: The Autograph Scores and Compositional Process," 188.

33. Butt, *Bach: Mass in B Minor,* 18.

34. Wolff, *Der Stile Antico,* 180.

35. Spitta, *Johann Sebastian Bach,* 3:41.

36. Smend, NBA II/1, KB, 178–187.

37. That a cantata, the second part of a two-part cantata, or some other concerted vocal music was performed during Communion in Leipzig is verified by the two Orders of Service that are handed down in Bach's hand. See *Bach-Dokumente* 1: nos. 178 and 181.

38. See Alfred Dürr's diagram of the fascicle structure in *Johann Sebastian Bach. Messe in H-Moll, BWV 232. Faksimile der autographen Partitur,* Commentary, 14–15.

39. Rifkin, Notes to Nonesuch recording no. *79036* (1982).

CHAPTER 6
The B-Minor Mass after Bach's Death

1. It is presumably one of "five passions" mentioned in the works list of the 1754 Obituary. Bach composed the St. Mark Passion, "Geh, Jesu, geh zu deiner Pein," for Good Friday, 1731. Its surviving madrigal text shows that it contained forty-six movements and was thus roughly equal in size to the St. John Passion. A handful of choruses, arias, and harmonized chorales can be reconstructed from secondary sources.

2. Yoshitake Kobayashi, "Franz Hauser und seine Bach-Handschriften-sammlung" (Ph.D. diss., University of Göttingen, 1973), 297.

3. Letter of December 6, 1846, to Carl Klingemann, printed in *Briefe aus den Jahren 1833 zu 1847 von Felix Mendelssohn Bartholdy*, ed. Paul Mendelssohn Bartholdy and Carl Mendelssohn Bartholdy (Leipzig: Hermann Mendelssohn, 1865), 471.

4. Hans-Joachim Schulze, ed., *Johann Sebastian Bach: Missa H-Moll, BWV 232¹. Faksimile nach dem Originalstimmensatz der Sächsischen Landesbibliothek Dresden* (Neuhausen-Stuttgart: Hänssler-Verlag, 1983).

5. The text is transcribed in *Bach-Dokumente* 1: no. 27 and translated in *The Bach Reader*, 128–129; a photograph is given in *Bach-Dokumente* 4: no. 459.

6. *Bach-Dokumente* 3: no. 666.

7. *Bach-Dokumente* 3: no. 754, Commentary.

8. Schering, "Die Hohe Messe in h-moll," 22; Dadelsen, "Friedrich Smends Ausgabe der h-moll Messe von J. S. Bach," 318–319.

9. The binding was discarded in the 1930s during a restoration.

10. The intrigues of the purchase are related in marvelous detail by Smend in NBA II/1, KB, 66–71.

11. BG 44, ed. Hermann Kretzschmar (Leipzig: Breitkopf & Härtel, 1895), plates 89–124.

12. *Hohe Messe in h-moll. Faksimile-Ausgabe der Handschrift* (Leipzig: Insel-Verlag, 1924).

13. *Johann Sebastian Bach. Messe in h-Moll BWV 232. Faksimile der autographen Partitur,* with Commentary by Alfred Dürr (Kassel: Bärenreiter Verlag, 1965; reprint, 1984).

14. Christoph Nichelmann, *Die Melodie nach ihrem Wesen sowohl, als nach ihren Eigenschaften* (Berlin, 1755), 138. Reprinted in *Bach-Dokumente* 3: no. 668.

15. Johann Philipp Kirnberger, *Die Kunst des reinen Satzes* 2, part 2 (Berlin and Königsburg, 1777), 172, and idem, *Die Kunst des reinen Satzes* 2, part 1 (Berlin and Königsburg, 1776), 118, respectively. Kirnberger's treatise is available in an English translation, *The Art of Strict Musical Composition*, trans. David Beach and Jurgen Thym (New Haven: Yale University Press, 1982).

16. Johann Friedrich Agricola, review in *Allgemeine deutsche Bibliothek,* part I, vol. 25 (Berlin, 1775), 108.

17. *Bach-Dokumente* 3: no. 870.

18. Emanuel's Introduction is reproduced in full in the new Peters edition.

19. *Staats- und Gelehrte Zeitung des Hamburgischen unpartheyischen Corres-*
pondenten, 1786, no. 57 (April 11). Reprinted in *Bach-Dokumente* 3: no. 911.

20. As Joshua Rifkin has demonstrated in "'. . . wobey aber die Singstimmen
hinlänglich gesetzt seyn müssen . . .': Zum Credo der h-Moll-Messe in der
Aufführung Carl Philipp Emanuel Bachs," *Bach-Tage Berlin 1986* (Berlin, 1986),
104–116.

21. See the pay receipts reproduced in Heinrich Miesner, *Philipp Emanuel*
Bach (Leipzig: Breitkopf & Härtel, 1929; reprint, Wiesbaden: M. Sandig, 1969),
121–128; and the discussion in Rifkin, "'. . . wobey aber die Singstimmen hinlänglich gesetzt seyn müssen . . .,'" 104–116. A group of *Chorknaben* is also mentioned in the Hamburg documents, but its role seems to have been very limited. In
the 1786 Credo performance the use of female dilettantes means that there may
well have been people singing who did not get paid. Thus the group may have
exceeded Emanuel's normal vocal ensemble in size (though the parts do not point
in that direction).

22. To the five listed in NBA II/2, KB, 17–20, and the *Bach Compendium*
4:1162, I can add two more: a manuscript owned by Alan Tyson of London and a
manuscript, copied by one of C. P. E. Bach's Hamburg scribes (Anonymous 305),
owned by Michael D'Andrea of Princeton, N.J.

23. Charles Burney, *A General History of Music* 4 (London, 1789; reprint,
London: G. T. Foulis, 1935), 591–592.

24. The title page of the copy contains the remark (in English): "Nicene creed
by Sebastian Bach."

25. Christoph Daniel Ebeling, "Lobgesang auf die Harmonie," reprinted in full
in NBA II/2, KB, 401–403, and in abridged form in *Bach-Dokumente* 3: no. 940.

26. A late eighteenth-century manuscript copy written by a Viennese scribe, *P*
11-P 12 in the Berlin State Library, reflects the text of *Am.B. 1-Am.B. 2* from
Princess Amalia's Collection and may stem from van Swieten's circle.

27. Johann Nikolaus Forkel, *Über Johann Sebastian Bachs Leben, Kunst und*
Kunstwerke (Leipzig, 1802; reprint, Berlin: Henschelverlag, 1982), 127.

28. There can be no doubt that Beethoven was familiar with *Die Kunst des*
reinen Satzes, for he cited music examples from it in his personal studies of counterpoint. See Richard Kramer, "Notes to Beethoven's Education," *Journal of the*
American Musicological Society 28 (1975): 72–101 (pp. 86 and 97, in particular).

29. Breitkopf's stock of Bach manuscripts is surveyed in Ernest May,
"Connections Between Breitkopf and J. S. Bach" and Hans-Joachim Schulze,
"Johann Sebastian Bach's Vocal Works in the Breitkopf Nonthematic Catalogues of
1761 to 1836," both in *Bach Perspectives II: J. S. Bach and the Breitkopfs*, ed.
George B. Stauffer (Lincoln, Nebraska: University of Nebraska Press, 1996), 11–26
and 35–49, respectively.

30. The picture of the *Singakademie* sketched here is derived principally from Georg Schünemann, "Die Bachpflege der Berliner Singakademie," *Bach-Jahrbuch* 25 (1928): 138–171. Schünemann's account is by far the most important, since many of the archival documents cited by him were subsequently lost in World War II.

31. Zelter's score is discussed in Christoph Albrecht, "Zum 'größten musikalischen Kunstwerk, das die Welt gesehen hat,'" *Deutsches Bachfest Berlin 1976*, 145–154. The library of the Berlin *Singakademie* is lost, though parts of it are rumored to have survived in the former Soviet Union.

32. Schünemann, "Die Bachpflege der Berliner Singakademie," 145.

33. Fascinating examples are given in Schünemann, "Die Bachpflege der Berliner Singakademie," 149–150 and 154–155. Forkel, too, preferred simpler versions of Bach's works and incorrectly considered the early, less embellished version of the Inventions and Sinfonias to be the composer's refinement of the later, more ornate version.

34. Letter of June 9, 1827, cited by Smend in NBA II/1, KB, 398, n. 26.

35. *Leipziger Allgemeine musikalische Zeitung*, 1818, "Intelligenz-Blatt," no. 3, col. 28. Nägeli also distributed the solicitation in the form of a single sheet, which is reproduced in facsimile in NBA II/1, KB, 215.

36. Johann Nepomuk Schelble, letter to his family, quoted in *Hundert Jahre Caecilien-Verein in kurzer Fassung zusammengestellt nach den in dem Archiv des Vereins niedergelegten Protokollen und Schriftstücken* (Frankfurt, 1918), 10.

37. Adolf Bernhard Marx, review in the *Berliner Allgemeine musikalische Zeitung* 5 (1828): no. 17, 138.

38. Which Spontini borrowed from Georg Poelchau, who had obtained them from C. P. E. Bach's estate.

39. Gerhard Herz, "The Performance History of Bach's B-Minor Mass," in Herz, *Essays on Bach* (Ann Arbor: U.M.I. Research Press, 1985), 193.

40. Adolf Bernhard Marx, review in the *Berliner Allgemeine musikalische Zeitung* 5 (1828): no. 18, 146, and no. 19, 152–154.

41. Ludwig Rellstab, review in *Vossische Zeitung Berlin*, no. 102 (May 2, 1828), and *Leipziger Allgemeine musikalische Zeitung*, 1828, no. 30, 365. Both reviews are cited in NBA II/1, KB, 400–401.

42. Fanny Mendelssohn, letter to Carl Klingemann of April 14, 1828, quoted in Martin Geck, *Die Wiederentdeckung der Matthäuspassion* (Regensburg: Gustav Bosse, 1967), 23.

43. This is obvious not just from Marx's influential review of Spontini's concert but from later comments on the B-Minor Mass. For instance, the Berlin manuscript *P 182*, a nineteenth-century copy of the B-Minor Mass, contains the remark: "On April 23, 1843, the Sanctus from this Mass was performed under Mendelssohn's direction as the closing piece in a concert for the Bach Monument. One names Beethoven's Mass in D and that of Bach in B minor as the two greatest creations of this type, even though the approaches in the two are different." See NBA II/1, KB, 20–21.

44.   As first suggested by Smend, NBA II/1, KB, 184–185.

45.   Written out by Poelchau and other scribes in November and December of 1827. The "old" (1786) and "new" (1827) portions of *St 118* are described by Smend in NBA II/2, KB, 17, 41, and 231–234, and more accurately by Rifkin in "'. . . wobey aber die Singstimmen hinlänglich besetzt seyn müssen . . .,'" 107 and 114, n. 33.

46.   Berlin, Staatsbibliothek, *St 595.*

47.   Smend already deduced such numbers for the voices and strings but believed that only the newly made wind and brass parts were used in the performance (NBA II/2, KB, 44). Marx's comments on the "Crucifixus," cited below, seem to indicate, on the contrary, that all the woodwind parts, old and new, were used. It would seem equally likely that all the brass parts were utilized as well.

48.   Adolf Bernhard Marx, review in *Berliner Allgemeine musikalische Zeitung* 5 (1828): no. 19, 154.

49.   Nikolaus Harnoncourt, "Zu Problemen der Wiedergabe von Bachs Chor-Orchester-Werken," *Österreichische Musikzeitschrift* 24 (1969): 78.

50.   *Leipziger Allgemeine musikalische Zeitung,* 1834, no. 14 (April 2), 227.

51.   According to Smend's calculations in NBA II/2, KB, 47.

52.   Herz, "The Performance History of Bach's B minor Mass," 202, n. 42.

53.   Preserved in the Musikbibliothek der Stadt Leipzig, Leipzig, Rudorff Sammlung, *Ms.R. 16.*

54.   *Leipziger Allgemeine musikalische Zeitung,* 1834, no. 14 (April 2), p. 227.

55.   Spitta, *Johann Sebastian Bach,* 3:52–53.

56.   Schweitzer, *J. S. Bach,* 2:414.

57.   Schweitzer, *J. S. Bach,* 2:417–418.

58.   Arnold Schering, "Verschwundene Traditionen des Bachzeitalters," *Bach-Jahrbuch* 1 (1904): 104–115.

59.   Arnold Schering, "Über die Kirchenkantaten vorbachischer Thomas-kantoren," *Bach-Jahrbuch* 9 (1912): 86–123.

60.   Arnold Schering, "Die Hohe Messe in h-moll," 7–8.

61.   Friedrich Smend, "Bachs h-moll-Messe: Entstehung, Überlieferung, Bedeutung," *Bach-Jahrbuch* 34 (1937): 1–58.

62.   Smend, "Bachs h-moll-Messe: Entstehung, Überlieferung, Bedeutung," 30–31.

63.   Abstract in *Bulletin of the American Musicology Society* 7 (1943): 2–3.

64.   Wilhelm Ehmann, "'Concertisten' und 'Ripienisten' in der h-moll Messe Johann Sebastian Bachs," *Musik und Kirche* 30 (1960): 95–104, 138–147, 227–236, 255–273, and 298–309.

65.   Notes to RCA recording no. *LM 6157* (1961).

66.   Telefunken *Das Alte Werk* recording no. *SKH 20/1–3* (1968).

67.   Nikolaus Harnoncourt, "Zu Problemen der Wiedergabe von Bachs Chor-Orchester-Werken," 79. Translation from Harnoncourt, *The Musical Dialogue: Thoughts on Monteverdi, Bach and Mozart,* ed. Mary O'Neill (Portland, Oregon: Amadeus Press, 1989), 188.

68. Rudolf Klein, review in *Österreichische Musikzeitschrift* 24 (1969): 60.

69. *High Fidelity/Musical America* 19 (1969): July, 76–78.

70. *High Fidelity/Musical America* 19 (1969): July, 77.

71. "The Best Records of the Year: An International Jury Decides," *High Fidelity/Musical America* 19 (1969): December, 67–72.

72. In a later interview, printed in the liner notes to his 1986 recording of the B-Minor Mass, TELDEC *8.35716* (1986).

73. This is evident from archival records of church choirs. Bach sang soprano in the Lüneburg Mettenchor until his fifteenth year, for instance. See *Bach-Dokumente* 2: no. 5 and 3: no. 666.

74. Nonesuch recording no. *79036.*

75. Deutsche Grammophon recording no. *ARC-415514–2* (Gardiner) and Angel recording no. *CDCB 47292* (Parrott). In the liner notes Parrott acknowledges an indebtedness to Rifkin.

76. Notes to TELDEC recording no. *8.35716* (1986).

CHAPTER 7
Issues of Performance Practice

1. Joshua Rifkin, "Bach's 'Choruses'—Less Than They Seem?" *High Fidelity* 32 (1982): 42–44; idem, "Bach's Chorus: A Preliminary Report," *The Musical Times* 123 (1982): 747–754; and idem, "Bachs Chor—ein vorläufiger Bericht," *Basler Jahrbuch für historische Musikpraxis* 9 (1985): 141–155. Rifkin's views were challenged by Robert L. Marshall in "Bach's 'Choruses' Reconstituted," *High Fidelity* 32 (1982): 64–66, 94; and idem, "Bach's Chorus: A Preliminary Reply to Joshua Rifkin," *Musical Times* 123 (1982): 19–22.

2. Joshua Rifkin, "'. . . wobey aber die Singstimmen hinlänglich besetzt seyn müssen . . . ,'" 114, n. 33.

3. Alfred Dürr, *Zur Chronologie der Leipziger Vokalwerke J. S. Bachs,* 93.

4. Schulze, ed., *Johann Sebastian Bach, Missa h-Moll BWV 232ᴵ*, Commentary.

5. Giovanni Lorenzo Gregori, *Concerti grossi a più stromenti* (Lucca, 1698), Preface.

6. Walther, *Briefe*, 72.

7. Reproduced in *Bach-Dokumente* 1: no. 22, and translated in *The Bach Reader*, 120–124.

8. Translation from *The Bach Reader*, 121.

9. The roster is reproduced in facsimile in *Bach-Dokumente* 4: no. 490.

10. Horn, *Die Dresdner Hofkirchenmusik*, 194.

11. *Bach-Dokumente* 1: no. 22; translation from *The Bach Reader*, 121.

12. In the diary of St. Thomas School rector Jacob Thomasius for the years 1676–1684, cited in *St. Thomas zu Leipzig: Schule und Chor*, ed. Berhard Knick (Wiesbaden: Breitkopf & Härtel, 1963), 110–111.

13. See the facsimile in *St. Thomas zu Leipzig: Schule und Chor,* 132.

14. See NBA I/17.1, KB, 77–78. The parts were written out by Johann Andreas Kuhnau; the solo and tutti indications were added by Bach.

15. *Ordnung der Schule zu S. Thomae* (Leipzig, 1723; reprint Leipzig: Zentralantiquariat der Deutschen Demokratischen Republik, 1987), 72.

16. Gorke Collection, No. 303, Bach-Archiv, Leipzig. The manuscript and its marginalia are described in *Sammlung Manfred Gorke,* ed. Hans-Joachim Schulze (Leipzig: Veröffentlichungen der Musikbibliothek der Stadt Leipzig, 1977), 74–75.

17. *Bach-Dokumente* 2: no. 432.

18. *Bach Compendium* 4: 1488.

19. Horn, *Die Dresdner Hofkirchenmusik,* 37–38.

20. Horn, *Die Dresdner Hofkirchenmusik,* 109 and 195.

21. BG 5^1: xviii.

22. Arnold Schering, "Die Besetzung Bachscher Chöre," *Bach-Jahrbuch* 17 (1920): 77–89.

23. Ehmann, "'Concertisten' und 'Ripienisten' in der h-moll-Messe Joh. Seb. Bachs," 95–104, 138–147, 227–236, 255–273, and 298–309.

24. Alfred Dürr, "Zum Problem 'Concertisten' und 'Ripienisten' in der h-moll-Messe," *Musik und Kirche* 31 (1961): 232–236.

25. Dürr, "Zum Problem 'Concertisten' und 'Ripienisten' in der h-moll-Messe," 233.

26. We will not take into account here two additional instruments that Bach used on occasion, the *Lautenwerk* and the gamba, since they do not seem to have played a role in the B-Minor Mass.

27. Laurence Dreyfus, "Zur Frage der Cembalo-Mitwirkung in den geistlichen Werken Bachs," *Bachforschung und Bach Interpretation heute,* ed. Reinhold Brinkmann (Kassel: Bärenreiter, 1981), 178–184; and idem, *Bach's Continuo Group,* 10–71.

28. Dreyfus, *Bach's Continuo Group,* 170–172.

29. Dreyfus, *Bach's Continuo Group,* 67–68.

30. Walther, *Musicalisches Lexicon,* 647.

31. According to Arthur Mendel, editor of the St. John Passion for the NBA, Bach used lute for the first two performances of the work (in 1724 and 1725), harpsichord for a third performance (in 1739), and organ for a fourth performance (in 1749). See NBA II/2, KB, 96–98. The dates given by Mendel have been adjusted here according to more recent findings, given in Kobayashi, "Zur Chronologie der Spätwerke Johann Sebastian Bachs," 44 and 63.

32. *P 22* and *St 118,* respectively, in the Berlin State Library. Emanuel's figures are discussed in Bernhard Stockmann, "Der bezifferte Generalbass von C. Ph. E. Bach zum Credo der h-Moll-Messe J. S. Bachs," *Carl Philipp Emanuel Bach und die europäische Musikkultur des mittleren 18. Jahrhunderts,* ed. Hans-Joachim Marx (Göttingen: Vandenhoeck und Ruprecht, 1990), 451–458, and they are reproduced in the new Peters edition of the B-Minor Mass edited by Christoph Wolff.

33. On this point see Peter Wollny's comments in "Ein Quellenfund zur Entstehungsgeschichte der h-Moll-Messe," 166.

34. Dreyfus, *Bach's Continuo Group*, 164–165.

35. Though one must note that Bach did drop the violone during solo episodes in the Harpsichord Concerto in A Major, BWV 1055. See the discussion in Christoph Wolff, "Bach's Leipzig Chamber Music," *Early Music* 13 (1985): 170–172. There is no evidence that this practice was carried over into vocal works, however.

36. Ulrich Prinz, in "Zur Bezeichnung 'Bassono' and 'Fagotto' bei J. S. Bach," *Bach-Jahrbuch* 67 (1981): 107–122, makes the case that whenever copyists produced bassoon parts for Bach, they simply reproduced the continuo line of the score. Whenever Bach wrote out the part himself, he made a more refined, independent line.

37. The oft-voiced notion that Bach used bassoon in the continuo whenever a movement contained oboes does not hold up under scrutiny. See Konrad Brandt, "Fragen zur Fagottbesetzung in den kirchenmusikalischen Werken Johann Sebastian Bachs," *Bach-Jahrbuch* 54 (1968): 65–79.

38. Dreyfus, *Bach's Continuo Group*, 126.

39. In the recent Peters edition, Christoph Wolff proposes that the bassoon should sound half notes on the first and last beat of each measure, in the manner of Bach's scoring in the "Weinen, Klagen, Sorgen, Zagen" model. One might question whether Bach would have carried over the heterogeneous scoring of Cantata 12, a Weimar work, into the B-Minor Mass, a piece compiled thirty years later, when he was taking a more homogeneous approach to scoring (as we noted in Chapter 3).

40. Horn, *Die Dresdner Hofkirchenmusik*, 195–197.

41. Albert Schweitzer, *J. S. Bach*, 2:324 and 325.

42. Rilling, *Johann Sebastian Bach's B-Minor Mass*, 103; *Bach Compendium*, ed. Hans-Joachim Schulze and Christoph Wolff (Frankfurt: C. F. Peters; Leipzig: Edition Peters, 1985-present) 4:1179.

43. Though even here Alfred Dürr has at least raised the possibility that the vocal parts in the "Credo" were doubled by instruments, in *Johann Sebastian Bach*, "zu Blatt 72."

44. Johann Joseph Fux, *Gradus ad Parnassum*, 183–192.

45. This is discussed in detail in Horn, *Die Dresdner Hofkirchenmusik*, 109–118 ("Die praktische Einrichtung der a-cappella-Werke").

46. Walther, *Musicalisches Lexicon*, 4.

47. Cited in Karl Gustav Fellerer, "Der stile antico," *Geschichte der katholischen Kirchenmusik* (Kassel: Bärenreiter, 1976), 91.

48. Daniel R. Melamed, "Eine Motette Sebastian Knüpfers aus J. S. Bachs Notenbibliothek," *Bach-Jahrbuch* 75 (1989): 191–196.

49. "NB müßte ein ganzes Orchestre dazu gesezt werden." See NBA III/1, KB, 32–33.

50. Fux, *Gradus ad Parnassum*, 182.

51. A fine example of Bach's concern that all musicians be occupied is the Renaissance-style chorus "An dir, du Fürbild großer Frauen" from Cantata 198 ("Trauer-Ode"), in which he put the two lute players in his ensemble to work doubling the vocal bass, much in the fashion of a *colla parte* bassoon.

52. Wolff, *Der Stile Antico*, 108–112.

53. Rilling's suggestion, in *Johann Sebastian Bach's B-Minor Mass*, 103, that the *colla parte* wind instruments would drop out only during the "Et expecto" bridge seems less plausible.

54. As seen in the manuscript *Mus. 2358-D-24* in the Saxon State Library.

55. Kirnberger, *Die Kunst des reinen Satzes*, 2:106. Translation from Beach and Thym, *The Art of Strict Musical Composition* (New Haven, Conn.: Yale University Press, 1982), 376.

56. The synonymity of "neutral" *tempo ordinario* and *allegro* in Bach's music was first demonstrated convincingly by Robert L. Marshall in "Tempo and Dynamic Indications in the Bach Sources: A Review of the Terminology," *Bach, Handel, Scarlatti: Tercentenary Essays*, ed. Peter Williams (Cambridge: Cambridge University Press, 1985), 259–275.

57. Kirnberger, *Die Kunst des reinen Satzes*, 2:107. Translation from Beach and Thym, 377.

58. Kirnberger, *Die Kunst des reinen Satzes* 2: 107. Translation from Beach and Thym, 377.

59. This phenomenon was first outlined by Marshall in "Tempo and Dynamic Indications in the Bach Sources," in which he pointed to several instances in which Bach used two different tempo or *Affekt* indications simultaneously. In my own survey of the original materials, which included not only the scores checked by Marshall but the original performance parts as well, I found forty-nine such cases.

60. Walther, *Musicalisches Lexicon*, 9.

61. No. 71 in BG IV; no. 61a in NBA II/5.

62. Walther, *Musicalisches Lexicon*, 355.

63. Walther, *Musicalisches Lexicon*, 598.

64. Walther, *Musicalisches Lexicon*, 35.

65. Walther, *Musicalisches Lexicon*, 27.

66. Kirnberger, *Die Kunst des reinen Satzes* 2: 118.

67. Agricola, review in *Allgemeine deutsche Bibliothek*, 108. One cannot help but wonder whether Agricola was referring to the early G-mixolydian version of the "Credo," which survives solely in a manuscript copy in his hand (see Plate 2–2 in Chapter 2).

68. Arthur Mendel, "A Note on Proportional Relationships in Bach Tempi," *Musical Times* 100 (1959): 683–684.

69. Butt, *The Mass in B Minor*, 72–73.

70. Kirnberger, *Die Kunst des reinen Satzes*, 2:120.

71. Kirnberger, *Die Kunst des reinen Satzes*, 2:118.

72. Walther, *Musicalisches Lexicon*, 464–465.

73. Häfner, "Über die Herkunft von zwei Sätzen der h-moll-Messe," 73–74.

74. Doris Finke-Hecklinger, in fact, classifies the "Et in Spiritum" as a "Giga-Pastorale" in *Tanzcharaktere in Johann Sebastian Bachs Vokalmusik* (Trossingen: Hohner-Verlag, 1970), 113.

75. See Dürr's comments in NBA I/10, KB, 102–104. It should be pointed out that the corrupt ¢ signatures are often "corrected" to C signs without comment in modern editions. Even as scholarly a publication as the *Bach-Compendium* assigns the 1724 version of the Sanctus a C meter rather than the ¢ found in the original score (see under *E12*, vol. 4, 1229).

76. Bernard Rose, "Some Further Observations on the Performance of Purcell's Music," *Musical Times* 100 (1959): 385–386.

77. Arthur Mendel, "A Note on Proportional Relationships in Bach Tempi," 683.

78. Kirnberger, *Die Kunst des reinen Satzes*, 2:130.

79. The *molt' adagio* appears only in the solo oboe part, which makes one suspect that it was not in the original score (which is no longer extant).

80. Bach's approach to articulation has recently been scrutinized in remarkable detail by John Butt, in *Bach Interpretation: Articulation Marks in Primary Sources of J. S. Bach* (Cambridge: Cambridge University Press, 1990). I am indebted to this source for many of the broad points presented here.

81. Georg Muffat, for instance, treated slurs and staccato marks within the discussion of ornaments in the preface to *Florilegium Secundum* (Passau, 1698).

82. Butt, *Bach Interpretation*, 94–96.

83. See Smend, NBA II/1, KB, 42, or Herz, "The Performance History of Bach's B Minor Mass," 188.

84. Georg von Dadelsen, "Friedrich Smends Ausgabe der h-moll-Messe von J. S. Bach," 331.

85. Gerhard Herz, "Der lombardische Rhythmus im 'Domine Deus' der h-Moll Messe J. S. Bachs," *Bach-Jahrbuch* 60 (1974): 90–97. Revised English version: "Lombard Rhythm in the *Domine Deus* of Bach's *B minor Mass*," in Herz, *Essays on J. S. Bach*, 221–229.

86. Johann Joachim Quantz, *Versuch einer Anweisung, die Flöte traversiere zu spielen* (Berlin, 1752; reprint, Leipzig: VEB Deutscher Verlag für Musik, 1983), Hauptstück XVIII, § 58 (pp. 309–310).

87. Gerhard Herz, "Der lombardische Rhythmus in Bachs Vokalschaffen" in *Bach-Jahrbuch* 64 (1978): 148–180. Revised English version: "Lombard Rhythm in Bach's Vocal Music," in Herz, *Essays on J. S. Bach*, 233–268.

88. Saxon State Library, *Mus. 2358-D-27*. Horn, in *Die Dresdner Hofkirchenmusik*, 182, cites this movement as well as a second example, the "Christe eleison" from a 1735 Mass in D Major by Johann Gottlob Harrer (Bach's successor in Leipzig).

89. C. P. E. Bach, *Versuch über die wahre Art, das Clavier zu spielen* (Berlin, 1753 and 1762; reprint, Leipzig: VEB Breitkopf und Härtel, 1978), Part I, Hauptstück III, § 24 (p. 128).

90. Quantz, *Versuch einer Anweisung*, Hauptstück V, § 23 (p. 59).

91. Quantz, *Versuch einer Anweisung*, Hauptstück XI, § 12 (p. 106).

92. A most useful guide to regional pronunciations of Latin is Harold Copeman, *Singing in Latin* (Oxford: Ipswich Book Co., 1990).

93. As correspondence between the Vatican and the Dresden Court reveals. See Horn, *Die Dresdner Hofkirchenmusik*, 13–31.

CHAPTER 8
"The Great Catholic Mass"

1. On the cadential structure of *Clavierübung* III, see Peter Williams, *The Organ Music of J. S. Bach* (Cambridge: Cambridge University Press, 1980–1984) 2:181; on that of the first version of the Art of Fugue see Douglass Seaton, "The Autograph: An Early Version of the 'Art of Fugue,'" *Current Musicology* 19 (1975): 54–59.

2. Butt, *Bach: Mass in B Minor*, 99.

3. The "Gloria in excelsis," the "Et in terra pax," and the "Et incarnatus" may also be torsos, but that is less certain.

4. The folio structure of the *P 180* autograph reveals that Bach removed a page from the manuscript at the juncture of the "Domine Deus" and the "Qui tollis," raising the possibility that he initially concluded the "Domine Deus" in a different fashion. See Alfred Dürr's diagram of the folio structure in *Johann Sebastian Bach. Messe in H-Moll, BWV 232*, Commentary, 14–15.

5. Friedrich Smend, "Die Johannes-Passion von Bach," *Bach-Jahrbuch* 23 (1926): 105–128, and idem, "Bachs Matthäus-Passion," *Bach-Jahrbuch* 25 (1928): 1–95; Eric Chafe, "J. S. Bach's *St. Matthew Passion:* Aspects of Planning, Structure, and Chronology," *Journal of the American Musicological Society* 35 (1982): 49–114, and idem, *Tonal Allegory in the Vocal Music of J. S. Bach*, chapters 11 and 14 in particular.

6. Bitter, *Johann Sebastian Bach*, 3:1.

7. Spitta, *Johann Sebastian Bach*, 3:46.

8. Schering, "Die Hohe Messe in h-moll." See the discussion of Schering's theory in Chapter 2 of the present work.

9. NBA II/1, KB, 124–127, 163–165, and 186–187.

10. Dadelsen, "Bachs h-Moll Messe," 139.

11. Christoph Wolff, "Bach the Cantor, the Capellmeister, and the Musical Scholar: Aspects of the B-Minor Mass," in *The Universal Bach. Lectures Celebrating the Tercentenary of Bach's Birthday* (Philadelphia: American Philosophical Society, 1986), 45.

12. Kobayashi, "Zur Chronologie der Spätwerke Johann Sebastian Bachs," 61–65.

13. Horn, *Die Dresdner Hofkirchenmusik*, 191.

14. Horn, *Die Dresdner Hofkirchenmusik*, 194.

15. Wolfgang Osthoff, "Das 'Credo' der h-moll-Messe: Italienische Vorbilder und Anregungen," in *Bach und die italienische Musik*, ed. Wolfgang Osthoff and Reinhard Wiesend (Venice: Centro Tedesco di Studi Veneziani, 1987), 109–140.

16. Horn, *Die Dresdner Hofkirchenmusik*, 49.

17. Christoph Wolff, ed., *The New Grove Bach Family* (New York: W. W. Norton, 1983), 111.

18. See Horn's remarks in *Die Dresdner Hofkirchenmusik*, 192–193.

19. Horn, *Die Dresdner Hofkirchenmusik*, 194.

20. As reported by Laurie H. Ongley in "Liturgical Music in Late Eighteenth-Century Dresden: Johann Gottlieb Naumann, Joseph Schuster, and Franz Seydelmann" (Ph.D. diss., Yale University, 1992).

21. Quoted in Snyder, *Dieterich Buxtehude: Organist in Lübeck*, 312.

22. Forkel, *Über Johann Sebastian Bachs Leben, Kunst und Kunstwerke*, 117.

23. The theme of universality in Bach's music is explored in Robert L. Marshall, "On Bach's Universality," in *The Music of Johann Sebastian Bach: The Sources, the Style, the Significance* (New York: Schirmer Books, 1989), 65–82.

24. Finke-Hecklinger, *Tanzcharaktere in Johann Sebastian Bachs Vokalmusik*, 132–143.

25. Thrasybulos G. Georgiades, *Musik und Sprache. Das Werden der abendländischen Musik dargestellt an der Vertonung der Messe* (Berlin, 1954).

26. Georgiades, *Musik und Sprache*, 70–89.

27. Williams, *The Organ Music of J. S. Bach* 2:186.

28. Mellers, *Bach and the Dance of God*, 9.

29. As Charles Rosen convincingly demonstrates in *Sonata Forms* (New York: W. W. Norton, 1980), 27–68.

30. Quoted in *Source Readings in Music History*, ed. Oliver Strunk, vol. 5, *The Romantic Era* (New York: W. W. Norton, 1965), 35.

A Word on Modern Editions

1 Steuart Wilson, "The Text of the B Minor Mass," *The Musical Times* 73 (1932): 30–32, 120–123.

2 Dadelsen, "Friedrich Smends Ausgabe der h-moll-Messe von J. S. Bach," *Die Musikforschung* 12 (1959): 315–335. English trans.: "Friedrich Smend's Edition of the B-Minor Mass by J. S. Bach," tr. James A. Brokaw II, *Bach: The Journal of Riemenschneider Bach Institute* 20/2 (1989): 49–74.

Index

GENERAL INDEX

MASS IN B MINOR, BWV 232